# RE-WRITING THE FRENCH REVOLUTIONARY TRADITION

This book examines the politics of the French Revolutionary tradition during the Bourbon Restoration and the early July Monarchy. Robert Alexander argues that progressive political change was achieved by legal grassroots organization and persuasion – rather than the Revolutionary tradition of conspiracy and armed insurrection – and that, moreover, political struggle was not confined to the elite, as common material interests and values linked the electorate to the disenfranchised. Battle between the advocates of national and royal sovereignty constituted the principal dynamic of the period, and fostered significant developments in party formation previously unrecognized by historians. To substantiate his claims, the author analyses relations between the Liberal Opposition, ultraroyalists and the state, concluding that although Liberals triumphed in the 1830 Revolution, thereafter they contributed to the destabilization that produced an immobile Orleanist regime. Nevertheless, they had pioneered a model for change which could successfully adapt pursuit of reform to longing for civil order.

ROBERT ALEXANDER is Professor of History at the University of Victoria, Canada. He has previously published with Cambridge University Press *Bonapartism and Revolutionary Tradition in France* (1991), and has also published *Napoleon* (2001). He has also contributed to many journals, including *The Historical Journal, French History* and *Modern and Contemporary France.*

NEW STUDIES IN EUROPEAN HISTORY



This is a new series in early modern and modern European history. Its aim is to publish outstanding works of research, addressed to important themes across a wide geographical range, from southern and central Europe, to Scandinavia and Russia, and from the time of the Renaissance to the Second World War. As it develops the series will comprise focused works of wide contextual range and intellectual ambition.

*For a list of books in the series, please see back of book*

# RE-WRITING THE FRENCH REVOLUTIONARY TRADITION

ROBERT ALEXANDER

CAMBRIDGE
UNIVERSITY PRESS

PUBLISHED BY THE PRESS SYNDICATE OF THE UNIVERSITY OF CAMBRIDGE
The Pitt Building, Trumpington Street, Cambridge, United Kingdom

CAMBRIDGE UNIVERSITY PRESS
The Edinburgh Building, Cambridge, CB2 2RU, UK
40 West 20th Street, New York, NY 10011–4211, USA
477 Williamstown Road, Port Melbourne, VIC 3207, Australia
Ruiz de Alarcón 13, 28014 Madrid, Spain
Dock House, The Waterfront, Cape Town 8001, South Africa

http://www.cambridge.org



First published 2003

Printed in the United Kingdom at the University Press, Cambridge

*Typeface* Adobe Garamond 11/12.5 pt. *System* LaTeX 2ε [TB]

*A catalogue record for this book is available from the British Library*

*Library of Congress Cataloguing in Publication data*
Alexander, R. S., 1954–
Re-writing the French Revolutionary Tradition / Robert Alexander.
p. cm. – (New Studies in European History)
Includes bibliographical references and index.
ISBN 0 521 80122 2
1. France – History – Restoration, 1814–1830. 2. France – History – July Revolution, 1830.
3. France – Politics and government – 1814–1830. I. Title. II. Series.
DC256.A43 2003 2003043812

ISBN 0 521 80122 2 hardback

*Dedicated to the memory of my mother,*
*Helen Kathleen Richards*

# *Contents*

# *Maps*

# *Tables*

# *Acknowledgements*

Among the many who have helped me with this work, I would like particularly to thank the following. The Social Sciences and Research Council of Canada and the University of Victoria funded research for the project, and while in France and Switzerland I was greatly aided by many dedicated archivists and librarians who dealt admirably with my incessant requests and queries. Three of my colleagues, Angus McLaren, Perry Biddiscombe and Mariel Grant, kindly read through early drafts of the manuscript. Cameron Sinclair helped greatly with mapmaking, and, as usual, the technical expertise of David Zimmerman was invaluable to me. Elizabeth Howard, History Editor for Cambridge University Press, gave much appreciated, and patient, advice, as did two anonymous readers. I would also like to thank Cambridge University Press for permission to reprint map 1, entitled 'The departments of France and their capitals in 1814', which was initially published in A. Jardin and A.-J. Tudesq, *Restoration and Reaction 1815–1848* (Cambridge: University Press, 1983). Finally, I would like to express my sincere gratitude to Dr Emma Alexander for the support she gave while I was undertaking this project and to congratulate her upon her entry into the profession.

# *Abbreviations used in the notes*

| | |
|---|---|
| ADBR | Departmental Archives of the Bas-Rhin |
| ADHG | Departmental Archives of the Haute-Garonne |
| ADI | Departmental Archives of the Isère |
| ADSM | Departmental Archives of the Seine-Maritime |
| AN | (French) National Archives |
| BCUL | Cantonal and University Library of Lausanne |
| BMT | Municipal Library of Toulouse |
| BMUG | Municipal and University Library of Grenoble |
| BN | (French) National Library |
| BNUS | National and University Library of Strasbourg |

Figure 1 The departments of France and their capitals in 1814

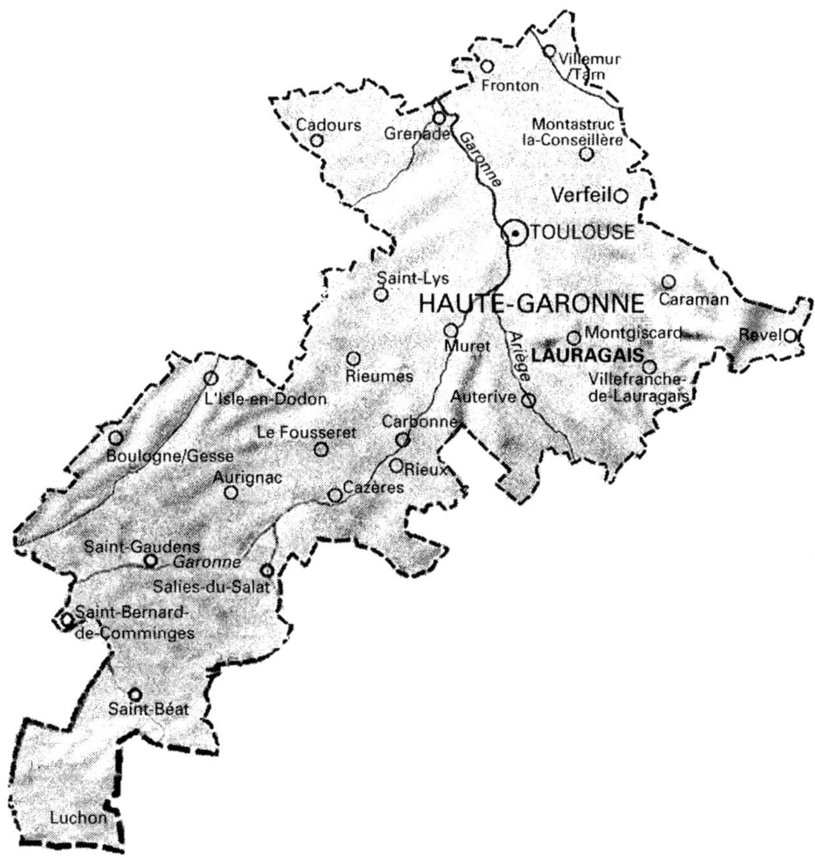


Figure 2 The Haute-Garonne

Figure 3 The Isère

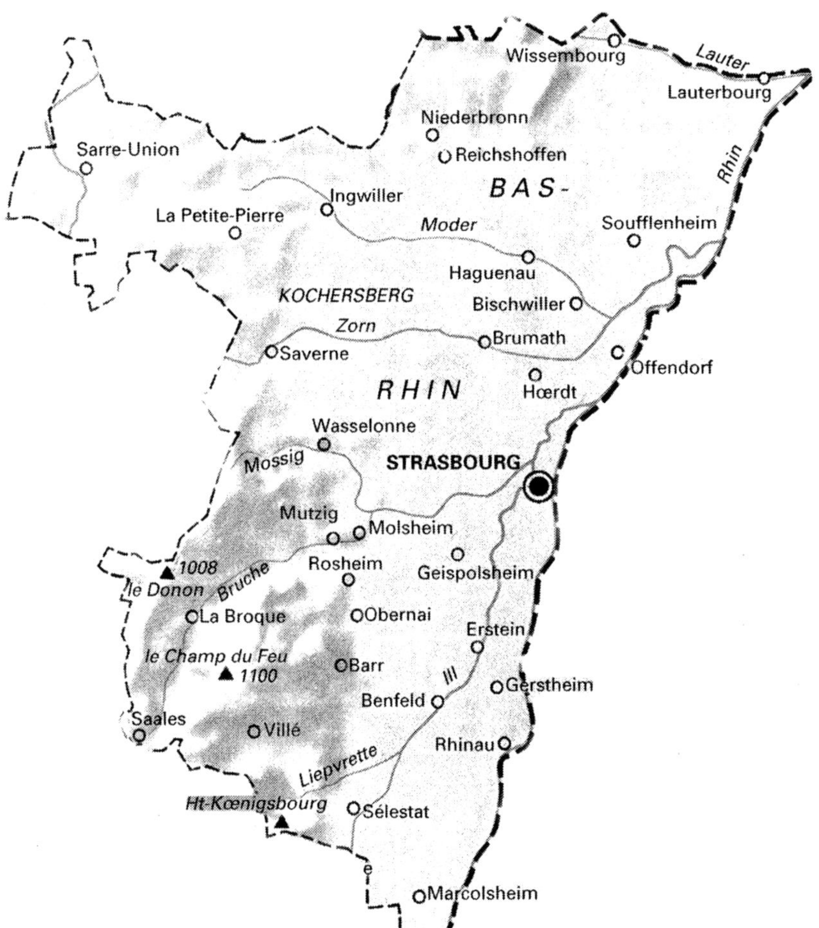


Figure 4 The Bas-Rhin

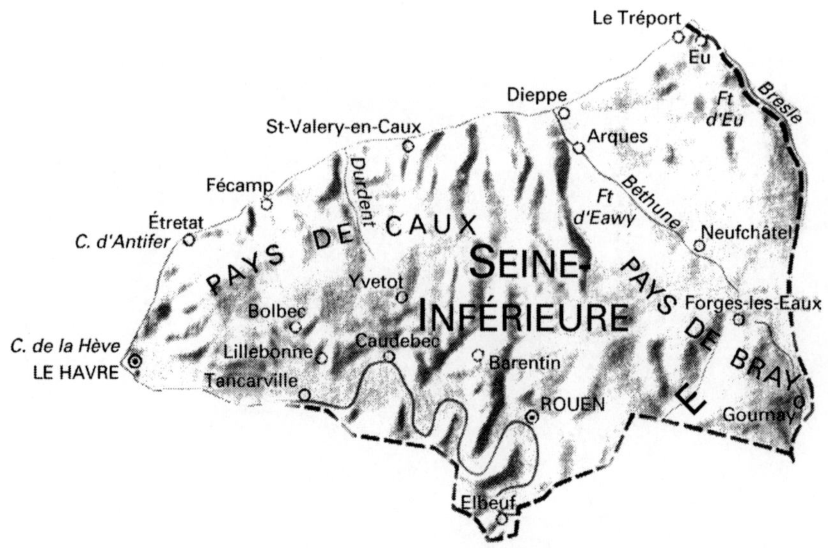


Figure 5 The Seine-Inférieure

INTRODUCTION

# Open questions

An experiment in government – such was how contemporaries viewed the Bourbon Restoration, according to Charles de Rémusat. Although partisan, Rémusat's observation was nevertheless insightful. For many, the political system established in 1814 was not necessarily definitive; it could be subjected to alteration, minor or major, and ultimately the public would decide whether the experiment was a success or failure.[1]

The chief embodiment of the Restoration experiment was the Charter of 1814, a constitution wherein elements of the changes brought to society and polity after 1789 were blended with elements of the *ancien régime*. Implementing the new constitution thus entailed, at least in part, putting into practice the ideals of the Revolution in an enduring and stable fashion. Yet, as the Charter was drawn up in haste, with many details left for subsequent elaboration, it was natural to look upon the new constitution as at most a blueprint.

In many regards the Charter was ambiguous, leaving much open to interpretation. Given the fragility of the new regime, ambiguity served a certain purpose in that it allowed various groups to view the regime differently, but still give their approval. From its origins, however, the Charter was interpreted in two fundamentally different ways. For royalists, the constitution was entirely a product of royal sovereignty – it was granted by Louis XVIII of his own free will. For those who came to oppose this interpretation, the Charter was a contract between the monarch and the nation. Thus the Restoration's founding principle was contested, and battle between the advocates of royal or national sovereignty would provide the period's central political dynamic.

The new regime was also a product of foreign intervention, and consequently certain parts of the public were disposed to view the 'experiment'

[1] Rémusat was a highly influential journalist and played a significant role in organizing Parisian Liberal Opposition. See C. de Rémusat, *Mémoires de ma vie*, 5 vols. (Paris, 1958), I, p. 150.

with hostility from its onset. In destroying the First Empire, the leaders of the Sixth Coalition had proclaimed in December 1813 that they were waging war against Napoleon, but not the French nation. Consultation with the nation over a successor regime was, however, very limited indeed. By early 1814 the Allied powers had decided that no compromise could be reached with the Bonaparte dynasty, and hence there would be no Imperial regency with Napoleon's son as king. Similarly, there was little likelihood that France might again become a republic, given the First Republic's association with international revolution.

In their search for a royal alternative, the Allied powers opted for the Count of Provence (Louis XVIII), because restoration of the Bourbon dynasty appeared to hold the best prospect for French stability and international peace. They had been encouraged to make this decision by royalist demonstrations at Bordeaux and Paris orchestrated by a secret organization known as the Chevaliers de la Foi. While such manifestations were in fact very limited, in combination with the advocacy of Charles Maurice de Talleyrand, a legendary 'political survivor' of the Revolution and Napoleon's former Foreign Minister, they were enough to push aside weak claims made by potential rivals such as Marshal Jean-Baptiste Bernadotte and Duke Louis-Philippe of Orleans.

Allied confidence in the Bourbon dynasty was, however, far from unqualified. As a means of fostering acceptance, Allied leaders called upon the Imperial Senate to formulate a new constitution in April 1814. Given that they had been appointed, Napoleon's Senators had little claim to represent France, but they did include much of the Imperial elite. Under pressure from Allied leaders, especially Czar Alexander I, Louis XVIII agreed to accept the Senate's proposals in principle, but a new committee was then created to reformulate the proposals along lines acceptable to the monarchy. The Charter was then proclaimed on 4 June.

Upon the surface, the new regime had a distinctly British appearance. France would have a bicameral parliament composed of a Chamber of Peers and a Chamber of Deputies. Legislative initiative would rest with the government, but laws would have to pass through both houses prior to royal proclamation. Of crucial importance was the influence parliament could exert over government budgets. Proposed tax bills must gain the approval of the Deputies before passing on to the Peers, and while indirect taxes could be voted for several years, land taxes must be approved annually. Peerage would be hereditary; of the 155 original members, 84 were drawn from the Imperial Senate, while the king appointed the rest. In the future, the king would appoint all new Peers, whereas Deputies would be elected.[2]

While the Charter's provisions for a parliament represented a grafting of British institutions onto French polity, other elements of the regime were distinctly indigenous. The Restoration preserved much of the legacy of the Revolution of 1789, but it did so through the filter of reforms instituted under Bonaparte. Retention of the Napoleonic Codes meant that legal equality (in social, but not gender, terms) would be maintained, and there would be no return to *ancien régime* fiscal or officeholding privileges. Freedom from arbitrary arrest, freedom of expression (though subject to unspecified restraints against abuses) and the inviolability of property ownership (including nationalized lands that had been expropriated by the state and sold to private citizens during the Revolution) were all proclaimed. So too was freedom of religious opinion, although Catholicism was specified as the religion of the state.

A third feature of the new regime put it more in line with the continental powers than with Britain. Retention of the Napoleonic state apparatus meant that France would possess a highly centralized governmental system, with a chain of command reminiscent of the military. Power would be concentrated in a central government composed of a Council of Ministers and Council of State (which prepared legislation), both appointed by the king and responsible solely to him. In accord with the law of 7 February 1800, crown-appointed officials would administer government in the provinces. This system held for consultative bodies of notables (such as municipal and departmental councils) and agents with real decision-making powers (though only with ministerial approval) – prefects, mayors, police commissioners, and officers of the military and *gendarmerie*. Members of the judicial system were also appointed by the central government. According to the Charter, judges held life tenure and the jury system would be maintained, but justices of the peace could be removed. Although judges thus theoretically could act with a measure of independence from the central government, the constitution afforded little opportunity for the judiciary to act as a counterweight to executive power. By the law of August 1790, judges were prohibited from interfering in, or taking cognizance of, acts of the administration. Charges against state administrators could only be lodged with the Council of State, which meant that government agents could be judged only by the government itself.[3]

[2] See P. Rosanvallon, *La monarchie impossible* (Paris, 1994), pp. 15–104.

[3] On the Napoleonic state, see S. Woolf, *Napoleon's Integration of Europe* (London, 1991) and I. Woloch, *Napoleon and his Collaborators* (New York and London, 2001).

Contemporary commentators were particularly struck by the Restoration's parliamentary system, but the new regime lay somewhere between British parliamentary government and continental authoritarianism. Despite the narrow confines of the electorate, the British House of Commons could claim to represent the nation and parliament did hold powers independent of the crown. Limited as its application was, the principle of representative government was entrenched in the British system, whereas it had no place in the regimes of continental powers other than France. Representative government was, however, anything but secure within the Bourbon Restoration. The Charter stated explicitly that Louis XVIII had voluntarily granted the new constitution. It was thus entirely a product of the royal will. According to royalists, the Bourbons had always been the legitimate rulers of France, despite the creation of the First Republic in 1792 and the subsequent execution of Louis XVI. Thus in 1814 the dynasty had simply returned to resume its rule; it had not been called back to the throne by the French nation and its legitimacy had nothing to do with the will of the people.[4]

If the Charter thus was simply an expression of royal generosity, what was to prevent a monarch from revoking it? In what sense was the Charter a contract, if the legitimacy of one contracting party (the crown) was recognized and the other (the French people) was not? From this fundamental ambiguity flowed a host of related uncertainties. Given that the Chamber of Deputies was elective, to what extent would the regime be guided by public opinion? The Charter did make provision for petitions to either Chamber, although they must be presented in writing and not in person. Was this a mechanism to allow the public to express its will? If public opinion was to play a part in the political system, what constituted the public? Did the public consist only of the enfranchised? Would public opinion be expressed simply through elections? Or would there be some place for the press and political associations? Concerns over the press and political association, in turn, gave rise to the most burning issue of all – how to maintain stability while admitting a measure of pluralism. Pluralism necessitates toleration of dissent. What would be the acceptable parameters for dissent?

In time Louis XVIII would come to view the Charter as the product of his own wisdom. Hence the constitution would gain a measure of security under his rule, although the issue of parliamentary independence would remain very much at play. Even this limited level of security would not,

[4] By way of contrast, see N. McCord, *British History 1815–1906* (Oxford, 1991), pp. 1–76, and B. Simms, 'The eastern empires from the challenge of Napoleon to the Restoration, c. 1806–30', in P. Pilbeam, ed., *Themes in Modern European History 1780–1830* (London, 1995), pp. 85–106.

however, necessarily remain upon the succession of the heir to the throne, the Count of Artois, brother of the king and a notorious advocate of unmitigated royal sovereignty. Thus the limited application of representative government in France rested upon shaky foundations.

The vagaries of royal will were not the only danger to representative government in France. The Napoleonic state had been designed for the provision of order rather than the safeguarding of political liberty. In this regard it was akin to other continental states and, indeed, a large number of Restoration European governments would adopt parts of the Napoleonic state for authoritarian purposes. Moreover, among Napoleonic officials an ethos of benign despotism held sway; administrators viewed themselves as the true representatives of the people. The state was the vector of progress and to do its work it should be untrammelled by politicians whose claims were based on the ignorance of voters, rather than the professionalism of government agents.[5]

Since the election of the Convention in late 1792, confidence in representative forms of government had varied in relation to fear of civil disorder. While elite preoccupation with social order was a crucial variable in the fortunes of representative government, it was not only the elite that had an interest in maintenance of the rule of law; support for Napoleonic order was by no means confined to the elite. When confronted by widespread civil disorder, French society generally turned to strong government as a remedy. As part of this tendency, the French turned against representative government due to its association with factionalism. Such had been the case at the end of the eighteenth century, and this tendency would remain until at least the 1870s.

For Restoration royalists, the chief threat to royal sovereignty lay in the establishment of a parliament capable of challenging the royal will. Advocates of parliamentary government inevitably based their claims on national sovereignty, although their plans of how to represent the nation were seldom very democratic. In this contest over ultimate power, royalists gradually grasped that the Napoleonic state could provide a means to check attempts to assert national sovereignty through the establishment of parliamentary government.

Given the inclination of royalists to denounce everything associated with the Revolution or Napoleon, there was irony in Bourbon governments adopting the Napoleonic political system for the purpose of establishing unchecked royal sovereignty. The reason for such apparent heresy becomes

[5] See David Laven and Lucy Riall, eds., *Napoleon's Legacy* (Oxford, 2000).

clear, however, if we consider the basic elements of the Restoration regime. Judges, Peers and members of the government were all ultimately appointed by the king and derived their authority from the monarchy. Only the members of the Chamber of Deputies derived their authority from a source other than the throne. Should the Deputies challenge the king's appointees in some regard, the potentially explosive issue of ultimate authority might very well arise.

The best way to ensure that no such challenge arose lay in securing a lower house which would comply with government, or royal, will. Towards this end, Bourbon governments consistently turned to the administration as a means to establish control over the electorate, so as to secure the election of 'suitable' Deputies. In the pursuit of control, governments either altered electoral laws, or simply broke them. Had the objective of control been achieved, the result would have been similar to the political system of the First Empire, wherein parliaments gave an impression of representing the nation but possessed neither the will nor the capacity to challenge or check the executive.

Restoration pursuit of despotism did not entail plans for the abolition of parliament, which would have smacked too loudly of disdain for public opinion and probably triggered revolution. Thus the Restoration drive for despotism should not be confused with *ancien régime* absolutism. Removal of parliamentary independence, nevertheless, was designed to prevent any serious challenge to royal authority from arising in the one body that could, and frequently did, claim to represent the nation.

Like Napoleon, royalists put forward the claims of strong executive government as the means to secure civil order. In essence, these were the arguments of all authoritarian states, and in this sense all the contemporary powers had a certain interest in the French Restoration experiment. Conversely, for the partisans of national sovereignty, the crucial question lay in how to combat authoritarianism without triggering fears of disorder. Royalists were by no means reluctant to label opponents as agents of disorder, and much would pivot on whether the public accepted such allegations.

Constitutional arrangements were one thing, and political practices another. If the Restoration experiment was troubled by the ambiguities of the Charter, the heritage of French political culture was even more problematic.

The Revolution of 1789 had seen the rise of two great traditions of political change. The two often overlapped, but for analytical purposes we can distinguish them along the following lines. The first consisted of creating public demand for change through argument and persuasion. The second lay in the application of force and coercion. These two modes could be employed for the purposes either of reform (changes which adjust a political system without altering its basic foundations) or revolution (change in the fundamental principles and structures of a system). While we tend to associate revolution with violent coercion, we should not discount the extent to which the successful application of force depends upon persuasion both before and after the event. Similarly, even reform has often entailed physical coercion, whether through direct violence or through intimidation.

Neither the political Left nor the political Right held a monopoly over either of the two great traditions. On one hand, not long after the convening of the Estates General in 1789, Louis XVI and his more conservative advisers decided to use the army to put an end to the demands of the more intransigent Deputies of the Third Estate. Thereafter the leaders of counter-revolution frequently sought to destroy Revolutionary governments by force – through civil war and by foreign intervention. On the other hand, proponents of the Revolution fought fire with fire from the fall of the Bastille onwards. While the Red Terror may have marked the zenith of Revolutionary coercion, the employment of violence remained characteristic of Revolutionary politics until Bonaparte's seizure of power in 1799.[6]

Both sides combined persuasion with coercion during the 1790s; neither the Right nor the Left was shy about propaganda and, when they could, they set about organizing groups who shared their objectives. The stakes were so high, and fundamental antagonisms so deep, however, that no regime could establish a system wherein differences could be resolved through recourse to public opinion via elections, no matter how narrowly the 'public' was defined. For a brief interlude during the Directory royalists did seek to regain control of government through election of (closet) sympathizers. Nevertheless, their intention was to overthrow the regime, and hence Directorial governments responded with purges of duly elected candidates. Not long afterwards, successful Jacobin candidates also had their elections annulled.[7]

Thus elections had offered no remedy to the discord within Revolutionary France prior to the coup d'état of Brumaire. Many members of the elite had come to associate elections and even the most modest forms of representative government with endemic strife, and there was remarkably

[6] For surveys of the Revolution, see D. M. G. Sutherland, *France 1789–1815* (London, 1985) and W. Doyle, *The Oxford History of the French Revolution* (Oxford, 1989).

[7] See M. Crook, *Elections in the French Revolution: An Apprenticeship in Democracy, 1789–1799* (Cambridge, 1996) and I. Woloch, *The New Regime* (New York, 1994), pp. 60–112.

little opposition to Bonaparte's subsequent destruction of political liberty. Napoleon left the forms of representative government in place, but while France retained a parliament and local councils of notables, these bodies had little by way of independent power. To give credit where it is due, one must acknowledge that Napoleon did stop the French from killing each other by the thousands, and that by 1814 habitual recourse to violence was much less a part of political culture. The Napoleonic regime's antidote to civil disorder, however, had consisted of depoliticization, partly based on governmental control of expression of opinion.[8]

The Charter of 1814 did make provisions for public opinion to play a part in the political system. For example, Frenchmen were granted the right 'to have their opinions printed and published, in conformity with the laws necessary to restrain the abuse of such liberty'. Moreover, the Chamber of Deputies would be determined by elections. Deputies would be elected to five-year terms, but the Chamber would be renewed by one-fifth each year. Electoral colleges, the organization of which would subsequently be determined by law, would choose the Deputies. Half of the Deputies had to reside in the department in which they were elected, and each college would have a president appointed by the king. The Napoleonic *corps législatif* would form the initial Chamber of Deputies, until the first renewal of one-fifth in 1816. While Peers would gain pensions of anywhere from 12,000 to 30,000 francs, Deputies would receive no salary. Thus Deputies would need to be well heeled. To be eligible a candidate must be male, over the age of forty, and pay a direct tax of at least 1,000 francs. Should fewer than fifty men paying 1,000 francs reside in a department, the required sum would be reduced until a total of fifty qualified individuals was reached.

The franchise would also be highly exclusive: one must be male, over the age of thirty, and pay over 300 francs in direct taxes. The latter was a hefty sum, requiring a personal revenue of roughly 1,200 francs and restricting the franchise to at most some 90,000 *censitaires*. These basic provisions ensured that the electorate would consist mostly of a plutocracy of landowners, although much remained to be determined concerning the electoral regime.

The Chamber of Deputies, despite the narrowness of its claims to represent the nation, did embody the representative principle in government and it immediately became a focus of public attention. Fascination with the lower house was partly due to its ability to criticize the government (a capacity shared with the Peers), but interest was magnified by the fact

[8] See Sutherland, *France*, pp. 333–5, and Woloch, *Napoleon*, pp. 3–9.

that Deputies were chosen by the public (however minimally defined) rather than appointed by the crown. The Chamber of Deputies possessed real power, especially over fiscal matters, and elections would be hotly contested.[9]

Despite such signs of willingness to play the political 'game' as outlined in the new constitution, a central question hovered from the origins of the Restoration: would the provisions for political liberty be sufficient to prevent the French from returning to the tradition of political violence? The Charter called upon all Frenchmen to bury the resentments of the past and begin anew. Whether the institutions set in place would provide sufficient means to resolve disputes through persuasion was, however, an open question. Closely related was the issue of whether Frenchmen would choose to confine themselves to such means. Armed revolt against unwanted regimes, or governments, had been characteristic of opposition groups in the past. Conversely, groups in power had often used the state to repress dissent.

Because the Restoration ended in the fall of the dynasty, it has been tempting to view the experiment as a failure. Such an interpretation is valid, provided that one adds certain qualifications. There was a fair measure of continuity between the Restoration and the subsequent regime, the July Monarchy, and hence one must conclude that certain aspects of the Restoration experiment were deemed successful, in so much as they were continued. Nevertheless, the political changes implemented in the aftermath of the Revolution of 1830 were of a fundamental nature. In effect, 1830 removed the central ambiguity of the Restoration. For those who had argued all along that the monarchy ruled by virtue of a contract with the nation, 1830 marked a confirmation of their interpretation of the Charter. For the proponents of this view, the Liberal Opposition, the ruling dynasty was in fact not integral to the political system, whereas the embodiment of national representation, parliament, was. This did not mean elimination of monarchy itself, but it did mean rejection of royal despotism; 1830 confirmed that France would be a genuine constitutional monarchy. Among the continental powers at the time, this was no small departure.

Thus 1830 marked the triumph of one interpretation over another in terms of polity, and this confirmation was managed rapidly and with relative ease. For those who think revolution must be a product of massive turmoil, the Revolution of 1830 hardly deserves the name. The relative absence of violence in overturning the regime points, however, to extensive

[9] See P. Mansel, *Paris between Empire 1814–1852* (London, 2001), pp. 103–6.

consensus in a public confronted by the necessity of choosing between the two interpretations of the Charter. The Liberal Opposition had created the consensus that brought an end to Bourbon rule.

## THE STATE OF PLAY

To this point in time, historians have discussed the Liberal Opposition in a number of contexts, but seldom as a subject in its own right. General surveys give us a narrative of the struggle waged between Restoration governments and their opponents. They have the virtue of covering the entire period, so that one can trace in broad outline the development of the Opposition and identify its main phases. The fortunes of Liberals ebbed and flowed and long-term narratives allow us to analyse the dynamic element of politics – response to circumstance and the relation change bore to public opinion. Such works, however, focus almost exclusively on 'high politics' – the actions and speeches of parliamentarians and the Liberal Parisian press.[10]

Complementary, in that they pursue lines of investigation touched on in the classic narratives, are the many biographies of major figures and studies of leading newspapers and journals. The Restoration was fruitful in the writing of political theory and history, and hence the *idéologues*, Germaine de Staël, Benjamin Constant, François Guizot, François Mignet, Adolphe Thiers and many others have long exercised the minds of intellectual historians. Resultant literature tells us something about the Liberal message, but largely leaves aside the subject of those who received it.[11]

The Liberal Opposition has also come under consideration in works on its component parts. Works on republicanism, liberalism, Bonapartism, democracy and radicalism to some extent can find roots in the Restoration. Such studies do contribute to an understanding of the Liberal Opposition, but their subjects are only parts of a greater whole. Moreover, in their search for doctrinal origins, they tend to give short shrift to doctrinal 'impurities' that were in fact central to the Opposition. In this sense, the search to give ideological definition leads to approaches that ignore the character of the Opposition as it actually existed. Liberal Opposition was in fact ideologically ambiguous in many regards, and politically heterogeneous in terms

[10] See A. de Vaulabelle, *Histoire des deux restaurations*, 8 vols. (Paris, 1847); P. Duvergier de Hauranne, *Histoire du gouvernement parlementaire en France*, 10 vols. (Paris, 1857–72); F. Artz, *France under the Bourbon Restoration* (Cambridge, Mass., 1931); G. de Bertier de Sauvigny, *The Bourbon Restoration* (Philadelphia, 1966); A. Jardin and A.-J. Tudesq, *Restoration and Reaction* (Cambridge and New York, 1984); and E. de Waresquiel, and B. Yvert, *Histoire de la Restauration 1814–1830* (Paris, 1996).

[11] See D. Bagge, *Les idées politiques en France sous la Restauration* (Paris, 1952) and A. Jardin, *Histoire du libéralisme politique* (Paris, 1985).

of the usual categories of analysis. One searches in vain for a specifically republican, liberal or Bonapartist movement during the Restoration. Yet members of the Opposition did have certain common beliefs and objectives that can be identified if one looks for them. Moreover, ideology is but one, and not necessarily the most important, part of politics.

Historians have frequently underlined divisions within nineteenth-century France. Without denying the existence of significant fissures, one can, however, ask whether the emergent picture does not partly reflect the analytical approaches taken. One can, for example, view the Liberal Opposition in terms of potential doctrinal divisions restrained only by the context of shared opposition. Conversely, one can also view the Opposition as a modern political phenomenon based on a coalition of diverse elements. Unless one wishes to study division only, one needs to pay equal attention to elements that bring unity. Doctrine can, of course, be a unifier, but so too can political traits such as moderation, gradualism, pragmatism, opportunism and willingness to compromise. All of these features were to be found in the Liberal Opposition, and they were integral to the consensus that brought about the fall of the Bourbon dynasty.

Identification of the Liberal Opposition with doctrine has at times led to serious misrepresentation. Perhaps the most general of mistakes has been to think that Liberals were liberal in the classical sense of the term. In truth, there was much about the Opposition that was illiberal, and figures such as the *doctrinaire* Guizot, often taken as representative of liberalism, fell well short of being typical. The emphasis that *doctrinaires* placed on finding a middle way between royal and national sovereignty positioned them to the political right of Liberals. A similar error has been to think that the political theory of, say, Constant can somehow be taken as characteristic. As a politician rather than a theorist, Constant was much more central to the Liberal Opposition than, say, the *doctrinaires*, but this was largely because Constant was frequently willing to compromise where ideological principles were concerned. The notorious twists and turns of Constant's political career begin to make sense if one takes context into account; Constant had a good, and pragmatic, political nose and followed it.[12]

Inclination to define politics in terms of doctrine has contributed to the absence of studies devoted to the Opposition as a political movement in

[12] See P. Pilbeam, *Republicanism in Nineteenth-Century France* (London, 1995); L. Girard, *Les libéraux français* (Paris, 1984); F. Bluche, *Le Bonapartisme* (Paris, 1980); J.-T. Nordmann, *Histoire des radicaux 1820–1973* (Paris, 1974); P. Rosanvallon, *Le sacre du citoyen: histoire du suffrage universel en France* (Paris, 1992) and the same author's *Le moment Guizot* (Paris, 1985); and D. Wood, *Benjamin Constant* (London, 1993).

its own right. The one exception, P. Thureau-Dangin's *Le parti libéral sous la Restauration*, thus has been highly influential, partly because it has had so little competition. Written in the 1870s, when the nature of the French regime was again in question, Thureau-Dangin's work castigated Liberals for failure to compromise with royalists for the preservation of the Bourbon monarchy. Thureau-Dangin, however, asserted an inappropriate criterion for judging the Opposition, in that he placed retention of the dynasty above establishment of even a limited measure of representative government. To Liberals, the reigning dynasty was a secondary matter, whereas the nature of the regime was of the essence. In July 1830 most of the public viewed the constitutional crisis from the same perspective, and it had not been 'tricked' into doing so by Liberals conniving at the removal of the Bourbons.

Thureau-Dangin derived his conclusions from the sources of high politics – memoirs, parliamentary debates and Parisian newspapers – and thus his work tells us little about the provincial voters who sent Liberal Deputies to the Chamber. Who were they? Why did they choose to vote Liberal? Did they simply read Parisian journals such as the *Constitutionnel*, or a brochure penned by Guizot, and then trot off to electoral colleges to cast their ballot? The impression created by Thureau-Dangin is that provincial voters were the marionettes of their Parisian masters. Were there no battles, or initiatives taken, at the local level?

*Le parti libéral* does contain valuable insights, despite such flaws. One cannot help but be struck by the point that Thureau-Dangin blazed paths that would be followed subsequently by many historians. Sympathy for royalism, despite its despotic inclinations, can be seen in the classic works of G. de Bertier de Sauvigny and, to a lesser extent, in a recent study by E. de Waresquiel and B. Yvert. Moreover, Thureau-Dangin was very much alive to the politically heterogeneous character of the Opposition, although he tended to view this as a sign of hypocrisy. In underlining the element of Bonapartism, he pointed in a direction later followed by F. Bluche and myself, and in downplaying republicanism he reached conclusions similar to those of E. Newman and P. Pilbeam.

More striking still is the pattern that Thureau-Dangin established for the interpretation of the dynamic of politics. Until 1824 old men, basically intent on overthrowing the monarchy, directed the Opposition. By 1824 they had been thoroughly defeated. Thereafter the Opposition changed in appearance, if not substance. Aided by the infusion of a younger generation, partly inspired by a vast diffusion of works on the Revolution, the Opposition publicly took on an essentially defensive image, while concentrating on improving its political organization. Simultaneously, ultraroyalists, whom Thureau-Dangin viewed with equal displeasure, became overly confident, pushing a counter-revolutionary agenda and alienating much of the public until the July Ordinances brought an end to the regime. Readers familiar with Restoration literature will recognize in this brief summation themes subsequently explored by S. Mellon (the use of history for political conversion), A. Spitzer (the younger generation), and P. Pilbeam (a revolution triggered by defensive reaction). To have had such influence, even if indirectly, constitutes no small achievement.[13]

Yet a great deal of broad interpretation would seem to rest on slim foundations. Historians have long recognized the Restoration's seminal influence as the first extended French experience of parliamentary government, but little attention has been paid to this seminal influence at the grassroots level, where the votes were counted. If one considers the depth of local study for, say, the Revolution, the contrast is striking.

Several reasons for what seems an obvious lacuna can be offered by way of explanation. The first lies in the elitist nature of the political regime. Only a tiny minority of male landowners possessed voting rights, and this particular group holds limited appeal for academics primarily interested in the development of mass democracy. The inclination of historians of the Left has been to view the period between the coup d'état of Brumaire of 1799 and the Revolution of 1848 as a sort of popular interregnum, worthy of scant attention.

Historical approaches based on assumptions of class struggle re-enforced the inclination to look elsewhere. If one posits that politics simply expressed class interests, then whatever struggles existed were of little significance for those outside the political elite. At most, the period consisted of the triumph of one small group (the bourgeoisie) over another (the nobility), a process that was preordained by the law of historical materialism and that had, in fact, largely been achieved in the Great Revolution. Bourgeois triumph was important, but the Restoration was mostly an 'Indian summer' for the nobility, and the most interesting of social groups had yet to return to centre stage. Presumptions concerning the social origins of political behaviour also coloured the limited number of studies conducted on the electorate. One can find statistical analyses of various departmental electorates, informing

[13] P. Thureau-Dangin, *Le parti libéral sous la Restauration* (Paris, 1888). See also the works previously mentioned by Bertier de Sauvigny, Pilbeam and Bluche; S. Mellon, *The Political Uses of History* (Stanford, 1958); E. Newman, 'Republicanism during the Bourbon Restoration in France, 1814–1830' (Ph.D. dissertation, University of Chicago, 1969); R. S. Alexander, *Bonapartism and Revolutionary Tradition in France: The fédérés of 1815* (Cambridge and New York, 1991); A. Spitzer, *The French Generation of 1820* (Princeton, N.J., 1987), and P. Pilbeam, *The 1830 Revolution in France* (London, 1991).

one of their socio-professional profile, but the cut and thrust of political battle is absent.[14]

## TOWARDS REINTERPRETATION: RECONSIDERING REVOLUTIONARY TRADITION

There have been exceptions to approaches that draw broad conclusions simply on the basis of doctrine or social character, and these do provide useful materials for building a general study of the Liberal Opposition. Much attention has been given to the Revolutionary tradition as an agent of change, and the element of armed insurrection has held particular fascination, apparent in a relative wealth of literature on the French Carbonari. The latter were, effectively, an offshoot of the Liberal Opposition of rather limited duration, but, because they formed conspiratorial societies designed for armed seizure of power, historians have focused on the Carbonari as part of a long tradition of insurrection. They were heirs of the Jacobins, and forerunners of the Society of the Rights of Man of the July Monarchy, and the various formulations of revolutionary vanguard organized by 'professional' revolutionaries such as Auguste Blanqui and Armand Barbès.[15]

The best study of the Carbonari, A. Spitzer's *Old Hatreds and Young Hopes*, reveals that it was largely middle-class, ambiguous in terms of political objectives, and ineffectual. Spitzer goes much further than previous authors in assessing the dimensions of the organization, a task made difficult by the interest members had in not leaving a trail for the police, but even in *Old Hatreds* we find relatively little information concerning the composition of the Carbonari in the provinces. Spitzer's study does, however, reveal the close relationship of the Carbonari to the Liberal Opposition; the former was derived from the ranks of the latter. Moreover, the Carbonari were the product of a combination of associations, some insurrectionary and some not, which dated back to the earliest stages of the Restoration. In other words, the insurrectionary tradition was a significant component of the Liberal Opposition, and hence must form part of the subject matter of this monograph.[16]

The Left by no means held a monopoly on covert political organization. Bertier de Sauvigny's *Le Comte Ferdinand de Bertier* demonstrates the extent

[14] See A.-J. Tudesq, 'Les comportements électoraux sous le régime censitaire,' in Daniel Gaxie, ed., *Explication du vote: un bilan des études électorales en France* (Paris, 1985).

[15] For an important exception, see the emphasis Rosanvallon places on 'liberal tradition' in his *La monarchie*, pp. 7–11, and *Le moment*, pp. 11–31.

[16] A. Spitzer, *Old Hatreds and Young Hopes: The French Carbonari against the Bourbon Restoration* (Cambridge, Mass., 1971).

to which ultraroyalism was organized in the form of secret societies, which, at times, used armed violence to achieve their objectives. What this alerts us to is that part of the experience of the 1790s, armed struggle between Revolutionary and Counter-Revolutionary groups, was continued into the Restoration. In comparison to the Revolution, the dimensions of this struggle were limited, but the mode of conspiratorial organization did persist. More to the point for our purposes, the nature of ultraroyalism had a direct impact on the Liberal Opposition and, in truth, the character of both was a product of the dynamic between them.[17]

Bertier de Sauvigny's *thèse* went some ways towards sketching the organization of ultraroyalism, and subsequently several works have put flesh on the bones of the initial outline. Much remains to be done, however, in that the organization of ultraroyalism was national and not restricted to the heartland of the Midi. The only way to grasp its full dimensions and character lies in a great deal more study at the local level, where battle between groups such as the Chevaliers de la Foi and the Liberal Opposition took place. All the same, it is at least true that there are good studies of ultraroyalism where it lived and fought for power.[18]

Conspiratorial organizations thus were a part of Restoration politics. Yet, if we know more about these means of struggle, this does not mean that they were the most important. For most of the Restoration, political wars were fought publicly rather than in the shadows of secret societies. Part of the complexity of unravelling Restoration history lies in the point that illegal and legal modes of contestation were often closely bound and, indeed, waged by the same individuals at different points in time. Gaining a true appreciation of the nature of politics becomes more difficult still when one knows very little about the legal forms of organized struggle.

Many analysts have approached post-Revolutionary France as a long project in 'terminating' the Revolution. There is much to be said for this, and certainly the Restoration French were preoccupied by what they understood of the Revolution. Nevertheless, while contemporaries may have viewed political issues in this light, there is little reason to follow their example. The Revolution, no matter how interpreted, offered no promised land wherein all problems would be rectified. The very idea that one could achieve such a state was a trap: the central task of the Restoration, as with

[17] G. de Bertier de Sauvigny, *Le Comte Ferdinand de Bertier (1782–1864) et l'énigme de la congrégation* (Paris, 1948).

[18] See J. Roberts, *The Counter-Revolution in France 1787–1830* (New York, 1990), pp. 77–111; D. Higgs, *Ultraroyalism in Toulouse* (Baltimore, 1973); G. Lewis, *The Second Vendée* (Oxford, 1978); and B. Fitzpatrick, *Catholic Royalism in the Department of the Gard* (Cambridge, 1983).

all subsequent regimes, was to set in place mechanisms capable of coping with the perpetual need for change.

It is something of a commonplace to point out that the term 'party' was used pejoratively during the Restoration, due to connotations of Revolutionary factionalism. It is also true that the notion of the 'General Will', often ascribed to the Enlightenment *philosophe* Jean-Jacques Rousseau but rampant in French political thought generally, tended to undermine ideas of pluralism and loyal opposition. How could one achieve unity and yet tolerate dissent? Moreover, many of the features associated with modern parties (party discipline, programmes, card-carrying membership and the like) either did not exist, or existed only in rudimentary form. Party is, however, but a form of a more general phenomenon – political organization – and, as will be demonstrated repeatedly in this work, the Restoration had a rich history in this.

Analysis of texts – speeches, publications or visual representations – can yield insight, but it can also be misleading if not viewed alongside behaviour and action. Very few of us would judge a politician simply by his or her speeches or symbolic gestures. In this case, rhetoric warning of the dangers of 'factions' was often a means of attacking another group's organization to the advantage of one's own. Organization was in truth a key to power during the Restoration and over the course of fifteen years it became increasingly sophisticated. Given its partisan nature, the government administration itself played a leading role in the development of political organization, but it was Opposition groups – ultraroyalists early in the Restoration and the Liberal Opposition thereafter – that progressed furthest.

Political association was often justified on the defensive grounds that the opponent was organized, but when organization succeeded, its objectives seldom proved to be simple maintenance of the status quo. Organization was, therefore, a vehicle for change. There was nothing new in this; organization had been the motor of the Revolution and the Counter-Revolution in the 1790s. Almost uniformly, Restoration general histories point to the development of the Aide-toi Le Ciel t'aidera electoral organization of 1827 as a first startling initiative. According to Pouthas, the 'fecund idea' of Guizot awakened 'all the latent forces at risk, for want of occasion [to manifest themselves], of dying in provincial inertia'. There was, however, very little about the Aide-toi that was novel, and that so much weight has been placed on it indicates how little research has been directed towards legal modes of organization.[19]

[19] See C. Pouthas, *Guizot pendant la Restauration* (Paris, 1923), pp. 369–80.

Acceptance of dubious generalization can partly be attributed to a narrow definition of politics that has either confined it to the electorate or divorced electoral politics from other forms of contestation. Voters did not, however, live in a vacuum. When they gathered at the colleges they were well aware of anticlerical demonstrations and the Catholic missions that triggered them. Tumult in theatres, petitions gathered on behalf of arrested journalists, battles to sustain mutual schools against ultramontane hostility, seditious Bonapartist tracts, market riots, and endless rumours over restoration of *ancien régime* privileges – all of this and more provided the context in which Restoration voters cast their ballots. Moreover, the assumption that an essentially conservative electorate was divorced from the disenfranchised simply does not hold up to scrutiny. In tracing the alliance between the 'blouse and the frock coat' in support of the Liberal Opposition back to 1820 in Paris and Rouen, E. Newman uncovered what was just the tip of the iceberg.[20]

One of the more recent developments of analysis, the study of political culture, holds great potential for reaching beyond narrow approaches to study of the Restoration. This becomes especially the case if political culture is considered to include practice as well as ideals. Issues of how the state sought to represent itself through festival and commemoration have increasingly come to the fore, and works by S. Kroen and M. Lyons have pointed to just how closely religion and politics were connected in the provinces. Kroen, in particular, through analysis of the cultural practices of anticlericalism, has taken a major step towards breaking rigid conceptions of what constituted politics during the Restoration.[21]

Of equal importance was patriotism. Questions of foreign relations have long been out of vogue in French history, but Restoration domestic and foreign politics were closely tied. How could matters have proved otherwise when the regime was twice established by Allied intervention? Moreover, patriotism was one of the most important means by which contemporaries formulated their identity. Like religion, patriotism had a politically innocuous aspect – very few claimed to be atheists, or proclaimed their detestation of France – but patriotism was largely the domain of the Left during the Restoration and it provided a means by which republicans, Bonapartists

[20] See E. Newman, 'The blouse and the frock coat: the alliance of the common people of Paris with the liberal leadership and the middle class during the last years of the Bourbon Restoration', *Journal of Modern History*, 46, n. 1 (1974), pp. 26–69.

[21] M. Lyons, 'Fires of expiation: book-burnings and Catholic missions in Restoration France', *French History*, 10, n. 1 (1996), pp. 240–66, and S. Kroen, *Politics and Theater: The Crisis of Legitimacy in Restoration France, 1815–1830* (Berkeley, 2000).

and liberals could unite. As with opposition to clerical privilege, patriotism was a great unifier for the Left and knew no class bounds.

If the emergent sub-discipline of political culture brings advantages, it can also bring liabilities. Within a rapidly burgeoning literature there is a certain penchant for using works of fiction as historical sources. Fiction can be useful for illustration, but it pivots on stereotype and for the Restoration, stereotypes, often derived from Balzac and Stendhal, have too often served as justification for conclusions that do not hold up well against archival enquiry.

By way of illustrating some of the stereotypes, we can turn to Bertier de Sauvigny's highly influential survey of the Restoration. According to the author, politics 'concerned only the upper level of the nation' and was 'outside the purview of the masses'. Politics came to life 'only on the eve of a national election or . . . a political visit or a sensational political trial. Parties in the local communities were made up of a circle of a few friends.' With brief exceptions in 1819, the provincial press counted for virtually nothing; there could be 'no political life in the provinces except as it . . . [was] . . . connected to the capital'. Elections were 'orderly and quiet; however hot the political passions became, the campaign was conducted among gentlemen'. Thus while the stability of institutions did enable France to undergo 'an apprenticeship in constitutional government, permitting the nation to have a real participation in political affairs', a characteristic of the Restoration 'was the narrowness of this political activity, which was limited to a very small minority of the privileged rich'.[22]

From this image of rustic backwaters, come many related stereotypes. Uninformed as it was by doctrine, provincial politics was simply a matter of nepotism and pursuit of local material interests; the candidate who best dispensed patronage could expect to represent local interests in Paris. Beyond providing contacts to secure contracts or, better yet, government office, the Deputy was largely free to follow whatever course he chose while in parliament. Certainly there was nothing that bound a Deputy to his local supporters in terms of ideology. Then again, why should there be? There were no official campaigns, prospective candidates inevitably disavowed intention of running, and there was no party organization – just whispering in local salons. All of which was very much as Stendhal and Balzac described provincial political life.[23]

[22] Bertier de Sauvigny, *Restoration*, pp. 288–99.

[23] See Artz, *France*, pp. 44–9, 73–4 and 80–2, and A. Pilenco, *Les moeurs électorales en France* (Paris, 1928). For two famous fictional representations, see Balzac's *Le député d'Arcis* and Stendhal's *Lucien Leuwen*.

One could go on, but there seems little need, given how standard such conventions have become. There are, however, several works that do not rest comfortably with such interpretation. Fragments of information often are to be gleaned from local studies, but even in as valuable a study as S. Fizaine's *La vie politique dans la Côte-d'Or sous Louis XVIII* evidence is largely restricted to election results and newspaper reports; one needs to dig deeper to gain a satisfactory view of local personnel and strategies. P. Lévêque's *Une société provinciale*, while it concentrates on Burgundian departments during the July Monarchy, does at times point to a Restoration political life which was far from 'dormant'. The latter point can also be made of P. Leuilliot's *L'Alsace au début du XIXe siècle*. Spitzer, in his study of the Carbonari, noted that political animosities probably ran deeper in the provinces than in the capital, and has recently turned to analysis of the electorate of the Doubs. While S. Kent's *The Election of 1827 in France* did not include study at the local level, the author did recognize that what made the Aide-toi successful was, at least in part, a rich tradition of local political experience.[24]

In addition to Kroen, two authors in particular have made notable contributions to breaking the grip of Parisian high politics. Contemporaries often noted the role of Charles Goyet as the 'Grand Elector' of the Sarthe, but not until recently has a historian, S. Neely, provided serious analysis of Goyet's pioneering work in electoral organization. In her article, Neely reveals many of the strategies employed by Liberals to combat administrative domineering, and challenges the view that political life 'failed to generate much interest'. As Neely notes, however, the question of whether the Sarthe was typical remains, and the article is largely confined to the period up to 1824. Conversely, P. Pilbeam has investigated the Opposition in many departments, analysing ideological character, social composition and economic interests. Her work enriches our knowledge greatly, but it is based primarily on the Opposition as it existed from 1827 onwards and does not direct much attention to electoral organization, which leaves a good deal yet to be investigated.[25]

Neely notes how much the Liberal Opposition in the Sarthe drew upon the leadership of former Jacobins, and, in a work which traces the fate of

[24] S. Fizaine, *La vie politique dans la Côte-d'Or sous Louis XVIII, les élections et la presse* (Dijon and Paris, 1931); P. Lévêque, *Une société provinciale: la Bourgogne sous la Monarchie de Juillet* (Paris, 1983); P. Leuilliot, *L'Alsace au début du XIXe siècle* (Paris, 1959); A. Spitzer, 'The elections of 1824 and 1827 in the Department of the Doubs', *French History*, 3, n. 2 (1989), pp. 153–76, and S. Kent, *The Election of 1827 in France* (Cambridge, Mass., 1975).

[25] S. Neely, 'Rural politics in the early Restoration: Charles Goyet and the Liberals of the Sarthe', *European Historical Quarterly*, 16, n. 3 (1986), pp. 313–42, and Pilbeam, *1830*.

the *fédérés* of 1815 up to the July Monarchy, I have found similar evidence of the importance of Jacobin organizational skills. If one combines this observation with Bertier's comments about the (relative) stability of parliamentary politics, an important feature of the Restoration begins to emerge. Old Jacobins had long experience of the difficulties of accommodating Revolutionary principles to desire for civil order and the rule of law. Many had concluded that too rapid an advance to the promised land of liberty had led straight to Napoleonic despotism.

Figures such as Goyet believed that liberty and order could be wedded by appeal to public opinion and legal political organization. Goyet also had strongly democratic tendencies based on confidence in the common sense of the 'people', who only disdained order when they could no longer bear oppression. In these regards he was a vector of the Revolution who remained both optimistic and tempered by experience. He would have no truck with the politics of coercion, thereby distinguishing himself from the famous general (the Marquis de Lafayette) for whom he orchestrated election. Goyet was, however, at the centre of a Revolutionary tradition, developed by the Liberal Opposition, best calibrated to promote, rather than retard, progressive change.[26]

Despite the contributions of the authors previously mentioned, a great deal of work must still be undertaken before a clear picture of Restoration opposition at the grassroots level can emerge. We know little about the 'rank and file' of the Liberal Opposition – those who voted for Liberal candidates, the activists who organized local voting, and those whose support enabled Liberals to win the constitutional struggle of 1830. Memoirs offer few clues. Rémusat, for example, does cite some of the figures who secured his election in the Haute-Garonne in 1830, but he views local politics with the disdain of a Parisian intellectual. At the other end of France, the Bas-Rhin, Jean-Jacques Coulmann was more gracious in recognizing his debts to local supporters, but he said very little about the work they did.

Largely based on accounts of 'high politics', secondary literature depicts departmental politics as a playground for notables who pulled the levers of patronage. Politics being politics, there is some truth to such observations. Yet such images do not go very far towards explaining why, for example, the abbé Henri Grégoire was elected in 1819 in the Isère, where he had no local 'roots' and no prospect of offering patronage. His victory was not a product of parochialism, and much the same could be said of the many

[26] See R. R. Palmer, ed., *From Jacobin to Liberal: Marc-Antoine Jullien, 1775–1848* (Princeton, 1993), and E. Harpaz, ed., *Benjamin Constant et Goyet de la Sarthe: correspondance 1818–1822* (Geneva, 1973).

Deputies elected in colleges far from their personal bases. More than the parish pump was at play, and there are many questions to be posed about the relationship between Deputies and their local supporters.[27]

In sum, then, the current state of Restoration literature calls for certain lines of enquiry that can be briefly summarized as follows. Study of the Liberal Opposition must take both the violent and non-violent wings of Revolutionary tradition into account and assess their role in promoting, or hindering, change. Similarly, evaluation of the Liberal Opposition should include analysis of Liberal relations with their opponents in terms both of ideology and means employed to secure objectives. In undertaking such an investigation, we should eschew narrow definitions of what constituted politics so as to explore the connections between electoral and non-electoral opposition, and to assess the ways in which sentiments such as patriotism and anticlericalism united Liberals, while dividing them from royalists. Ultimately, such lines of enquiry should yield a much better understanding of why the Bourbon Restoration fell in 1830, and also clarify the role that Liberals played in creating an almost equally short-lived successor regime.

## METHOD AND STRUCTURE

Who were the Liberals? Questions of personnel can be pursued in depth only at the local level, where one can accurately identify the groups that supported Liberal Deputies, and seek to determine what motivated them. Moreover, it is only by rooting politics in its context that one can uncover its dynamic element – decision-making.

The logical unit for studying grassroots Liberalism is the department. That the Opposition was largely organized on a departmental basis sprang from the electoral regime. In the early Restoration, voters gathered at the *chef lieu* to form departmental colleges and choose their Deputies. Such assemblies fostered a good deal of horse-trading among voters of the various localities and accustomed different groups to working in common. Thereafter, in 1820, the Law of the Double Vote renewed the departmental college for the wealthiest quarter of voters, while also creating *arrondissement* colleges. Crucially, battles developed over voter registration, and Liberal electoral committees, operating on a departmental basis, took charge of conducting registration campaigns. Liberal organization was not, however, limited to the departmental level. Contacts could extend throughout

[27] Rémusat, *Mémoires*, II, pp. 381–9; J.-J. Coulmann, *Réminiscences*, 3 vols. (Paris, 1862–9), II, pp. 232–4 and 241–4, III, pp. 139–40 and 183–7.

regions and indeed Deputies could provide the means for a degree of national coordination in Paris. The latter remark could also be made of the Parisian press, although the local press, where it existed, played a more direct role in organization. Assessment of the extent to which the Liberal Opposition was a national organization will form a continuous theme throughout this study, but for now we can note simply that the basic political unit was the department, in terms of both organization and initiative.

Selection of which departments to analyse is not easy. One cannot hope to please all historians who have conducted studies in the various regions of an exceptionally diverse country, but one can, at least, offer certain points by way of explanation. Having previously conducted case studies in Dijon and Rennes that to some extent share common ground with this monograph, I have rejected the otherwise attractive thought of returning to the Côte-d'Or and Ille-et-Vilaine. Other departments, such as the Bouches-du-Rhône, have been eliminated for technical reasons – the absence of the organization of the crucial archival series 'M' when this study was commenced.

In choosing departments on more positive grounds, I selected two where the Opposition was particularly successful: the Isère and the Bas-Rhin. Moreover, while the Isère was constantly a focus of national attention, not simply because of the election of Grégoire, so too was the Bas-Rhin, due partly to the triumphs of Benjamin Constant. Both departments were witness to the impact of the Carbonari revolts and both subsequently were in the forefront of the organization of legal modes of opposition.

Very different from the first two choices was the third. Bastion of an ultraroyalist network deeply implanted in the Midi, the Haute-Garonne did not elect a single Restoration Liberal. It thus provides a good example of what Liberals were struggling against. Not only was the Haute-Garonne the heartland of counter-revolution, in Joseph de Villèle it possessed the man who progressed furthest in implementing administrative depotism. To a degree Villèle's strategies as *premier ministre* constituted a departure from the initial decentralist tendencies of ultraroyalism. Nevertheless, his version of ultraroyalism, based on using the central government to eliminate rivals, represented the greatest threat confronted by Liberals.

To some extent, one must shape a monograph in terms of the primary materials still existing. In this regard the Isère and the Bas-Rhin offer particular assets in the form of substantial collections of personal correspondence. Through such materials one can enter into the world of grassroots organization in a way not possible through reading official correspondence or published memoirs. For the Haute-Garonne, the *France Méridionale*, an excellent source for tracing Liberal ideas and strategies, provides rewarding reading for the researcher.

Finally, it should be noted that for certain issues extensive research has been conducted in what was then known as the Seine-Inférieure, although this department is not given the sustained treatment of the other three. In terms of success rates, the Seine-Inférieure was not as strongly Liberal as the Bas-Rhin or the Isère, but it was much more favourable terrain than the Haute-Garonne. At a certain point, however, the gains of further research begin to diminish, and there are limits as to the number of examples one need put forward.

Politics is a product of the combination of local and national concerns and the nexus of these two is a preoccupation of this study. The Liberal Opposition was a national phenomenon, however, and the focus of this monograph will be on features common throughout France. Thus case studies are employed as a means towards investigating national issues, and great effort has been made to determine to what extent local developments exemplified national trends. Towards these broader objectives, the findings of local study are integrated with materials drawn from published literature and sources at the National Archives that cover all of France for subjects such as the Carbonari, subscription or petition campaigns, or the organization of potential tax revolts.

Towards integrating local and national politics, the first five chapters have been organized into four parts. Each chapter commences with discussion of the broad progression of national politics. Such discussion partly consists of rehearsing major developments, but, more importantly, it also serves to introduce a pattern which characterized national politics, but which can be most readily traced at the local level. The pattern consisted of brief phases of tripartite political division that ended in crisis as politics was reduced to bipolar struggle. A first phase of tripartite politics began in late 1816, but by 1819 it was already giving way to bipolar politics as the issue of ultimate sovereignty rose to the fore. Royalism triumphed in this first crisis of the early 1820s, and this ushered in a period of relative calm until the general election of 1827 began a second phase of tripartism. The latter proved even shorter than the first, and by the summer of 1828 the Restoration had entered into a second period of bipolar struggle that culminated in the Revolution of 1830.

Failure to break away from bipolar politics brought the fall of the Bourbon monarchy. In broad terms, we can identify three main groupings in Restoration politics: the Right, the Centre and the Left. The Centre, however, was always a fragile construction, utterly dependent upon the state for its formation, organization and direction. Herein lies a key to understanding Restoration politics: the state administration took on the role of a political party in seeking to control elections. This was the path of despotism and, as we shall see, the state went well beyond traditional methods of patronage in pursuit of its objective. For the moment, however, it is more important to note that the state apparatus could be put to different ends according to the objectives of the king and his government. During the phases of tripartism, two cabinet leaders, Elie Decazes and Jean-Baptiste de Martignac, sought to use the administration to create a moderate royalist block among the voters and the public generally. Both failed and in both cases government then passed into the hands of the Right, triggering the return of bipolar politics.

For most of the Restoration, politics was characterized by a dynamic of state initiative followed by Opposition response. This dynamic was, however, reversed in the early years of the Second Restoration. For this reason, the second part of chapter 1 will consist of discussion of ultraroyalism, and the third will analyse state response to ultraroyalism. In the fourth part the emerging character of Liberal Opposition will be traced.

Thereafter, consideration of state attempts to control elections forms the second parts of chapters 2 to 5. Herein methods the state deployed in acting as a political party, and responses by opposition groups, are analysed. State initiatives and opposition counter-initiatives formed the most dynamic element of politics, underpinning the pattern previously described.

Discussion of response to the state entails consideration of all parts of the political spectrum. For the Left, the fight against despotism was permanent, whereas for the Right, reaction to state control depended on who held power. As we will see, there were many divisions within the Right. All members did place priority upon royal sovereignty. Some royalists were willing to follow the lead given by Louis XVIII in granting the Charter, with its vague provisions for parliamentary government. Thus they were crucial to attempts to form a moderate royalist block. However, they splintered during periods of crisis, realigning either with the Left or, more frequently, the extreme Right.

Ultraroyalists formed the extreme Right. In a sense, ultraroyalism was like Bonapartism – as much a sentiment as a body of coherent ideas. Nevertheless, it can be identified as the heir of the Counter-Revolution. Ultimately, ultraroyalists were advocates of royal sovereignty untrammelled by any notion of national sovereignty. This did not necessarily mean that their devotion to the Bourbon dynasty knew no bounds; they saw in monarchy the means to enhance their social, cultural and political domination. On the whole, ultraroyalists were disposed to look upon the *ancien régime* as a golden age wherein the monarchy relied upon the 'superior' elements of society (principally the nobility and clergy) to provide good government based on a value system which was hierarchic in social terms, and closely attached to Catholicism.

Ultraroyalists were more than willing to contest the royal will when it did not appear that the government was working to re-establish social and political organization along the lines of their vision of the *ancien régime*. Ultraroyalist opposition was frequent, and at its most strident, whenever the king and his government appeared to be willing to compromise with the Left, or disposed to establish a non-ultraroyalist power base by creating a centrist following of moderate royalists: under such circumstances, ultraroyalists worked to destabilize compromising government ministries, and they were good at it. Polarization was the favoured means for defeating centrist initiatives because it forced a rallying of all royalists, including the crown, into a single camp. Fear of disorder was central to this strategy, and in the long run it served not only to block the development of moderate royalism, but also to ensure ultraroyalist political domination for most of the period.

Drawing upon methods initially devised during the Revolutionary and Napoleonic periods, ultraroyalists became adept at grassroots organization. Such strategies made them more independent of the state than moderate royalists, and when they were in opposition ultraroyalists developed modes of resistance to state control that, ironically, included championing constitutional liberties that they otherwise despised. One should not, however, confuse short-term strategies with fixed principles; to defend liberty while in opposition was not the same as respecting it while in power. Ultraroyalists did teach the Left a great deal, and the two extremes occasionally combined for immediate objectives, but the two were at odds over the fundamental issue of sovereignty. Despite occasional alliances born of expediency, the Left and the extreme Right were always enemies. Thus the character of the Left was shaped not just by battle against state despotism, but also by struggle with ultraroyalism.

The Left was not solely defined by what it opposed; it had its own positive character. Parts 3 and 4 of chapters 2 to 5 consist of analysis of the Liberal Opposition. The third parts concentrate on modes of opposition; they trace the process of development, particularly in terms of organization. The fourth parts analyse character in terms of ideology, material interests, social background, temperament and political culture. Especially in terms of political culture, the relation between enfranchised Liberals and the disenfranchised elements of the general public is probed.

The final chapter takes us beyond the Restoration and breaks from the previous organizational structure. In formal terms, Liberal Opposition ended with the Revolution of July 1830. Liberals did not, however, simply disappear; they realigned in new formations that slowly emerged under the July Monarchy. Thus the sixth chapter analyses the role of the Liberal Opposition in the July Revolution, the extent to which the Revolutionary Settlement reflected their objectives, and the mixed heritage Liberals brought to the politics of the new regime.

## NOMENCLATURE

Before we commence, certain matters of terminology and definition should be clarified. Even naming the subject of this study poses problems that Thureau-Dangin broached rather ambiguously. Having put forward the expression 'the opposition of fifteen years', he then dropped it, alternating between 'liberal party' and 'liberal opposition'. This was wise; while 'opposition of fifteen years' underlined continuity, it failed to recognize diversity. Moreover, it implied stasis, whereas the Opposition reformulated itself several times. Thureau-Dangin also noted that the Opposition assumed different titles at different stages – Independents, Opposition of the Left, *constitutionnels* and patriots. Nevertheless, he did not pay sufficient attention to the element of coalition sometimes hidden in these titles and, hence, lumped together Liberals and allied moderate royalist groups such as the Agier 'defection'.

Problems of nomenclature are further complicated by the penchant of royalists for applying a variety of labels to their opponents. Many of these were of historical derivation – Jacobin, Bonapartist, revolutionary or anarchist – but some of them referred to temperament or perceived place in the current political spectrum – moderate, ultraliberal or radical. The term that links the entire period, however, is that of liberal, which presumably explains why Thureau-Dangin adopted it.

One must make choices. Most historians have chosen the name 'liberal', and that precedent will be partly followed here. Only a handful of members of the Opposition, however, were truly liberal. Thus the most appropriate way to describe this group is to term it the Liberal Opposition, taking care to capitalize both words. The intention here is to recognize that, taking the Restoration as a whole, there was a certain unity that bound the Opposition. Contemporaries recognized this unity, and it went beyond simply dividing the political spectrum between Left and Right.

Liberal Opposition was defined by two essential characteristics. Unity was not based on simple preservation of the status quo as embodied in the Charter. It was based on a reading of the Charter which emphasized national sovereignty and gave rise to plans to 'develop the representative principle' within the constitution. Emphasis on national sovereignty distinguished Liberals from royalists and intermediary groups such as the *doctrinaires*.

Liberal conceptualization of national sovereignty was implicit in the emphasis Liberals placed on defending the nation from alleged threats. The most obvious danger lay in foreign influence over the French government, and the role of the Allied powers in restoring Bourbon rule was never forgotten by Liberals as they clamoured for an independent foreign policy. Appeal to patriotism was by no means monopolized by the Opposition, but Liberal championing of the past achievements of the Revolutionary and Imperial armies was calculated to embarrass royalists and sustain suspicion that the Bourbons were agents of reactionary foreign rulers determined to prevent the French nation from fulfilling its mission as vector of world progress.

Still more contentious was Liberal 'defence' of the nation from royal despotism. Liberal interpretation of the Charter as a contract entailed belief that the nation retained independent authority. Such authority was institutionalized in the Chamber of Deputies. Although the franchise might be narrow, Liberals maintained that the electorate represented the nation, as did the Deputies whom the voters elected. Such representation would be meaningless should the royal government gain control over the electorate, and hence Liberals demanded that voters and their Deputies must remain independent of the will of the executive and its agents.

Liberal emphasis on independence was also apparent in their opposition to formal social privilege. To Liberals, granting privilege to any group amounted to a form of enslavement of the nation because it allowed the privileged to dominate the non-privileged. In terms of Liberal rhetoric, privilege was the means by which the First and Second Estates had oppressed the Third prior to 1789, and groups calling for a return to the laws and institutions of the *ancien régime* were 'anti-national'. Defence of national sovereignty thus entailed opposition to any measure that appeared to conflict with the principle of equality in social, though not gender, terms. Liberals were at their most strident in denouncing what they perceived to be a drive by the Catholic Church, abetted by royal government, to establish domination over French society. Attacks on clerical despotism, by which the Church allegedly sought control of the nation through covert influence over the government, did serve partisan political purposes, but Liberals did sincerely believe that they were struggling to save the nation from clerical tyranny.

For much of the Restoration, Liberals and royalists alike sought to avoid direct confrontation over the issue of ultimate authority, but Liberal belief in national sovereignty underlay their insistence on the independence of the nation. Particularly in 1820 and 1830, periods of constitutional crisis clarified the fundamental division between royalists and Liberals. Groups such as the *doctrinaires* could try all they liked to find a constitutional balance between royal and national sovereignty; when push came to shove, Liberals proclaimed that ultimate authority derived from the nation, not the monarchy. When they enshrined this principle in the revised Charter of 1830, Liberals effectively repeated what many of them had told Napoleon in 1815 during the Hundred Days: thrones or governments are made to serve the nation, and not the reverse. Although statement of it may have at times been muted due to force of circumstance, belief in national sovereignty defined Liberal Opposition.

If a certain interpretation of the Charter united Liberals, there were differences among them. Studies at the high political level reveal two main Liberal blocks within the Chamber of Deputies – a Centre-Left and a Left. Similar distinctions were apparent at the local level, but here it is useful to employ terminology that is not typical of Restoration literature. At the grassroots level one can discern two broad groups that at times acted in concert but at times diverged. One cannot define them with absolute precision; one must resort to the impressionistic terminology of tendency and patterns of behaviour. One can, however, distinguish between moderate and radical Liberals clearly enough.

In national politics, the term 'radical' was used only occasionally and without much specificity. It entered into parlance in 1819 when royalist newspapers such as the *Conservateur* deployed the term to indicate what they considered extremism – the political ideas of men such as Constant and Alphonse Rabbe, publisher of the *Phocéen* of Marseilles – which, because they were relatively democratic, would surely lead to anarchy. Minister of the Interior Count Joseph Siméon referred to 'radicals' in the heated parliamentary debates following the assassination of the Duke of Berry as he vaguely linked French Liberals with British radicals and international conspiracy. Thereafter 'radical' connoted advocacy of reform, particularly expansion of the franchise, and it was in this sense that the term was defined in a dictionary published in 1823. Radicalism did not, however, extend to full manhood suffrage, something of which even republicans, with whom radicals were loosely associated, were wary. Thereafter the term went out of general usage until the aftermath of the 1830 Revolution, when conservatives again used it as a blanket description of all those who wanted further reform.[28]

It is only in its general sense that the term radical is used here. There were, however, differences at the local level between moderates and radicals, rooted in a combination of temperament and ideology. Individuals could at times slip in and out of either camp, but the two groups were remarkably consistent in their approach to minor and major issues. Radicals, as a rule, were more democratic. They were also much more likely to take the path of direct confrontation, including insurrection. In essence, they were less patient about the pace of change. Moderates also wanted change, but were more concerned by stability. Their approach tended more towards gradualism and, if possible, compromise; for these reasons they kept more rigorously to the path of 'legal liberty' with its reassuring emphasis on respect for the rule of law.

The dynamic between radicals and moderates could be fruitful. If radicals were at times too eager to push, moderates could be too timid in pressing for reform. While moderates were often more adept in persuasion when it came to broad public opinion, it was radicals who more often demonstrated the energy necessary to put into effect strategies broadly mapped out by the two groups. This is not to say that either side possessed more conviction, but it is to say that the Liberal Opposition worked most effectively when the two groups acted in unison. When the two sides took differing courses, the results could be catastrophic. When moderates failed to prevent them from taking the insurrectionary path, radicals contributed to periods of disorder that played into the hands of reaction. The one exception came in July 1830, when resort to force was considered defensive, and hence justified, by the public. Even then, radicals drew the wrong conclusion and wound up blocking change rather than advancing it.

This pattern was hardly specific to the Restoration; the periods preceding the Revolutions of 1830, 1848 and 1870 were not characterized by political insurrection, but the periods following these landmarks were, and they led, more or less directly, to repression. The Liberal Opposition thus provides an example with broad implications.

[28] See Nordmann, *Radicaux*, pp. 25–6 and J. Kayser, *Les grandes batailles du radicalisme* (Paris, 1962), pp. 6–9.

I

# *False starts and uncertain beginnings: from the First Restoration (May 1814) to the elections of September 1816*

## PART ONE: TUMULTUOUS POLITICS AT THE NATIONAL LEVEL

Uncertainty shrouded the First Restoration. Most historians have concluded that the First Treaty of Paris, signed on 30 May 1814, was relatively lenient: France was reduced to her 1792 frontiers and lost colonies in the West Indies and the Indian Ocean, but would not have to pay reparations. The French, however, had grown accustomed to victory under Napoleon and what was lost was at least as apparent to them as what had been salvaged. Talleyrand would represent France at the Vienna Congress, but it was by no means clear that *la grande nation* would have much say in the post-war settlement. Wounded patriotism, thus, posed unsettling questions for a regime installed by the Allied powers.[1]

Perhaps the prospect of peace might have enabled the Bourbon monarchy to entrench itself, had the government not exacerbated tensions by committing a series of errors. There was little immediate administrative purge at the start of the First Restoration; 76 per cent of the Imperial corps was maintained. By February 1815, however, the Minister of the Interior, the abbé François-Xavier de Montesquiou, was asking prefects for lists with comments on the worthiness of *fonctionnaires*, and change was accelerating. More potentially explosive were alterations in the army. Reduction by about three-fifths was perhaps not a great danger where common soldiers were concerned; many of the latter had simply melted away in the face of defeat. Nevertheless, 12,000 officers were put on half-pay and sent to cool their heels in the provinces while awaiting recall. To add salt to their wounds, the Minister of War, General Pierre-Antoine Dupont, known mostly for a

[1] For background, see Bertier de Sauvigny, *Restoration*, pp. 3–145; Jardin and Tudesq, *Restoration*, pp. 3–31; Waresquiel and Yvert, *Restauration*, pp. 11–195, and P. Mansel, *Louis XVIII* (London, 1981), pp. 170–343. On electoral procedures, see G.-D. Weil, *Les élections législatives depuis 1789* (Paris, 1895), pp. 60–121; P. Bastid, *Les institutions politiques de la monarchie parlementaire française (1814–1848)* (Paris, 1954), pp. 211–40, and Rosanvallon, *Le sacre*, pp. 209–49.

humiliating defeat at Baylen in 1808 during the Penisular War, handed out plum positions to returned émigrés who had fought against France.

Expiatory ceremonies to honour royal 'martyrs', such as Louis XVI, Marie-Antoinette and the Duke of Enghien, gave the opposite message of the Charter's call to forget. While the state might have preferred not to dwell on regicide, emphasizing royal 'forgiveness' more than suggested that something to forgive was remembered. All civil servants were expected to attend and the sub-text of these ceremonies, often made explicit by local clergymen, was that the Revolution was one great sin. Did ceremonies in Brittany honouring former *chouans* not suggest that some Frenchmen were in a privileged position where royal favour was concerned? Why was it necessary to ban all work on Sundays? Doubts increased when, in introducing legislation to restore unsold nationalized lands to the original owners, Minister of State Count Antoine de Ferrand (a notorious advocate of counter-revolution) praised émigrés who had remained in exile with their king to the bitter end. Perhaps there was a link between such sentiments and disappointing implementation of the Charter's proclamation of freedom of expression? Censorship would continue for writings of less than twenty pages; newspapers would have to apply for a permit prior to publication, and bookshops and printers must obtain a licence.[2]

Uncertainty over the evolving nature of the regime was greatly exacerbated by the counter-revolutionary inclinations of the king's brother Artois, and the circle of intransigent émigrés who clustered round the apparent heir to the throne. The two brothers had lived separately through most of their period of exile from France, and the royal household, and patronage network, of Artois was almost as large as that of the king. In essence, Artois stood for royalists who longed for the good old days of the *ancien régime*, and he and his entourage, often referred to as the Pavillon de Marsan (after the wing of the Louvre occupied by the count), could be viewed as a less compromising alternative to Louis XVIII waiting in the wings.

Evidence of surging alarm was manifest in rumours of a return to feudal dues and the Church *dîme* sweeping through the countryside in late 1814 and early 1815. Sensing the vulnerability of the regime, a number of former Imperial and Revolutionary notables began plotting revolt in favour of some alternative regime – perhaps Orleanist or republican. Such conspiracies were then swept aside when the leading threat to the Bourbon monarchy returned to France. Napoleon's decision to escape from exile at Elba was undoubtedly

[2] See Kroen, *Politics*, pp. 63–75, and F. Waquet, *Les fêtes royales sous la Restauration* (Geneva, 1981), pp. 79–81 and 130–1.

a gamble, but it was a calculated one. The Bourbon government had failed to pay pensions promised to him as part of his abdication in 1814, and the dignitaries at Vienna were pondering whether to distance him further, to the Azores. Emissaries from France had informed him of growing public apprehension and he decided to roll the dice. Leading a band of roughly 1,200 men, he landed close to Antibes on 1 March 1815 and began his 'Flight of the Eagle'.

Napoleon hoped the Allied powers would accept his return, and to further this end he proclaimed his intention to abide by the First Treaty of Paris. Appreciation of the weakness of his position could also be seen in proclamations declaring he had returned to rescue the new France that had emerged from 1789 onwards from the clutches of the past. Should priests and nobles not desist from seeking to enslave the nation, Napoleon would hang them from the lampposts!

The message held appeal. That the army rallied was no surprise; the fervour of the rank and file ensured that forces sent to arrest the former emperor merely joined in his Flight. More telling was the upsurge of public support apparent among peasants who joined in the march, and the rapturous receptions given at Grenoble and Lyons. To be sure, not all were pleased. At Paris, liberals such as Benjamin Constant likened Bonaparte to Attila the Hun, and, as Bonaparte's march took on the character of a triumphal parade, Louis XVIII saw fit to assemble parliament and promise to uphold the Charter. He also promised to die rather than flee, but departed for Ghent shortly before Napoleon's arrival at the Tuileries on 20 March.

More serious resistance was launched when Duke Louis-Antoine of Angoulême, elder son of Artois and nephew of the King, organized royalist forces for an attack upon the usurper. Angoulême was made Lieutenant General of the Midi, and Baron Eugène de Vitrolles, a former royalist secret agent who had become a provisional Secretary of State early in the Restoration, sought at Toulouse to organize a royalist government in the south and west. Angoulême's volunteers were, however, almost surrounded close to Valence and capitulated at La Palud on 8 April; Vitrolles had been arrested five days before. As part of the capitulation, Angoulême was allowed to retire to Spain.

The final episode of Napoleonic rule, the Hundred Days, exacerbated the polarization already apparent during the First Restoration. Allied refusal to deal with Napoleon soon made renewal of war inevitable. Many of the French preferred not to choose sides, but France clearly was not the aggressor in the looming conflict and, while it had been short, previous invasion had left bitter memories. Napoleon only partially fulfilled the promises of renewed liberty made during the Flight of the Eagle, and hence a revision of the Imperial constitution known as the *Acte additionnel* gained a relatively lukewarm response when put to a plebiscite. Deputies elected to a Chamber of Representatives included Bonapartists, but also liberals and republicans less dedicated to the dynasty. Rallying in a federative movement was, however, substantial; perhaps half a million *fédérés* joined, and recruitment gained pace until the cause was lost at Waterloo.

Royalist attempts at subversion were, in the main, unimpressive. Vendean royalists did manage to raise a revolt, but the Imperial government was well on the way to reasserting control prior to Waterloo, and it was defeat abroad that brought Napoleon's second fall. Liberals and republicans in parliament pressured Bonaparte into a second abdication on 22 June, and set up a provisional government led by the Minister of Police, Joseph Fouché, a notorious Terrorist of the Revolution who had become a duke under Napoleon.

The circumstances surrounding the foundation of the Second Restoration were even more volatile than those of the First. Louis XVIII returned to Paris 'in the baggage train of the Allies', strengthening an association that became all the more debilitating as some 1,200,000 Allied troops poured into France, occupying sixty-one departments. Requisitions, rape and plunder ensued. The Second Treaty of Paris, signed in November, proved far harsher than the first. France was reduced to her 1790 borders, ceding strategic territories along the north and eastern frontiers to the Netherlands, Prussia, Bavaria and Sardinia. This time reparations were set at 700 million francs to be paid in instalments over five years. In addition, the French would pay the costs of military occupation by 150,000 Allied troops until the reparations were liquidated.

For Louis XVIII, equally distressing was that Fouché, a regicide, and Talleyrand had played integral roles in engineering his return. Fouché had convinced the provisional government to capitulate rather than fight, and thrown his lot in with a Second Restoration during negotiations with Wellington, commander of the Allied forces. Talleyrand was all too prone to view himself as a 'kingmaker'. The royalist writer François-René Chateaubriand dubbed Talleyrand and Fouché 'sin and vice', but both had to be included in the Second Restoration's initial government.

The king gained deliverance from such unwanted allies by calling for general elections in August. The elections, in turn, yielded the *Chambre introuvable,* wherein extreme royalists held a large majority. In a sense, the king had leapt from the frying pan into the fire in that he now had to compromise with ultraroyalists in order to secure effective government. He was, however, able to form a cabinet more to his liking on 24 September, and Duke Armand-Emmanuel of Richelieu became head of the new government. An émigré initially thought to be a 'pure' (an ultraroyalist), Richelieu certainly had no love for the Revolution or Napoleon, but his moderate temperament put him more in line with the wishes of the king than with ultraroyalist leaders. Also in the cabinet, as Minister of Police, was Elie Decazes, whose subsequent rise to prominence was based almost solely upon royal favour. The ambitious Decazes soon concluded that the less the king relied on others, including ultraroyalists, the more he would come to rely on his personal favourite.[3]

The first year of the Second Restoration was marked by struggle in which Louis XVIII gradually sought to free his rule from dependence upon ultraroyalism. During his exile at Ghent, the king had moved closer to the intransigent attitudes of his brother Artois, leader of ultraroyalism. The king realized the dangers of plunging headlong into counter-revolution, and he did intend to abide by the Charter, as he interpreted it; in these regards he differed greatly from his brother. Louis XVIII and his government also intended, however, to root out the Revolutionary and Bonapartist elements in the administration and military upon which the First Restoration had relied; such intentions gave the government a certain amount of common ground with ultraroyalists. Moreover, several members of the cabinet, including Minister of the Interior Count Vincent-Marie Vaublanc (an adviser to Artois), had distinctly 'pure' tendencies. Thus it is not quite accurate to view this period simply as one wherein a moderate government sought to temper the demands of an ultraroyalist Chamber of Deputies. Certainly the cabinet was less extreme and in time it would increasingly distance itself from ultraroyalism, but the White Terror, hardly a product of moderation, was partly its own doing, and something which it intended to direct for its own purposes.

The White Terror of 1815–16 can be divided into legal and illegal components. Illegal White Terror consisted of retribution conducted by individuals or groups allegedly motivated by royalism. Murder and pillage were meted out to a host of victims, usually those who had been most pronounced in supporting Bonaparte during the Hundred Days. The extent to which figures of the Left had rallied made them vulnerable, recommencing

[3] Armand-Emmanuel du Plessis, Duke of Richelieu, had emigrated from France in October 1789 and subsequently served Czar Alexander as governor at Odessa. Decazes had earlier been attached to the household of Napoleon's mother, but had refused to take an oath of allegiance to the Emperor during the Hundred Days. Thereafter Decazes assiduously cultivated the affection of Louis XVIII, gaining the pejorative nickname *le favori* among his opponents.

cycles of violence that in some regions predated the Revolution. Thus politics was bound up in a variety of animosities, ranging from confessional differences to clan rivalries, and to this mix was added simple criminality. Illegal White Terror occurred mostly in parts of the Midi; perhaps some three hundred people were murdered and thousands more fled from the region.[4]

Legal Terror had several elements. On 28 June Louis XVIII issued a proclamation granting amnesty to subjects who had been led 'astray', but also vowing punishment of 'the instigators of treason'. To Fouché fell the task of drawing up a list of traitors, and this was then pared back in the ordinance of 24 July to fifty-four leading figures, including seventeen generals to be tried by military tribunal, and thirty-seven others to be placed under house arrest until parliament had decided their fates. Simultaneously, a massive purge of administrative and military personnel began; ultimately, perhaps 80,000 civil servants and 15,000 military officers would be punished.

Thereafter, from October to January 1816, parliament passed a series of punitive laws. A law of public security enabled the arrest of individuals on suspicion of conspiracy, and laws against seditious speech and writing complemented this measure. Special courts (*cours prévôtales*) were then established to judge offenders and they would eventually sentence some 6,000 individuals. Finally, an ironically named amnesty law excluded from clemency individuals placed under house arrest by the ordinance of 24 July, including regicides who had rallied to Napoleon in 1815, and any other individuals who had been indicted for treasonous actions committed during the Hundred Days. While most of the targeted individuals were subjected only to imprisonment or exile, several, including Marshal Ney, whose rallying to Napoleon during the 'Flight' had made him a symbol of treachery, were executed.

Legislative initiative for Terror came from ultraroyalists in the Chamber of Deputies, but the laws placed extraordinary power in the hands of the state and, ultimately, enabled the government to wrest control over White Terror away from ultraroyalists in the provinces. There was irony in this process in that ultraroyalists had thus created the means by which the government regained control over coercion. In this regard, however, it should be kept in mind that the dividing line between the cabinet and ultraroyalism was unclear when the laws were passed. Moreover, at that

[4] D. Resnick, *The White Terror and the Political Reaction after Waterloo* (Cambridge, Mass., 1966), and Alexander, *Bonapartism*, pp. 219–47.

stage ultraroyalists expected to grasp the reigns of power exclusively for themselves. Extreme measures could then be used to eliminate all those to whom the king might turn by way of alternative to the 'pures'. It took time before the cabinet's inclination to temper vengeful initiatives became fully apparent to ultraroyalists, who then reacted with steadily mounting anger.

During the First Restoration leading ultraroyalists had proclaimed their distaste for the Charter. When presented with a Chamber of Deputies to their liking in August 1815, however, they rethought their position. If parliament truly did possess power, control over it could be used to counter the compromising proclivities of the king. Ultraroyalists therefore championed parliamentary prerogative, as Vitrolles and Chateaubriand argued that the cabinet must represent the majority in parliament. Although this objective was not achieved, the *Chambre introuvable* did establish important conventions in terms of initiating and amending legislation. Moreover, ultraroyalist obstruction over the budget in 1816 forced the government to concede the right of parliament to approve state expenditures. Thus, in one of the great paradoxes of the era, ultraroyalists who had begun the Restoration by denouncing the Charter's limited provisions for parliamentary government wound up helping to entrench parliament's role within the new regime.[5]

Equally significant were the organizational strides ultraroyalists made in the two Chambers, and crucial to such organization was the secret society known as the Chevaliers de la Foi. The Chevaliers had mobilized support for the First Restoration, had been disappointed by the result, and had then reactivated their network during the Hundred Days. By the Second Restoration most Chevaliers were determined that the mistake of compromise would not be repeated and thus prior to the parliamentary session they purged moderate Chevaliers. A new cell was then formed to act as an ultraroyalist parliamentary steering committee.

Meanwhile, meetings of the mass of ultraroyalists at the salon of the Deputy Jean-Pierre Piet could draw upwards of 228 parliamentarians. It was here that Joseph Villèle began to establish ascendancy over many ultraroyalists, while the star of older Chevalier leaders such as Mathieu de Montmorency (an honorary aide-de-camp of Artois and closely tied to the

[5] Bertier de Sauvigny, *Le Comte*, pp. 184–5, 212–16, and J. Barthélemy, *L'introduction du régime parlementaire en France* (Paris, 1904), pp. 166–81, 246–65. See also E. Waresquiel, 'Un paradoxe politique. La Chambre "introuvable" et la naissance de parlementarisme français (octobre 1815–avril 1816)', *Commentaire*, 15, n. 58 (1992), pp. 409–16, and R. S. Alexander, '"No Minister": French Restoration rejection of authoritarianism', in D. Laven and L. Riall, eds., *Napoleon's Legacy* (Oxford, 2000), pp. 29–47.

Count) waned. Son of a minor provincial noble landowner, Villèle did not possess the social prominence, or the long-term connections to the court, of the aristocratic Montmorency, but his organizational skills and ability to speak in parliament soon drew followers to him. Nothing like full party discipline was achieved among ultraroyalists, as most Deputies voted according to their own lights and sometimes in accord with the government, but divisions within the ultraroyalist camp were basically a product of strength. Meetings held by a small *ministériel* (pro-government) group of moderate royalists, and by a handful of left-wing Deputies, who gathered at the home of the republican Marc-René Voyer d'Argenson, were much less impressive.[6]

For opponents of the extreme Right, the most promising development of the winter of 1815–16 was that growing ultraroyalist criticism of cabinet moderation angered Louis XVIII. Thus the influence of Decazes waxed, leading ultraroyalists to denounce him in the Chambers after Count Antoine-Marie de Lavalette, the Imperial Postmaster General convicted of treason for his actions during the Hundred Days, escaped from prison. All this did, however, was convince Decazes that the leading threat to his own prospects, and hence those of the crown, was the extreme Right.[7]

Just how weak the Left and Centre were could be seen when Vaublanc presented a first electoral law in December 1815. The bill called for maintenance of indirect elections, but with a narrow franchise in which a high proportion of voters would be government officials, civil servants or clergymen. To the minister's chagrin, ultraroyalists, led by Villèle, attacked the proposal for the power it placed in the hands of the administration. They then presented a counter-proposal also calling for indirect elections, but with a broader franchise at both levels. On the one hand, Vaublanc's proposal was a first sign of government desire to control the electorate – hardly a recipe for free expression of opinion. On the other hand, Villèle's counter-proposal was calibrated to favour domination of the electorate by wealthy landowners, perceived to be an ultraroyalist stronghold. For tactical reasons, centrist and left-wing Deputies actually supported the government bill, but fortunately for them, nothing came of either proposal.[8]

By the early months of 1816 public discontent with ultraroyalists demanding the death penalty for individuals found in possession of the tricolour

[6] Bertier de Sauvigny, *Le Comte*, pp. 187–90; comte de Villèle, *Mémoires et correspondance du Comte de Villèle*, 5 vols. (Paris, 1887–90), I, pp. 349–52, 366–72, 378–9, 397, II, 40–7, and baron de Pasquier, *Histoire de mon temps: mémoires du Chancelier Pasquier*, 6 vols. (Paris, 1893–96), IV, pp. 59–67.

[7] R. Langeron, *Decazes, ministre du roi* (Paris, 1960), pp. 77–80.

[8] Vaulabelle, *Histoire*, IV, pp. 175–89.

was reaching serious proportions. Nevertheless, moderates in the cabinet could not move precipitously to reign in extremism. For one thing, ultra-royalist approval of the budget had to be gained, and to secure this Louis XVIII had virtually to promise not to call for general elections prior to the next parliamentary session. Moreover, compromise had to be made with some of the theocratic aspirations of ultraroyalism: divorce was abolished, although a bid to transfer control over civil registers back to the clergy was blocked by the Peers.

Worse still for proponents of national reconciliation was that ultraroy-alist warnings against compromise were given credence by the discovery of several left-wing plots to overthrow the regime. Most of the conspiracies were minor, far-fetched affairs, but rebellion at Grenoble in May 1816 was another matter. Didier's revolt took on serious proportions, and briefly seemed to substantiate allegations of imminent revolution.

More significant in the long run, however, was public outrage at the severity of ensuing repression at Grenoble led by the ultraroyalist General Donnadieu. Also significant for the cabinet, though less publicized, was another affair at Nancy in July; subsequent court testimony revealed that a police spy and the local prefect had in fact provoked an alleged conspiracy. Meanwhile, prosecution of four leading *fédérés* for 'conspiracy' at Dijon during the Hundred Days went badly awry, much to public satisfaction. Decazes and Louis XVIII rightly assessed that White Terror was binding the regime to ultraroyalist fanaticism in the perception of much of the French public, and at this point they moved directly towards winding down repression.[9]

To maintain pressure on the government during the parliamentary interim, ultraroyalists presented themselves as the true representatives of public opinion in the summer of 1816. Mass gatherings were organized to receive leaders arriving from Paris, and in the most notorious episode Villèle passed through a triumphal arch upon his return to Toulouse in late May. The houses of the city were bedecked with white flags, church and municipal bells rang, and Villèle enjoyed an escort of the National Guard as his cortege wound through the streets. For Louis XVIII, wrapping partisan politics in state ceremonial was the last straw, and Decazes was able to convince the king to call for general elections in September.[10]

[9] Alexander, *Bonapartism*, pp. 175–6, 258, and G. Richard, 'Une conspiration policière à Nancy en 1816', *Annales de l'Est*, 10, n. 3 (1959), pp. 173–88.

[10] AN, F7 9659, 16 May 1816. See also P. de Rémusat, ed., *Correspondance de M. de Rémusat pendant les premières années de la Restauration*, 5 vols. (Paris, 1883–4), II, pp. 1–10, 34, 72–6; Villèle, *Mémoires*, II, pp. 49–52 and III, p. 15, and E. Daudet, *Louis XVIII et le duc Decazes* (Paris, 1899), pp. 115–49.

That ultraroyalist roots were shallow was the message of the elections of September. One should not underestimate 'pure' successes: the north and east thoroughly rejected ultraroyalism, but the Midi remained a bastion and elsewhere results were close to even. A rough final count yielded 92 ultraroyalist Deputies and 150 *ministériels*. Given the threat posed by ultraroyalism, the Left was generally content to throw in its lot with Decazes and combined with government followers in an electoral block known as the *constitutionnels*. The term *constitutionnel* indicated defence of the Charter against ultraroyalist hostility, but, as time would tell, such a defence left little room for liberty.[11]

Thus the prospects for a successful Restoration 'experiment' looked dim after the first two years of Bourbon rule. Association with the Allied powers was an inevitable liability for the monarchy, but more telling was fear that the Bourbons would favour the interests of the former privileged orders. Bonaparte had exploited such association and fear to engineer his Flight of the Eagle, but he had not created them. Moreover, it was the military might of the Allied powers, not the strength of internal French royalism, that had overthrown the Imperial regime of the Hundred Days. Without Allied intervention, or fear of further intervention, the Bourbon regime could not have withstood assault by its leading rival.

In the immediate aftermath of Waterloo, Louis XVIII and his government had collaborated with ultraroyalists to strike against Bonapartist and Revolutionary elements accused of having betrayed the First Restoration; it was only towards the end of 1815 that Richelieu's cabinet's inclination to temper ultraroyalist calls for retribution had become apparent. Gradually the regime had managed to substitute legal state repression for illegal ultraroyalist-dominated White Terror, but polarization between royalists and their opponents had only increased in the meantime. In his electoral triumph of September 1816 Decazes had managed to cobble together a coalition based on expedience and fear of ultraroyalism, but whether this could provide a foundation for future stability remained very much in question.

## PART TWO: POLITICAL WAR AT THE GROUND LEVEL: THE RISE OF ULTRAROYALISM

For much of the Restoration, politics consisted of government initiative followed by opposition response, but ultraroyalists, especially members of the Chevaliers de la Foi, reversed this order from May 1814 to September 1816.

[11] Bertier de Sauvigny, *Le Comte*, pp. 185–6, 214–16, 243–5.

During the First Restoration, Chevalier organization was uneven nationally: it was already significant in the Midi, but cells in departments such as the Isère, Doubs, Côte-d'Or and Seine-Inférieure were at most embryonic. Nevertheless, ultraroyalist groups did generate fear throughout France.[12]

Because of their social prominence and penchant for aggressive public pronouncements, ultraroyalists could provoke alarm even in regions where they were relatively few in number. A visit to Grenoble in October 1814 saw Artois surrounded by 'pures' who criticized compromise with the Revolution, sparking anxieties over whether any Bourbon ruler would adhere to the Charter. Such doubts were exacerbated by affronts to wounded patriotism throughout the Isère as banquets and balls given to Allied officers and potentates led to the fatal association of royalism with 'anti-national' interests. Ostentatious displays in a time of hardship were also tactless; subsequently there would be a widespread tax revolt when the regime sought to collect indirect consumption taxes (*droits réunis*) that Artois had promised would be abolished. Tensions were equally apparent in the Bas-Rhin, where alarm over the apparent ascendancy of émigrés and the 'anachronistic pretensions' of clergymen led to rumours of an end to religious toleration and revocation of nationalized land sales. While the Protestant Consistory rallied to the new regime, in June the prefect had to instruct the crown prosecutor general to take measures against anyone threatening owners of nationalized lands.[13]

Ultraroyalists were just a small core of malcontents in the Isère and Bas-Rhin, but matters were otherwise in the Midi, where the Chevaliers had given royalists an organizational structure. The Chevaliers were essentially a continuation of counter-revolutionary groups that dated back to the 1790s; continuities in personnel with, and similarities in practice to, groups such as the Philanthropic Institutes were pronounced. At points such groups had sought to achieve their objectives through insurrection, but they had also taken a legal path when it seemed efficacious, seeking to gain restoration by the election of royalists. As part of the latter non-violent tradition, they had sought to sway public opinion, although repression had often forced them to resort to covert distribution of writings.

It was no coincidence that prior to the formation of the Chevaliers in 1810, Ferdinand de Bertier and his brother Bénigne-Louis, sons of the royal

[12] On ultraroyalist theory and response to legislation, see N. Hudson, *Ultra-Royalism and the French Restoration* (Cambridge, 1936) and J.-J. Oechslin, *Le mouvement ultra-royaliste sous la Restauration* (Paris, 1960).

[13] ADI 52M5, 25–8 February and 3 March 1815; ADBR, 3M11, 9 May 1814 and 24 January 1815; A. Gras, *Grenoble en 1814 et 1815* (Grenoble, 1854), pp. 15–23, and P. Leuilliot, *La Première Restauration et les Cent-Jours en Alsace* (1958), pp. 29–175.

intendant murdered by the Parisian crowd on 22 July 1789 and thereafter repeatedly involved in counter-revolutionary organization, had joined a masonic society to learn freemasonry's structure. As good royalists knew, Jacobinism sprang from 'masonic conspiracy', and while ultraroyalists denounced organization among others, they were keen to employ it themselves. Among the first initiates in Paris were Jules de Polignac (whose mother had been attached to Marie-Antoinette) and Mathieu de Montmorency; thus the fledging society reached into the highest levels of the *ancien régime* nobility, was closely tied to Artois, and was resolutely counter-revolutionary. Although the Bertiers gave the Chevaliers an organization modelled upon freemasonry, the association was designed to combat the latter and, indeed, from its origins the society possessed the character of a religious order – allegiance to the Papacy was as strong as loyalty to the Bourbon dynasty.[14]

Covert reorganization at Toulouse began in 1812 when Mathieu de Montmorency arrived to implant a chapter of the Chevaliers that ultimately extended as far as Montpellier. Among active agents were leading nobles and clergymen such as Baron Guillaume de Bellegarde, Robert de MacCarthy and the abbé Nicolas MacCarthy, and membership included men who, as we shall see, would provide the Haute-Garonne's ultraroyalist leadership: d'Escouloubre, de Limairac, Joseph de Villèle, Count Montbel and Léopold de Rigaud.

In the Midi, ultraroyalism possessed a mass base. Religious discontent with the anticlerical policies of Revolutionary governments had been central to the Institutes, and refractory priests had encouraged recruitment into the Institute's secret armies. Perhaps more importantly, royalist Catholics had been able to maintain domination of provision of charity to the poor. Given Napoleon's clash with the Papacy, such ties were potentially threatening and the years 1812 and 1813 saw extensive correspondence between Imperial officials over worker mutual aid societies organized by clergymen. Attempts to remove the religious elements of the associations foundered, however, against opposition from the societies themselves. Correspondence does not reveal how many such associations existed, but there were over thirty in Toulouse alone, with memberships ranging between seventy and one hundred.

Charity thus fostered royalist influence, but it was resistance to conscription that provided the Chevaliers with a rank and file for their secret armies. While nobles led the secret armies, commoners conducted recruitment.

14 See Bertier de Sauvigny, *Le Comte*, pp. 29–65, and J. Godeschot, *The Counter Revolution* (Princeton, 1971), pp. 141–296, 327–83.

Inflated estimates of membership ran as high as 50,000, but probably most of these individuals could be counted on only after victory. As Montbel and Villèle pointed out, Bonaparte did not fall because of royalist insurrection in 1814; more important was general indifference to the Imperial regime resultant from the burdens of incessant warfare. Nevertheless, when Wellington entered Toulouse after the battle of 10 April 1814, crowds sporting white cockades supplied by the Chevaliers greeted him as a liberator.[15]

Ultraroyalists expected to gain the spoils of victory, and Wellington appointed a member of the Chevaliers, Louis-Gaston d'Escouloubre, as interim mayor in place of Baron Joseph-François Malaret, who had retreated with the French army. What such an appointment might herald became apparent during speeches celebrating the arrival of Angoulême in late April; Escouloubre's greeting implied that the only true French were those who had always awaited the return of the Bourbons. In such a context Jules de Polignac, who reached Toulouse as *commissaire du roi* in early May, perhaps appeared an apostle of reconciliation. He called for past conflicts to be forgotten, although he surrounded himself with fellow Chevaliers. Then again, news had yet to arrive of the proclamation of Saint-Ouen, wherein Louis XVIII promised France representative government.[16]

Ultraroyalist disenchantment with the government grew amidst discussions leading to the Charter, and Villèle gained prominence with a pamphlet lauding the institutions of the *ancien régime* and arguing that to make the sale of nationalized lands irrevocable was 'to consecrate an injustice'. Discontent was also fuelled by failure to gain monopoly over government office. Alexandre Hersant-Destouches was retained as prefect and Malaret resumed his post as mayor. Matters improved, however, when Louis Beaupoil de Saint-Aulaire replaced Destouches in November 1814. Beaupoil was a former Imperial court chamberlain and ultraroyalists had little confidence in him, but he did at least appoint a 'pure' as sub-prefect at Muret and, better yet, he soon departed for Paris, leaving the running of the prefecture to an ultraroyalist. A purge of mayors accelerated, but clearly much remained to be done.[17]

When news arrived of Napoleon's escape from Elba, leading Toulousains rallied to the monarchy, contributing funds to the organization of a mobile

[15] Correspondence on the mutual aid societies can be found in AN, F15 3618. See also P. Wolff, ed., *Histoire de Toulouse* (Toulouse, 1974), pp. 428–38; Higgs, *Ultraroyalism*, pp. 50–3; comte de Montbel, *Souvenirs du Comte de Montbel* (Paris, 1913), pp. 65–103, and Bertier de Sauvigny, *Le Comte*, pp. 72–3, 102–12.

[16] See the speech of Lannéluc in BMT, LmC 8799. See also M. Albert, *La Première Restauration dans la Haute-Garonne* (Paris, 1932), pp. 13–52, and Bertier de Sauvigny, *Le Comte*, pp. 133–49.

[17] Albert, *Restauration*, pp. 13–52 and 77–93, and Villèle, *Mémoires*, I, pp. 218–23 and 499–509.

National Guard. By 23 March 1815 a voluntary battalion of 400 men had set off. Crown officials described the masses as unpredictable, but reported that members of the local councils and National Guard remained devoted to Louis XVIII. Enthusiasm mounted when it was learned that Angoulême had been named Lieutenant General of the Midi, and that Toulouse would be the centre of royalist operations. On 26 March, Vitrolles arrived to set up a new government dedicated to waging war against Bonaparte. He quickly converted the *Journal de Toulouse* into a new *Moniteur Universel*, and sent instructions to the prefects of the Midi. Control of the post could not, however, keep news of Napoleon's triumphs from reaching Toulouse, and General Bertrand Clausel's securing of Bordeaux proved to be the last straw. Royalist ardour cooled, and on 4 April General Delaborde had Vitrolles arrested.[18]

Toulouse was, nevertheless, the last major city to recognize the emperor's return, and the majority of officials soon resigned. Although the *arrondissements* of Villefranche and Saint-Gaudens were quicker to acknowledge the returned Imperial regime, outside Toulouse men who remained in place were at least as much a concern as those who departed. Through the remainder of April, reports stressed the almost uniform hostility of Toulousain nobles to the emperor, and the clergy's refusal to hold prayer services for Napoleon until 23 April was equally worrisome. Most ominous of all was that officers who had returned from their futile mission to confront Napoleon were maintaining relations with the men who had marched with them.[19]

Throughout the Hundred Days, Imperial officials remained alarmed by the threat posed by secret royalist organization as National Guardsmen openly recruited for volunteer armies. An antidote to royalist organization was, however, found with formation of the Federation of the Midi at Toulouse on 26 May. Royalists in the surrounding countryside had been busy: guns had been procured and perhaps some 800 Toulousains had been recruited. After news of Waterloo, rebellion was attempted on 26 June, but *fédérés* and soldiers responded immediately, and within several hours all monarchist demonstrations had been brought to a halt. In consequence, royalist forces were not mobilized until 17 July – after General Charles Decaen had ordered the *fédérés* to disband and departed with his troops for

[18] AN, F7 3785, 27–30 March 1815; F7 9659, 23 March – 6 April 1815; F1C III Garonne (Haute-), 14, lists of volunteers, and Albert, *Restauration*, pp. 95–164.

[19] AN, F7 9659, 8–13 April 1815; F7 3785, 9–13 April, 5–17 May 1815; F1B II Garonne (Haute-), 7, 7–19 April and 26 May 1815; F1C III Garonne (Haute-), 14, 6–9 May 1815; ADHG, 2M20, 5 May 1815; 13M57bis, 7 September 1815; Albert, *Restauration*, pp. 157–64.

Narbonne. By then the Second Restoration had already commenced, and, indeed, Louis XVIII had returned to Paris by 8 July.[20]

Ultraroyalism thereafter made great strides in the first months of the Second Restoration. With the monarchy scrambling to reassert authority, the time was ripe for those who were unquestionably royalist to advance their claims. In the Midi, forces that had rallied to Angoulême during the Flight of the Eagle seized control over local government. Elsewhere, ultraroyalist societies, often linked by the Chevaliers, rapidly formed to organize the royalist vote in the elections of August.

Gaining control over the National Guard was central to the takeover of local power, as disarray in the regular army meant that provision of order fell largely to the Guard. At the national level, Artois became Commander of the Guard and his personal followers, including Polignac, dominated a committee of inspectors. Below this was a sub-structure of inspectors at the departmental and *arrondissement* levels, and, crucially, the inspectors were subordinate to neither the civil administration nor the regular army.

To be put to full effect, the Guard had to be rendered unquestionably royalist. Everywhere the officer corps could be purged, although in many parts of France there was a limited pool of ultraroyalists upon which to draw. Especially in the Midi, however, total purging could be combined with merging the rank and file of the secret royalist armies into the Guard. These steps made the Guard very effective for the elimination of political rivals. Much of this was conducted by illegal White Terror, which was largely confined to the south. Elsewhere ultraroyalists had to advance their interests through legal Terror, and they were less able to entrench themselves in local government.[21]

In subsequent accounts, ultraroyalists claimed that illegal White Terror was simply a product of spontaneous mass anger, but there can be no doubt that ultraroyalists directed violence to serve their own ends. When Angoulême departed France after the failed attempt to block Napoleon's return, he retained his powers as Lieutenant General of the Midi and left behind agents who would organize a provisional government in the event of the tyrant's overthrow. Jurisdiction was divided along departmental lines: the Marquis Charles de Rivière de Riffardeau would organize government for the Bouches-du-Rhône, Count René de Bernis for the

[20] AN, F7 3785, 29 April, 8–26 May, 10–19 June 1815; F7 9659, 22 June 1815; F9 515–16, 20–22 May, 5 June–1 July 1815; F1B II Garonne (Haute-), 7, 26 May 1815; F1C III Garonne (Haute-), 6, 15–27 May 1815; ADHG, 4M34, 18 May 1815; 4M35, 10–15 June; 4M37, 18 May 1815. See also J. Loubet, 'Le gouvernement toulousain du duc d'Angoulême après les Cent-Jours', *La Révolution Française*, 64 (1913), pp. 149–55.

[21] L. Girard, *La garde nationale 1814–1871* (Paris, 1964), pp. 58–70.

Gard, the Marquis Hippolyte de Montcalm for the Hérault, and Marshal Dominique de Pérignon for the Haute-Garonne. Local committees were then formed under these delegates, and the Chevaliers de la Foi played a major role in coordinating the committees and recruiting secret armies.

Angoulême's alternative government played a negligible role in the liberation of France. Roughly one week after Waterloo, the commanding general, worried by the presence of the British fleet, retired the Imperial garrison from Marseilles, leaving the port to the tender mercies of Rivière, who duly seized control against little resistance. Rivière's plans to liberate Toulon then foundered, however, when Marshal Guillaume Brune proved more obdurate. It was only on 24 July that Brune and his garrison evacuated Toulon. Elsewhere, royalist advance was similarly mixed. Although Beaucaire rapidly followed the example of Marseilles, Nîmes did not fall under royalist control until 17 July. Results were similar at Montpellier, which held out until 15 July.

The importance of Angoulême's supporters thus lay in what they did after victory. Mass violence was perpetrated by bands, such as the *verdets* in the Haute-Garonne or the *miquelets* in the Gard, which had been recruited into the secret royalist armies. They were acting under the directions of ultraroyalist committees, and even after Angoulême's special powers had been revoked by the royal government in late July, they continued to slaughter and pillage well into 1816. Claims by Rivière and Bernis that popular desire for vengeance was beyond their control were, in fact, a cover for their own complicity. Rivière and his committee, for instance, imprisoned all those who otherwise might have suffered 'popular' vengeance, but the crown-appointed prefect found it necessary in August to release them because concentrating potential victims simply facilitated massacre.[22]

White Terror served a purpose, and the Haute-Garonne provides an instructive example of how ultraroyalists used it to secure local domination. Hard upon the departure of Decaen, royalist forces under the command of Léopold de Rigaud (a Chevalier) swept into Toulouse on 17 July. Initially there were about 600 soldiers, although only a small minority had guns. Rigaud and a Toulousain committee then set up a suitably noble, ultraroyalist provisional government. Villèle become mayor, Charles-Antoine Limairac (brother-in-law of Villèle) prefect, Louis-Maurice Delpy secretary general of the prefecture, and Jean-François de Savy-Gardeilh lieutenant general of police. Royalists who by right of appointment during the First Restoration should have resumed their positions were pushed aside. The

[22] See Resnick, *White Terror*; Lewis, *Second Vendée*, pp. 187–218; Fitzpatrick, *Catholic Royalism*, pp. 33–59, and Alexander, *Bonapartism*, pp. 219–47.

same fate awaited Auguste-Laurent de Rémusat, an *ancien régime* noble who had served in the Napoleonic prefectoral corps, when he arrived on 21 July. Although Rémusat had been named prefect by the cabinet in Paris, Marshal Pérignon, who had accompanied Angoulême to Spain and subsequently been appointed governor of the tenth military division, informed him that only orders from Angoulême were valid. Cabinet orders from Paris putting an end to the Duke's authority, received on 25 July, were ignored.[23]

A 'military' commission was established to judge *fédérés*, who were ordered to turn in their guns within twenty-four hours. It appears that none of them did so, but at any event the order was simply a pretext for *verdets* to go about their work. Some ninety to a hundred arrests soon followed, and *verdets* made a point of looting and extortion, but there was no slaughter. Although *fédérés* had frightened royalists, the one fatality during the Hundred Days had been the work of soldiers. Moreover, given there were at least 1,200 *fédérés* and the Toulousain crowd was far from uniformly royalist, a certain measure of restraint made sense.[24]

When questioned by cabinet ministers about the lengthy imprisonment of *fédéré* leaders thereafter, Villèle deployed the argument about potential mass violence should hated individuals be released. If we look at two incidents of crowd agitation, however, we begin to see how convenient 'popular' revenge was for the ultraroyalists of Toulouse. The most notorious was the assassination of General Jean-Pierre Ramel. As garrison commander of Toulouse, Ramel possessed control over the National Guard, and he was twice attacked by *verdets* after he had refused their demands to be included into the Guard as entire units (rather than be integrated as individuals and hence be divided) and to draw their pay from the Guard. Ramel had decided that the government must bring the *verdets* into line, and his reason for doing so brings us to a closely related prior incident.

The leniency he had shown royalists as mayor during the Hundred Days perhaps led Malaret to believe all would be forgiven; at any event, when the government appointed him president of the departmental electoral college in August 1815, he decided to return from Paris. Even before he had reached Toulouse, however, lieutenant general of police Savy-Gardeilh had advised Rémusat that 'popular' discontent would make it difficult to protect Malaret. Upon his arrival, the former mayor found that a petition opposing

23 AN, F1B II Garonne (Haute-), 7, 22 July 1815, F7 3786, 8 August 1815; ADHG, 1M75, 25 July 1815, 13M57bis, 23 July 1815; Loubet, 'Le gouvernement', pp. 165, 339–50, and Resnick, *White Terror*, pp. 20–40.

24 AN, F7 3786, 9 August; ADHG, 4M35, 1–22 August and 19 September 1815; Loubet, 'Le gouvernement', pp 149–65, 337–66, and Higgs, *Ultraroyalism*, pp. 56–63.

his appointment as college president, undersigned by thirty 'pures', had been presented to Angoulême. Crowds demonstrated outside his house on the evenings of 13 and 14 August, and Malaret fled. Given that one of the leaders of the crowd was Savy-Gardeilh's son, it is rather obvious why the police were of no aid.

These developments led Ramel to rebuke Savy-Gardeilh *fils*, while Rémusat attempted to read the riot act to Savy-Gardeilh *père*. On 15 August, Ramel was attacked and left badly wounded, though not dead. National Guardsmen and police then stood aside while a second visit of *verdets* finished Ramel off on the night of 17 August. Subsequent investigations did lead to the punishment of several *verdets*, but they failed to reveal the role of the upper echelons of the ultraroyalist organization.

Certain points do, however, emerge from official reports. No one in a position of authority could claim much credit for his part in the affair. Neither Villèle nor Rémusat, for example, spoke to Ramel after the first attack. Although the prefect did go to Ramel's residence, he did not enter, seeing Pérignon 'in control'. Villèle's account in his memoirs ignored the period between the two attacks, giving the impression that it was all a single incident, but such was not the case and the fact that the small number of guards posted after the first attack conveniently went away strongly suggests an arrangement by which *verdets* were enabled to complete their mission.

Between the assaults, Ramel had informed justices of the peace that Savy-Gardeilh and Rigaud were responsible for the attacks, although he had been unable to identify his assailants. It was not, however, in any local official's interest that all matters should come to light; after all, Savy-Gardeilh and Rigaud were Chevaliers who had accompanied Angoulême into exile, and were key figures in the latter's provisional government. Nor was full revelation likely. Initial investigations went nowhere under the guidance of the crown prosecutor Jean-Antoine Miègeville, son of a councillor of the Toulousain *parlement* and a notorious 'pure' who had refused to take office during the Empire.[25]

Ultimately, struggle for local control was at the heart of White Terror. Malaret and Ramel had posed no threat to royalism, and their actions during the Hundred Days had not made them likely targets for popular revenge. They had, however, challenged ultraroyalist ascendancy at a time when elections were taking place.

[25] AN, F7 9659, 16 August 1815; F7 3786, 22–4 August 1815; F9 515–16, 24 August 1815; ADHG, 4M35, 3–19 August and 19 September 1815; Bertier de Sauvigny, *Le Comte*, pp. 193, 274–6; Louis Eydoux, *L'assassinat du général Ramel à Toulouse* (Toulouse, 1905), and Villèle, *Mémoires*, 1, pp. 298–303.

When Louis XVIII called for elections in August 1815, recourse was had to the Imperial system, with modifications. The Imperial system stipulated indirect elections: voters in colleges of the *arrondissements* would vote a list of candidates, and members of a departmental college, gathered at the *chef lieu*, would then elect Deputies, half of whom must be chosen from the list of the *arrondissements*. There would be one elector in the departmental college for every thousand inhabitants of the department, and the electors must belong to the 600 leading departmental taxpayers. The king could add twenty individuals to the departmental college and ten to each of the colleges of the *arrondissements*. The minimum age for voters was lowered to twenty-one and that of candidates to thirty, and the number of Deputies was raised from 258 to 402.

In most colleges, only ultraroyalists were organized; leading left-wing figures were in hiding, or found their influence negligible after having backed a losing emperor. In the Seine-Inférieure, the prefect called on voters to eschew candidates who could 'again attract the hatred and mistrust of Europe'. Better still for ultraroyalism, the administrative chain of command was at low ebb, so that the wishes of the Talleyrand–Fouché ministry counted for little. Repeated purges and transfers meant that most prefects either had barely arrived on the scene, or were yet to appear. Even where prefects were willing to follow the cabinet line, their influence over lesser officials was often far from secure. Moreover, many ultraroyalist prefects simply ignored the wishes of a cabinet they despised.[26]

Thus ultraroyalists had exceptionally favourable circumstances in which to operate. At Toulouse, Limairac took charge of adjusting voter lists, and did so to full ultraroyalist advantage. Rémusat's first choice as replacement for Malaret as college president was in fact Villèle, who, however, declined. The presidency therefore fell to the lawyer Mathieu Espinasse, on Villèle's recommendation. Given that Villèle's attack on the Charter was still circulating, Rémusat's reliance on the mayor was striking.[27]

While Ramel was being attacked, Villèle was attending a pre-election meeting of royalist voters directed by the Chevaliers de la Foi. During voting on 16 August, messages were delivered to Espinasse informing him that crowds were preventing voters from entering the hall. According to the official college minutes, measures were taken to ensure that troops secured passage for troubled voters, but this was contradicted by the commander

[26] See *Journal de Rouen*, 14 August 1815, and N. Richardson, *The French Prefectoral Corps, 1814–1830* (Cambridge, 1966), pp. 44–69.

[27] AN, F1C III Garonne (Haute-), 6, 9–13 August 1815 and 7 October 1816, and F7 3786, 24 August 1815.

of the *gendarmerie*, who reported that members of the Legion of Honour had been so harassed that they had departed.[28]

In the event, elections went in a predictable direction. All the new Deputies were wealthy nobles and confirmed royalists, but there were nuances among them. Limairac, Hippolyte d'Aldéguier (a former councillor of the Toulousain *parlement*) and Baron Jean-Pierre de Marcassus de Puymaurin (a son of a former Toulousain *capitoul*) would sit with the Right and take directions from Villèle. The Marquis Jean-Antoine de Catellan, also a former member of the Toulousain *parlement*, would, however, break ranks and sit with the Centre-Right. As president of the departmental college, he had called for the election of men who loved the throne, but were also committed to the Charter. Villèle secured victory by the slimmest of margins on the third ballot, a sign that he was not yet established as a leader over local ultraroyalist rivals.[29]

Ultraroyalists were similarly aggressive at Mende, where a volunteer royalist army also intimidated voters, so that the crown-appointed college president could not block the election of candidates chosen by a Chevalier committee. Such means, however, were not usually necessary. Intimidation certainly was not restricted to the Midi, but in truth the composition of the *Chambre introuvable* was more a product of the disarray of local rivals, and an electorate hopeful of reducing reprisals through selection of the seemingly most royal of royalists.[30]

In the Isère, the Casino, a branch of the Chevaliers, directed royalist strategy. Largely noble in composition, but using priests as agents, the Casino had been formed in late July and early August. At Grenoble Jacques-Pierre de Chaléon, departmental inspector of the National Guard, and his son-in-law Charles de Pujol, who sent reports to Artois by means of Count MacCarthy, ran the Casino. Correspondence was also maintained with Polignac and Vitrolles, but it would appear that Viscount François-Joseph Dubouchage was the leading patron of the Casino. Dubouchage was a former minister of Louis XVI who had emigrated in 1792 and then returned under Bonaparte to live on his estates. He had not, however, publicly rallied to Bonaparte and had been placed under police surveillance for suspected conspiratorial plotting in 1805. Louis XVIII had made him Minister of the Marine, where he distinguished himself primarily by the appointment of

[28] AN, F7 3786, 17 August 1815; F1C III Garonne (Haute-), 6, 18 August 1815; ADHG, 2M19, 16 August 1815, and Bertier de Sauvigny, *Le Comte*, pp. 184–90.

[29] ADHG, 2M19, college minutes for August 1815; Rémusat, *Mémoires*, 1, pp. 229–33, and Villèle, *Mémoires*, I, pp. 306–7.

[30] See T. Beck, *French Legislators 1800–1834* (Berkeley, 1974), pp. 50–8.

inexperienced and incompetent émigrés to leading positions in the navy. In the Isère the Casino secured election of three of its members – Gabriel Dubouchage, nephew of the Viscount, Gaspard Du Boys, an émigré who had returned after Brumaire and entered the justice system, and Charles-Laurent Planelli de Lavalette, another returned émigré who had retired as *adjoint* at the Grenoble *mairie* during the Hundred Days and been appointed mayor in July. In a department closely associated with opposition to monarchy, this was no small achievement for the fledgling Casino.[31]

Although ultraroyalism triumphed in August, success was not universal. Allied non-cooperation prevented Bourbon authorities from completing elections in the Bas-Rhin until 24 August. Difficulties of communication meant that electoral organization was minimal, and what little direction was given to voters came from François Barbé-Marbois, acting as president of the departmental college. A former minister of Napoleon, Barbé-Marbois was a moderate royalist who would soon become Minister of Justice. Moreover, the National Guard had yet to be purged and hence could not be used as an ultraroyalist power base. Under these circumstances, the department elected Deputies who would all sit with the minority in the *Chambre introuvable*.[32]

At the national level, right-wing success was partly a product of immediate circumstance in that both the Left and the central government were in disarray in the aftermath of the Hundred Days. Due largely to the work of the Chevaliers, ultraroyalists had been able to seize the electoral advantage through superior organization. Principally in the Midi, they had employed coercion when they deemed it useful, but in most of France such tactics were neither necessary nor likely to prove efficacious. A potentially dominant position in the Chamber of Deputies (roughly 78 per cent of the members sat with the Right) would thereafter present further opportunities, provided that organizational superiority was consolidated. Ultraroyalist organizational advantages would not, however, go unchallenged.

## PART THREE: STATE RESPONSE TO ULTRAROYALISM

Election of the *Chambre introuvable* ushered in the first Richelieu ministry. Its character was mixed: while Decazes would emerge as moderate, Vaublanc would not, and Richelieu hovered somewhere between the two. This meant that initially there was no clear direction given by the cabinet, and no clear division between moderate and extreme royalists.

[31] BMUG, R9109 and R9466; M. Rolland, *Le département de l'Isère sous la chambre introuvable* (DES, University of Grenoble, 1955), pp. 45–7, and Bertier de Sauvigny, *Le Comte*, pp. 190–3, 278.

[32] AN, F1C III Rhin (Bas-), 3, 22 July, 7–28 August 1815; Leuilliot, *L'Alsace*, I, pp. 86–90.

A second result of the elections was parliament's creation of the legal apparatus of the White Terror, beginning in October. In theory, the laws of general security, sedition and 'amnesty' were designed to enable the regime to take preventive measures against rebellion, but they could also be used for the elimination of political rivals. Moreover, they placed extraordinary power in the hands of state officials. Prefects could arrest, incarcerate and exile 'suspects' without recourse to the normal process of law. In addition, the definition of sedition was broadened to include any public utterance or sign of dislike of the regime.

In the autumn of 1815, ultraroyalism was well placed to prosper. Where the prefect was a 'pure', such as Ferdinand de Bertier in the Calvados, Joesph de Kergariou in the Seine-Inférieure, Guy-Pierre de Kersaint in the Meurthe, or Hervé-Clérel de Tocqueville in the Côte-d'Or, ultraroyalists could penetrate all levels of local government. In the absence of clear cabinet direction, ultraroyalist committees could also pressure leading officials into making appointments along desired lines. In the Isère, prefect Casimir de Montlivault, a veteran of the Imperial administration, was not an ultraroyalist, but he followed the advice of the Casino, which prepared lists of undesirables and suitable replacements, and Jules Pasquier took a similar line in the Sarthe.[33]

In the Haute-Garonne, Rémusat tried to combat ultraroyalist domination, but failed. When Angoulême finally recognized that his extraordinary powers were no longer legitimate, some of his appointees, such as Savy-Gardeilh, did retire from their offices. Others, such as Villèle and the majority of members of the prefectoral and municipal corps, carried on. To some extent this was inevitable. While purging men who had served Bonaparte, Rémusat had to rely on committed royalists – individuals who might have wished to occupy the centre ground could easily understand the lesson of Ramel.[34]

*Verdets* were incorporated into the National Guard, but this fusion only confirmed the latter's unreliability. In August *verdets* attacked lawyers defending *fédérés* in the courtroom; on 10 October Guardsmen ransacked the country house of a Toulousain judge, and in mid-November, after a *fédéré* had been acquitted, three judges were warned by Guardsmen not to return to the courtroom. Only one was willing to continue.[35]

[33] Bertier de Sauvigny, *Le Comte*, pp. 226–39, R. Perrin, *L'esprit public dans le département de la Meurthe de 1814 à 1816* (Paris, 1913), pp. 84–96 and Fizaine, *La vie*, pp. 47–52.

[34] AN, F7 9659, 9–28 November and 14–23 December 1815.

[35] AN, F7 3786, 29 August 1816; F7 9659, 9–21 November, 19 December 1815, 9 January and 10 February 1816, BB3 155, 23 December 1815.

Ultraroyalist attacks on the Charter during the election of August 1815 had worried Rémusat; yet he consistently collaborated with Villèle. Reliance upon Villèle, in combination with ultraroyalist intimidation of their opponents, ensured that power remained vested in 'pure' hands. Guard forces were increasingly despatched into rural communes, where, according to Savy-Gardeilh, most mayors, *adjoints* and judges connived in conspiracy against royal government. Surveillance became a pretext for illegal arrest and forced requisitions at Muret and Villeneuve. House searches of ten members of the federation central committee at Salies netted only a couple of *tricolores*, but this simply led the mayor to request a detachment of *gendarmes* so as to force 'obstinate' *fédérés* to yield guns they must have hidden.[36]

Administrators appointed during the Hundred Days automatically yielded their authority, and officials who had retained their positions during the Hundred Days were purged as well. The mayor of Cintegabelle was thought by the prefect to be a good royalist, but he had made the mistake of visiting Madame Clausel. Although Madame had assured officials that her husband the general had departed for the United States, this had not prevented *verdet* pillaging. At Toulouse, members of the ultraroyalist committee thought the expeditions led by their henchman Philippe Barthélemy salutary; they taught revolutionaries and peasants that there was 'a force' which could 'reach them' should they prove 'insolent'.

By 1816 Rémusat had begun to doubt the efficacy of continued repression. An ordinance in March, however, swept 'impures' from the royal court and replaced them with ultraroyalists. Shortly thereafter the prevotal court began operations. Count Joseph-Thimoléon d'Hargenvilliers, the provost, and Pierre-Donat Martin-Bergnac, the presiding civil judge at Toulouse, were not particularly vengeful; both were moderate royalists who had served under the Empire. The court meted out decisions from 21 June 1816 to 13 December 1817, and only twenty-six of its forty-four cases were political in nature. Then again, there was little need for further repression given the previous labours of the regular courts. There had been 178 political cases in the Haute-Garonne between July 1815 and June 1816, a figure dwarfing those of most other departments.[37]

36 AN, F7 3786, 29 August 1815; F7 9659, 14 November 1815; F9 515–16, 17 October 1815; ADHG, 4M34, 29 July – 24 August, 31 October, and 4–6 November 1815.

37 On administrative purge, see ADHG, 1M72 and 2Mbis 2. Information on the prevotal court has been drawn from D. Higgs's unpublished 'Bonapartism lower-class in the Haute-Garonne', and Resnick, *White Terror*, pp. 83–115 and 132.

Denunciations poured in, and Rémusat took action when he deemed it appropriate. Matters were complicated by an ultraroyalist 'counter-police' which was quick to forward allegations to the Minister of War. Worse still, Barthélemy, recently named a Chevalier de Saint-Louis, had become an ultraroyalist agent at Paris, presenting charges directly to cabinet ministers. After a round-up of suspects following the Didier affair, Rémusat wearily expressed the hope that such measures would render ultraroyalists less inclined 'to draw extreme conclusions'.[38]

Elsewhere, ultraroyalist use of Terror to seize local control was less successful. When appointed to the Bas-Rhin in September 1815, prefect Constantin de Bouthillier-Chavigny faced the opposite problem confronting Rémusat – ultraroyalists were thin on the ground. Bouthillier was a leading 'pure' favoured by Artois; whether he was a Chevalier is unclear, but he did encourage formation of a departmental Casino, organized by the barrister Simon-François Demougé. Using the code name 'Ferret', Demougé had been involved in counter-revolutionary organizations since the early 1790s, principally through his contacts with General Pichegru, and had acted as a spy for the Austrian and British governments. Although the prefect refused to preside over meetings of the Casino, he relied on Demougé's network of 274 members for denunciations and recommendations from throughout the department.[39]

Despite prefectoral mistrust of most officials, change had to be gradual; otherwise the entire administration would have collapsed. Top levels were the first affected. Antoine de Kentzinger became mayor of Strasbourg; he was an old émigré who, however, had an annoying tendency to resist Bouthillier whenever he felt the prefect was intruding on his patch. Ultraroyalist sub-prefects at Sélestat and Saverne were more reliable, but Bouthillier never could find a suitably hard-line sub-prefect for Wissembourg.

Thereafter the prefect concentrated on the forces of repression. Bouthillier placed the *gendarmerie* under an ultraroyalist and overcame the reluctance of Allied commanders to have the force fully armed, all the while noting that it was 'entirely bad'. To impose order in the countryside, Bouthillier also created a special police force composed of members

38 AN, F1C III Garonne (Haute-), 6, 19 September 1816; F1C III Garonne (Haute-), 14, 18 May – 10 August 1816; F7 3737, 1–2 September, 14–30 August 1816; F7 3787, 22–30 June, 13–20 July 1816; F7 9659, 31 May – 23 July 1816, 6–14 August 1816; ADHG, 4M39, 24 May – 13 June 1816; 4M40, 11 July and 24 September 1816.

39 BNUS, Mss. 1169, 1170, 1172, 1178, and marquis de Frénilly, *Recollections of Baron de Frénilly* (New York, 1909), pp. 279, 317 and 338.

of the National Guard 'known for their morality and loyalty'. The Guard at Strasbourg nevertheless had to be handled carefully, if only because of its size – over 4,500 strong in January 1816. Bouthillier did manage a minor purge among officers in February 1816, but he hesitated over ordering more sweeping changes for fear of creating dangerous discontent.

Similar problems arose in the lower ranks of the administration. Bouthillier conducted a massive purge of mayors, appointing émigrés whenever possible, but allowance had to be made for the virtues of being bilingual, and in communities of mixed faith the convention of alternating between Protestants and Catholics could not be ignored. At a higher level, in February Bouthillier found he had to work with a lieutenant general of police, Albert de Permon, who numbered Fouché and Metternich among his acquaintances and was the brother of Laure Junot, the Duchess of Abrantès. While such contacts were attributes when it came to spying beyond the Rhine, they did not impress the prefect, and relations between the two were uneasy. Nor was Bouthillier enamoured of the commander of the Fifth Military Division, General Jean-Louis Dubreton. Although he had resigned from the army during the Hundred Days, Dubreton was famous for his defeat of Wellington at Burgos (Spain) in 1812 and, worse still, he was popular with local moderates. Unfortunately for the prefect, moderates were the only realistic option for royalism in the Bas-Rhin.[40]

Ultraroyalist penetration of the state at both the national and local levels, thus, was far from complete by the end of 1815, and this uncertain state of affairs made the emerging struggle between moderates and extremists in the cabinet crucial. Louis XVIII began the Second Restoration by frequently agreeing to ultraroyalist demands, but he had to weigh concessions against the destabilizing impact of counter-revolution upon the nation as a whole. Ultraroyalist preference for Artois angered the king, and Allied leaders increasingly expressed alarm as the White Terror unfolded. It was these factors that enabled Decazes to lead the king slowly to a break with ultraroyalism.[41]

In essence, Decazes developed three lines of attack. Firstly, direction within the cabinet would have to shift. Secondly, ultraroyalist influence over the administration must be weakened. Thirdly, the administration should be put to the purpose of securing a more amenable, moderate royalist, Chamber of Deputies.

40 ADBR, 3M15, 11 October 1815; AN, F7 9693, 1 November 1815 and 6 February 1816, and Leuilliot, *L'Alsace*, I, 92–128.

41 Bertier de Sauvigny has estimated that between 50,000 and 80,000 civil servants were dismissed; see his *Restoration*, p. 136.

Alteration of the cabinet had to be performed discreetly if the government wished to pass its budget. Thus it was not until 7 May, a week after the close of the parliamentary session, that Count Joachim Lainé replaced Vaublanc as Minister of the Interior. Lainé had gained fame in late 1813 by authoring a highly critical address in which the Legislative Corps called on Napoleon to negotiate peace, but he was a moderate royalist. Even so, the dismissal of Vaublanc had to be balanced by the replacement of Minister of Justice Barbé-Marbois with Chancellor Charles-Henri Dambray, an arch-conservative, though no friend of Artois.[42]

Subsequently, Lainé would facilitate the appointment of moderates, and this change in the composition of the administration would complement steps Decazes had already taken. In December 1815 the Minister of Police had issued a circular reminding local officials of the illegality of secret societies, whether left- or right-wing in orientation. With Vaublanc still at the Interior, however, the message had been muted. The Chevaliers do not appear to have been affected, although a second secret royalist association known as the Francs-régénérés was terminated. The circular did not have much impact in the Midi, but elsewhere it began to loosen the ultraroyalist grip. In the Bas-Rhin it served to confirm the wavering of fair-weather 'pures' who rapidly lost interest in the Casino, and in the Isère Montlivault began to think twice about accepting ultraroyalist proposals.

Vital to Decazes's campaign was public reaction to the White Terror. Repression of the Left did serve a purpose, but lawless application of it increased the likelihood of further revolution. To prevent the latter, repression had to be made a state monopoly, and wayward officials must be brought into line. Too many prefects were failing to exercise their extraordinary powers with discrimination. It was perhaps no surprise that men were left to rot in prison for well over a year in the Gard and Haute-Garonne, but the way in which Montlivault wielded his powers in the Isère did not differ greatly.

As in the Haute-Garonne, suspicion became a pretext for arbitrary arrest, house search and harassment in the Isère. Moreover, harsh application of sedition laws did more damage than good because punishments were disproportionate to alleged crimes. Three months' imprisonment and fines of up to 100 francs were the going price for *cris séditieux*, but penalties could rise much higher: a former soldier living just outside Bourgoin was

[42] See baron de Barante, *Souvenirs du Baron de Barante, 1782–1866*, 8 vols. (Paris, 1890–1901), II, pp. 177–81, 238–40, 248–66, and Mansel, *Louis XVIII*, pp. 320–43.

imprisoned for five years for having led a crowd which insulted royalists with cries of 'Long live Napoleon!'[43]

Departmental registers indicate that 106 individuals had been convicted of sedition between the period of 6 December 1815 and the end of April 1816. It should be borne in mind, however, that many of the vast number of arrests did not lead to trial. Prefects could incarcerate suspects without ever lodging an accusation and Montlivault frequently did so, although such tactics created tensions between the judiciary and administration. Many magistrates were troubled by a system wherein charges were withheld from the accused, and wherein, even when judicial enquiries determined there was no basis for prosecution, suspects remained in jail simply upon the prefect's orders. Nor did judges appreciate prefectoral hectoring when they failed to secure convictions from juries inclined to clemency.[44]

The answer to such problems lay in the appointment of men willing to exercise caution in implementing repressive legislation. There was no obvious purge in the summer of 1816, but public reaction to the Didier affair in May did allow Decazes to accelerate emphasis upon moderation. Sadly for all concerned, Didier's assault upon Grenoble exacerbated royalist paranoia just after Montlivault had broken with the Casino. The latter society, meanwhile, had found a new darling in the military commander General Gabriel Donnadieu. Known both for his courage and eagerness to plunder, Donnadieu had risen quickly through the ranks in the Revolutionary and Napoleonic armies, but he had indulged several times in conspiratorial intrigue and had been placed under police surveillance by Napoleon in 1811. Thus he had been quick to rally to the Bourbons in 1814 and had joined Louis XVIII at Ghent during the Hundred Days.

What Didier intended by the revolt of May has been the source of much speculation, but given the absence of solid evidence to the contrary, it seems best to take the former Imperial *doyen* of the Grenoble law faculty at his word. He had hoped to act as a catalyst for the resentments he had found during travels throughout the east, and to establish a regency government with Napoleon II as sovereign.

The extent of conspiracy was vast, stretching to the southernmost points of the Isère and also reaching northwards along the valley of the Grésivaudan to Savoy. A fortuitous clampdown by Montlivault on suspects immediately

43 These examples have been extracted from ADI, J529, 52M4, 52M12 and 52M13.

44 Trial registers are in ADI, 52M16. See also 52M4, 30 September and 15 November 1815; 52M5, 7 December 1815; 52M9, 31 December 1815, 3 January and 8 April 1816; 52M10, 16 March 1816, and 52M18, 2 April 1816.

prior to the revolt, however, sowed confusion within rebel ranks and led Didier's main agents to take flight. The latter circumstance largely explains why Grenoble itself remained quiet on the night of 4–5 May. Didier narrowly missed gaining the support of several hundred armed customs agents at Pontcharra, and the fires that burned along the mountainsides of the northern Grésivaudan suggested a much greater support base than was indicated by the number who actually participated in revolt.

What was clear was that while Didier had little trouble raising an armed band (estimates vary anywhere from 400 to 4,000) that 'took' Vizille, his plans badly misfired at Grenoble. The authorities had learned that something was afoot at least twenty-four hours in advance, and so General Donnadieu sent some of his forces outside the gates to confront the rebels, but also held many back to watch over Grenoble. Didier's bands, which had counted on the gates of the city being opened to them, repulsed an initial foray, but were then easily routed. Outside Grenoble eleven rebels were killed and another thirty captured.

Donnadieu immediately requested permission from Paris to put the department in a state of siege, and at a meeting on 5 May civil and military officials discussed what to do with the captured rebels. Donnadieu was for rapid justice, but Colonel Bernard Falquet de Planta, president of the prevotal court and a founding member of the Casino, insisted on regular trial procedures. Donnadieu asked de Planta whether he was part of the conspiracy, and next day de Planta submitted and ordered the first executions.

By 8 May eighty-four rebels had been captured and Donnadieu had received permission to place the department in a state of siege. The general and prefect had both signed proclamations threatening summary execution of any individual harbouring a rebel or found in possession of a gun, and Colonel Victor de Vautré (another favourite of the Casino who had been imprisoned during the Hundred Days and was spoiling for revenge) had begun a military expedition into the countryside, rounding up the relatives of captured rebels and marching them back to Grenoble. Donnadieu then set up a military commission to take over the trial of rebels on 9 May. By 15 May, twenty-one executions had occurred, with fourteen of them taking place in villages so as to impress residents. During the trials military judges insulted the accused and their lawyers, and ignored requests for clemency from leading local notables.

House searches, arrests and letters of denunciation again became the order of the day. Prevotal courts were held in the communes where the revolt had originated, and by 30 May the prisons of Grenoble were so overloaded that resort had to be made to dungeons. The 'affair' also became a pretext for exiling from the department prominent figures such as Charles Renauldon *fils* (son of the former mayor and a sub-prefect during the Hundred Days), Jacques Berriat-Saint-Prix (a distinguished jurist), and Alphonse-Marie Bérenger (de la Drôme), a former Imperial *avocat-général* who had been elected in the Drôme to the Chamber of the Hundred Days. Although no evidence of participation in the revolt could be found to justify legal action against them, each of these individuals was considered hostile to the regime.

Cabinet alarm at public reaction to the extent of repression put a term to this savage state of affairs. On 14 May the Minister of War rebuked Donnadieu for creating a military commission, which was unconstitutional, and for threatening to raze entire towns, which was irrational. One month later, Decazes rejected Montlivault's request to incarcerate 'circumspect' agitators who could not be stopped by regular judicial procedures. Correctly reading the shifting winds, Montlivault abruptly changed tack and sailed into an internecine battle with Donnadieu based on disavowing responsibility.[45]

Alarm over frequent reports of massacre in the south, and revulsion at ultraroyalist bloodlust in the Isère, led many officials to respond eagerly to signs of moderation emanating from the cabinet. To encourage such trends, Decazes moved to neutralize use of the National Guard as a political base. In July, royal ordinances banned political demonstrations by the Guard, while prohibiting mayors or *adjoints* from membership. Meanwhile requests from inspectors for increased funding languished, encouraging a downward spiral in enthusiasm for the Guard.[46]

Such measures posed problems for ultraroyalist prefects who were out of line with the sentiments of the local elite. In a review in October 1815, Bouthillier had been mortified when cries of 'Long live the king!' were met with frosty silence by the Strasbourg National Guard. Changes in the officer corps in February 1816 did not improve matters; in June notices from the prefect and mayor lamented reluctance to serve. In August artillery guards threatened refusal to join in the fête of Saint-Louis unless a royalist officer who allegedly specialized in denunciation was removed. Bouthillier forced the guards to march and purged six officers. The dismissals were reversed,

[45] See H. Dumolard, *La Terreur Blanche dans l'Isère* (Grenoble, 1928). I have supplemented this with the documentation in ADI, 52M14, 52M16, 52M22 and 52M23; BMUG, R7906, R8772, R9676, and AN, F1C III Isère 9.

[46] See Girard, *La garde*, pp. 77–91; Bertier de Sauvigny, *Le Comte*, pp. 190–216; Langeron, *Decazes*, pp. 85–115, 208–13, and Pasquier, *Mémoires*, IV, pp. 117–32.

however, when Police Commissioner General Permon reported to Decazes that the royalist officer had previously been brought to court for defamatory remarks.[47]

The final step in breaking ultraroyalist influence consisted of the application of state despotism. Beginning with the elections of September 1816, the administration would be put to the task of securing results that were favourable to the current executive. Recourse was again had to the Imperial electoral system, although the age limits specified in the Charter were restored and the number of Deputies was reduced back to 258. Notions of electoral neutrality were abandoned as the administration sought to orchestrate support for official candidates approved by the cabinet. In this sense, the administration began to act as a political party.

The call for elections was a great gamble because the loyalty of administrators was far from uniform at this stage. To improve the chances of success, Decazes convinced the king to intervene directly, calling upon voters to elect candidates who were loyal to both the monarchy and the Charter. Despite recent ultraroyalist posturing, the public well knew what ultraroyalists truly thought of representative government, and the battle lines were clear. In response, 'pures' fell back on the stratagem of arguing that the king had fallen under the sway of evil ministers. Such was the message of Chateaubriand's *La monarchie selon la Charte* and it was immediately banned, but ultraroyalists still hawked it about, sometimes with the aid of prefects.

As part of his campaign, Decazes sought to encourage the development of a *constitutionnel* party of moderates. The thrust of this could be read in brochures arguing that the Charter granted France all she had fought for in 1789, but that 'the cornerstone of our new social edifice' was inseparably tied to the reigning dynasty. The chances for a broad coalition based on opposition to ultraroyalism, however, pivoted on several factors. Much depended on the willingness of prefects to follow cabinet orders. To address this problem, Decazes despatched agents to organize the vote, but this ran aground against prefectoral opposition in the Aude, Calvados and Ardèche, and was counter-productive generally.[48]

Coalition also required a Left capable of rallying. While Rémusat did not prove very adept in the Haute-Garonne, the main factor there was that ultraroyalism had dismantled the Left so thoroughly that it would take

[47] AN, F7 9693, 1 November, 5 and 30 December, 1815; ADBR, 3M15, 10 June 1816; Leuilliot, *L'Alsace*, I, pp. 128–36 and his 'La dissolution de la garde nationale de Strasbourg en 1817', *Revue d'Alsace*, 81 (1934), pp. 385–6.

[48] See Duvergier de Hauranne, *Histoire*, III, pp. 508–18.

years to recover. An ultraroyalist network of noble country homes was a major advantage, not simply for negotiations among various 'pures', but also for influencing other voters at appropriate times. Domination of the local press could also be an asset; *L'Ami du Roi* pumped out the ultraroyalist message and alerted voters to their responsibilities. Most important, however, was ultraroyalist domination of local government. Ability to pull the levers of government patronage, in combination with Church influence, gave ultraroyalism advantages in the Haute-Garonne far greater than elsewhere.[49]

Rémusat appears to have been insufficiently aware of what surrounded him. Prone to lament the difficulty of establishing the king's rule, he nevertheless had relied heavily on Villèle's advice. In doing so, he had fallen into the hands of an ultraroyalist more cunning than his less astute rivals. Unlike Polignac, a more prominent but less subtle ultraroyalist, Villèle had accepted the necessity of swearing allegiance to the Charter and had even posed as champion of parliamentary rights. Such manoeuvring was at times more than extremists could comprehend and local rivalries emerged, but by and large Villèle was able to keep a lid on them.

Rémusat approached the elections optimistically and confided presidency of the colleges of the *arrondissements* to men who were 'tied to no faction'. Hence Chateaubriand attacked all four in a brochure. Voting results soon shattered illusions. None of the four presidents gained nomination as candidates in the *arrondissements.* Meanwhile the 'pure' slate of Villèle, Limairac, Puymaurin and d'Aldéguier swept the nominations at Toulouse and Villefranche. Intimidation was again at play in Toulouse, where the prefect was informed of voters being insulted and threatened. For the departmental college, Armand Bastard de l'Etang, lieutenant general of police at Grenoble during the Didier affair but in fact attached to Decazes, was appointed as president. He gave a suitably *ministériel* speech, lauding the *Chambre introuvable* for its 'loyalty' but alluding to excessive zeal. This was not music to ultraroyalist ears and the voters responded by electing the ultraroyalist slate by a wide margin.[50]

Outside the Midi, the electorate was more disposed to vote according to its own inclinations. Voter independence, in turn, made elections more difficult to predict and transactions (arrangements wherein rival candidates agreed to transfer support to whichever of them led after a ballot) often

[49] Higgs, *Ultraroyalism*, especially pp. 71–137.

[50] ADHG, 2M19, election minutes; AN, F1C III Garonne (Haute-), 6, 14–24 September and 7 October 1816; F7 3787, 29 October 1816, and J. Fourcassié, *Villèle* (Paris, 1954) pp. 106–24.

became crucial to success. As prefect of the Calvados, Ferdinand de Bertier ignored cabinet directions and arranged a transaction between a moderate and an ultraroyalist candidate, thereby defeating the left-wing candidate. Matters could have been otherwise had *constitutionnels* not been discouraged from aligning with the Left.

In the Bas-Rhin, opportunities for the prefect to orchestrate such an arrangement were minimal. Bouthillier did successfully back staunch royalists as presidents of the colleges of the *arrondissements*, but was disappointed by the crown's appointment of the prefectoral councillor François Levrault to the departmental college. Levrault was an old Patriot of the 1790s and, besides, just a bookseller and publisher; all four of the prefect's appointments were nobles. The Bas-Rhin responded by electing four centrist Deputies – François-Ignace Metz, a councillor at the prefecture, Claude-Henri Kern, a former member of the Imperial Legislative Corps and Chamber of the Hundred Days, Claude-François Reibel, a wealthy Strasbourg proprietor and member of the hospice commission, and Jean-Charles Magnier-Grandprez, a merchant who subsequently shifted leftwards.

Information as to electoral organization is sparse. One might have expected better ultraroyalist results given the formation of the Casino, but the latter carried very little influence within the elite, and does not appear to have met much beyond 1815. In certain regards, however, the indirect electoral system did foster organization. For example, Kern was nominated in three *arrondissements*, and Metz and Magnier-Grandprez in two each, thus reducing the number of rival candidates and virtually assuring subsequent election. This must have encouraged the ambitious to seek support blocks throughout the department. Backing from the Church could be useful: while Kern was associated with Protestants, the Catholic clergy were said to work for Metz and Magnier-Grandprez, who was accused of adopting piety for that very reason. Metz was also thought to have the support of tobacco growers, whereas Reibel was elected on the final ballot essentially as a rebuff to Bouthillier's ultraroyalist candidate.[51]

In the Isère, Montlivault was largely a bystander as a combination of *constitutionnels* and the Left negotiated an arrangement with ultraroyalists. Judging by an electoral pamphlet lauding the feudal system, local 'pures' had not changed. Meanwhile the Left had been busy, with future Liberals

[51] AN, F1C III Rhin (Bas-), 3, 12–28 September, 6–8 October, 1816; F7 9693, 16 September 1816, and Leuilliot, *L'Alsace*, I, pp. 172–81.

such as the liquor manufacturer Camille Teissère (a Montagnard leader during the Revolution) travelling from place to place, holding meetings with individuals whom police spies immediately labelled Jacobins. Police agents were, however, all too inclined to mistake political lobbying for conspiratorial plotting. While there was reason to suspect Camille and Hector Gauthier, both of whom were implicated in the Didier affair, when the industrialist Augustin Perier parleyed with them the talk was of legal politics. Such combinations enabled the Left to combine with moderates to secure the election of Jacques-Fortunat Savoye-Rollin, a former Imperial prefect and member of the Perier clan, and Claude Lombard, a wealthy landowner at Saint-Symphorien, and force ultraroyalists to throw their support behind two relatively moderate men of the Right (Planelli and Jean-Laurent de Regnaud de Bellescize, a member of the departmental general council who resided at Satolas).[52]

At the opening of the college, matters were in flux. On the first ballot, only Planelli gained the necessary majority. Savoye-Rollin and the ultraroyalist Joseph Faure, outgoing Deputy of the *Chambre introuvable*, were the next best-placed candidates, with the former leading the latter by one vote. Supporters of Savoye then conducted an overnight search for eligible voters who had not appeared for the first ballot and helped Savoye secure victory by a margin of two votes.

Seeing that they had been outmanoeuvred, ultraroyalists then suggested compromise. They would drop their support of Faure for the more moderate de Bellescize; in return the Left would vote for the moderate Lombard, rather than the more radical Bérenger de la Drôme. The proposal was accepted and Lombard and Bellescize were easily elected. Essentially moderate in nature, the Deputation was satisfactory to Montlivault, but the administration had exercised little control over the voters, and already an independent Left within the *constitutionnel* block was emerging.

A similar pattern unfolded in the Doubs, where the Left secured one Deputy, while reaching an agreement with ultraroyalists as to another, but avoided an extreme 'pure' and cut out the *ministériel* candidate. In the Côte-d'Or no such agreement between the political extremes was reached, but this did not work to the benefit of the cabinet. Even in 1815 the Left had registered resistance at the *arrondissement* level, despite the absence of

[52] Minutes of the election are in ADI, 8M3. See also 53M12, undated report probably written in September 1816, 22 October 1816; 52M13, 22 September 1816; 52M20, 3 June 1817, and BMUG, R9676, 28 September and 23 October 1816.

imprisoned leaders. By 1816 former *fédérés* were back on the scene, organizing a meeting of some fifty voters. Meanwhile an ultraroyalist committee, secretly favoured by prefect Tocqueville, was also busy. Intransigence was such that Decazes's agent could arrange no transaction for the *ministériel* candidate with either the Left or Right, and the elections were nullified through abstention.

At Versailles, Count Matthieu Molé, a former émigré who had rallied to Bonaparte and had eventually become Minister of Justice in 1813, soon learned that some voters would not simply follow directions from prominent notables. An ultraroyalist committee was much in evidence, and Artois actually addressed his supporters just outside the college assembly while voting took place. Artois's presence, however, alienated as many as it pleased, and there was little chance of notorious extremists such as Colonel Anne-Pierre de Bertier gaining re-election. Nevertheless, Molé found it difficult to direct anti-ultraroyalist voters towards the transactions he favoured. The stumbling block was a group of farmers and millers who did not trust him because he did not own nationalized lands. Comparison of preference lists did yield one candidate in common – Jean-François Delaitre, a former prefect of the Hundred Days who was the sole candidate elected on the first ballot. This result forced ultraroyalists to compromise, enabling Molé to take part in transactions which yielded a *ministériel* and two of the less intransigent ultraroyalists. Given the easy victory of Delaitre, however, the end result was less than what a Molé-led *constitutionnel* block would have gained, had not the independent character of part of the Left manifested itself.[53]

The upshot of the 1816 elections was a majority of *constitutionnels* in the lower house. For the time being, Decazes had reversed the ultraroyalist tide of 1815. Backed by Louis XVIII, he had done so by easing the cabinet towards the political centre, by challenging ultraroyalist organization with measures against secret societies and use of the National Guard as an electoral agent, and by directing the administration to mobilize non-ultraroyalists within the electorate. His work had been facilitated by a public backlash against extremism and, even at this early stage, parts of the electorate had begun to show independence of both the administration and ultraroyalism. Nevertheless, much hung in the balance. Ultraroyalism still possessed sizeable support in both Chambers, was predominant in the royal

[53] Fizaine, *La vie*, pp. 111–19; Charles Weiss, *Journal, 1815–1822* (Besançon, 1972), pp. 130–5, marquis de Noailles, ed., *Le Comte Molé*, 6 vols. (Paris, 1923), II, pp. 262–6, and Beck, *Legislators*, pp. 58–62.

family, and remained deeply implanted in the administration and local government.

### PART FOUR: THE EMERGING CHARACTER OF LIBERAL OPPOSITION: THE CRUCIBLE OF THE HUNDRED DAYS

It was not until 1817 that an independent opposition of the Left became apparent in the Chamber of Deputies, but one can detect what were to become the bases for this opposition in the period under discussion. The depth of anti-Bourbon sentiment could be seen in the extent of rallying to the Imperial regime during the Hundred Days. Such rallying was not simply Bonapartist; it contained a broad array of political groups. In ideological terms this coalition was based on the principle of national sovereignty. The latter, however, had several components. National sovereignty entailed at least some recognition, and implementation, of representative government. It also included rejection of social privilege. Moreover, because the Restoration was a product of foreign intervention, it was all the easier to identify the regime with 'anti-national' social and political reaction.

Napoleon's return tore apart an already fraying illusion of reconciliation cultivated by the First Restoration. It was possible not to choose between the two regimes, and many opted to divorce themselves from the struggle, but adopting such a position necessitated a fine weighing of interests, especially when ultraroyalist demands were taken into account. Moreover, fence-sitting became increasingly precarious when the prospect of renewed war, with its potential for a second invasion, arose. Conversely, patriotic sentiments had to be weighed against the possibility of defeat and potentially dire consequences for those who had chosen the losing side. Under these circumstances, it took gumption to rally publicly to the returned Emperor.

Royalists subsequently attributed Napoleon's 'Flight' to conspiracy, but this was to ignore the mass anxiety that royalists themselves had created. In the Isère, Napoleon did have agents working for him, most notably the military surgeon Appolinaire Emery and the Grenoblois glove manufacturer Jean Dumoulin. Dumoulin sent reports on public opinion to Elba. Emery joined Bonaparte after the landing on 1 March, and then raced to Grenoble to distribute the emperor's proclamations.

It was also true that Napoleon could hardly have advanced had the army held firm, but here the conspiracy argument breaks down. Despite the notorious rallying of officers such as Marshal Michel Ney, it was the rank and file that led the 'betrayal' of the monarchy. Even if officers had wanted to fight Bonaparte, it was unlikely that their troops would have obeyed. Moreover, the army came under tremendous popular pressure not to stand in his way. Throughout his march Napoleon was accompanied by bands of peasants; inside Grenoble workers chastised royalist efforts to prepare defence. When he arrived at Grenoble on 7 March, it was the populace that threw open the gate.[54]

Further evidence could be seen in reaction to news of the advance of royalist forces from the Midi in late March and early April. Volunteer battalions were immediately formed and armed at Grenoble, Vizille and La Mure. Notable for their enthusiasm were largely middle-class *jeunes gens*, and workers and artisans of Grenoble's *faubourg* Très-Cloître. More revealing still was ferment in the countryside. The approach of royalists almost set off a repeat of the Great Fear of 1789 in the Isère; subsequent reports from administrators at Moirans, La Sône and Voiron warned of rural anti-noble and anticlerical agitation. Only the intervention of a police commissioner prevented Grenoblois crowds from sacking a seminary and the home of de Chaléon, and similar disturbances occurred at Bourgoin. In late April National Guardsmen returning from Valence threatened to pillage a noble chateau and demanded a 'patriotic' contribution; one suspects that compulsion was also exercised at Châte, where the wealthy donated 770 francs to peasant volunteers.[55]

Agitation was also apparent in the Bas-Rhin, where rumours of revolt were ubiquitous by January 1815. Prefect Kergariou sought to censor news of Napoleon's advance, but private correspondence rendered this futile. While officials adopted an *attentiste* position, restiveness within the army became increasingly obvious. Marshal Louis-Gabriel Suchet held out until the last moment before rallying to Bonaparte, but news of the successful completion of the 'Flight' was greeted by a widespread outpouring of joy. Mixed with avowals of patriotism was a Revolutionary Bonapartism stirred by Napoleon's proclamations. It could be heard in the singing of the 'Marseillaise' in streets and taverns, and seen in a hanging effigy of Louis XVIII at the *lycée* in Strasbourg.[56]

Discontent could also be heard in the Haute-Garonne, where the barrister Jean-Antoine-Dominique Romiguières had expressed disgust with

[54] ADI, J529; BMUG, T3938, pp. 2–8; J. Berriat-Saint-Prix, *Napoléon I à Grenoble* (Grenoble, 1861), and Gras, *Grenoble*, pp. 21–31.

[55] See reports in the *Journal de Grenoble*; BMUG, R7906; R7976, 8–13 April 1815; ADI, 52M5, 5–17 April 1815; 52M7, 17 and 29 April 1815.

[56] AN, F1C III Rhin (Bas-) 8 and 14; ADBR, 3M11, 9 May 1814 and 24 January 1815, and Leuilliot, *Première Restauration*, pp. 29–175.

royalist sycophancy towards the Allies, and thereby gained banishment from Toulouse. For similar reasons, another dozen or so patriots, including the wealthy merchant-banker Antoine Chaptive, had been arrested by Savy-Gardeilh. Although the Charter had been greeted with approval by some middle-class elements, many others were displeased by what they considered its illiberal character.[57]

There was also widespread mass disenchantment with the First Restoration. Resumption of the *droits réunis* produced riots at Toulouse; at Saint-Gaudens 150 troops had to be deployed to protect collectors. Meanwhile food shortages, a poor harvest, price inflation, and rural brigand bands provided a volatile backdrop to the lavish *fêtes* royalists threw. Opposition spread among owners of nationalized lands, former Imperial officers and old Jacobins. As royalists girded themselves for battle with the returned tyrant in March 1815, officials reported that Toulousains noted for revolutionary principles had posted seditious placards at churches. Disturbances at Saint-Lys, Auterive, Cintegabelle, Blagnac, Montastruc and Montesquiou were, however, described as Bonapartist. One way or another, the Restoration had made many enemies.[58]

In the Isère, certain notables kept their distance from the returned Emperor during the Hundred Days. Alphonse Perier refused appointment as Commander of the National Guard and Savoye-Rollin rejected the post of prefect, despite having been one for much of the Empire. Other leading figures, however, came forward. Jean-Joseph Fourier renewed his career as prefect (of the Rhône); tax receiver general Pierre Giroud became mayor of Grenoble, and Baron Charles Renauldon accepted election to the Chamber of Representatives, although he had lost his position as mayor of Grenoble. Sceptical as he was, even councillor-*auditeur* Félix Faure found himself mesmerized during the 'Flight' by Bonaparte's adumbration of plans for a more Revolutionary future in a long discussion with the judicial corps at Grenoble. Most of the younger members, particularly Bérenger de la Drôme, responded with enthusiasm. Bonaparte also cast his spell in a meeting with the academic corps, where Berriat-Saint-Prix and several other professors were 'electrified'. Jean-François Champollion *le jeune*, another leading *savant*, was also galvanized. After a long interview, Champollion emerged as editor of the *Journal de Grenoble*.[59]

[57] BMT, LmC 13232; AN, F7 9659, 1–8 April 1815, and Villèle, *Mémoires*, 1, pp. 217–8.

[58] AN, F7 9659, 23 March 1815; F7 3785, 30 March 1815, and Albert, *Restauration*, pp. 13–116.

[59] BMUG, N1925, 21 March 1815; J. Félix-Faure, *Un compagnon de Stendhal: Félix Faure pair de France* (Aran, Switzerland, 1978), pp. 181–95; J.-J. Champollion-Figéac, *Fourier et Napoléon* (Paris, 1844), pp. 224–32, and Berriat, *Napoléon*, pp. 31, 83–4.

Among many addresses of loyalty, that of the Academic Council was particularly revealing. Napoleon had 'solemnly declared that the nation does not belong to the throne'. He had 'called upon the nation itself to revise its fundamental laws'. The nation could therefore expect that he would 'undertake everything in that great work, in concert with its representatives'. Placing his own promises before him was a means of reminding Bonaparte that support would be based on his acting upon his word. The lawyer Joseph Rey achieved a similar effect in a brochure entitled 'Address to the Emperor'. The message was clear enough: Napoleon's successful return was due not to personal popularity, but because the Bourbons had waged war on the liberal ideas of the Revolution.[60]

In the Bas-Rhin, a new prefect, Jean de Bry, began a purge which Baron François de Pommereul, Imperial *commissaire extraordinaire*, accelerated in late April and early May. All sub-prefects were dismissed, many mayors were replaced, and the judiciary was revamped. Later the municipal council of Strasbourg and councils of the department and *arrondissements* were also changed. Probably all of this went too far; General Jean Rapp, commander of the Army of the Rhine, commented that so many changes wounded more pride than caused satisfaction. Appointment of de Bry, an experienced Imperial prefect but also a regicide, caused fears of Terror in certain quarters. In fact, de Bry tempered anticlerical proclamations by Pommereul and joined forces with the vicars general to reduce conflict between Catholics and Protestants.[61]

Polarization was apparent everywhere, but the stakes were especially high in areas where royalism was strong. Among those who rallied in the Haute-Garonne, one group can be considered traditional Bonapartists – individuals who had made their careers in the service of Napoleon and were motivated by personal loyalty. Probably the best example was Pierre-François Dantigny, an anticlerical former military officer who had become secretary general of the prefecture in 1800. Dantigny took on the position of interim prefect and played a crucial part in selecting new administrative personnel. Most replacements had to be drawn from the middle class: Guillaume Bastide, who became sub-prefect of the *arrondissement* of Toulouse, had been an Imperial sub-prefect at Rodez and had been dismissed during the First Restoration due to his devotion to the Emperor.[62]

60 BMUG, T3940, pp. 100–14; R. Espié, *La conspiration du 19 août d'après les mémoires inédits de Joseph Rey de Grenoble* (DES, University of Grenoble, 1965), p. 2.

61 Leuilliot, *Première Restauration*, pp. 29–175.

62 AN, F1B II Garonne (Haute-), 7, 7–19 April 1815; F9 515–16, 23 May 1815, and F7 9659, 1 April 1815.

Careerism was surely a factor in determining which side one chose. At first glance this would appear to apply to Baron Malaret, who decided to retake his post as Imperial mayor. There may, however, have been some truth to Malaret's subsequent claim that he had done so out of fear that some other individual might have acted with less restraint. A similar desire to maintain stability amidst potential chaos may also have motivated the rallying of Baron Philippe Picot de Lapeyrousse, an internationally renowned naturalist.[63]

Not all men who rallied were associated with Bonapartism or the Empire. Jean-Antoine Romiguières *père*, appointed a councillor of the prefecture, had purchased nationalized lands, and was valued for his influence over other owners of *biens nationaux*. Also associated with the Revolution was his son Dominique, appointed lieutenant general of police. Over the course of the Revolution, the Romiguières had managed to anger royalists and Montagnard Jacobins alike; they were in essence Girondins.[64]

The mixed nature of Napoleon's support could be seen in response to the *Acte additionnel* to the Imperial constitution. Previously, the Charter had been generally well received in the Isère, although reservations had been expressed in pamphlets written by the lawyers Hippolyte Duchesne and Joseph Rey. Rey and Duchesne had agreed that the Charter was an improvement over the First Empire, but they had also argued that it was acceptable only as a first step: national sovereignty should be enhanced through increased constitutional powers for a Chamber of Deputies made more representative by an expanded franchise.

Duchesne questioned by what right Louis XVIII had 'granted' the Charter. Representatives of the nation should have been summoned to give approval of a new constitution, and the two Chambers as constituted in 1814 had possessed no such qualification. Duchesne then attacked some of the Charter's basic provisions: guarantees of individual liberty and of previous sales of nationalized lands were insufficient; there should be no official religion of the state; preliminary censorship should be banned, and the legislative powers of the throne were too great. Elections should be direct, and age qualification for Deputies should be lowered from forty to thirty years. The *cens* of 1,000 francs for candidates would create an 'aristocracy of fortune', and Deputies should be salaried.[65]

[63] AN, F7 3785, 14 May; F1B II Garonne (Haute-), 7, 19 April – 31 May 1815; F1C III Garonne (Haute-), 6, 19 May 1815, and ADHG, 4M34, 10 May 1815.

[64] AN, F7 9659, 1 and 13 April 1815; F1B II Garonne (Haute-), 7, 18 April 1815; F1C III Garonne (Haute-), 14, 26 April and 6 June 1815; M. Lyons, *Revolution in Toulouse* (Berne, 1978), pp. 54, 60, 80 and 115.

[65] A.-L.-H. Duchesne, *Nouvelles réflexions* d'un royaliste constitutionnel (Paris, 1814); Rolland, *L'Isère*, pp. 8–11.

Duchesne's assessment of the *Acte additionnel* also contained criticism, but was more favourable. The *Acte* was better than the Charter; indeed it was better in some regards than the best of constitutions, that of the English. Provisions for freedom of the press needed to be strengthened and the *Acte* should have been an entirely new departure, not simply an addition to the Imperial regime, but such flaws could be rectified by subsequent reform. Although the franchise was only slightly more generous than that of the Charter, two fundamental points were established in the *Acte*: national sovereignty and direct elections. Thus Duchesne gave his approval.[66]

While the *Acte* gained more consent in the Isère than in most departments, reservation was apparent in relatively low voter turnout (28,104 voted in favour and 35 voted against). Nor was the number of voters in elections to the new Chamber of Representatives reassuring – 163 for Grenoble, 83 for La-Tour-du-Pin and 91 for Vienne. Nevertheless, the Deputation was not unimpressive. Most eye-catching was the election of Lucien Bonaparte, brought about by his old secretary Charles Sapey. Knowing that this 'sign of homage' to the emperor might not entirely please him, the voters also chose Duchesne as a substitute. Sapey was a prominent figure, having sat in the Imperial Tribunate. Baron Renauldon, Champollion *le jeune*, Romain-Yves Perrin, an *adjoint* at the *mairie* of Grenoble, and the lawyer Jean-Pierre Duport-Lavillette *père*, a Girondin leader of the federalist revolt of 1793, were also among the Deputation. Chosen as representative for industry and commerce, Augustin Perier preferred not to attend.[67]

Relative to the rest of France, 25,600 votes in favour and 6 opposed was not a bad return for the *Acte* in the Bas-Rhin, but de Bry blamed nobles and priests for what he considered a poor result. The *Acte*'s provision of hereditary peerage was not popular, and *attentisme* had appeal. What, however, was most evident was that the *Acte* gained the most positive reception in Protestant cantons. Voter turnout for elections to the Chamber was not high either; 88 of 116 registered voters of the *arrondissement* of Strasbourg participated, but the figure for the departmental college was a dismal 103 of 272.[68]

The Deputation was, nevertheless, largely satisfactory to the regime. At Strasbourg a former Patriot of the early 1790s, the surgeon Anselme Marschal, defeated another Patriot, Philippe-Gaêtan Mathieu-Faviers, a

66 A.-L.-H. Duchesne, *Vote d'un Dauphinois sur l'Acte Additionnel aux Constitutions de l'Empire, du 22 avril 1815* (Grenoble, 1815), and Rolland, *L'Isère*, pp. 18–20.

67 AN, F1C III Isère 3, results of the elections and plebiscite, Beck, *French Legislators*, pp. 38–43; R. Avezou, 'Un grand parlementaire dauphinois Charles Sapey', *Evocations*, 33–8 (1948), pp. 370–5, 396–401, 434–42.

68 AN, F7 9693, 23 May 1815.

military engineer and administrator who had become a member of the Legion of Honour in 1804. At Saverne the victory of François Martinez, a court magistrate, was a repudiation of Pommereul's purge. Wissembourg chose Jean Boell, a former Deputy of the Five Hundred who had supported the coup of Brumaire, but not the Consulate for Life. If this was not Bonapartism, neither was it royalism. On the other hand, Sélestat provided Pierre Beaudel, an Imperial magistrate. At the departmental level, Imperialism was apparent in the election of Strasbourg's Mayor Jacques Brackenhoffer and Police Commissioner General Georges Popp, but the triumph of Metz represented another rebuff, and Reibel was an unaligned moderate.[69]

Correspondence concerning preparations for the plebiscite on the *Acte* in the Haute-Garonne was marked by pessimistic predictions largely borne out by results. By 9 June approval of the *Acte* had been gained from 13,793 voters, while 63 had voted against. Among the *arrondissements*, Toulouse and Villefranche had yielded, respectively, figures of 2,472 for and 14 against and 1,641 for and 10 against. As one travelled towards Spain, support grew; figures for Muret and Saint-Gaudens respectively were 4,327 for and 4 against and 5,353 for and 35 against.[70]

Reports on elections were also full of foreboding. The number of electors who gathered at the *arrondissement* colleges gave little cause for confidence: sixty at Toulouse despite the inclusion of sixteen members of the Legion of Honour, forty-six at Muret, forty-eight at Villefranche, and a more respectable ninety-five at Saint-Gaudens. At the departmental college in Toulouse, only fifty-four electors participated. Nobles were scarce, but so too were many middle-class officials, especially judges. Among the elected were Picot de Lapeyrousse, Malaret, Romiguières and Louis Loubers, *doyen* at the Toulousain court. Also chosen were Louis Dupuy, a military officer and member of the Legion of Honour, Baron Jean Calès, a retired colonel elected for Villefranche, Dr Etienne Sengez, sub-prefect at Saint-Gaudens, and the leather merchant Bernard Lignières, elected to represent commerce. When compared to ultraroyalist Deputies of the Second Restoration, the *représentants* of 1815 were perhaps less illustrious, but they did have social standing, experience and a certain local following.[71]

For all of France, the *Acte* gained roughly 1,550,000 votes of approval (about twenty-one per cent of the electorate), against 5,740 votes of

[69] AN, F1C III Rhin (Bas-), 3, 15 May 1815, and F1C III Rhin (Bas-), 14, 12 June 1815.

[70] ADHG, 2M20, 5–8 May 1815 and voting returns for the *Acte*, 25 May – 12 June 1815.

[71] AN, F1C III Garonne (Haute-), 6, 9 May 1815.

rejection. This was much less than support registered in the plebiscites of 1802 and 1804. Circumstances were, however, very different; a Napoleonic future was far less apparent. Abstention was the most favoured response, but it could mean one of several things: royalism, desire not to make a choice publicly, or rejection of the *Acte* itself, though not necessarily of Napoleonic rule.

The *Acte* disappointed many individuals who had been 'electrified' by Napoleon's promises during the Flight of the Eagle. Some had expected an entirely new constitution; many wanted a more generous franchise, and provisions for a hereditary Senate provoked widespread disenchantment. Thus while his rhetoric had been sufficiently Revolutionary, Bonaparte's actions had not. One did, however, have to make hard choices in the bipolar world of the Hundred Days, and it was in this context that the federative movement arose.[72]

When on 14 May an Imperial *commissaire extraordinaire* appealed to patriots in Dauphiny to form a counterpart to the *fédération lyonnaise*, response was immediate. A royalist whispering campaign that the Empire would again soon fall was hampering recruitment to the mobile National Guard, and, although the Isère would ultimately see some 15,000 Guardsmen transferred to the front, no hands available could be spared and remaining units needed bolstering. Thus a pact for a *fédération dauphinoise* was drawn up, and a central committee established at Grenoble. Deputies were despatched throughout the Isère, Drôme, Hautes-Alpes and Mont-Blanc, and very quickly a substantial organization was achieved.

*Fédérés* consistently sought prefectoral approval, and they would act as a semi-official police, patrolling streets. Close relations with authorities did not, however, constitute government control – membership in the central committee was elective, not appointive. The *fédérés* drew up their own statement of intention to support the Imperial government, posted copies and instructions for admission, and entered into correspondence with federative associates inside and outside the department. Moreover, while patriotic speeches at meetings gave little cause for official alarm, authorities were troubled by several aggressive actions designed to intimidate royalists.

A register for Grenoble lists 495 members and a similar document for the commune of Goncelin reveals that 116 men, mostly peasants, had taken the oath of allegiance. Of the individuals named on the Grenoble register, the occupation of 397 can be determined with some precision. Roughly

[72] See F. Bluche, *Le plébiscite des Cent-Jours* (Paris, 1980), and Alexander, *Bonapartism*.

58 per cent of the association derived from upper- or middle-class occupational groups, whereas only 42 per cent were drawn from the popular levels of society. Unfortunately, it is impossible to ascertain whether the registers were complete, or whether all those who attended meetings and thought of themselves as members were actually listed. One does wonder, however, whether recruitment among the lower classes was to some extent limited by the central committee. Certainly the association had enough lower-class members to frighten royalists; perhaps Imperial officials and middle-class leaders thought that sufficient.

*Fédéré* leadership did have a radical hue. Notable by their absence were certain bourgeois luminaries. The Perier clan (including Savoye-Rollin, Camille Teissère, and Duchesne), Baron Renauldon and the magistrate Jean Michoud were not part of the association. We can also note the absence of the lawyers Duport-Lavillette (father and son) and the merchant Félix Penet. All of these men would subsequently emerge as leaders of Second Restoration opposition, but with the exception of the Duport-Lavillettes, their tendency was towards moderation.

Deference to Imperial authority was perhaps embodied in the president of the association, mayor Giroud. More striking, however, was the presence of former Revolutionary mayor and current first president of the court of appeal Joseph-Marie de Barral, the wool merchant Joseph Chanrion, leader of Grenoble's Revolutionary popular society, and the notary Vincent Rivier. These three, along with two *fédérés* who were not on the central committee, the newspaper publisher and bookseller Guillaume Falcon and André Réal, who had sat in the Convention, had been leading Jacobins. Particularly aggressive in speeches and action were several other figures of local prominence: Champollion *le jeune*, the surgeon Claude Ovide-Lallemand, and Berriat-Saint-Prix. Again with an eye to the future, we can also note figures such as the lawyer Félix Réal and Colonel Camille Gauthier, Augustin Blanchet (scion of one of the wealthiest industrial families in the department), the merchants Augustin Thévenet and Hughes Blanc, and the lawyers Alexandre-Marie Crépu and Perrin. These men would lead a radical brand of Second Restoration opposition.

The political character of the association was Revolutionary Bonapartist: speeches mixed patriotism with allegiance to the gains of the Revolution. The secretary of the association, Champollion, who supplemented the *Journal de Grenoble* with the *Bulletin des Fédérations de l'Empire*, caught the spirit of the federation in a series of revealing articles. One article argued that Hughes Capet, to whom French kings had traced their lineage, had a weaker claim to the crown of France than Napoleon because the latter was the choice of the French people. A second criticized timid souls who objected to the revived popularity of the 'Marseillaise' among the people.[73]

The federative movement also received a warm welcome in the Bas-Rhin, but here it was government-orchestrated. An assembly saw delegates from the towns and villages of both Alsatian departments converge on Strasbourg for a series of ceremonies on 5–6 June. De Bry and General Rapp treated some 4,000 *fédérés* of 'all social levels' to harangues and the whole affair was designed to give foreign despots a show of resolution. A patriotic outburst was useful, as defence of the department fell largely to mobile National Guardsmen. In the end, the Bas-Rhin furnished 11,856 Guardsmen, a good turnout.[74]

The federation of the Midi was also a product of government initiative, organized to shake middle-class elements out of their lethargy as royalists recruited for secret armies. As part of this mobilization of support for the Empire, artisans, 'more generous and devoted than the higher social classes', were allowed to enter the National Guard. The industrialist François-Bernard Boyer-Fonfrède played the leading role in forming the federation at Toulouse on 26 May; plans were immediately made to extend the organization throughout the Midi, and on the following day there were already 800 members.[75]

It appears that Second Restoration officials destroyed the minutes of association meetings, but we do have a list of the more notorious members, extracted from the federation registers. The list cites 428 individuals, of whom 71 lived in communes outside the *chef lieu.* Contemporary descriptions of the association uniformly pointed to its popular base, but the list demonstrates that there was a sizeable middle-class contingent. Of the 206 Toulousains whose occupations are cited, 98 fall into middle-class categories. Among the leaders of the association were Romiguières, Chaptive, the surgeon Guillaume Viguerie, the lawyer Bernard Tajan, and Boyer-Fonfrède. All five of these men considered themselves liberals rather than Bonapartists plain and simple.[76]

[73] Federation registers can be found in ADI, J514 and to this can be added the reports in the *Journal de Grenoble* from 21 May 1815 onwards.

[74] AN, AFIV 1937, *Acte Fédératif des Alsaciens*, 17 May 1815, and BN Lb46 396, *Fédération Alsacienne: relation des journées.*

[75] AN, F7 3785, 21–3 May and 4–10 June 1815; F9 515–16, 22 May 1815; F1B II Garonne (Haute-), 7, 26 May 1815; F1C III Garonne (Haute-), 14, 27 May 1815; ADHG, 1M65, 10 May 1815; 4M34, 18 May 1815, and 4M37, 18 May 1815.

[76] This analysis is based on the *Etat pour faire suite* . . . in ADHG, 4M35; see also the report of Savy-Gardeilh of 30 July 1815.

The claims of Boyer-Fonfrède to liberalism were strong. Brother of a Girondin executed during the Montagnard purge of 1793, Boyer-Fonfrède had found the Charter disappointing. In a series of pamphlets, he had argued that sovereignty rested with the nation, and that it was the nation's right to present a constitution to the king, not the reverse. Such a constitution would recall to former privileged groups that all were equal in rights. While vague concerning franchise, Boyer-Fonfrède clearly wanted a powerful parliament to which government ministers would be responsible, which would control the budget, and which would initiate legislation.[77]

It was not, however, liberal *fédérés* who most alarmed royalists. Only nine listed *fédérés* were linked specifically to Bonapartism. On the other hand, thirty-nine were given the blanket description 'revolutionary' and twenty-seven others were termed Jacobin. If we look at the backgrounds of these individuals, we find that Napoleon's supporters in 1815 were drawn from all phases of the Revolution. At least two were on the federalist committee of early 1793, nine were on the Terrorist revolutionary committee established in September 1793, and five were on the Thermidorean Committee of Year III. The most famous *fédéré*, the regicide Marc-Guillaume-Alexis Vadier, had been a member of the Jacobins at Toulouse and president of the mother society at Paris.[78]

The list of *fédérés* focuses on individuals thought to have held influence and thus probably gives excessive weight to middle-class elements. Only eighty-five individuals whose occupations are cited fall into lower-class categories; yet much recruitment was conducted in the impoverished area around the Place Saint-Michel. Blaise Faure and Louis Savés were artisans smitten with Bonapartism, whereas Etienne Projet, a retired military officer since 1791, was reported to have been a Terrorist. In turn, these men had a host of connections among lower-class Toulousains.[79]

Thus the Hundred Days witnessed extensive rallying to the Imperial regime, but motivation for support was complex. Napoleon's supporters cannot be labelled as simply Bonapartist or Revolutionary, but they did consistently espouse the principle of national sovereignty, opposition to restoration of *ancien régime* social privilege, and patriotism based on willingness to fight foreign intervention. Whether the defeat of Bonaparte would alter such sentiments remained to be seen.

[77] See BMT, LmD 3129, and J.-J. Hemardinquer, 'Affaires et politique sous la Monarchie censitaire. Un Libéral: F.-B. Boyer-Fonfrède (1767–1845)', *Annales du Midi*, 54 (1961), pp. 165–218.

[78] Many of these individuals crop up repeatedly in Lyons, *Revolution*.

[79] See ADHG, 4M39, 13 September, 17 December 1815 and 4–7 January 1816.

## DEFEAT, CONTINUITY AND SHARED EXPERIENCE

News of Waterloo produced exasperation in the Isère. While Duchesne called in the Chamber for Napoleon to abdicate in favour of his son, rising royalist hopes were quickly dampened at Grenoble by *fédérés* roaming the streets calling 'To arms, citizens!'[80]

Allied armies were approaching by late June. During a brief armistice, work on fortifications accelerated, and the *fédéré* Ovide-Lallemand oversaw a general distribution of arms. On 4 July the renewal of hostilities was announced, and on the following day Austro-Sardinian forces began canon fire. Allied troops then sought to enter, but were caught in a crossfire unleashed by French troops, National Guardsmen, *fédérés* and students, and the Austrians were forced to request a ceasefire so that they could cart away perhaps 500 casualties. On 9 July, two days after the Allies had entered Paris, the Grenoble municipal council convinced the commanding general to send emissaries to negotiate capitulation. The defence of Grenoble would thereafter become a great source of pride throughout the department.[81]

No such action was seen in the Bas-Rhin, as General Rapp enclosed the bulk of French forces behind Strasbourg's city walls. Once again the fortified towns came under blockade and peace negotiations conducted between the Allies and representatives of the provisional government achieved nothing in late June and early July. This in turn encouraged capitulation. By 13 July the Bourbon *drapeau blanc* fluttered at Saverne, though Strasbourg held out until 30 July and Sélestat did not recognize Bourbon rule until 7 August. Announcement of the Second Restoration sparked little enthusiasm in Strasbourg, and the fête of Saint-Louis of August was marred by shouts of 'Long live the emperor!'[82]

At Toulouse the federation outgrew its original meeting place, and made its transfer to a new locale the occasion for a procession of some 1,200 marching behind a bust of Bonaparte. General Decaen then gave the association permission to form a battalion as an auxiliary of the National Guard. The battalion was comprised of six companies, each composed of thirty-two *fusiliers* and thirty-two *lanciers* armed with pikes. *Fédérés* and troops of the line checked the initial attempt by royalists to seize power, and as late as 17 July *fédérés* were still demanding cries of 'Vive l'Empereur' from all whom they met. At Paris on 3 July Romiguières had been one

[80] BMUG, R7906, 27–30 June 1815; ADI, J514, 28 June 1815, and the *Journal de Grenoble* for the same period.
[81] BMUG, R7906; ADI, 51M21, 9 July 1815; 52M4, 4 July 1815, and Gras, *Grenoble*, pp. 50–63.
[82] Leuilliot, *Première Restauration*, pp. 179–269.

of the authors of a declaration in which the Chamber informed foreign monarchs of the necessity for 'legal and political equality, freedom of the press and religious opinion, and the representative system as the form of government'. The voices of those who had chosen to side with Napoleon counted for little, however, in Allied ears.[83]

Accounts of the Hundred Days generally stress division. Beyond the obvious parting of ways between royalists and those who supported Napoleon, opposition to the Bourbons can also be sub-divided into Bonapartists, liberals and Jacobins. Among Jacobins, one can note differences between former Montagnards and Girondins, and among Girondins one can make countless distinctions. Yet such emphasis has liabilities. There were tensions apparent in relations between Bonaparte and a Chamber wherein liberals were determined to assert parliamentary independence. Ultimately, however, such tensions did not turn into open conflict, partly due to the threats posed by insurgent royalism and Allied invasion, and partly because the regime fell so quickly. Unity among non-royalist elements thus became the decisive experience.[84]

The main expression of unity was the federative movement. The federations were formed after publication of the *Acte additionnel*, when the allegedly divisive shortcomings of the latter were known, but the associations succeeded in emphasizing common goals and heritage among Bonapartists, liberals and Jacobins alike. Because the federations were public, they drew on individuals with a fair measure of commitment. Moreover, their paramilitary nature meant that beneath the federative rhetoric of 'spreading enlightenment' lay the use of force, drawing on lower-class elements when it was deemed propitious.

Figures who had organized opposition to royalism became the primary targets of White Terror. Underpinning both legal and illegal White Terror was a desire to remove whatever influence such men might have possessed. Repression was not, however, restricted to individuals who had come forward during the Hundred Days; anyone associated with the Revolutionary and Napoleonic regimes was suspect. Thus a wide range of groups gained a shared experience of persecution.

Royalist disinclination to distinguish between the groups that had rallied to Napoleon could be seen in a war of caricature engravings that

[83] AN, F7 9659, 22 June 1815; F7 3785, 10–19 June 1815; F9 515–16, 5 June – 1 July 1815; ADHG, 4M35, 10 and 15 June 1815; 4M37, 18 May 1815, and Loubet, 'Le gouvernement', pp. 149–55.

[84] See H. Housaaye, *1815* (Paris, 1902); E. Le Gallo, *Les Cent-Jours* (Paris, 1923), and J. Chaumié, 'Les Girondins et les Cent Jours', *Annales Historiques de la Révolution Française*, 43, n. 205 (1971), pp. 329–65.

erupted in 1815 and would continue well into the 1820s. On the royalist side, Bonaparte was depicted as a Revolutionary Jacobin on horseback. In response, opponents of royalism demeaned Louis XVIII as a stupid pig, engrossed in consumption while his followers, clergymen and émigré nobles, requested their share in the despoliation of France. Perhaps more tellingly, royalism was depicted as subordinate to, and dependent upon, the Allied powers, which were equally interested in plundering *la patrie*. The material deprivation of the early years of the Second Restoration would empower such images among all parts of society, strengthening the ties that had been formed during the Hundred Days.[85]

Unwillingness to overlook the past underlay a vogue for 'outing' leading individuals who had not remained consistently loyal to one political side or the other, especially during the Hundred Days. From 1815 onwards works on *girouettes* (political weather vanes) became especially popular, and in this case wounding satire was aimed at individuals associated with either the Left or the Right. Such a perspective did not bode well for a regime seeking stability through consensus-building.[86]

Similar points can be made concerning the iconoclastic onslaught that the restored Bourbon state launched upon all signs and insignia of the Revolutionary and Napoleonic regimes. In the autumn of 1815 prefects began to organize the removal of all reminders from public edifices and this attempt to purge memory was extended to all symbolically charged possessions – busts or statues, tricolour flags or ribbons, buttons with the Imperial eagle on them, or church catechisms with reference to Napoleon in them. Throughout France, such items were then burnt in a ritual of cleansing in which the public was encouraged to participate.

That the ritual burnings were accompanied by official speeches condemning both the Revolution and Napoleon served to strengthen association of the two. The destruction of objects found in the public domain, however, simply added to the emotive value of items that were carefully hidden away, and very soon there would be a rapidly growing commerce in seditious objects. Moreover, ritual iconoclasm occurred amidst massive physical and material oppression, indelibly linking the symbols destroyed with resistance to such oppression. By such means, the White Terror ensured that opponents of the regime of all social classes would continue to

[85] See A. Duprat, 'Une guerre des images: Louis XVIII, Napoléon et la France en 1815', *Revue d'Histoire Moderne et Contemporaine*, 47, n. 3 (July–September 2000), pp. 487–504, and R. S. Alexander, *Napoleon* (London, 2001) pp. 146–57.

[86] See A. Spitzer, 'Malicious memories: Restoration politics and a prosopography of turncoats', *French Historical Studies*, 24, n. 1 (2001), pp. 37–61.

be linked in the future, partly by the value they all placed on seditious symbols.[87]

In the short term, White Terror did serve to disorganize opposition to the monarchy. Most of the Left was too busy dodging reprisal to play much of a role in political organization, and the results could be seen in the elections of August 1815. Thereafter, some former opponents retired from active politics, while others saw the wisdom of converting to royalism. Most, however, simply bided their time, waiting for more propitious circumstances. Two options remained: armed resistance or participation in the political system offered by the Charter.

Ultimately, the Didier affair revealed the unpromising prospects for revolt. If we turn to it again, however, we can see how closely legal and illegal modes of opposition remained intertwined. When Decazes informed parliament in January 1817 that the rebellion involved little more than 300 peasants misled by a madman, his objective was to imply that the extent of subsequent repression was a product of ultraroyalist extremism, rather than an appropriate response to a serious threat to the monarchy. Such a description was not, however, an adequate account of all that had transpired. It did have a certain veracity concerning the rank and file of the revolt if we substitute 'country people' for the term peasants and note that recruiting was done primarily in the small towns south of Grenoble. Not all those who conspired, however, actually participated in the events of 4–5 May.

In his account of the affair, Joseph Rey wrote that prior to the revolt Didier had asked Louis Brunet, a wealthy notary at Adrets, and Berriat-Saint-Prix for support. Both Brunet and Berriat were members of a secret society, known as the Union, which Rey had helped found in early 1816. According to Rey, his fellow Union members had denied Didier's request, but Brunet, a former *fédéré*, did in fact help Didier recruit rebels. Moreover, Didier's main lieutenants, the military officers Jean-Baptiste Biolet and Alexandre Arribert, Colonel André Brun, Louis-Martin Durif, former mayor of Vaujany, and Pierre-Joseph Dussert, former mayor of Allemont, had all been members of the federation. Rey's account also indicates that Didier received loans from Perrin, a former Representative in the Chamber of the Hundred Days and a member of the federation central committee. While the policing activities ordered by the authorities ensured that no revolt occurred within Grenoble, the actions of individuals such as Renauldon *fils* also strongly suggested complicity. South of

[87] See Kroen, *Politics and Theater*, pp. 39–62.

Grenoble, middle-class agents such as Pierre Genevois, who had been mayor of La Mure since 1789, also gave Didier assistance. At La Mure the notary Louis-Joseph Guillot, president of the local federation, and his three sons – a lawyer, a professor at the *lycée* of Grenoble, and a military officer – had conducted recruitment. At Vizille, Didier held meetings at the home of the notary François Boulon, former mayor during the Empire, and closely tied to Charles Sapey.[88]

Thus the Didier affair revealed widespread middle- and lower-class discontent and willingness to conspire against the regime. Popular defiance continued over the course of the summer of 1816: buttons with the image of Napoleon II circulated, royalist soldiers were insulted, and rumours continued to swirl. Alienation was also deepened in the middle and upper levels of society, as the affair became a pretext for exiling yet more prominent figures, including Renauldon *fils*, Berriat, the lawyers Duport-Lavillete (father and son) and Bérenger de la Drôme, former *avocat-général* and member of the Chamber of Representatives in 1815. A telling sign of elite resentment at Grenoble came on 24 August when the bar elected its new council of discipline. Among those who received the most votes were four men in exile, two Representatives of the Chamber of the Hundred Days, and two leading *fédérés*.[89]

The impact of the White Terror was also apparent in *De la justice criminelle en France*, commenced by Bérenger while in exile and published in 1818. The author attacked the exceptional laws of 1815 as a violation of the Charter, and used the military tribunal of the Didier affair for examples of illegality. Bérenger argued for the clear division of executive and judicial authority and directed much of his invective at Imperial laws that had made judges servants of the government. Central to the work was its appeal to the legal fraternity to guide development of 'constitutional principles', through political activism.[90]

Bérenger's tome was a clarion call for legal opposition at a time when this appeared the best option. As such, it was part of a development begun in late 1815 when future Liberals and moderates in the Isère had commenced meetings in the salon of Champollion *le jeune*. The group was predominantly middle-class, including merchants, manufacturers and members of the legal and medical professions. Among them were moderate royalists Achille de Meffray, a wealthy landowner, and Louis Royer-Deloche, a Girondin leader of the 1790s who had become Prosecutor General under Napoleon, but

88 See the sources in note 46.

89 The election results can be found in BMUG, R8473.

90 A.-M. Bérenger, *De la justice criminelle en France* (Paris, 1818), especially pp. 1–79, 106–40, 220–56, 257–310 and 342–62.

lost the post during the post-Waterloo purge while remaining a prefectoral councillor. Also included were centrist future Liberals (the Periers, Teissère, Lombard and Penet) and men of a more radical stamp (the Renauldons, Barral, Antoine Français de Nantes (a Revolutionary Montagnard who had comfortably evolved into an Imperial Senator and been appointed a *commissaire extraordinaire* during the Hundred Days), Sapey, the Duport-Lavillettes, Perrin, Félix Réal, Thévenet and Champollion).[91]

There were, however, wheels within wheels. In February 1816 several members of the radical wing of this group (including Réal, Perrin and Champollion) joined with Rey, Berriat and Bérenger in forming the Union. Although not conspiratorial at this point, the Union had pronounced republican or Revolutionary Bonapartist tendencies. For the time being, ideology was tempered by pragmatism and the Union's strength as an electoral pressure group could be seen in the alliance between *constitutionnels* and the Left in the elections of October 1816. Upon learning of the results, Champollion *le jeune*, in exile at Figeac, expressed the hope that friends of the Charter would not use their victories to strike ultraroyalists too roughly; those who preached moderation in 1816 should practise it in 1817. Time would tell; the bonds of illegal and legal modes of opposition were loosened for the moment, but they were not broken.[92]

While the means of opposition had yet to be determined, certain core values among the Left were already apparent. *Fédérés* had frequently invoked the principle of national sovereignty, successfully appealing to previously divergent groups. As expressed by the federative movement, belief in national sovereignty entailed defence of France from foreign influence, opposition to social privilege, and demand for a regime wherein elected representatives of the nation exercised independent power. Whether belief in national sovereignty could be accommodated to the Bourbon monarchy remained an open question, but the repression meted out to former Bonapartists, liberals and Jacobins during the White Terror gave them common grievances that strengthened the ties formed during the Hundred Days.

91 See Rolland, *L'Isère*, pp. 92–3.

92 BMUG, T3938, T3939, T3940; N1549, 8 February 1817, and G. Weill, 'Les mémoires de Joseph Rey', *Revue Historique*, 157 (March–April 1928), pp. 291–307.

2

# *Battle commences: from September 1816 to July 1820*

## PART ONE: THE DECAZES EXPERIMENT

During verification procedures for the new parliament, Villèle denounced Louis-Antoine Malouet for interfering in elections in the Pas-de-Calais and, as evidence, gave the press a prefectoral letter urging voters not to support Deputies of the previous Chamber. In the Peers, Chateaubriand called for investigation of ministerial corruption.[1]

While out of power, ultraroyalists attacked executive despotism, criticizing the practice of making Deputies civil servants, or promoting Deputies who already held government office. Such 'favours' enhanced cabinet influence by reducing parliamentary independence. In 1816 an ultraroyalist Deputy proposed a complete ban on holding both positions, and in January 1817 Villèle suggested adoption of the British model, whereby Deputies must seek re-election after appointment or promotion. Both propositions were designed to hamper the cabinet from corrupting elections, and both ran aground against warnings of the danger of restricting royal prerogative. Even the *doctrinaire* Pierre-Paul Royer-Collard, generally associated by historians with advocacy of constitutional checks and balances, argued against excessive division of powers. Villèle replied that he wanted to secure a Chamber sufficiently independent to inform the king of the truth. Subsequently, the electoral law of 1817 did establish that prefects and military commanders were ineligible to run in the departments they administered, but went no further.[2]

The first two years of the Restoration deeply influenced left-wing opposition by entrenching resistance to ultraroyalism, but a more complex dynamic emerged after the elections of 1816. Within the cabinet, the

[1] For background, see Bertier de Sauvigny, *Restoration*, pp. 141–65; Jardin and Tudesq, *Restoration*, pp. 32–46, Waresquiel and Yvert, *Restauration*, pp. 197–292, and Mansel, *Louis XVIII*, pp. 344–73.

[2] See L. Girard, 'La réélection des députés promus à des fonctions publiques (1828–1831)', in *Mélanges offerts à Charles H. Pouthas* (Paris, 1973), pp. 227–31.

influence of Decazes rose, and until 1820 policy was characterized by reforms designed to attract moderate elements of both the Left and Right. Decazes sought to stake out a centrist ground, and thus the period has come to be known as one of 'liberal experiment'. His programme, however, was essentially despotic, and hence resistance to state despotism became a second defining characteristic of left-wing Opposition.

For the Left, response to Decazes was complicated by cabinet instability. The 'experiment' actually began under a centre-right government, with Richelieu heading the cabinet, Decazes retaining the position of Minister of Police, and Lainé at the Interior. By January 1817 the extreme-right Dambray had given way as Minister of Justice to the centre-right Baron Etienne-Denis Pasquier, a former Imperial prefect of police who had remained loyal to the monarchy during the Hundred Days; in June Molé replaced the ultraroyalist Dubouchage as Minister of the Marine. Cabinet unity remained fragile, however, as failure to negotiate a new Concordat with Rome corroded relations between Decazes and conservatives, and as elections shifted the Chamber of Deputies leftwards. By late 1818 Richelieu had decided that 'liberalism' had gone far enough, and it said a great deal about the position of Decazes that Louis XVIII initially turned to Richelieu to form a new government.

Richelieu had served France well by negotiating liberation from occupation by the end of November 1818 at the Congress of Aix-la-Chapelle, but he could not carry enough of the Centre into alliance with ultraroyalism to secure a majority in the Chamber of Deputies. Thus the king called on Decazes to form the new government. Decazes added the Ministry of the Interior to his portfolio, and shifted cabinet orientation towards the Centre-Left with the inclusion of Baron Joseph-Dominique Louis as Minister of Finance and Count Hercule De Serre as Justice Minister. An émigré who had rallied to Napoleon and served in the Imperial treasury, Louis had been Finance Minister during the First Restoration; De Serre had also emigrated during the Revolution, had subsequently entered the Imperial judiciary, and had thereafter refused to serve Bonaparte during the Hundred Days. Because both were advocates of national reconciliation, neither minister was popular with ultraroyalists. Indeed, Decazes's unpopularity with the Right by this stage was such that the royal favourite felt obliged to mask his leadership of the government. General Jean-Joseph Dessoles, a political nullity, was named as head of the cabinet and Foreign Minister.

To foster middle ground based on reconciliation, Decazes oversaw a series of reforms. The first Restoration electoral law was proposed by Lainé, with help from the *doctrinaires* Guizot and Royer-Collard, and in February 1817 the Lainé Law established direct elections, to be held in a single departmental college at the *chef lieu*. The government projected that there would be 90,878 voters and 16,052 *éligibles* qualified to run as candidates. Despite the narrowness of the franchise, the law was popular, largely because ultraroyalists argued for indirect elections. Behind the bill, however, lay partisan considerations: it was thought that forcing large landowners to travel away from their rural bases would reduce their influence and thereby benefit *constitutionnels* – candidates who avowed loyalty to both king and Charter.

More volatile was the Saint-Cyr Law of March 1818. This reorganized the army on the basis of the annual conscription of 40,000 men. Service would last for six years; thereafter veterans would be placed on reserve. Appointment was regulated so as to ensure that officers had at least two years of experience as non-commissioned officers, or had passed through the military schools at Saint-Cyr or Metz. Two-thirds of promotions up to the rank of lieutenant colonel would be based on seniority, with the remaining third left to royal patronage. Ultraroyalists objected to most of the law's provisions. They preferred a professional army of volunteers to conscription, and they found the prospect of a reserve composed of Imperial veterans especially frightening. In arguing that appointment and promotion should be left entirely to royal prerogative, 'pures' hoped to re-establish the officer corps as a noble monopoly.

Increased freedom of expression was achieved more stealthily. Initially, change came mostly by way of allowing the repressive laws established in 1814–15 to fall into neglect, but by May of 1819 De Serre was ready to propose new press statutes establishing that expression of opinion could be prosecuted only if it was libellous, or provoked a crime against an individual, public or religious morality, the king, or constituted authorities. Indicted authors would undergo trial by jury, and newspapers would be free of preliminary censorship, provided they posted a bond and declared their managers and owners.

Thus reform was substantial, but Decazes had little respect for division of power and his 'liberalism' should not be overestimated. Decazes believed that the Chambers should be no more than consultative bodies, and that government should be highly centralized. He wanted to popularize the monarchy by detaching it from counter-revolution, but in seeking to build a centrist following he had no intention of creating an entity independent of government control.[3]

[3] Langeron, *Decazes*, pp. 116–248, and B. Yvert, 'Decazes et la politique du juste-milieu: "royaliser la nation, nationaliser la royauté" (1815–1820)', in Roger Dufraisse and Elisabeth Müller-Luckner, eds., *Révolution und Gegenrévolution 1789–1830* (Munich, 1991), pp. 193–210.

Rallying to Decazes, therefore, risked sacrifice of representative government. The Left did frequently cooperate with the royal favourite, but there was to be no yielding on this essential point. They appreciated Decazes's attack on ultraroyalist influence, but they could also see that extremism continued to prevail in the royal family, most particularly in the person of Artois, the heir to the throne. Meanwhile, as power flowed away from them, 'pures' raked over the past to link the Left with Revolutionary atrocities in the *Conservateur*, a journal initially funded by Artois. Given this scenario, what good could be expected of the future unless parliament was capable of checking royal extremism?[4]

With the vengeful nature of ultraroyalism still on display, the value of Decazes's gradual tipping of the balance of power in the cabinet was often lost upon the Left. Slow progression away from the White Terror only added to frustration by allowing limited revelations about the Didier revolt, the assassinations of Ramel and Marshal Brune (at Avignon), the Fualdès affair, and a host of other scandals. The sad truth was that powerful figures were involved, and Decazes could not probe too deeply. Nevertheless, pressure mounted: the role of agents provocateurs bent on vengeful reaction was again evident in a second alleged conspiracy at Lyons in June 1817.[5]

The inadequacies of the Decazes programme encouraged the Left to assert its independence. Formation of left-wing Opposition to some extent followed the path of ultraroyalism, but it was a product of different conditions. Given the weakness of their position, insistence on orthodoxy was not an option for the Left. Thereafter, the Left began to perceive administrative despotism as a greater immediate threat than ultraroyalism, and hence the emergence of a group known as the Independents. For a Deputy, being an Independent meant voting on the merits of a proposed bill, rather than automatically accepting cabinet direction. Due to their penchant for defending liberties gained during the Revolution, the Independents came to be known as Liberals.

Alignments initially took shape in salons. Ultraroyalist meetings *chez* Piet were exceptional in size and, perhaps, in their direct relation to parliamentary organization, but other salons were also linked to political affiliation. There was a certain amount of fluidity in the composition of most salons so that contacts could be made in the process of recruitment and patronage

4 G. de Bertier de Sauvigny, 'L'image de la Révolution Française dans "Le Conservateur", in *Révolution und Gegenrévolution 1789–1830*, pp. 143–53.

5 Fitzpatrick, *Catholic Royalism*, pp. 44–57; P. Darmon, *La rumeur de Rodez* (Paris, 1991), and J. Lucas-Dubreton, 'Le complot de Canuel à Lyon (1817)', *Revue des Deux Mondes*, n. 19 (1959), pp. 443–9.

essential to politics, but not everyone was welcome. When he returned from England after dissolution of the *Chambre introuvable*, Benjamin Constant found the *doctrinaires* could not forgive his having helped write the *Acte additionnel*. Hence he became a denizen of the salon of Madame Davillier, where Bonapartist, republican and liberal luminaries mixed, 'united by defeat, persecution and resistance'.[6]

In parliament, the first sign of an independent left-wing block came with the elections of September 1817 when members of the salons of the wealthy bourgeois Guillaume-Louis Ternaux and the banker Jacques Laffitte combined to form a committee and adopt the title 'Independents'. November marked the founding of the Société des Amis de la Presse, initially to defend Opposition journalists undergoing prosecution. Thereafter, however, the Amis took on the same function as the Piet salon, with leading Deputies frequently attending. At the end of the parliamentary session in May 1818, the Amis hosted a banquet to honour Deputies who had spoken against the press laws; some 400 voters attended. Meetings of the Amis were public, but within the organization there was a secret steering committee of twenty members who plotted parliamentary tactics.

Despite such promising signs, there were differing tendencies within the Left, which the cabinet exploited to block the election in 1817 of General Marie-Joseph-Paul de Lafayette, the republican 'hero of two worlds' (and two revolutions), and which resurfaced in the autumn of 1818 when Ternaux accepted official support to defeat Constant at Paris. During the 1818 contests, a radical block within the original electoral committee of 1817 made a first step towards party formation with the *Correspondant Electoral*, a publication that recommended slates of candidates to departments undergoing renewal. In the capital, coordination extended to election of college bureaux, but for the provinces the Parisian press settled for recommending candidates. By 1819, the Opposition journal the *Constitutionnel* had progressed to publishing an 'official' list of Liberal candidates for the departments.

Growth in Opposition ranks brought complications. At Paris, infusion of Deputies such as Claude Tircuy de Corcelles, a Lyonnais former émigré who had rallied to Napoleon and become a fierce critic of the Bourbons, pushed the Amis in an increasingly aggressive direction. When radicals at the Amis passed a motion to support ultraroyalist candidates rather than *ministériels* where Liberals could not win, Decazes responded by forcing closure of the

[6] E. Schermerhorn, *Benjamin Constant* (Boston and New York, 1924), pp. 317–18, Coulmann, *Réminiscences*, I, pp. 172–210, and Mansel, *Paris*, pp. 120–40.

Amis and prosecuting two members of the electoral committee after the elections of November. Moreover, this tactic increased tensions within the Parisian Liberal leadership; Constant and his fellow journalist Charles-Guillaume Etienne both denounced the resolution and subsequently left the Amis. Nevertheless, during the parliamentary session of 1819–20 Liberal Deputies continued to meet *en bloc* on a regular basis; potential for rupture existed, but Deputies such as Constant helped to assure that no definitive break occurred.[7]

Each annual parliamentary renewal saw Liberals advance, initially at the expense of ultraroyalism, but increasingly at the expense of the Centre too. Estimates of the three main parts of the Chamber vary, but it would appear that about twenty Independents were added in 1818. By December 1819 the Liberal Opposition held perhaps 110 seats in a Chamber of 257. Roughly fifty-four of these Deputies belonged to the more radical *réunion* Laffitte, and fifty-six to the centre-left *réunion* Ternaux. They were short of a majority in the lower house, but the crux of the issue lay in momentum: in November 1819 Liberals had gained twenty-four seats while ultraroyalists and *ministériels* lost eighteen and six seats respectively. Liberal growth was even more striking in terms of percentage; annual renewal saw the Left progress between 1817 and 1819 from 29 per cent to 70 per cent of the vote. In regional terms, the Left consolidated its position in the east while making massive inroads in the west and south-west.[8]

Electoral results had steady impact upon high politics. After the elections of 1818 the Centre-Right tied to Richelieu broke with Decazes and fragmentation of the Centre then prompted Decazes to woo the Left. Meanwhile, left-wing advances forced ultraroyalists to drop previous championing of parliamentary independence and they became staunch defenders of royal prerogative. Advocacy of crown constitutional power did not, however, necessarily indicate loyalty to the current monarch, and initiatives such as Vitrolles's *note secrète* and the Affair at the Water's Edge revealed little by way of confidence in Louis XVIII. The *note secrète*, written upon the request of Artois, described France as on the verge of revolution and requested that the Allied powers remove Decazes before ending occupation. It is difficult to discern whether the Affair at the Water's Edge amounted to anything more than ultraroyalist minions spinning tales of plans to seize the king,

[7] Duvergier de Hauranne, IV, pp. 153–60, 223–9, 469–87, V, 68–9, 112–20, 215–23, 252–8, 314; Vaulabelle, *Histoire*, IV, 448–506, V, 40–71; E. Harpaz, *L'école libérale sous la Restauration, le Mercure et la Minerve, 1817–1820* (Geneva, 1968), pp. 74–5, and R. Huard, *La naissance du parti politique en France* (Paris, 1996), p. 49.

[8] Vaulabelle, *Histoire*, IV, pp. 71–80, V, pp. 11–39, and Beck, *French Legislators*, pp. 64–70.

but, one way or another, Decazes exploited both affairs through publication of tendentious accounts, thereby tarnishing ultraroyalism. In doing so, he played into the hands of the Left.

By speculating on the ramifications of these affairs, the Opposition press developed a strategy that proved crucial to periods of Liberal success. In effect, Liberals entered into a war of conspiracy theory based on contrasting their own highly public and legal activities with the secret machinations of their opponents. The impact of their allegations was, in turn, heightened by revelations about the White Terror. While court proceedings frequently raised questions about the role of ultraroyalist organizations in directing violence in 1815–16, repeated travesties of justice demonstrated that there were limits as to how far Decazes could, or would, go in pursuing the ultimate perpetrators of crime. Thus Liberals gained plenty of material by which they could shift attention from previous left-wing insurrection to ultraroyalist covert operations.[9]

Desire for a return to legal order was strong in Restoration France; less strong was acceptance that future justice might have to rest on ignoring past injustice. Ultraroyalists had been unwilling to accept this proposition from 1814 onwards, and during the 'liberal experiment', Liberals demonstrated similar reluctance. Decazes was thus caught between two extremes, but the extremes represented very different things. Ultraroyalism had gained its primacy during the White Terror by exploitation of organizational opportunities denied to others. Thereafter they found themselves surpassed in organization by the administration and the Liberal Opposition, but of the three contending parties, it was only Liberals who championed the freedom of voters to choose whomever they preferred.

Ultraroyalists always, and moderate royalists increasingly, argued that they were fighting revolution, but such claims should not be taken at face value. There was a certain amount of hostility towards the dynasty within the Opposition, but this rose and fell according to the proximity of the throne to counter-revolution. After the alleged conspiracy at Lyons in early 1817, insurrection went into steep decline because Liberals had opted for working within the political system. When royalists spoke of revolution, they included anything that shifted power away from the monarchy and, given that the crown appointed the executive and the administration, any measure reducing their powers could be construed as a threat to the throne. The real danger, however, lay in Liberal advocacy of the principle of representative government. Arguments for securing parliamentary

[9] Harpaz, *L'école*, pp. 145–63.

independence, by forcing Deputies to seek re-election if appointed to government office, now came from Liberals.[10]

From 1817 onwards, royalists increasingly denounced the Lainé Law. According to such critics, holding elections in departmental centres enhanced the influence of left-wing urban commercial groups at the expense of more conservative landed interests. Yet when Richelieu's followers put forward the Barthélemy proposal in early 1819, they did not settle for merely reducing travel by establishing *arrondissement* colleges. From its very inception, the royalist counter to the Lainé Law was based on giving the wealthiest segment of the electorate a greater percentage of the vote by raising the *cens* (the level of tax payment necessary to qualify).[11]

Decazes opposed the Barthélemy proposal and Louis XVIII backed him by creating a batch of sixty new Peers in March 1819. In the lower house, Liberals fought by means of petitions against change in the electoral regime. Liberal committees organized collection of signatures, often with help from prefects, and by way of reciprocation, Liberals generally limited themselves to signing the enfranchised. The same alliance of Liberals and the government could be seen in May during passage of the de Serre press laws. Shortly thereafter, however, came Liberal demand for a blanket pardon of all individuals exiled during the White Terror, again supported by a batch of petitions. At this point the Decazes programme began to unravel.

The elections of September 1819 revealed the possibility of a Liberal majority after the next round. Such a prospect brought in its train the question of whether the cabinet would have to be shaped along lines agreeable to Liberals in the lower house, putting Decazes's own position in jeopardy. Moreover, while for tactical reasons Decazes had been willing to accommodate a developing convention of forming cabinets that loosely reflected the majority in the lower house, he by no means accepted the tenet of cabinet responsibility to parliament. Thus Decazes took criticisms of the Lainé Law on board. Even so, while his decision to alter the electoral law provoked a break with left-leaning cabinet members, he still hoped to rebuild a coalition of the two Centres. When Decazes formed his new cabinet in November, General Victor de Latour-Maubourg replaced Marshal Gouvion Saint-Cyr as Minister of War, Baron Louis gave way to the banker Count Antoine Roy as Finance Minister, and Pasquier succeeded Dessolles at Foreign Affairs. De Serre retained his position as Justice Minister.

10 Girard, 'La réélection', pp. 231–2.

11 Duvergier de Hauranne, *Histoire*, v, pp. 34–65, and Vaulabelle, *Histoire*, v, pp. 11–39.

De Serre put forward the new line: holding single departmental colleges in the *chef lieu* gave too much influence to urban interests. Furthermore, the current franchise gave preponderant influence to the part of society that paid between 300 and 500 francs; the latter composed three-fifths of the electorate and could hold sway whenever it chose. To rectify such deficiencies, the government proposed establishment of two types of college based on different franchise qualifications. There would be 258 Deputies elected by colleges of the *arrondissements*, and 172 Deputies elected by departmental colleges composed of men with a *cens* of 1,000 francs or more.

Liberals launched another petition campaign against the proposed changes, arguing that they constituted a violation of the Charter. Given that they remained a minority, Liberals were in effect using extra-parliamentary means to pressure the majority of *ministériels* and ultraroyalists. At this critical juncture, however, the Duke of Berry, younger son of Artois and the sole Bourbon capable of producing an heir to the throne, was assassinated on 14 February 1820. Although the murder was the work of an isolated fanatic, ultraroyalists exploited the assassination, associating it with an alleged Liberal desire to destroy the dynasty, and the war of conspiracy theory swung very much in their favour.

Decazes became the first victim of reaction as ultraroyalists successfully linked past compromise with the fostering of revolution. Under intense pressure, Louis XVIII gave in, calling on Richelieu to replace the favourite while otherwise maintaining the cabinet, on 21 February. The king, however, also wished to accelerate Decazes's swing to the right with exceptional laws. Even Villèle was reluctant over granting emergency powers that might well be trained against either political extreme, but the violence of Liberal rhetoric in the Chamber strengthened ties between the moderate and extreme Right. Thus in late March the second Richelieu ministry was able to pass reactionary legislation that would remain in effect until the end of the parliamentary session of 1821. A law of 'general security' enabled the government to incarcerate any individual suspected of conspiracy against the king or state for three months without charges being filed. New press laws re-established preliminary censorship, and, in the event of prosecution, the government could immediately suspend publication until the trial verdict, and for six months afterwards.

The capstone to reaction was the Law of the Double Vote, passed on 12 June as riots outside the Chamber gave credibility to charges of Liberal revolutionary intent. Count Joseph-Jérôme Siméon, who had replaced Decazes as Minister of the Interior, initially proposed a return to indirect elections, with departmental colleges composed of the most heavily taxed one-fifth of the colleges of the *arrondissements*. This proposal was, however, too extreme, and several amendments formulated the legislation along the lines originally outlined by Decazes. Direct elections were retained, and most *arrondissements* became colleges for the remainder of the Restoration. For a small number of departments where fewer than 400 voters were registered, voters were obliged to travel to the departmental *chef lieu*. Otherwise, the departmental colleges became marginally more inclusive than called for by Siméon; they would be composed of the top quarter of *arrondissement* franchise-holders. The wealthiest quarter of the electorate would vote in both types of college, and hence the name 'Double Vote'.

Calls for revision had been buttressed by arguments concerning voter participation, and reducing the travel burden did perhaps serve to enhance turnout. By the end of the Restoration rates in the *arrondissements* had shot up to 84.3 per cent, whereas abstention had run to close to one-third of the electorate in 1817 and 1818. Improved participation may, however, have been more a product of increasing organization; voters in the departmental colleges still had to travel to the *chef lieu*, but rates of 81.9 per cent were equally impressive.[12]

As intended, departmental colleges became conservative bastions, but Charles de Rémusat was correct in criticizing Liberal resort to violence after passage of the Law of the Double Vote: 1827 and thereafter showed that organization, persuasion and legality were the better strategies. Liberals did themselves great harm by adopting the wrong means to pursue their objectives. Nevertheless, this did not mean that their opposition to change in the electoral regime was unjustified in principle.

For long after 1820, Liberals would ponder whether they had demanded too much too quickly, or whether the principal fault lay with royalists unwilling to play by the rules of the Charter. There was, in fact, nothing illegal about changing electoral laws, but the essence of Liberal argument was that proposed changes violated the spirit of the Restoration contract. If we leave aside questions of measuring the franchise to meet partisan interests, Liberals were essentially correct. Decazes, and subsequently the second Richelieu ministry, introduced the Double Vote to enhance official control over elections; royalist government would allow public choice only in so much as it suited the executive.[13]

[12] See A. Spitzer, 'Restoration political theory and debate over the law of the double vote', *Journal of Modern History*, 55, n. 1 (1983), pp. 54–70, and Rémusat, *Mémoires*, 1, p. 431.

[13] Langeron, *Decazes*, pp. 129–32, 213–18 and 248–52.

Much has been made of the fear of revolution caused by the election of figures such as the Bonapartist Jacques-Antoine Manuel, Lafayette and Grégoire in the years 1817–19. None of them were known for devotion to the Bourbons, but one wonders about the nature of the threat they actually represented. Grégoire was put forward as a candidate shortly after de Serre had rejected a Liberal proposal that all exiles, including regicides (with whom Grégoire was associated), be granted royal pardon. Liberals had argued all along that the White Terror, including the 'amnesty law', had violated liberties guaranteed by the Charter. Royal pardon had allowed certain exiles to return, but with no implication that the 'amnesty law' had been wrong in principle. What Liberals were pushing for was tantamount to recognition that the powers exercised by the executive had been unconstitutional; had the cabinet accepted this, its ability to garner Centre-Right support would have immediately vanished. Thus, there were purely partisan reasons for the cabinet's decision to force annulment of Grégoire's election on the grounds that it was an outrage to the monarchy in December 1819.[14]

Some Liberals thought at the time that they were pushing too hard, but the question of whether to fight annulment placed them in an awkward position. On the one hand, opposition to annulment would have terminated the possibility of any future collaboration with Decazes. On the other hand, the decision to promote Grégoire had come from local Liberal organizers, and Deputies could ill afford to alienate grassroots supporters if they aspired to future election. The embarrassment of the Parisian leadership could be seen in their decision to accept annulment on the basis of an electoral technicality – Grégoire was the third departmental non-resident elected when there were supposed to be only two. By this means they managed to avoid annulment based on Grégoire's past conduct, but such face-saving did little to dampen growing frustration among the Liberal rank and file.[15]

In parliamentary terms, the election of Grégoire was a mistake, but it was hardly an irreparable one. Louis XVIII was not unduly alarmed; his anger was directed more towards alleged ultraroyalist connivance in the abbé's election. While they screamed of the affront to Louis XVIII represented by the election of a man who had favoured the execution of Louis XVI in 1793, in truth ultraroyalist fostering of polarization had more to do with fear that punishment for the crimes of the White Terror might finally include leading 'pures'.

[14] See *ibid.*, pp. 242–8.

[15] S. Neely, *Lafayette and the Liberal ideal 1814–1824* (Carbondale and Edwardsville, Ill., 1991), pp. 120–5, and Harpaz, *Constant et Goyet*, pp. 169–213.

Referring to the assassination of Ramel, de Serre in the spring of 1819 had spoken of subsequent mistrials, giving Villèle much to ponder. Indeed, at that point Ferdinand de Bertier and the Chevaliers had begun to consider fomenting counter-revolutionary insurrection, informing Artois as to potential for success. Ultraroyalist alarm was then heightened in December when a second trial of alleged assassins of Fualdès raised serious questions about the testimony upon which previous convictions had been based. If the men convicted were not the actual culprits, who should have been brought to trial? For their part, Liberals came closest to exposing the Chevaliers in early 1820, when Joseph Madier de Montjau, court councillor at Nîmes, presented a petition to the Chamber denouncing a secret ultraroyalist organization in the Gard, linking it to the White Terror, acquittal of the psychopathic small landowner Jacques Dupont (better known as Trestaillons), and alluding to Vitrolles and Artois. Fortunately for 'pure' royalists, however, Decazes had by then given way to Richelieu, and Pasquier could argue successfully for refusal to give the petition consideration.[16]

Ultimately, it was the potential consequence of representative government that forced Decazes to end the 'liberal experiment'. Further Liberal electoral progress held dire implications for many prominent royalists, including members of the court. The chief threat lay not in Liberal revolution, but in the possibility of Liberals gaining control of the Chamber of Deputies and insisting on a thorough investigation of crimes committed during the White Terror. Given such a prospect, Decazes joined with ultraroyalists to promote a law designed to assure royalist control over elections.

Royalist attitudes towards representative government were also evident in battles over the use of petitions. The right to petition was stated in the Charter, but royalists were highly ambivalent over this liberty because petitions provided a means by which parliament could exert influence over the executive. The mechanism was simple enough. A petition raised questions about some action of the executive or administration allegedly infringing civil rights. If it so decided, the Chamber could create a committee to consider the petition, and then vote on its report. If the Chamber voted to send the matter on to a ministry, it thereby expressed disapproval of governmental conduct.

During the *Chambre introuvable*, when they held a majority in the lower house and wished to pressure the cabinet, ultraroyalists had been keen advocates of such use of petitions, and moderate royalists had opposed

[16] Darmon, *La rumeur*, pp. 183–221; Pasquier, *Mémoires*, IV, pp. 381–9, and Bertier de Sauvigny, *Le Comte*, pp. 301–13.

it. Thus it was largely due to ultraroyalists that by 1816 a convention had been established that the government would respond to requests for further information. Attitudes changed, however, when Liberals began to enter the Chamber in increasing numbers. Initially, moderate royalists followed the direction of the cabinet and accepted the Liberal use of petitions to lobby the government, whereas ultraroyalists developed a marked aversion to the practice. Ultraroyalists were champions of parliamentary prerogative only when they dominated parliament. Moreover, there were limits to moderate royalist, and cabinet, acceptance of the Liberal use of petitions; in January 1819 Liberals failed to secure a bill that would have forced the government to report on its actions after Chamber recommendation for further attention to a petition.[17]

Royalist ambivalence over petitions derived from the fact that they were being used as a means by which the Chamber could seek to control the executive. More troubling still was that Liberal Deputies claimed they had a right to do so because the Chamber represented the public: a claim perilously close to assertion of the principle of national sovereignty. According to royalists, however, the Charter gave no formal recognition to the principle of national sovereignty, and government derived its legitimacy solely from the king's will. Thus the issue of whether ultimate sovereignty rested with the nation or the monarchy was implicit in differing attitudes to the use of petition.

Few royalists wished to attack assertions of national sovereignty publicly in 1819–20. Moreover, when faced with Napoleon's return, in March 1815 Louis XVIII had promised parliament to adhere to the basic principles of the Charter. He had thereby underlined the contractual nature of the constitution, between the nation, through its representatives, and the dynasty. Louis XVIII, however, interpreted the Charter to mean that while the Chamber of Deputies represented the nation in proposing laws, the government, in executing them, did not. This formulation was as liberal a construction of the Charter as royalism ever managed, but it ignored the question of where ultimate sovereignty lay should the national and royal wills collide. In periods of stability it is probably wise to ignore such points, but Decazes's decision to alter the Lainé Law made this impossible.[18]

The centrepiece of opposition to the new Decazes programme was another petition campaign, but this time petitions were designed to block government legislation; thus in 1820 most prefects sought to obstruct

[17] Barthélemy, *L'introduction*, pp. 18–39, 41–70, 166–98, 234–51.
[18] Rosanvallon, *La monarchie*, pp. 44–54.

signature collection. More significantly, some Liberals began to collect signatures from the disenfranchised, thereby strengthening their claim to represent the nation. In the Chamber in mid-January, Pasquier commented that 139 petitions with 19,000 signatures did not represent much. Corcelles responded that the figure would soon rise to 29 million.

What proved decisive was an agreement between the Centre and Right to vote the order of the day rather than consider the petitions. This gave a first indication that reactionary legislation would be passed, but the margin of victory was a slender five votes. Nor did it stop Liberals from continuing to collect signatures. In some parts of France collection began to reach outside the electorate – from tiny Burgundian villages to the Normandy countryside, where Liberals at Neufchâtel sent emissaries to disquiet the 'inferior classes'. In the Haut-Rhin, manufacturers carried petitions into rural areas, where labourers were 'encouraged' to sign. By 2 March, the Liberal Deputy Jacques-Charles Dupont de l'Eure could report the reception of 442 petitions with over 52,000 signatures from seventy departments, which the Chamber again refused to consider. Corcelles had overstated matters, but we will never know how far this development might have progressed had the government not intervened. Repression started with orders to all local officials not to participate, followed by the usual drawing-up of lists for sacking. Thereafter came prosecution of journalists.[19]

Liberals then ensured royalist victory by plunging into insurrection. The issue of ultimate sovereignty was only temporarily resolved, however, and would return more forcefully when Liberals found better ways to advocate it.

## PART TWO: THE DECAZES PROGRAMME AT THE LOCAL LEVEL

Decazes's attempt to create a moderate Centre pivoted on reducing antagonisms exacerbated by severe economic distress, as a combination of unfavourable climatic conditions, invasion and occupation reduced many regions to the brink of a subsistence crisis in 1816 and 1817. In the north, bands of brigands reappeared in the countryside, necessitating a mix of repression to secure grain markets and state-coordinated welfare in the form of *greniers d'abondance*. These initiatives ostensibly could have encouraged political fusion among notables in the shared interest of public order, but

[19] Correspondence on petitions can be found in AN, F7 6740, dossiers Côte-d'Or and Ille-et-Vilaine, and F7 6741, dossiers Rhône and Haut-Rhin, and ADSM, 1M174, dossier *Libéraux*, 12–13 February 1820. See also Duvergier de Hauranne, *Histoire*, v, pp. 332–49.

royalists remained suspicious of contacts between well-heeled members of the Left and the masses.

One should not be hasty in linking political and economic discontent; grain riots were often simply an expression of material desperation. Nevertheless, there is abundant evidence that some opponents of the regime did see in misery an opportunity to launch revolt. Popular agitation remained a source of alarm virtually everywhere in 1817 and early 1818, especially as the month of March approached. Miniature statues of Napoleon, Napoleon II and Marie-Louise were in high demand throughout the east, and in the Bas-Rhin Bouthillier fretted over seditious remarks made by half-pay officers at Wissembourg and Sélestat, and tavern-keepers at Strasbourg. In the Isère, tricolour flags and ribbons kept reappearing, and rumours swirled of the return of seigniorial obligations.[20]

By the summer of 1818 economic crisis was abating, and prefects began to report that the people were more interested in reaping bountiful harvests than political agitation. Stabilization, however, should not be attributed solely to economic recovery. By 1818 ultraroyalism had disappeared from the cabinet, and was less prevalent in the administration. Arrests for sedition thus diminished, partly as a result of moderate officials looking the other way. Moreover, seditious cries would return in force in 1820, in the midst of relative prosperity.[21]

Officials served the regime well by shifting emphasis from repression to poor relief. At Strasbourg, prefect Bouthillier directed the municipal council to organize a society to create a *grenier d'abondance*, but here a crucial feature of the Decazes experiment became apparent. France stabilized as the regime peregrinated leftwards. This improved relations with left-wing elite elements, who were further encouraged to reject sedition by the progress they made in elections. The Strasbourg subsistence society was private, and led by a committee of leading merchants including Louis Schertz, president of the chamber of commerce, Baron Charles Turckheim, Georges Humann and Athanase-Paul Renouard de Buissière. Of these notables, Renouard was the sole conservative.[22]

There was a contradiction in an ultraroyalist prefect relying upon middle-class elements; relations between Bouthillier and the National Guard were in free fall. When bread rations for the poor were reduced by a third

[20] See, for example, M. Vergnaud, 'Agitation politique et crise de subsistances à Lyon de septembre 1816 à juin 1817', *Cahiers d'Histoire*, 2 (1957), pp. 163–77.

[21] See B. Ménager, *Les Napoléon du peuple* (Paris, 1988), pp. 15–83.

[22] BMUG, R90630; *Journal de Grenoble*, 7 November 1816; BNUS, Ms. 1176, 5 November 1816; *Courrier du Bas-Rhin*, 17–20 April 1817, and F. Ponteil, *Georges Humann, 1780–1842* (1977), pp. 22–6.

in June 1817, the Guard refused to take part in distribution any longer. The colonel in command duly ordered sixty-eight Guardsmen to attend to their duty, but this produced a crowd, estimated at a thousand, bent on preventing the sixty-eight from serving. The *gendarmerie* was called in; several arrests resulted, and Bouthillier ordered demobilization of the Guard. Police Commissioner Permon and General Dubreton thereafter warned the cabinet that Bouthillier was doing the monarchy great harm.[23]

It was Permon who had the ear of Decazes. Between January and April 1817 Permon reported that the department had responded favourably to the king's dissolution of the *Chambre introuvable.* Alsatians expressed satisfaction with the discussion of proposed new electoral laws, and hoped that press laws would be liberalized, although ultraroyalist intransigence hurt the monarchy by blocking the rallying of moderates. After the events of June, Permon toned down his rose-coloured analysis, admitting that Alsatians were not 'enthusiastic' about the regime, but he continued to maintain that liberalization would encourage a majority who wanted both king and constitution. Such was the route Decazes had taken, and stabilization would continue as long as he stayed on it.[24]

In the provinces, Decazes's programme had three main components: removal of extremist officials, encouragement of mutual schools (to be discussed in detail shortly), and assertion of administrative control over elections. The first two alienated the Right, whereas the third proved unacceptable to the Left, leading the regime to fall back on the Right as compromise collapsed.

Removal of ultraroyalists was by no means fully accomplished during the period under consideration, and the extent of the purge varied from region to region. In the Isère, Ferdinand de Bertier ended his brief tenure as prefect by resigning in August 1817; the founder of the Chevaliers was no partisan of reform. He had enjoyed friendly relations with the Marquis Calixte de Pina, mayor of Grenoble and a fellow Chevalier, and Donnadieu, but had quarrelled with lieutenant general of police Bastard de l'Etang, who was very much tied to Decazes. Bertier's replacement, Augustin Choppin d'Arnouville, a veteran of the Imperial administration, more accurately reflected cabinet intentions and thus he immediately ran afoul of Donnadieu, but he gained an important ally in October 1818 when Royer-DeLoche, a centrist, was named mayor of Grenoble.[25]

[23] See Leuilliot, 'Garde Nationale', pp. 388–98.
[24] AN, F7 9693, 9 September 1817, and ADBR, 3M15, January–April 1817.
[25] AN, F7 3790, 31 August 1818, and Bertier de Sauvigny, *Le Comte*, pp. 248–69.

Choppin undertook to build bridges to disaffected elements by supporting the return of exiles such as Champollion and Berriat, and then publicly treating them with respect, but he could not heal wounds ultraroyalists insisted on reopening. Choppin endured consistent harassment; ultraroyalists posted placards insulting to the prefect, and relations with Donnadieu soon reached a point where they could not meet without risk of a duel. Donnadieu's officer corps refused to visit the prefecture, and the general himself did his best to antagonize members of the Legion of Honour. Nobles snubbed prefectoral balls and refused to take part in celebrations when Allied occupation ended. Thus, because the Casino cast such dark shadows, finding moderates who were committed royalists proved no easy task.[26]

In the Haute-Garonne, the central government moved slowly against extremists, and for a time this seemed to have an impact, but here too accumulated grievances made the formation of a constitutional royalist party virtually impossible. Rémusat suspected that it was *verdets* who organized grain riots on 8 and 11 November 1816, and concluded that ultraroyalists were as bad as Bonapartists for sowing discord. Nevertheless, a grain crisis did contribute to long-term weakening of popular royalism. In September 1815 Villèle had set up a *grenier d'abondance*, but stocks had run down by November 1816. Local nobles were keen free traders when it came to personal profit, and large supplies had soon departed for the Bas-Languedoc and Provence. Moreover, when *ateliers de charité* were established, ultraroyalist-dominated councils took an increasingly hard line over aid. After the closure of the *dépôt de mendicité* in October 1818, the departmental council decided to transfer indigents to prisons. When the Protestant banker Isaac Courtois suggested that the poor be employed in workshops, the municipal council replied that the city need not 'sacrifice religious and political principles on the subject of interest or money'. Such attitudes made Rémusat's task of establishing stability very difficult indeed, and he happily departed in February 1817.[27]

Prefectoral lament continued under Louis-Marie de Saint-Chamans, who reported that local officials expressed devotion to the king, but refused to enact 'orders of which the dominant party did not approve'. Yet it was difficult to find suitable replacements; moderates wished to avoid 'trouble

[26] AN, F7 3789, 12 March and 29 May 1818; F7 3790, 12 June 1818; BMUG, R7453, 12–22 March, 10–24 December 1818; R9676, 18 January and 21 February 1819.

[27] AN, F1C III Garonne (Haute-), 6, 7 October 1816; F7 3787, 29 October, all of November, and 1–16 December 1816; F7 9659, 12–14 November 1816; F1C III Garonne (Haute-), 14, prefectoral proclamation of 12 November 1816 and 12 December 1816; ADHG, 1M75, ordinance of 24 December 1816. See also D. Higgs, 'Politics and charity at Toulouse, 1750–1850', in J. Bosher, ed., *French Government and Society, 1500–1850* (London, 1973), pp. 200–7.

and intrigue', whereas those who were 'willing to brave all' had been justly purged in 1815. A dramatic change seemed to occur when Villèle retired as mayor and was replaced in March 1818 by Baron Guillaume de Bellegarde, whom Saint-Chamans considered 'frankly constitutional'. It would be unwise, however, to conclude that 'pures' had been dislodged; Bellegarde was, after all, a Chevalier, and reports that members of the municipal council had changed their stripes lack credibility.[28]

Pursuit of the assassins of Ramel began in something resembling earnest. An initial hearing before the civil court at Toulouse saw eighteen men accused, but in the process judges were threatened and witnesses 'convinced' not to testify. Eleven of the accused were released for lack of evidence, including Savy-Gardeilh *fils*. The initial response from Paris was incredulity; subsequently the trial was transferred to Pau. When the trial reopened in August 1817, intimidation continued and, in the event, two minor figures were sentenced to five years imprisonment and the rest were released.[29]

Toulousains were also involved in the most notorious scandal of the period as Dominique Romiguières led the defence of Charles Bastide-Gramont, one of several individuals accused in the Fualdès affair. The affair involved the murder at Rodez in 1816 of a former Imperial prosecutor who had led the departmental federation. He thus was well qualified for vengeance, but Antoine-Bernardin Fualdès' fate had been sealed by his intention to expose ultraroyalist financing through robbery. Initially the accused were brought before the prevotal court at Rodez, but Romiguières challenged the competence of the court and gained transfer to the court of assizes. Nevertheless, the jury of the assizes reached a guilty verdict. Romiguières then appealed on a technicality, and the case was transferred to Albi, where retrial began in February 1818.

The government desperately wanted a conviction. Lurking behind the proceedings were Fualdès' plans to expose leading Chevaliers, a potential bombshell. The prosecution was encouraged by Justice Minister Pasquier to do whatever was necessary to put an end to the matter, and neither crown prosecutor general Baron Alexandre-Gaspard de Gary (of Toulouse) nor prefect Joseph-Léonard Decazes (brother of the royal favourite) showed much concern over the rights of the accused, or the obviously dubious testimony upon which charges were based.

[28] AN, F7 3788, 12 and 29 March 1817; F7 3789, 29 July 1817; F7 9659, 28 May 1817, 31 March, 2 August, 22 September, 15 December 1818, 13 March and 13 April 1819; ADHG, 1M75, 5 March 1818; *Journal de Toulouse*, 14 January 1820.

[29] AN, BB30 190, 25 October 1817; F7 3788, 18 March and 19 April 1817; F7 9659, 28 May 1817 and 26 April 1818, and Eydoux, 'L'assassinat'.

Conviction was secured and followed by the hasty execution of several of the accused, including Bastide, in May 1818. In a second retrial that ran into 1819, however, the prosecution's case began to unravel as key witnesses recanted. Matters could have gone much further had high politics not given Decazes reason to realign with the Right and had Pasquier not duly orchestrated another cover-up in 1820. For Liberals such as Romiguières, the upshot of the Fualdès and Ramel affairs was to harden their conviction that no justice could be expected of Restoration government.[30]

During the 'liberal experiment' reconciliation was also pursued through government support of mutual schools. The latter employed various forms of the Lancastrian method, whereby advanced students, under the guidance of their instructors, taught beginners. Such methods were not intrinsically secular, but many advocates saw in them a way to challenge the Catholic monopoly of publicly funded primary education.

Although the government of the First Restoration had shown interest, it was Lazare Carnot, perhaps the most famous of Revolutionary republicans to have rallied to Napoleon, who had first introduced a state programme to spread mutual education during the Hundred Days. The Second Restoration saw the state drop Carnot's programme in favour of expansion supervised by cantonal committees under the direction of the clergy, but the first Richelieu ministry did encourage a private association, the Société pour l'Instruction élémentaire, which sought to spread mutual schools.

Decazes believed that mutual schools should be supported simply as a cheap means to expand education, and in 1818 he personally funded the first mutual school at Libourne. More to the point, however, was that he also hoped that spreading education through state-endorsed private organizations would provide a common, non-partisan, cause and promote reconciliation within the elite.[31]

In the Isère, Choppin used the *Journal de Grenoble* to laud the mutual school system. Who better to enlist in the cause than professors Champollion *le jeune* and Berriat, even if they had previously been exiled? Moreover, it was natural that philanthropists such as the Periers, Teissère and Duchesne should be drawn in, but the key was that confirmed royalists were also recruited: Planelli de Lavallette, and crown prosecutor general Alexandre Achard-de-Germane gave credibility to educational societies, although Liberals dominated them.

30 AN, BB30 190, 13 November 1818; BMT, LmC 13232 (3), and Darmon, *La rumeur.*

31 See R. Tronchet, *L'enseignement mutuel en France de 1815 à 1833*, 3 vols. (Lille, 1973).

Subsequent expansion was recounted in the *Journal*. In October 1817 there were only two mutual schools in the department; one at Bourg d'Oisans had 200 students, and another at Vizille, for the sons and daughters of textile workers, prospered under the patronage of Augustin Perier. By February 1818 a school had been established at Grenoble with the help of the prefect, despite criticism by the Frères des Ecoles chrétiennes. In December Choppin personally set up a society for the propagation of elementary education. Although by this stage noble support was declining, the movement continued to grow, so that in May 1819 Choppin established regulations to ensure that schoolmasters had actually been trained in the method. Similar developments were apparent in the Haute-Garonne in 1818, where the *Journal de Toulouse* followed the founding of three mutual schools with satisfaction, especially given that the prefect, mayor and rector of the Academy had declared themselves protectors of the new institutions.[32]

Such protection became necessary because ultraroyalists soon began to fight mutual schools by promoting teaching congregations, to which they directed as much municipal funding as possible. In the Ille-et-Vilaine, theocrats attacked mutual schools as the work of the 'Prince of Darkness', and the ultramontane Félicité de Lammenais linked them to republicanism and atheism. In the Côte-d'Or, determined resistance continuously troubled prefect Stanislas de Girardin's efforts to expand mutual schools. By the end of 1819 he had overseen the establishment of nine schools, but support had come almost entirely from the Left. Expansion in the Nord was more striking, but it was confined to areas where the influence of the Compagnie des Mines d'Anzin (and the Periers) was great, and Liberals dominated. In the Gard, the prefect's hopes that mutual schools might bridge confessional divisions proved illusory; the schools became entirely a Protestant concern. Conversely, a school at La Rochelle did threaten to erode confessional divisions, providing ultramontanes with greater reason for vituperation.[33]

Denunciation of mutual schools was but part of a broad onslaught and correspondence from virtually everywhere testified to the embarrassment of officials confronted by religious extremism. Refusal to grant Christian

[32] AN, F7 9667, 22 September 1817; ADI, J515; BMUG, 90630; *Journal de Grenoble*, 4 October 1817, 27 January, 12 February, 29 December 1818 and 29 May 1819; *Journal de Toulouse*, 6 December 1819 and 19 January 1820.

[33] Tronchet, *L'enseignement mutuel*, II, pp. 103–288; R. Gildea, *Education in provincial France 1800–1914* (Oxford, 1983), pp. 37–9, 51–4, 71–3, 89–92; Langeron, *Decazes*, p. 285; Fizaine, *La vie*, pp. 158–69; J. Moulard, *Le Comte Camille de Tournon* (Paris, 1914), pp. 70–2, and C. Day, 'The development of Protestant primary education in France under the constitutional monarchy, 1815–1848', *Canadian Journal of History*, 16, n. 2 (1981), pp. 215–36.

burial repeatedly troubled public order. In one instance at Grenoble, a priest informed a crowd of mourners that in a vision he had seen the deceased hurtling towards the abyss of hell. Such was the consequence of owning nationalized lands; that the deceased was popular among his workers meant something to Choppin's administrators, but little to uncompromising zeal. Conversely, burial without civil authorization of the grand *seigneur* de Bertier in a church at Toulouse was a calculated provocation, as was the abbé Jean-Joseph Berger's refusal of communion to anyone who had sworn allegiance to the Charter.

Especially troublesome was the missionary movement by which the Church sought to re-Catholicize souls lost during the Revolution. The movement had been born out of the general conviction, shared by Louis XVIII, that Catholicism needed revitalization. In 1814 the king had provided funds to restore Mont-Valérian, which would become the national centre for the missionary movement, legalized in September 1816. Thereafter funding of the Church would take an increasing toll on state revenues, but more problematic for Decazes was that the movement immediately took on a counter-revolutionary character. Adding to the alarm was that missionaries made little distinction between spiritual and secular concerns, advocating Bourbon rule as a restoration of theocracy. Nothing could have been better calculated to prevent left-wing groups from rallying to the monarchy.

References to the troubled consciences of owners of nationalized lands, derogatory comments about the Imperial army and the lionizing of Donnadieu were hardly likely to promote calm at Grenoble in 1818. At Toulouse, attendance at the mission of 1819 became a litmus test of more than spiritual orthodoxy. While the ultraroyalist commander of the tenth military division participated, he was unable to convince artillery units to follow suit and duly punished recalcitrant officers. Judges of the civil court graced initial proceedings, as did much of the National Guard, but there was no official presence during the final ceremonies in May. Perhaps this could be attributed to the missionary who dramatized his sermon by tossing a skull into an open grave, reputedly causing fainting fits.[34]

It is impossible to say exactly how much harm the missionary movement did to the prospects of the monarchy, but the damage was substantial.

[34] AN, F7 3788, 19 February 1817; F7 3789, 30 September 1817 and 6 February 1818; F7 3790, 10 June, 1–19 July, 24 September, 21 November 1818 and 12 March 1819; F7 3792, 3 November 1819; F7 9659, 26 April, 28 May 1817, 22 September 1818, 22 January and 6 March 1819; F7 9667, 14 November 1817; BMT, LmC 4756, and E. Sevrin, *Les missions religieuses en France sous la Restauration (1815–1830)*, 2 vols. (Saint-Mandé, 1948–59), II, pp. 88–106 and 381–401.

Over the course of the Restoration, some 1,500 missions were held in the departments. Proceedings could last for months, and they drew numbers in the tens of thousands. Theatrical staging and the mass singing of canticles complemented marathon preaching sessions, and ceremonies culminated in processions in which massive crosses (up to twenty metres in height) were carried by hundreds of the faithful and then erected in public squares. Through association of regicide with the crucifixion of Christ, missionaries linked royal legitimacy to divine right.

According to the ordinance legalizing the movement, the missions were placed under the authority of the bishops, and, ultimately, the king himself. Decazes's administration did seek to influence proceedings, but missionaries frequently ignored requests that they moderate aggressive practices, and local officials were left without clear direction from the central government. At the heart of this irresolution lay Louis XVIII. The king had chosen to begin the Second Restoration on 3 May 1815, thereby associating his rule with the Catholic feast day of the 'Finding of the Holy Cross' and symbolism wherein no line was drawn between Church and state. Louis XVIII thus opened the door to charges that the regime was inclined towards theocracy. Although such allegations would take on much more substance under the subsequent rule of Artois, the failure of Louis XVIII to restrain the missionary movement during the Decazes era did play a major part in the failure of the 'liberal experiment'.[35]

Ties between political and religious extremism meant that polarization could not be overcome even as ultraroyalist influence in the government receded. The Parisian 'Conspiracy at the Water's Edge' sent shockwaves through the Isère due to ongoing fear that political advocates of religious 'purity' might again seize power. Meanwhile Decazes pondered on reports that the Church was continuing to aid *verdet* recruitment in the Haute-Garonne. That ultraroyalism had not changed its spots became apparent when, in the July 1817 commemorations of the Second Restoration, students of the free schools of the Christian brothers paraded through the streets of Toulouse holding white flags with green crosses, the colours of the *verdets*.[36]

In the short term, religious zealotry worked to the benefit of ultraroyalism, as threatening anticlerical responses at all points of the realm drove centrist Deputies towards the Right. Indeed, one notorious episode

[35] See Kroen, *Politics and Theater*, pp. 76–108, and J. Phayer, 'Politics and popular religion: the cult of the cross in France, 1815–1840', *Journal of Social History*, 11, n. 1 (1978), pp. 346–51.

[36] AN, F7 3788, 27 March 1817; F7 3789, 18 July and 4–15 February 1818; F7 3790, 27 August 1818 and 26 March 1819; F7 9659, 3 January, 13 March, 13 April 1819, 17–28 May, and 2–18 June 1819, and ADI, 52M22, 22 July – 1 August 1818.

at Brest occurred in late October 1819 just as Decazes was deciding whether to change the electoral law. After the departure of Decazes, the second Richelieu ministry briefly encouraged the further expansion of mutual schools, so that by 1821 their number exceeded 1,500. Shortly thereafter, however, the advent of ultraroyalist government in December heralded a rapid contraction. State funds were directed solely to teaching congregations, and cabinet hostility was made obvious to local councils. Thus, far from serving as a means towards reconciliation, mutual schools had become yet another battleground.[37]

The Left was deeply troubled by the inability of the government to rein in the extreme Right, but the main breaking point between Liberals and Decazes lay in his attempts to stifle parliamentary independence. The electoral system gave the government several advantages in this regard. The king appointed college presidents who were often 'official' candidates, and naturally they made full use of the opening address to voters. More of an issue was the secrecy of the ballot, upon which the Charter and the Lainé Law were silent. The law of 29 June 1820 did subsequently specify that a voter should write out his ballot, fold it, and then hand it over to the president for deposit in the voting urn, but all of this had to be done in front of the president. Voters could cover their efforts with their hands, but government supporters developed a convention of loudly proclaiming their choice and one could readily draw one's own conclusions about those who made no such declaration. To combat this pressure tactic, Liberals demanded that cartons be placed at the voting desk and criticized public declarations, but no legal regulations were drawn up and so college presidents could respond to such demands as they chose.

Elections lasted for a minimum of two days and could extend to ten. A provisional bureau, consisting of a president appointed by the government, and a secretary and scrutineers appointed by the president, initially conducted proceedings. The appointments of the president were, however, provisional and they could be overturned in the election of the definitive bureau. Given that these officials sat at the front table with the president, election of an opposition scrutineer or secretary soon became a means to block violation of secret voting. Moreover, voting for the bureau often became a first trial of strength that might sway uncommitted voters, and hence the first day of operations was often lively.

On the second day voters settled down to the task of choosing Deputies, following the rules of *scrutin de liste* established by the Lainé Law. For the

[37] See Tronchet, *L'enseignement mutuel*, II, pp. 423–552.

first two ballots a voter could write down the name of any *éligible*, but an absolute majority of votes cast was required for a candidate to succeed. After the second ballot, the bureau drew up a list of leading candidates, the number of whom had to be twice the number of Deputies to be elected. Thereafter the principle of run-off was applied until a candidate seeking the final seat gained a majority.

As Decazes re-established a chain of command, the administration emerged as a powerful electoral agent for the cabinet. To give credit where it is due, one should recognize that under Decazes intervention did not extend to wide-scale fraud in the compilation of voter lists, or to the degree of intimidation employed by subsequent governments. In the Isère, for example, Choppin took care to make the lists accurate and, rather than threaten voters with loss of official favour, he relied on 'good sense', hoping that bringing moderates back into local councils would encourage the development of a constitutional royalist voting block.[38]

Official restraint did not, however, amount to neutrality. Prefects were expected to produce results favourable to the ministry, and all other officials were expected to lend support. Leading officials were to organize the *ministériel* vote by facilitating transactions among voter blocks, and as part of the battle, the cabinet provided prefects with pamphlets outlining the virtues of *ministériel* voting for distribution to voters. The pamphlets made great play of patronage for regions that voted correctly, and attacked candidates who claimed to be independent of government favour.[39]

Immediately after the elections of 1817, Decazes began to systematize despotism. The first step lay in the compilation of lists of voter preferences. Initially Decazes's personal agents did this work, but subsequently prefects took over the task, drawing upon the resources of the entire administration. Cabinet instructions were detailed and, although the precision of response varied by department, some analyses were remarkably painstaking. Thus information was gathered concerning political affiliation, wealth, occupation, influence and personal character. Such materials were then used to determine how to woo voters through patronage.

As a second step, Decazes prepared guidelines for prefects to follow in conducting elections in 1818. Prefects were thereby instructed to use promotions, surveillance lists and gradual purging as means to ensure discipline

[38] AN, F1C III Rhin (Bas-), 3, 30 July 1819; ADI, 8M5, 23 June 1819; BMUG, R7453, 1 July 1819, and *Journal de Grenoble*, 30 October 1817, 13 February and 8 June 1819.

[39] See Pilenco, *Les moeurs*, pp. 37–102.

among officials. 'Men of confidence' (whose loyalty to the cabinet was certain) should be assigned to mobilize voters, and funds should be disbursed to aid official candidates, particularly through the provision of banquets.[40]

Prior to the elections, Decazes also dealt another blow to ultraroyalism, but this did not necessarily work to the advantage of the cabinet. In September a royal ordinance suppressed the National Guard Committee of Inspectors and placed the Guard under the direction of the civil administration. A primary source of ultraroyalist organization was thus removed, but the electoral results of 1818 saw Liberal progress accelerate. Here again was a familiar problem: removal of ultraroyalists was apt to transform the institution into a bastion for the Left. At Rouen the refusal of Guardsmen to follow prefectoral orders could be attributed to the influence of men such as the merchant Henry Duhamel, whose sentiments were revealed by the Imperial bees adorning the sails of his ship.[41]

Decazes's 'liberal experiment' failed for three main reasons. Removal of extremists from government was insufficient to reassure elements terrified by the potential return of ultraroyalism to power. Meanwhile ultraroyalists rejected initiatives designed to promote reconciliation, and the Catholic Church played a crucial role in ensuring that polarization continued. Finally, although much legislation passed under Decazes held appeal for the Left, the 'favourite' was essentially an agent of state despotism. Confronted by his electoral strategies, the Liberal Opposition fought the government by an appeal to voter independence. Failure to detach moderate elements of the Left became increasingly clear in annual elections and hence Decazes changed course. France would then enter into political crisis, despite improving economic fortunes.

## PART THREE: LIBERAL RESPONSE TO THE DECAZES 'EXPERIMENT'

That provincial politics was restricted to brief electoral campaigns has become something of a shibboleth in historical accounts of the Restoration, and generally this limit to political life has been linked to absence of party formation. It is true that there were no parties in the full modern sense of the term. Deputies might choose to sit in the same section of the Chamber and vote as a block, but ultimately they voted as individuals. Liberals did

[40] See Girard, *La garde*, pp. 91–104; Langeron, *Decazes*, pp. 208–13, 220–3, and P. Fauchille, 'Comment se préparaient des élections en 1818', *Revue de Paris* (July, 1902), pp. 154–74.

[41] AN, F1C III Seine-Inférieure 16, 25 June 1817; ADSM, 1M176, dossier *emblèmes*, 5 September 1817; 4M2703, 19 November 1818, and Alexander, *Bonapartism*, pp. 140–1.

not carry membership cards, pay dues, draw up platforms to which they formally adhered, or issue party manifestos. Moreover, the practice of public candidature developed slowly; declarations were seldom made prior to the convening of the college assembly.

None of this, however, meant that no advances were made. From 1817 onwards, Liberal Deputies consistently stood for a corps of beliefs understood by voters, and prefects could often predict the main contenders months before the college assembled. Formation of electoral committees, salon and reading room negotiations, campaign stumping by activists, brochures and newspaper reports of slates of candidates – all clarified the main fighting lines.

Nor is it accurate to portray elections as simply a matter of patronage; being a wealthy local notable could argue as much against a candidate as for him. Few individuals could claim to represent all the interests of the electorate, and most could bring along a certain personal following. More importantly, the fundamental nature of the storms buffeting France ensured that voters could readily link immediate material concerns with national issues. Patronage was a part of politics, but it did not prevent election of outsiders such as Grégoire, Count Charles-Joseph Lambrechts, Constant, Lafayette, and many others.

From 1817 onwards, battle was waged among ultraroyalists, the Decazes-orchestrated Centre, and the Opposition of the Left. Candidates of the Left generally continued to use the appellation *constitutionnel*, and only occasionally adopted the term Independent or Liberal. To the outside observer, this could cause confusion, because official candidates frequently used the same name. Taken at face value, *constitutionnel* simply connoted loyalty to both king and Charter, but significant difference could lie in emphasis placed on one or the other component. For their part, voters had little trouble distinguishing whom the prefect was backing.

The emergence of the Liberal Opposition was a watershed in that it brought the Left to the forefront of the battle against despotism. Even in 1816 blocks of left-wing voters had demonstrated their independence of prefectoral wishes in certain departments, and when the Independents emerged as a separate group in the Chamber in 1817, it was to such voters that they appealed.

Liberal progress thereafter resulted from a combination of message and means. The Liberal message consisted of the development of what the Left termed the 'representative principle' in the Charter. Such a position was not new in 1817; it could be seen in earlier brochures wherein Duchesne, Joseph Rey, Boyer-Fonfrède and Marc-Antoine Jullien, a former

Montagnard Terrorist turned liberal journalist, couched acceptance of the Charter with the proviso that the 'representative principle' must be developed. Such development could be achieved by a wide variety of reforms: expansion of the franchise, increased powers for the legislature, election of local government officials, entrenchment of judicial independence of the executive, application of the jury system to all trials, or liberalization of press laws. Few Liberals expected the immediate achievement of all these goals, and not all of them supported each reform, but the total package was Liberal.

Liberal appeal to voters was based on the argument that Deputies should represent the wishes of the electorate, rather than those of the government. One can construe this as the rhetoric of men out of office seeking to force their way in, but this misrepresents the basic issue involved. The crux of Liberalism lay in establishing genuine representative government. It was in 1817 that the first Opposition brochure was written informing voters of their rights in registration procedures; the objective was to foster independence from the administration.[42]

A principal theme of Liberal writing was criticism of the extraordinary powers granted to the executive during the White Terror. In part, such criticism was a personal response to persecution; such had been the case when Bérenger de la Drôme wrote *De la justice criminelle en France*, and Jean-Pierre Pagès de l'Ariège, author of *Principes généraux du droit politique*, had been exiled from Toulouse by prefect Rémusat. Nevertheless, what underlay their works was an argument echoed in Constant's pamphlets – that exceptional laws corroded constitutional liberties by freeing the state to do whatever it pleased. At one level, *De la justice criminelle* and *Principes généraux* can be read as calls for a return to the rule of law. Law should be applied by those most qualified, with one set of rules for all. For justice to prevail, the judiciary must be independent of the executive, and capable of forcing the state to abide by the law. Liberals, however, also called on judges and lawyers to play a direct political role and join them in securing the 'representative principle'.[43]

While their calls for independence from the executive were the most striking departure of the period, Liberals also continued to train their guns on the 'anti-national' forces of the 'old France'. Distinctions between the state and

[42] Palmer, *Jullien*, pp. 119–50; Neely, *Lafayette*, pp. 42–58, and B. Constant, 'De la doctrine politique qui peut réunir les partis en France', in E. Laboulaye, ed., *Cours de politique constitutionnelle*, 2 vols. (Paris, 1872), II, pp. 285–308.

[43] See Bérenger de la Drôme, *De la justice*; J.-P. Pagès, *Principes généraux du droit politique* (Paris, 1817); Harpaz, *L'école*, pp. 40–2, and M. Bourset, *Casimir Perier* (Paris, 1994), pp. 89–91.

ultraroyalism were not always clear to Liberals and they often attacked both simultaneously, especially over state favouritism of the Catholic Church. Liberals were not anti-Catholic, which would have been self-defeating given that the vast majority of voters were at least nominally Catholic, but as ultramontanism became increasingly pronounced, the Opposition stepped forward as an enemy of clerical domination and critic of the growing ties between Church and state.

The best way to achieve reform lay in the election of left-wing Deputies through the organization of voting blocks by local committees, abetted by the press. To some extent, local committees acted in conjunction with Parisian organizations. Opponents screamed 'Jacobinism' and warned of a conspiratorial *comité directeur* seeking revolution, but charges of conspiracy were often no more than a rhetorical gambit, and neither the administration nor ultraroyalists were shy about organizing their own forces. Under Decazes laws banning more than one gathering of over twenty individuals were not rigorously enforced, allowing Liberal committees to go about their work.

A Liberal electoral *comité* did constitute a first attempt to coordinate efforts nationally by despatching agents from the capital. The idea was to maximize results by discouraging desirable candidates from running against each other, and by encouraging voters to take prospects for victory into consideration. To combat cabinet wooing, Liberal pamphleteers asked that candidates promise not to accept government office and, following an example set by the *doctrinaire* Camille Jordan at Lyons, left-wing candidates distinguished themselves with 'patriotic addresses'. These consisted of pledges to voters, often published, and their function was to make Deputies accountable for their subsequent performance in parliament. Agents from Paris did plump for certain candidates, but they were in no position to impose their will. Where there was a strong local committee, selection of candidates originated entirely at the departmental level. Nor did the Parsian *comité directeur* create local committees; these had already begun to form in 1815–16 in the face of ultraroyalism.[44]

The greatest of local activists was Charles Goyet, the 'Grand Elector' of the Sarthe who gained fame by orchestrating the election of Lafayette and Constant in what was thought to be a bastion of ultraroyalism. He was an old Jacobin and *fédéré* who knew how to network, particularly among owners of nationalized lands. Indeed, prior to putting Constant forward as a candidate in January 1819, he sought the written approval of

[44] Schermerhorn, *Constant*, pp. 320–1.

sixty-four of his 'colleagues'. Goyet's home was the centre for nightly meetings at Le Mans, but his organization spread throughout the department, with agents establishing sub-committees in each canton. Equally impressive were Goyet's efforts to turn out the vote, organizing travel and accommodation for Liberals, and ensuring that they would be protected from intimidation. Part of the committee's task was to decide which candidates to support, and national luminaries were balanced with local figures.[45]

How typical was the Sarthe? It was exceptional in the extent to which Goyet had centralized organization in one main committee. For this reason, Goyet received letters seeking information from Liberals at Rouen, Poitiers and other points. Moreover, the Parisian *comité* advised Liberals elsewhere to follow Goyet's prototype by forming their own coordinating committees, establishing agents in each canton, and then informing Paris of their candidates. In the summer of 1819 two Parisian journals, the *Censeur* and the *Renommé*, published extensive reports on Goyet's strategies for Liberal success.[46]

Organizational advances in the Sarthe were not unique. Prior to the election of 1817 at Dijon, two former Jacobins and *fédérés*, the barrister Gabriel Gabet and journalist Vivant-Jean-Baptiste Carion, had countered *ministériel* brochures with one of their own putting forward the Liberal line: the 'representative principle' of the Charter must be developed. Moreover, the Opposition slate of candidates was well known to voters: the lawyer Etienne Hernoux had been mayor of Dijon during the Hundred Days and had been subsequently acquitted of charges of treason against the monarchy in a notorious trial in 1816; Jacques-Etienne Caumartin was a wealthy Burgundian industrialist; and Marquis Bernard-François de Chauvelin had served the French Republic as ambassador to London. Voters demonstrated their independence at the start of the college by rejecting *ministériel* bureau candidates in three assembly halls. Thereafter, during the evening between the first and second days of the college, some 500 voters met to discuss candidates, reviewing the conduct of the three Independents. Ultimately Hernoux and Caumartin sailed through on the first college ballot; it took Chauvelin two turns, but then he was elected by a wide margin. One year later, Lyonnais Liberals applied a similar organization, with a network of agents throughout the cantons of the Rhône.[47]

45 Neely, 'Rural politics', pp. 313–42.

46 See Harpaz, *Constant et Goyet*, pp. 68–85, 120–30, and Neely, *Lafayette*, pp. 88–91 .

47 Gabet's brochure can be found in AN, F7 9649, October 1817. See also Alexander, *Bonapartism*, pp. 163–9.

Elsewhere the pattern was for several committees supporting individual candidates to develop simultaneously. Thereafter negotiations among committees could produce transactions, sometimes yielding slates of candidates and agreements concerning the college bureaux. Negotiations continued into the college assembly, where Opposition voters often, but not always, demonstrated more discipline than *ministériels*. Where transactions were not arranged, as in the Seine-et-Marne in 1818, divisions within the Left favoured the cabinet, especially when ultraroyalists combined with *ministériels*. Despite his fame and resources, Lafayette needed a local team with connections throughout the department to overcome governmental patronage.[48]

During the campaign of 1819 in the Bas-Rhin, prefect Decazes, recently transferred to the department, received reports from Jacques Lienhardt, of the canton of Truchtersheim. Described as a 'wily peasant', Lienhardt was modest about his own skills, blithely commenting that voters had 'spontaneously' gathered at his home to discuss candidates. In mid-June he forwarded their suggestions as to honourable *constitutionnels*. Many Patriots of the early 1790s were present and on the whole it was a left-leaning collection, but with the exception of Jacques Brackenhoffer, mayor of Strasbourg during the Hundred Days, it contained no individuals likely to offend the cabinet.

A second letter arrived in early September. Lienhardt was troubled to see other organizers in the field, which smacked to him of 'party'. Ultraroyalists and 'ultraliberals' had established committees at Strasbourg, and sent agents into the countryside. The chief activist of the Parisian *comité directeur* was a doctor who had come to direct local agents on behalf of non-Alsatians associated with the radical Left: Lambrechts, Etienne de Jouy or Charles-Guillaume Etienne. Lienhardt estimated that this group of radical Liberals would sway about one-third of the electorate, whereas ultraroyalists could hope to muster at most one-fifteenth. What most troubled Lienhardt was that insufficient official direction left a vacuum for *constitutionnels* like himself, and he concluded by offering to identify opposition committee members if granted an interview.[49]

No such revelation now exists, but we can reconstruct who the main activists were. The agent from the *comité directeur* had met Lienhardt while soliciting support and, more importantly, he had previously dined in Paris with Jean-Jacques Coulmann, a wealthy landed proprietor of Brumath.

48 Neely, *Lafayette*, pp. 77–85.

49 ADBR, 2M13, 16 June and 6 September 1819, and Leuilliot, *L'Alsace*, 1, pp. 225–35.

Coulmann had for several years graced the Parisian salon of Madame Davillier, becoming friendly with Constant and Jouy, a notoriously Bonapartist journalist and playwright. Coulmann had also taken up the pen in 1818 and published a brochure calling for an end to the banishment of political exiles, earning personal thanks from Prince Eugène de Beauharnais, stepson of Napoleon, at Baden. At home in both Paris and the Bas-Rhin, Coulmann was a key Liberal organizer.

Doubtless Constant would have been Coulmann's first choice as candidate, but he had opted to run in the Sarthe. With Constant unavailable, Coulmann plumped for Jouy, but while he, the merchants Louis Steiner and Henri-Engelhard Wappler, and Jean-François Walter, proprietor at La Robertsau, were negotiating support from the surgeon Anselme Marschal and the wine merchant Frédéric Teutch, word arrived from Jouy indicating that he would not accept election. Happily for local Liberals, this unfortunate situation was soon rectified when the Napoleonic spymaster Charles Schulmeister, one of the leading departmental landowners, arrived to coordinate support for Lambrechts, who apparently had the approval of Jouy.[50]

Advice in the Parisian press as to how to vote does not appear to have pleased Alsatians, at least judging by the response of Frédéric-Rodolph Saltzmann, editor of the *Courrier du Bas-Rhin.* Among candidates cited by the Parisian press, however, Lambrechts was elected on the first ballot and Florent Saglio, a wealthy Strasbourg landowner, on the second. Also elected on the first ballot was Brackenhoffer. The election of Brackenhoffer and Lambrechts boded ill for the monarchy, though in different ways. Described by the ultraroyalist spymaster Demougé as a democrat, Brackenhoffer had been president of the federation of 1815. Lambrechts had been the first Senator to call for Napoleon's abdication in 1814, but he was associated with republicanism, the abbé Grégoire, and, crucially for departmental voters, the strong advocacy of religious toleration.

That Schulmeister had lobbied on behalf of Lambrechts demonstrated that officials confronted an ideologically ambiguous Opposition. Historians also meet complications in assessing electoral wheeling and dealing: Saglio had been paired with Lambrechts in preference lists circulated among voters, yet prefect Decazes had also supported him. Given the realistic options in the Bas-Rhin, the prefect had lined up with the Centre-Left in supporting Saglio. He also supported the politically moderate Protestant merchant Baron Bernard-Frédéric Charles de Turckheim, who finally succeeded on the third ballot.

[50] Leuilliot, *L'Alsace*, I, pp. 217–25, and Coulmann, *Réminiscences*, I, pp. 98–106, 167–210, 261–85.

In his summary of the elections, Count Decazes expressed satisfaction, though this necessitated ignoring Lambrechts and apologizing for Brackenhoffer. The prefect had been obliged to appeal to voters to opt for Alsatians rather than outsiders (an attack upon Lambrechts), and to fortify Saglio and Turckheim when the fray made them hesitant. Press evaluations were rather different. While the ultraroyalist *La Quotidienne* lamented the absence of royalists at Strasbourg, the Liberal *Renomée* remarked that Lambrechts, Brackenhoffer and Saglio would sit with the Left, and that Turckheim's election was no cause for dissatisfaction. The *Courrier du Bas-Rhin* proclaimed that Alsace rejoiced in the results.[51]

Liberal coordination reached its highest level (prior to 1827) in 1819, but it could not guarantee victory. In the Doubs, Liberals had as candidates Jean-Baptiste Victor Proudhon, *doyen* of the faculty of law at Dijon, and General Claude-Pierre Pajol, both Bonapartists recommended by the *Minerve*. They also had as organizers a local correspondent for the *Constitutionnel* who had been purged from the *lycée* at Besançon, and a former Imperial magistrate who arranged a Liberal assembly at Besançon prior to voting. The department was also suitably deluged with brochures, but few inroads were made into the *ministériel* block.[52]

Only one seat was contested in 1819 in the Haute-Garonne, where the principal members of a Toulousain Liberal committee were the lawyer Pierre Roucole, the surgeon Viguerie, the merchants Chaptive, Jean-Joseph Duffé, Grégoire-Jean Barre and Jean Authier, and General Jacques Pelet. It said something that Toulousain Liberals chose Jean-Marie-Gabriel Durand, former mayor of Saint-Gaudens and former president of the local federation, as their candidate. As in Goyet's Sarthe, the virulence of local ultraroyalism concentrated Liberal minds.

The official candidate was crown prosecutor general Gary. After his performance in the Fualdès affair, Liberals had little reason to admire him, and ultraroyalists were ill disposed towards anyone who had acted as an agent of Decazes. Thus, between the 'caballing of these two opposite factions', attempts to establish a centrist coalition foundered. Indeed, the composition of the elected college bureau indicated conniving between the two extremes: alongside the ultraroyalist Savy-Gardeilh were found the Liberal merchant Joseph Cassaing and Baron Malaret. Gary gained a minuscule 38 votes on the first ballot, whereas the ultraroyalist Castelbajac held 645,

[51] ADBR, 2M13, *renseignements sur les élections*, 30 July – 16 September 1819 and the minutes of the electoral college in the same folder; *Courrier du Bas-Rhin*, 2–21 September 1819; Coulmann, *Réminiscences*, I, pp. 236–7, 270–85, and Leuilliot, *L'Alsace*, I, pp. 225–35.

[52] Weiss, *Journal, 1815–22*, pp. 247–61.

and Durand 632. Prior to the second ballot, Gary directed his supporters towards Barthélemy de Castelbajac, helping to ensure that the ultraroyalist candidate won by 691 votes to 653.

Given the wide majorities previously gained by ultraroyalists, the slim margin of Castelbajac's victory paid striking testimony to Liberal progress, but disunity in the ultraroyalist camp also played a part in the final tally. Castelbajac was the 'darling' of extreme ultraroyalists, enjoying the support of ultramontanes such as the abbé MacCarthy, and the Parisian *Drapeau blanc*. As a co-founder of the influential *Conservateur*, Castelbajac was also well placed to rival Villèle, who represented a less intransigent branch of ultraroyalism.

Factional struggles waged among Deputies in Paris thus became manifest at the local level, and Villèle initially backed another candidate. It was only to prevent Liberal victory that he subsequently shifted support to the victor. In response, two of the theocratic founders of the Chevaliers, Montmorency and Ferdinand de Bertier, wrote to Villèle congratulating him on 'his victory'. Shortly thereafter, however, relations again deteriorated as Castelbajac sought to prevent ultraroyalists from combining with *ministériels* in supporting the reactionary legislation tabled by Decazes in January 1820, whereas Villèle supported expedient coalition. Thus it was Villèle who chose the path that ultimately led to power and he would benefit by it.[53]

In addition to the formation of electoral committees, establishment of a sympathetic local newspaper often facilitated Liberal organization. Such a journal could aid the coordination of voting blocks through the announcement of meetings and, outside the campaign season, update readers as to the performance of Deputies or the activities of the administration. In the absence of a local rag, Parisian dailies and political brochures available in reading rooms or bookstores could also spread the word. Pamphlets, frequently based on the speeches of Deputies, were distributed in small-town cafés and rural market places. For a time in 1816 prefects had been inclined to repress brochure distribution in electoral colleges, but this liberty was generally conceded thereafter.

In the Isère, Parisian journals were the chief vectors of Liberalism until the summer of 1819, when the *Journal libre de l'Isère* and the *Echo des Alpes* entered the fray. The latter two then began to coordinate previously

[53] AN, F1C III Garonne (Haute-), 6, F7 9659, 18 September 1819 and 9 August 1820; F7 3677 (6), 4 October 1819; ADHG, 2M22, voter lists of 1819, 2M24, 28 September 1819; *Journal de Toulouse*, 8–15 September and 27 December 1819; Higgs, *Ultraroyalism*, pp. 66–7, and Bertier de Sauvigny, 'L'image', pp. 150–2.

disparate elements of opposition. Reports on debates in the Chambers were an obvious means, especially when editing enhanced the arguments of the Left. By 1819 Liberal Deputies hailed from all over France, and frequently citing them gave the impression that certain beliefs united all patriots. Reports on trials could also be shaped to reveal that oppression had struck the entire hexagon. Directed towards the same end was the *Journal libre*'s penchant for reporting audience response in theatres throughout the country to plays wherein lines could be construed as anti-governmental and vigorously applauded.

A corollary of free expression lay in the establishment of places where individuals could discuss mutual concerns. The salons of Champollion *le jeune* and the Duport-Lavillettes had long served this purpose at Grenoble. They were rallying points for activists, and became headquarters at election time. The same was true of Falcon's reading room, where one could read Parisian journals or a profusion of brochures. Because brochures deluged the countryside during critical moments, the administration monitored *marchands colporteurs* assiduously, and were keen to have dedicated royalists in the postal system. Falcon, whose bookstore served as a distribution point, was well known to post officers who monitored his mail. When police were informed of offending articles, it was to Falcon that they paid their first visits. There were other centres of investigation, however, most notably the *cercle* Arribert, a private reading club with a membership of several hundred. Composed largely of merchants, manufacturers and professionals, the *cercle* Arribert was not a Liberal 'operations centre', but it was a place where word of Liberal causes could be spread.

What the administration was up against could be seen in the *Echo des Alpes*. Published by a society of *gens de lettres*, the *Echo* was small in format, cheap in production, and irregular in publication. It was less impressive than its counterpart the *Journal libre* and it certainly was not the organ of a single Liberal Opposition; it represented a radical wing, but this did not stop it from raising issues of concern to all Liberals. Ultraroyalists and ultramontanes came in for incessant invective – 'seeing only themselves in the universe' these groups demanded 'privileges to reduce others to slavery'. Some examples were drawn from the present – refusals to grant religious burial – and others dredged up the White Terror, including a long narrative of the travails in pursuit of justice of the family of a wealthy landowner murdered by ultraroyalists in the witch hunt following Didier's revolt.[54]

[54] *L'Echo des Alpes*, 1 (August 1819); for discussion of reading rooms and their relation to public opinion at Lyons during the July Monarchy, see J. Popkin, *Press, Revolution and Social Identities in France, 1830–1835* (University Park, Pa., 2002), pp. 55–65.

Similar, though less pronounced, trends developed in the Bas-Rhin and Haute-Garonne. While other towns in the department were bereft of reading circles, Strasbourg had three. At two of the *cercles* the *Minerve Française* was much sought after. A mix of Bonapartism and liberalism, the *Minerve* featured articles by Etienne and Constant; the causes it supported included a subscription for exiles in Texas. Moreover, a shift could be discerned in the *Courrier du Bas-Rhin.* Royalist during the White Terror, in the autumn of 1817 it began to advocate mutual schools and, while the owner Saltzmann did not engage in direct political commentary, he did print letters from Lafayette and Constant.

In the Haute-Garonne, François Vieussieux cautiously moved the *Journal de Toulouse* leftwards. He also shied away from editorial, but his selection of speeches from the Chamber gave increasing play to Liberals. A certain antipathy towards Spain was apparent, denoting a form of patriotism potentially hostile to indigenous ultraroyalism. On the home front, the newspaper covered an *éloge* given to Picot de Lapeyrousse at the Royal Academy in September 1819, and praised Malaret for the tact with which he delivered a speech on the 'alliance of science and letters'. Although the report was not overtly political, the *Journal* would not have dared to praise Lapeyrousse or Malaret in 1816.[55]

By 1819 the *Journal* was quietly backing the Liberal candidate Durand. Vieussieux avoided partisan commentary, but he did publish a letter calling for voters to look for 'moderation' and 'disinterest' on the part of a candidate – someone who combined love of king and *patrie* and took the Charter as his guide. Later the *Journal* would report charges of libel brought by Durand against the editor responsible for the Parisian *Drapeau Blanc.* When the latter was found guilty and ordered to pay 1,000 francs in damages to Durand, the *Journal* informed readers that Durand would devote the funds to the restoration of the parish church of Saint-Gaudens. What better sign of 'disinterest'?[56]

Judging by subsequent reports, it would appear that Liberals put down significant roots in the period under discussion. A police survey of printers and booksellers at Toulouse in July 1822 reported that nine of twenty-two had 'bad opinions', while another four were 'equivocal' or 'highly suspect'. A similar exercise conducted in October and November found that four literary *cabinets* were either 'Liberal' or 'highly Liberal'. At Saint-Gaudens, four reading rooms were considered so bad that the sub-prefect doubted whether sending free subscriptions to royalist journals would serve any

[55] AN, F7 9693, 10 November 1818; *Courrier du Bas-Rhin,* 28 October and 25 November 1817, 20 April and 22 June 1819; *Journal de Toulouse,* 3 September 1819, and Leuilliot, *L'Alsace,* I, pp. 205–10.

[56] *Journal de Toulouse,* 8–15 September and 27 December 1819.

positive purpose, although the clientele of one was mostly composed of workers who were generally 'less perverted' than middle-class elements. At Toulouse twenty cafés receiving newspapers were listed as 'Liberal' or 'ultra-Liberal'; all took the *Journal de Toulouse* and nineteen also subscribed to the *Constitutionnel.* At Villefranche two Liberal *cabinets* took the *Journal,* whereas at Muret two Liberal cafés did not subscribe to newspapers. At Saint-Gaudens there were three Liberal cafés: one was 'slightly Liberal' and attended by artisans; one was 'moderate' and attended by army officers, and a third was 'very Liberal', with subscriptions to the *Courrier Français* as well as the *Journal.* Liberal cafés were also to be found in Saint-Martory, Montrejean, Saint-Béat and Bagnères de Luchon and the *arrondissement* of Saint-Gaudens thus confirmed its reputation as being particularly receptive to the Opposition.[57]

In theory, Liberal committees were supposed to spring into action only during election campaigns, but activists did find ways to demonstrate allegiance in the absence of elections. Such means enabled them to mobilize support while drawing public attention to Liberal causes.

News of the Barthélemy proposal initially produced stupor in Grenoblois salons in February 1819, but thereafter Liberals sprang to the defence of the rights of the nation from 'aristocratic attack'. When Liberals Michoud and Duschesne brought the prefect a petition opposing change in the electoral laws, Choppin responded that the right of petition was recognized in the Charter, but counselled moderation. Within three hours of its creation, the petition had 500 signatures, and the number had increased to 817 by 3 March.

Matters then took an unfortunate turn as ultraroyalists threatened to send a counter-petition to the Peers. At the same time, Lafayette wrote to Duport-Lavillette asking that the petition be sent to him. Duport-Lavillette did so against the wishes of Michoud and Duchesne, who had wanted the petition to be presented by the moderate Liberal Savoye-Rollin. Meanwhile a second petition at Voiron gained 300 signatures, whereas the counter-petition drawn up by the Marquis de Pina gained only seventeen in the entire department. While such activity posed no immediate threat to public order, Choppin concluded that ultraroyalists would be in great danger should mounting agitation reach the popular classes.[58]

Reaction to the Barthélemy proposal also spurred Liberals in the Haute-Garonne. Previously, members of the Left had been keen to lay their hands

[57] ADHG, 6T1, 19 July, 22 October, 15 and 22 November 1822.

[58] AN, F7 6740, 25 February – 5 March, and 10 March 1819; ADI, 52M22, 4 March 1819.

on the 1814 brochure in which Villèle had shown 'much different attitudes towards nationalized lands and the Charter' than he expressed in 1818. They had also disseminated copies of speeches by Independents in the Chamber, and in April 1819, the police reported Liberal distribution of an address of the chamber of commerce of Bordeaux, attributed to the nephew of Boyer-Fonfrède. More significantly, several merchants had signed a petition against change in the electoral laws. Given that Liberals in the Chamber immediately linked the Barthélemy proposal to the Ramel affair, triggering allegations highly embarrassing for Villèle, more than just revision of the electoral law was at play. It would, however, appear that the petition remained within a narrow circle.[59]

To sustain allegiance, Liberals also used subscription campaigns wherein seemingly benign generosity often served a partisan purpose. For example, subscription drives in November 1817 on behalf of the victims of the sinking of the frigate *Medusa* (subsequently immortalized in Jean-Théodore Géricault's *The Raft of the Medusa*) were designed to drive a wedge between *ministériels* and ultraroyalists. Hugues de Chaumareys, an émigré whose previous naval experience had been restricted to the counter-revolutionary Quibéron Bay disaster of 1795, was the commander of the expedition to Senegal of which the *Medusa* was part, and he had, in turn, been appointed by the ultraroyalist Viscount Dubouchage. Similarly, after Colonel Charles Fabvier had been brought to trial for publishing brochures revealing police entrapment at Lyons, a subscription drive to pay his fines was opened in early 1819. Again, such publicity was embarrassing both to the government and to ultraroyalism.[60]

Liberals also began to copy ultraroyalist methods for rallying the troops, including banquets, 'illuminations' (the practice of placing candles in windows to mark public approval of some event), and serenades (the practice of singing to an individual as a public expression of approval, often in recognition of some service rendered), usually combined with speeches. At Strasbourg, Georges Humann made himself popular by lobbying in Paris for restoration of the city's transit status, and received serenades outside his home by way of reward. The Opposition press became especially enthused over 'patriotic' banquets wherever they occurred. Such occasions usually transpired upon the return of a Deputy after a parliamentary session, and they were a means by which activists could signal which of their representatives had best expressed their wishes, but the passage of any luminary could

[59] AN, F7 3789, 3–6 February, 29 March 1818; F7 3790, 21 November 1818, and F7 9659, 13 April 1819.

[60] See Harpaz, *L'école*, pp. 74–5, 155–7, and Leuilliot, *L'Alsace*, I, pp. 214–9, 225–7.

trigger demonstrations. At Rouen in September 1818 Liberals honoured two Deputies from the neighbouring department of the Eure, Baron Edouard Bignon, former Imperial diplomat and future Napoleonic biographer, and the magistrate Dupont de l'Eure, former *représentant* of the Chamber of the Hundred Days and a member of the Legion of Honour, with a banquet that drew roughly 260 subscribers. It was all very legal and indeed programme organizers, including the obstreperous Henry Duhamel, invited the mayor to send a police commissioner to attend. Invitations were also sent to two Deputies of the Seine-Inférieure, but the intent was not so much to honour them, as to draw them towards the Left through association with their counterparts from the Eure.[61]

Thus, while the extent of Liberal organization varied regionally and much depended on whether a department had come up for annual renewal, significant strides were taken nationally prior to 1820. During campaigns electoral committees played a vital role in forming voter blocks in support of Liberal candidates. Such committees might extend throughout a department and back a slate of candidates, or they might be less spatially developed and simply back an individual. In the latter case, agreements could be reached with other committees so as to preclude potentially internecine conflicts.

Organization was not, however, confined to the campaign season and Liberal activists found many ways by which sustained allegiance could be mobilized and demonstrated – petitions, banquets and serenades among them. Devices such as the 'patriotic oath' were designed to ensure that a Deputy's commitment to the wishes of his supporters remained permanent, and the press, national and local, was very keen to monitor the parliamentary performance of Deputies. Especially where Liberals managed to establish a local newspaper, they gained a means by which organization could be facilitated and burning issues brought continuously to the public's attention.

## PART FOUR: THE CHARACTER OF LIBERAL OPPOSITION

Whether in the Morbihan or the Rhône, the organizational role of former Jacobins and *fédérés* of 1815 was obvious, but one should not jump to conclusions concerning ideology; former Jacobins were not necessarily

[61] AN, F1C III Seine-Inférieure 16, 13 September 1818; ADSM, 1M174, dossier *réunions*, 13–18 September 1818, and Ponteil, *Humann*, pp. 21–6. On political banquets during the early years of the July Monarch, see Popkin, *Press*, pp. 167–79.

republican or terribly democratic, although they did continue to advocate the principle of national sovereignty. According to Goyet, many patriots were more 'Bonapartist than liberal', whereas the prefect of the Gironde reported that republican ideas lurked below surface attachment to Napoleon.[62]

Jacobin tendencies were still apparent in Gabet at Dijon. A journalist for the Dijonnais popular society during the Revolution, Gabet had argued that the *Acte additionnel* of 1815 was provisional and that patriots should determine what sort of constitution they really wanted. In 1817 he saw in the Lainé Law an assurance that public opinion would become the basis for legislation, and believed that the right to petition enabled the sovereign nation to exercise its will. Gabet's preoccupation with bringing government within the rule of law was, however, quintessentially liberal. Cabinets must be responsible to the Chamber of Deputies and the latter must have control over budgets. The judiciary must be independent of the executive, and the enfranchised should determine the composition of juries by drawing lots among themselves.

Gabet also proposed that the Charter should contain an article renouncing conquest, and favoured a citizen army over a professional force. Still, one should not read too much into renunciation of conquest; according to the author, war at present would lead to the destruction of France. During the Hundred Days the Burgundian federation, of which Gabet was a committee member, had based its support of Bonaparte on his vow to give up wars of aggression, but this had not prevented the association from backing Napoleon up to Waterloo.[63]

Ambiguity was honed to a fine art by Boyer-Fonfrède at Toulouse. Within a month of his return from exile, in March 1817 he published a brochure in which he styled himself former president of the *fédérés*, and lauded the association for its patriotism. In 1818 he funded caricatures of priests and nobles, and followed this with a memoir attacking local ultraroyalists. Another brochure published in 1818 was typical of emerging Liberal Opposition: 'My enemies have called me republican when they have not been able to reconcile the epithet Bonapartist with my past political conduct, and because they are ignorant, they do not know that the institution of a republic excludes neither Kings nor senators. Look at Sparta!' In

[62] See J. Mouchet, 'L'esprit public dans le Morbihan sous la Restauration', *Annales de Bretagne*, 45 (1938), pp. 89–182; Moulard, *Le Comte Tournon*, p. 75; Ribe, *Lyon*, pp. 100–26; P. Gonnet, 'La société dijonnaise au XIXe siècle' (*thèse*, University of Paris, 1974), pp. 404–12; Alexander, *Bonapartism*, pp. 178–81, 260–70, and Harpaz, *Constant et Goyet*, pp. 21 and 41.

[63] See note 47.

Boyer-Fonfiède we can see elements of republicanism liberalism and, implicitly, Bonapartism all combined in a single package.[64]

Perhaps the best explanation for Liberal ideological ambivalence lay in Goyet's warning to Constant not to alienate Bonapartists, and a feature of newspapers was how rapidly doctrinal fine points gave way to the exigencies of political combat. There were differences among Opposition journals, with some, such as the *Constitutionnel*, less abrasive in pushing for rapid change. Early on, the *Censeur* of Charles Dunoyer and Charles Comte tried to draw a line between liberalism and Bonapartism and, under Guizot, the *Courier* sought to separate Liberalism from radicalism, be it in the form of republicanism or Bonapartism. Yet such attempts did not last, as the *Censeur*, *Mercure*, *Minerve*, *Courrier Français*, *Constitutionnel* and others all wove threads of Bonapartism, republicanism and liberalism into the Opposition.[65]

If anything, provincial journalists such as Carion at Dijon were even more aware that a *doctrinaire* attitude was a recipe for defeat. At Grenoble, the *Echo* offered a typical melange. On the one hand, if patriotism was the sole sentiment behind odes to the defence of Grenoble in July 1815, something more lurked in the poem 'Chant de Waterloo'. On the other hand the Revolution, at least in its principles, was lauded, although the Red Terror was condemned. Last but not least, a soupçon of liberalism was stirred into the mix: waste in government should be reduced through the abolition of sinecures and, in general, the less a nation was taxed, the more freedom it possessed.[66]

During the period under discussion, Liberals confined themselves largely to legal modes of opposition, and because their efforts focused on electing Deputies, it is tempting to assume that there was no connection between them and groups outside the electorate. Liberals did, however, claim to represent the nation, and they became increasingly disposed to organize demonstrations of broad support.

The federations had restored elite and popular left-wing connections, and this continued into the Second Restoration. In the Haute-Garonne,

[64] AN, F7 3677 (6), 11 September 1817; F7 9659, 12 November 1817, 29 March, 26 April and 20 August 1818; F7 3787, 7 September 1816; F7 3788, 18 March 1817; F7 3789, 29 March 1818; ADHG, 4M40, 27 July 1816; 4M47, 29 March 1818, and Hemardinquer, 'Boyer-Fonfrède', pp. 181–8.

[65] See I. Collins, *The Government and the Newspaper Press in France 1814–1881* (Oxford, 1959), pp. 1–30; L. Liggio, 'Charles Dunoyer and French classical liberalism', *Journal of Libertarian Studies*, 1, n. 3 (1977), pp. 153–78; P. Gonnard, 'La légende napoléonienne et la presse libérale: La Minerve', *Revue des Etudes Napoléoniennes*, 3, n. 1 (1914), pp. 28–49, and A. Shumway, *A Study of the Minerve Française* (Philadelphia, 1934), pp. 56–61.

[66] *L'Echo des Alpes*, 1 (August 1819).

Rémusat concentrated on attacking rumour-mongering, which he considered a tactic of destabilization. Suspicion naturally fell on retired officers, and after the Didier affair, a former officer and *fédéré* associated with Boyer-Fonfrède was put under surveillance. Meanwhile the authorities nabbed four Toulousain retired officers with copies of a false proclamation of Marie-Louise.[67]

Most such seditious activity was popular or lower middle-class in nature. Nevertheless, agitation also came from *fédérés* who, although not strictly speaking middle-class, had worked with middle-class *fédérés* in 1815. The innkeeper Paul Ressegeat was prone to praising Napoleon in public, and Louis Savés, a former military officer and clerk, allegedly possessed a black flag with the motto 'War to the death against royalists!' on it. A third *fédéré* with debts to settle was the court clerk Jean-François Gasc. Having been assigned the task of arresting a *verdet*, he took an escort of *gendarmes* and some forty additional men, most of whom were reputed to be old *fédérés*. Arrest became a pretext for pillage and, although the *verdet* was delivered to justice, so too was Gasc. Yet such activities did not prevent Gasc from subsequently becoming a key figure in the Liberal Opposition.[68]

Middle-class students also posed challenges. The most troublesome were law students, of whom there were roughly 800 registered at the faculty. Their preferred field of battle was Toulouse's city theatre, where over 159 held subscriptions, and their standard tactic was to applaud lines referring to liberty or making unflattering allusions to nobility. Royalists grew annoyed and fistfights ensued. Among the leading student agitators were officers on half-pay who were fond of the play '*Triumph of the Lion*', which eulogized Bonaparte, and which was performed exclusively at the law faculty.[69]

Students were but one part of deep-seated polarization. Prefect Saint-Chamans in November 1817 reported that all cafés and billiard halls were aligned with political factions. While some were royalist, others were republican or Bonapartist. Denizens feasted on a war of caricatures supplied by shopkeepers and they could also read Jean-François de Cugnet de Montarlot's provocative *Le nouvel homme gris*. In one incident officers pursued students into a café, slashed the proprietor with sabres, and tore most

[67] AN, F7 9659, 17 February and 14 May 1816; F7 3787, 5–13 July 1816; ADHG, 4M39, 3 and 16 January, 4–29 May 1816.

[68] AN, F7 3787, 24 October 1816, 27 March 1817; F7 3788, 18 March 1815; ADHG, 4M39, 6 April 1816; 4M46, 14 March 1817.

[69] AN, F7 3787, 13 July, 14 and 20 December 1816; F7 3788, 28 February, 15 April 1817; F7 3789, 25–6 April 1818; F7 3790, 11 September and 9 December 1818; F7 9659, 10 May 1818; ADHG, 4M39, 29 May 1816.

of the establishment apart. The proprietor had been a *fédéré* and was reputed to have led the 'assassins of June 1815'.[70]

The stereotype that partisan battle ceased outside the campaign season pivots on divorcing elections from other ways of expressing opinion: seditious shouts, iconographic battles, displays of allegiance in theatres, anticlericalism or simple refusal to participate during Catholic missions. Yet protests outside the campaign season formed the context for elections and contemporaries made little distinction between the two in evaluating public opinion.

Moreover, the relation between electoral and non-electoral opposition was apparent in a pattern. As Liberal electoral fortunes rose from 1817 to 1819, seditious forms of opposition diminished. When this progression was challenged, firstly by the Barthélemy proposal and then by Decazes's decision to change the electoral law, agitation again began to threaten public order. As the regime lurched towards constitutional crisis over a matter seemingly of little concern to the disenfranchised, popular Bonapartism bounded forward, and there was something more than faintly disloyal when actors took to miming Napoleon during performances of Casimir Delavigne's patriotic *Sicilian Vespers* from 1819 onwards. The same message was delivered to Swiss Guardsmen and French émigré officers at the Strasbourg theatre in early 1819. This is not to say that the same agents necessarily coordinated legal and illegal modes of opposition, but the various forms of expression were complementary because they sprang from the same concerns.[71]

An indication of opinion in the Bas-Rhin in 1817 could be seen in iconographic battles over General Jean-Baptiste Kléber. Matters began in June when royalists proposed a subscription for a monument to the Prince of Condé, a recently deceased counter-revolutionary leader. The Left responded that a monument to Kléber would be more appropriate. The municipal council of Strasbourg then ordered the creation of a committee to organize the transfer of Kléber's remains from Marseilles, and open a subscription for a statue. The committee was presided over by General Dubreton, with Brackenhoffer as vice-president, and thus held as little appeal for prefect Bouthillier as commemoration of a Revolutionary icon.

70 AN, F7 3788, 27 March 1817; F7 3789, 26 April and 16 May 1818; F7 3790, 8 June and 11 September 1818; F7 3792, 4 December 1819; F7 9659, 12 November, 1 December 1817, 10 May and 16 December 1818; F1C III Garonne (Haute-), 14, November–December 1817; ADHG, 4M46, 14 March 1817, and Hemardinquer, 'Boyer-Fonfrède', p. 189.

71 AN, F7 6772, dossier Seine, 13 September 1819; F7 9636, 18 February 1818, and Leuilliot, *L'Alsace*, I, pp. 214–9, 225–7.

Nevertheless, the cabinet gave approval, and mayor Kentzinger organized a funeral convoy. Dispute then arose over whether Kléber had been Catholic or Protestant. After documents revealed he had been born a Catholic, the government directed that his remains be placed in the cathedral, but as half-pay officers flocked to Strasbourg for the ceremony, Bouthillier sped into the countryside.

The question of the statue proved even more illustrative of public sentiment. Subscriptions were no problem; by October 40,000 francs had been offered. Among the leading donors, however, were Duke Louis-Philippe of Orleans, Prince Eugène, several leading Napoleonic generals, the cream of the Strasbourg bourgeoisie and liberal professors from the Academy. Bouthillier's contribution was a derisory 50 francs. Acrimony then broke out over whether the statue should be erected in a public square or placed in the cathedral. When the government chose the latter, the Strasbourg committee resigned, retiring the subscriptions. Perhaps it was just as well that the department did not take part in the elections of 1818. At Strasbourg news of the election of Lafayette and Manuel was greeted 'with great enthusiasm'.[72]

In the Isère, Choppin showed great tolerance when the Left decided to organize banquets celebrating the defence of Grenoble of 6 July 1815. In initial reports to Decazes, Choppin attributed the initiative simply to bourgeois civic pride, but the hostility to the regime symbolized by resistance to the Allies of Louis XVIII led the prefect to ask voters not to attend. While this appears to have worked in 1818, in 1819 celebrations took on embarrassing proportions. The banquets were held in open fields just outside Grenoble, with estimates of participation varying between 300 and 600. Festivities also included the distribution of food and the collection of money for the poor, fireworks, and an open-air ball, all designed to draw crowds of workers estimated at anywhere between 2,000 and 4,000. While 'good order' was maintained and Choppin continued to look the other way, many electors chose to attend in 1819, while radical Liberals lobbied on behalf of Grégoire.[73]

The connection between electoral and non-electoral politics was obvious in the Seine-Inférieure in 1819. In response to news of Barthélemy's proposal in February 1819, denizens of Rouennais literary *cabinets* expressed astonishment at government tolerance of the ultraroyalist *Conservateur*, but were eager to read a memoir on Saint Helena. Meanwhile local merchants

[72] AN, F7 9693, 10 November 1818 and Leuilliot, *L'Alsace*, 1, pp. 210–14.

[73] AN, F7 3793, 18 July 1820, and *Journal libre*, 8 July 1820.

sold engravings of Napoleonic battles and snuff boxes featuring images of Bonaparte and Marie-Louise. Seditious songs could be heard in a *guinguette* at Beausecours, and the *chef lieu* was treated to a former soldier parading at night with a candle and calling 'Long live the emperor, saviour of France'. Tricolour ribbons and *boutonnières* also reappeared. Anticlerical agitation was stimulated by a priest failing to perform funeral rites for a child at Gouy, by the temptation to mock twenty virgins dressed in white in the commune of Veulettes, and by Catholic insistence on a procession past a Protestant church at Bolbec.

All of the above sources of agitation preceded the elections of September, which saw Liberals overturn provisional bureaux prior to electing Stanislas de Girardin, a liberal member of the Napoleonic Legislative Corps and Chamber of the Hundred Days, and Lambrechts. That the subsequent fate of Lambrecht's friend was on local minds could be seen on a placard posted at the *mairie* of Rouen; it invited the archbishop to take his fanaticism back to the abbey, and concluded with 'Long live abbé Grégoire!' Revolutionary songs were to be heard at a café at Fécamp, a packet of tricolour *cocardes* appeared at the main public square of Montvilliers, and Bonapartism continued at Rouen in silk badges sold at a novelty shop, or a liqueur labelled 'elixir of Saint Helena'.[74]

Reaction against the missionary movement was crucial to the maintenance of middle- and lower-class ties. Although anticlericalism would not reach its zenith until the mid-1820s, its socially adhesive quality could be seen in the most notorious episode of the Decazes period. In early October 1819, songs and caricatures mocking the missionaries were widely disseminated at Brest, and concern over previous turbulence at other missions led prefect Joseph-Philippe d'Arros to conclude that it would be best to ban a forthcoming mission at Brest. The bishop of Quimper, however, refused. Crowds of between 2,000 and 3,000 chanting 'Down with the missionaries!' then staged a *charivari* outside the bishop's residence. At the same time hundreds of *pères de famille* pressured the municipal council to express opposition, which the mayor and thirteen other delegates duly registered with the bishop. To underline resistance, Molière's *Tartuffe* was staged at the theatre. After three days of agitation, the bishop finally gave in, and thereafter pamphlets described the events as a successful demonstration of popular will.

[74] Materials for the above discussion covering February 1819 to April 1820 have been taken from AN, F7 6706, ADSM, 1M175–7, 1M642, 3M152, 4M207, 4M636. See also Kroen, *Politics and Theater*, pp. 157–201; B.-A. Day-Hickman, *Napoleonic Art: Nationalism and the Spirit of Rebellion in France (1815–1848)* (Newark, N.J., 1999), and Alexander, *Napoleon*, 151–7.

In his report to the cabinet, d'Arros portrayed the missionaries as the true fomenters of discord and stressed how orderly and non-violent the protests had been. There had been no expression of sedition, and most of the protestors were 'respectable people'. Such an interpretation of the source of trouble had previously been acceptable to a cabinet willing to ban the mission, but suddenly local officials found themselves under criticism for capitulation to agitators and the prefect was directed to prosecute the leaders of revolt.

Several points arise from this episode. Liberals, many of whom were former *fédéré* leaders, were actively engaged in organizing the protests, which were neither simply middle-class nor popular in character. The author of two pamphlets defending the expulsion of the missionaries was Edmond Corbière, a leading Liberal activist whom we will again see at work at Rouen and Le Havre in the 1820s. Brought to trial and acquitted in January, he was then honoured with a banquet of eighty 'ultraliberals' – the same group that in October 1818 had secured the election of Jean-Pierre Guilhem, a former Revolutionary Girondin who had rallied to the Empire and helped found the original federation of 1815. Middle-class Liberals were not at all shy about the use of *charivari* when they wanted mass demonstration of opposition and their continued contacts with the non-electorate enabled them to use such tactics. In subsequent years the return of Guilhem from Paris would be accompanied by large Liberal banquets and *charivaris* directed against the crown prosecutors who had sent Marshal Ney and General Jean-Pierre Travot to their deaths during the White Terror.

The sympathy that prefect d'Arros showed for the anticlerical protests of October 1819 was by no means unique among officials prior to Decazes's decision to court the Right from November onwards. Thereafter, however, administrators rapidly changed their positions in accord with policy emanating from Paris or they were purged, as was the case with d'Arros. Yet what is most striking in all of this is that while the Opposition was applying pressure through mass demonstration, it avoided violence while arguing that its actions were orderly and law-abiding, unlike those of the missionaries. Such strategies, based on a posture of defending the Charter, were wise, but would be abandoned by part of the Left in July 1820.[75]

The elections of 1819 constituted a high water mark for early Liberal coordination of opposition, but one could detect potential division as blocks of radical Liberals emerged. Campaigning in the Isère began early in the

[75] Kroen, *Politics and Theater*, pp. 134–41, and Y. Le Gallo, 'Anticléricalisme et structures urbaines et militaires à Brest sous la Monarchie constitutionnelle', *Actes du 91e Congrès de la Société des Savantes, Rennes 1966*, 3 (1969), pp. 102–34.

summer, and it was unfortunate for Choppin that public attention was then fixed upon a pamphlet war waged between Montlivault and Donnadieu. That unhappy memories of White Terror stimulated organization could be seen in calls for electors to meet at Grenoble prior to the opening of the college.[76]

Naturally the *Echo* commented on the campaign, reviewing Chamber sessions so that voters could determine which Deputies had fulfilled their 'mandate'. The department would be honoured to have Grégoire as its Deputy, but moderates Savoye-Rollin, Sapey and Français de Nantes were *ministériels*. Many voters and leading Liberal activists did not, however, accept such categorization: Savoye-Rollin, Français de Nantes and Sapey all had solid centre-left credentials. Indeed the lawyer Jean Duport-Lavillette *fils* disagreed so heartily that he disassociated himself from the *Echo*, despite having helped found it.

The *Echo*'s account of how events unfolded within the college reveals certain points. The central question was whether moderates would align with the Right or Left. Ultraroyalists divided, as a group supporting Planelli wooed moderates with offers to drop an extremist in favour of Louis-Joseph Berlioz, a doctor at La Côte, and Augustin Perier. For their part, Grenoble radicals offered support for Français de Nantes and Sapey in return for votes for Grégoire. From the moderate camp came offers to Français de Nantes, presumably on behalf of Perier, Jean-Baptiste de Rogniat (prefect of the Ain and Choppin's favourite) or Berlioz; Savoye-Rollin, who had been named president of the college, had no need of help. Moderates, however, drew the line at negotiating with supporters of Sapey, which led Lucien Bonaparte's old secretary to throw his hand in with the advocates of Grégoire.

The first ballot secured victory for Savoye-Rollin, Français de Nantes and Sapey. Grégoire gained 480 votes and needed only 499 to win on the second ballot, although in the event he secured 512. Crucial was that supporters of Français de Nantes and Sapey continued to back Grégoire; this fostered a very left-leaning alliance of Liberals of Grenoble, Vienne and La-Tour-du-Pin. Rogniat finished second to Grégoire. He was a moderate royalist, but ultraroyalist vitriol poured upon Grégoire in pamphlets distributed in the college led at least some moderates to shift their support to the abbé on the second ballot.

Several ultraroyalists confused matters by voting for Grégoire. Historians have made much of this seemingly Machiavellian manoeuvre, but it is

[76] AN, F7 3679\6, 10 October 1819; F7 3791, 28 June 1819; F7 9667, 11 May 1819; ADI, 8M5, undated notice sent to electors; 52M23, 29 October 1819; BMUG, R7453, 10 October 1819; *Journal de Grenoble*, 14 October 1819, and Dumolard, *Didier*, pp. 235–55.

impossible to determine whether it was decisive, and subsequent claims may well have been simple face-saving. Humbert Dubouchage later denied that ultraroyalists had enabled Grégoire to win, and apparently the Chevaliers did not support voting for a man associated with regicide. Choppin was quick to latch onto the connivance explanation, but it was expedient for him to do so and he later backed away from it. Perhaps it is best to turn to Decazes's leading agent on the scene: according to the commander of the *gendarmerie*, Grégoire would have won without ultraroyalist support.[77]

What was clear was the muscle radicals were flexing. Election of the abbé was not a product of parochialism; Rogniat would have been a better vehicle of patronage. Electing the abbé, however, did serve as a repudiation of ultraroyalism and ultramontanism. Grégoire was known for egalitarianism (having rejected a title offered by Bonaparte) and republicanism; he had been an Imperial Senator, but had pushed for the first abdication. Like his friend Lambrechts, Grégoire had been among the minority of senators not named Peers in 1814. All of which is not to say that his supporters were social levellers, but the election of Grégoire was a strong warning against tampering with the Charter in anything but a liberal direction.

Who were these radicals? The Union, the secret society founded by Joseph Rey in early 1816, played a key role. The idea of Grégoire standing for election had originated with Bérenger de la Drôme, and Félix Réal had helped to secure Grégoire's approval and seen to publication of several addresses to the electors. The *Journal libre* had given support, and of the staff Renauldon *fils* and Crépu were probably members of the Union. Among the voters much of the work appears to have been done by Union members Perrin, Rey and Champollion *le jeune*. Given their close association with Champollion and Rey, it is likely that the merchants Hughes Blanc and Augustin Thévenet and the schoolteacher Jean-Baptiste Froussard joined in the effort. Duchesne contributed with a pamphlet in favour of the abbé, and it was the lawyers Duport-Lavillette (father and son) who negotiated the transaction with the supporters of Sapey. During the campaign Falcon's reading room and the Duport-Lavillettes' salon were used as headquarters.

Assigning specific ideological affiliation to this corps of radicals is difficult. Within the Union, Rey, Blanc, Froussard and Crépu were republicans, and Rey's arguments that Bérenger and Félix Réal also leaned in this

[77] AN, F7 3679\6, letters of Pascalis from June 1819 to January 1820; F7 9667, 13 and 20 September 1819; ADI, 8M5, college minutes; *Echo des Alpes*, 2 (September 1819); *Journal de Grenoble*, 16 September 1819, and *Journal libre*, 10 October 1820.

direction at the time are convincing. That the old Jacobin Falcon was republican hardly needs stating, but Falcon, the above-mentioned members of the Union, and Renauldon *fils* and Perrin had all rallied to Napoleon during the Hundred Days. Duchesne, while steering clear of the federation, had written in favour of the *Acte additionnel*. His selection as *substitut* for Lucien Bonaparte in 1815 had indicated close relations with Sapey, and this was also true of Renauldon and the Duport-Lavillettes. Conversely, one should not leap to the conclusion that Bonapartism was paramount; Sapey consistently maintained that national sovereignty must be represented in an institution rather than an individual. When all is said and done, what bound these men was belief in national sovereignty and desire to entrench it within the constitution.

A similar trajectory could be detected in the Bas-Rhin. To the left of the Opposition was a wing in which Coulmann, Schulmeister, Schertz, Steiner, Wappler and Walter played major parts. More centrist were figures whose position varied according to the nature of governing cabinets. Levrault and Turckheim were favourable to the Decazes ministry in 1819, but they would position themselves in opposition subsequently, and play key roles in a moderate wing of the Liberal Opposition. The Saglios (Michel and Florent) appear to have been consistently more to the left, though their ties generally pulled them more towards moderation than radicalism. Magnier-Grandprez journeyed leftwards over time, but Reibel headed in the opposite direction, until confronted by the Villèle government. Too young to stand in 1819, Georges Humann was already considered a 'born Deputy'. In time, his relations with radical Liberals would fray, but at this stage he supported Lambrechts.

Thus the Liberal Opposition had a mixed ideological character, combining elements of republicanism, liberalism and Bonapartism under the umbrella principle of national sovereignty, much as the *fédérés* of 1815 had done. While Decazes remained in power, Liberals confined themselves largely to legal modes of opposition, but there were differing tendencies among them and already one could detect groups of radicals who were markedly more confrontational when it came to relations with the state.

## REACTION AND CRISIS

Choppin reported that voters were ashamed of the election of Grégoire, but radical Grenoble Liberals were the opposite of abashed. Celebrations included serenades for the new Deputies and the reading of verse honouring Grégoire, which large crowds of workers attended. Thereafter a banquet attracted 250 participants and featured speeches by Rey and Duport-Lavillette, followed by a collection for the poor. Perhaps the latter accounted for the songs sung in favour of Grégoire by workers, but close relations between middle-class radicals and workers were further demonstrated at a banquet in which eight mutual aid societies commemorated their foundation. Guests of honour included Reynaud, a former health officer who, after toasting Grégoire, 'electrified' 200 workers with a speech praising them as 'the most useful citizens of the *patrie*'. Closely tied to Rey in a legal action brought against General Donnadieu, Doctor Reynaud's popularity among workers was all the more worrisome in that he had previously been arrested for having distributed Napoleon's proclamations during the Flight of the Eagle.[78]

News of the Chamber's rejection of Grégoire did not temper radicalism. Félix Réal and Champollion saw to the publication of two addresses from the otherwise silent abbé, and the *Echo* and *Journal libre* condemned his exclusion as unconstitutional, comparing Grégoire's fate to the parliamentary purge of Girondins in 1793, and reminding Count Lainé that he had been a representative on a mission for the Convention.[79]

When the crown speech of January 1820 announced plans to revamp the electoral law, Liberals began to divide over an appropriate response. A first step lay in the collection of petitions against revision, and this time some Liberals began to reach beyond the confines of the electorate. A committee of twenty radical Liberals launched the campaign at Grenoble, and the *Journal libre* helped to spread it throughout the Isère. Thereafter signatures were collected at La Mure, Rives, Saint-Geoire, Vizille, Bourgoin, Saint-Marcellin, Vienne and Voiron. At Grenoble petitions were distributed in the faubourgs inhabited mostly by poor workers, and law students drew up their own petition, gaining 120 signatures. In the canton of Vizille, former mayor Boulon travelled into the countryside to gain support from 'misled peasants'; at Saint-Marcellin Liberals visited cafés on market day, and at Saint-Geoire only sixteen of the seventy-two supporters were enfranchised. There were certainly not 300 voters among those who signed at Bourgoin, and Choppin reported that one-third of all signatures belonged to *gens du peuple*.

The point of the campaign, according to the *Journal libre*, was that tampering with the Charter affected the rights of all French people. Meanwhile the *Echo* asserted that Liberals wanted frank execution of the Charter and

[78] AN, F7 9667, 12 November 1819; F7 3679\6, 10 October 1819; ADI, 52M22, 14 September 1819, and *Echo des Alpes*, 3 (October 1819).

[79] See the correspondence in ADI, 8M4, and *Journal libre*, 1 January and 3–19 February 1820.

were awaiting institutions without which the constitution was an illusion. This time Sapey was chosen to present the petitions to the Chamber. Conversely, Français de Nantes received warnings from the *Journal libre* for laxity in attending Chamber sessions to oppose the ministry's projects. Français's supporters sprang to his defence, denying the allegation, and the *Journal libre* announced itself happy to withdraw its criticism. Nevertheless, the point had been made.[80]

The same tone was struck in the Liberal press elsewhere. At Dijon, Carion and Gabet wrote that proposed revision could open an era of revolution. More ominous than journalistic predictions, however, were crowds, reported from all points of the realm, chanting 'Long live the Charter!' while omitting the complementary 'Long live the king!' The meaning of this was apparent to all: the Charter stood for national sovereignty and tampering with it meant breaking the Restoration contract.[81]

Choppin vigorously fought the second petition campaign, using the *Journal de Grenoble* to denounce 'revolutionary practices'. According to the prefect, the Chamber had a right to alter institutions cited in the Charter; those who asserted the contrary were in effect calling for a Constituent Assembly, a dangerous argument that might well be extended to the Peers and the monarchy. Choppin initiated legal proceedings against the *Journal libre* for its defence of Grégoire, and the *Echo* was also brought to trial.[82]

Reaction also provoked strong emotions in the Bas-Rhin. Anger could be heard at the Strasbourg theatre, where performances of *Sicilian Vespers* were used to vent spleen against 'ministerial despotism', despite prefectoral orders prohibiting repetition of certain lines. Meanwhile Constant's 'On the current state of France and circulating rumours', in which he warned that the new cabinet would attack 'the single law that we have achieved in four years', ensured that discussion of the Lainé Law remained heated.[83]

Opposition took on a more aggressive character in January with the advent of the *Patriote Alsacien*, with Charles-Philippe Marchand as head editor. Former editor of the *Censeur Européen*, member of the Amis de la Liberté de la Presse in Paris and closely tied to Constant and Goyet, Marchand had previously written brochures charging the government with kowtowing to the wishes of the Allied powers and calling for the

80 AN, F7 6740, 6 December 1819 to 18 January 1820; ADI, 52M22, 26 January 1820; *Journal libre*, 6–29 January, 3–15 February 1820, and *Echo des Alpes*, 5 (December 1819).

81 See Fizaine, *La vie*, pp. 170–3.

82 AN, F7 9667, 2 December 1819; *Journal de Grenoble*, 9 and 11 December 1819; *Journal libre*, coverage of the trial of the *Echo*, beginning with the edition of 13 January 1820.

83 AN, F7 6693, 13 December 1819; BN, Lb 48 1355, B. Constant, *De l'état actuel de la France et des bruits qui circulent* (Paris, 1819), and Leuilliot, *L'Alsace*, 1, pp. 240–1.

development of the representative principle in the Charter. Published in both French and German and introduced by Lambrechts, the *Patriote* announced it would keep watch over German developments, denounce all abuses of liberty, and defend religious toleration. The paper was soon thereafter banned in Baden, Bavaria, Prussia and Hanover.[84]

Despite such signs of growing agitation, the petition campaign appears to have been largely confined to middle-class elements in the Bas-Rhin, and a petition published at Strasbourg by the *Courrier du Bas-Rhin* was cast in a cautiously defensive posture: 'hardly has a constitutional regime been established after the horrors of the laws of exception and reaction, than the enemies of order and liberty wish to plunge us into the nightmare of anarchy and revolution'. Placed at the *cercle* Alexandre, the petition was signed by 205 voters and close to 100 medical students. Similar efforts were made at Bischwiller, where forty signatures were gained. Thirty-nine names were appended to a petition at Wissembourg, wherein Liberals asserted that the Charter could not be changed 'without the express consent of the Nation'.[85]

Liberalism in the Bas-Rhin, thus, was radicalized, but it was less overtly aggressive than in the Isère, and there was wisdom in the rhetorically defensive stance Liberals took. When news arrived of the assassination of Berry, young men singing the 'Marseillaise' were duly arrested. A half-pay officer was sentenced to six months' imprisonment, but the authorities had to release most of the accused for want of evidence of revolutionary intent. Thereafter the courts proved less reactionary than the administration, and released a tailor and a teacher who had laughed at assertions that Decazes himself had killed Berry.[86]

After the formation of the second Richelieu ministry, departmental Deputies voted to a man against the security and press laws, although Turckheim broke ranks over the Double Vote. Polarization was even apparent in the *Courrier*, where a new editor, Jean-Henri Silbermann, had joined Saltzmann. The journal came out clearly against the press and electoral laws, and supported motions for the recall of exiles.[87]

Following the establishment of the new censorship commission in March, Marchand decided that the *Patriote* should go down with guns blazing. Most provocative was an allegory in which a father 'grants' rights

84 BN, Lc9.10 (15), prospectus for *Le Patriote Alsacien*; ADBR, 3M19, 10 February – 2 March 1820, and Leuilliot, *L'Alsace*, 1, pp. 235–49.

85 *Courrier du Bas-Rhin*, 19 December 1819, and Leuilliot, *L'Alsace*, I, pp. 247–8.

86 ADBR, 2M13, February–March 1820; *Courrier du Bas-Rhin*, 18 January 1820, and Leuilliot, *L'Alsace*, 1, pp. 253–61.

87 *Courrier du Bas-Rhin*, 4 January – 9 April 1820.

to his children which are not his to grant, and subsequently usurps them. In a final outburst on 5 April, Marchand asserted that sovereignty rested with the nation, while invoking the taking of the Bastille and the Declaration of the Rights of Man and Citizen as touchstones of French polity. Three days later, he was arrested.

Government officials had been pondering when to strike the Liberal press for some time. In the case of the *Courrier*, prefect Decazes followed advice that the editors would fall in line after the passage of recently proposed new press laws. The prediction proved relatively accurate and increased caution certainly became the order of the day at the *Courrier*, but the journal did at least survive to quote Liberal speeches in the Chamber, publish letters from radical Liberals, and report on the trial of Marchand.

The trial went badly for the government. Subsequently, failure to secure a conviction was attributed to the superior performance of defending lawyers Louis Liechtenberger and Philippe-Jacques Fargès-Méricourt, and Marchand's own careful self-defence. In contrast, the crown prosecutor confused jurors with complicated arguments, fell into unfortunate discussions of the king's gluttony, and pushed the jury towards clemency by asking for two years in prison. When a verdict of innocent of all charges was reached on 16 June, the presiding judge had to threaten spectators to stop cheering. This could not, however, prevent a crowd estimated at 2,000 from gathering close to Marchand's residence to express their approval. In a sense, acquittal constituted a pyrrhic victory. On the one hand, the *Patriote* would appear no more, and with Silbermann and Saltzmann largely reticent, Liberals no longer possessed a local organ to express opposition. On the other hand, displays of support for Marchand stood in stark contrast to the paucity of response to a subscription campaign for a monument to Berry.[88]

In the Haute-Garonne prefect Saint-Chamans reported that the Toulousain electoral committee of 1819 had begun to circulate a petition. Although he could not say whether these men 'of little influence' had organized a permanent 'party', the group supporting them was 'large enough'. They did nothing in public, but met frequently at the home of one or another, as they had done at the time of the elections. Moreover, on 31 December a placard inviting students to sign a second petition approved by a 'celebrated lawyer' had been posted on the door of the law

[88] AN, F7 9693, 2 April – 6 May 1820; BB30 260, 4 May – 13 June 1820; ADBR, 3M19, 10 February – 18 June 1820; *Courrier du Bas-Rhin*, 18 June 1820, and Leuilliot, *L'Alsace*, 1, pp. 256–65.

faculty. Romiguières had, in fact, helped write it. The prefect subsequently reported that 360 signatures had been gained, and that Dupont de l'Eure would present the petition to the Chamber of Deputies.[89]

Had matters rested at this point, the prefect would have had little cause for alarm, but Liberal merchants and lawyers then began to circulate their petition more widely, despatching agents throughout the department. According to Saint-Chamans, Liberals believed that only the widest possible protest could prevent the government from going through with proposed legislation. Thus they were reaching well beyond the confines of the electorate. The prefect's estimation of the members of the committee went up, as he perceived their influence. Roucoule was 'a distinguished jurisconsult', Viguerie a 'very celebrated surgeon', and Chaptive and Barre 'rich merchants and furious demagogues'. The petition was reputed to have gained 600 signatures, and would be presented by Manuel, a more aggressive advocate than Dupont.

To Saint-Chamans this was to open the floodgates of revolution; already the 'missionaries of anarchy' were speaking openly in cafés of Napoleon II. He was overstating matters; like many royalists, he was too eager to believe that the *comité directeur* could simply pull strings, bestirring agents who would trigger mass revolution. The Haute-Garonne was indeed entering a phase of agitation, but the most powerful signal issuing from Paris came from the cabinet.

While the future direction remained unclear, the *Journal de Toulouse* based its coverage on reports in the Parisian Liberal *Constitutionnel*, and, in a dramatic departure, Vieussieux published an editorial opposing change in the electoral law, arguing that only a 'party governed by passions' wanted alteration. Ultraroyalist unease became apparent in early February when a councillor in the *cour royale* wrote to the *Journal* declaring he was not responsible for an offensive letter attacking Durand and Malaret in the *Drapeau blanc*. For his part, Saint-Chamans opined that 'good men' remained mute because they feared that 'fidelity to the king might one day lead to persecution'. News of the assassination of the Duke of Berry on 14 February thus came at an opportune moment for ultraroyalism.[90]

The most striking manifestations of opposition to reactionary legislation occurred in Paris, as huge crowds gathered near parliament and riots, partly instigated by the Royal Guard, broke out. The participation of students and *jeunes gens* in the ensuing street battles was frequently remarked, as Lafayette

89 AN, F7 6740, 10, 20, 29, 31 December 1819, and 3 January 1820.

90 *Ibid.*, 3 January 1820, and *Journal de Toulouse*, 10 and 17 December 1819, all January 1820 issues and 4 February 1820.

and Constant cultivated a habit of claiming the 'younger generation' as their own. After a law student, Nicolas Lallemand, had been shot and killed on 3 June, some 6,000 students and *jeunes gens* turned his funeral procession and burial into a commemoration of protest, setting a precedent for similar subsequent expressions of public dissent.

Such manifestations were also widespread in the provinces. Students and *jeunes gens* were the most aggressive participants, and hence cities holding major educational institutions were particularly troublesome. Law students at Toulouse also sought to commemorate Lallemand's 'martyrdom', provoking another major clash with the authorities. Students were not, however, alone in challenging the regime; wherever the public gathered, or whenever the National Guard assembled, there were similar demonstrations.[91]

Royalists interpreted all this to mean that revolution was stalking the land. They were half right. Assertions that the Parisian Liberal *comité directeur* orchestrated public demonstrations were off the mark; local Liberals did not need instruction as to how to go about expressing support for the battle being waged by their Deputies in the Chamber. Indeed, had royalists been content to leave battle to the public, the results would not have been favourable to them. Realization of their weak position was the reason for rejecting petitions in the Chamber, altering the Lainé Law, and passing laws constricting individual liberty and freedom of the press. The assassination of Berry gave a pretext for such measures, but reaction was on the cards long before Louis-Pierre Louvel plunged his dagger. As the elections of 1817–19 had demonstrated, the more politics was based on public opinion, the weaker was the position of royalism. Thus royalists moved towards the control of opinion by repression of dissent, and thereby sparked the return of revolt in August 1820.

[91] See Fizaine, *La vie*, pp. 198–205, Alexander, *Bonapartism*, pp. 141–8, 179–80, and A. Ben-Amos, *Funerals, Politics, and Memory in Modern France, 1789–1996* (Oxford, 2000), pp. 88–9.

3

# *Self-defeating opposition: from July 1820 to February 1824*

## PART ONE: FAILED REVOLUTION FOSTERS REACTION

With the advantage of hindsight, one can characterize the second Richelieu ministry as essentially transitional in nature as power flowed from the Centre-Right to the Right. Such a perspective was not, of course, necessarily apparent to contemporaries, but for our purposes the main points of interest of the period lie in how this transition was brought about. In particular, the role of Joseph de Villèle in bringing ultraroyalism to power and the ways in which the Liberal Opposition unwittingly facilitated Villèle's triumph merit careful consideration.

Departmental colleges greatly fortified the Right in the elections of November 1820, but the Left also performed poorly in *arrondissement* colleges, partly because some 14,500 voters had been removed from the electorate by lowering of the basic land tax. Liberals were reduced to roughly 80 Deputies, the Centre-Right rose to 190, and the main beneficiaries were ultraroyalists, whose numbers increased to 160.[1]

Richelieu therefore had to accommodate ultraroyalism, and Villèle and his ally Count Jacques-Joseph de Corbière, a Deputy of the Ille-et-Vilaine known for his sharp debating skills, entered the cabinet as Ministers without Portfolio in December. Collaboration with the Centre-Right, however, left Villèle open to criticism from extreme ultraroyalists who raised difficulties before granting a three-month extension to censorship. While it was aimed principally at the Left, censorship also constrained ultraroyalist vituperation. To make his independence of Richelieu clear, Villèle refused to accept remuneration for serving in the cabinet, and he and Corbière demanded that 'pures' be appointed to the ministries of the Interior and War. When their demands were not fully met, they departed the cabinet in July 1821.

[1] For background see Bertier de Sauvigny, *Restoration*, pp. 168–96; Jardin and Tudesq, *Restoration*, pp. 47–62; Waresquiel and Yvert, *Restauration*, pp. 311–60, and Mansel, *Louis XVIII*, pp. 374–408.

Villèle's position required adroit manoeuvring. His future lay in delivering power to ultraroyalism, but this task necessitated exercising at least a measure of control over extremism. Meanwhile Louis XVIII slowly became detached from politics after the departure of Decazes, and the influence of the heir apparent, Artois, rose. Compared to Artois, Villèle was a moderate, although differences between them lay more in means than ends. Villèle preferred to take a gradual approach to securing ultraroyalist objectives, whereas the count was far less concerned about provoking a public backlash against aggressive measures.

To secure his position for the future, Villèle needed to make himself indispensable to Artois without completely antagonizing Richelieu and Louis XVIII. Villèle did possess an advantage in that Madame Zoë du Cayla soon replaced Decazes as royal favourite. Du Cayla was tied to Viscount Sosthènes de La Rochefoucauld, an aide-de-camp of Artois much given to court intrigue, who initially collaborated with Villèle. Du Cayla helped to overcome the king's reluctance to rely on ultraroyalists, but even this aid to Villèle was complicated by Du Cayla's inclination to favour the interests of a theocratic wing of ultraroyalism whose cooperation Villèle needed, but whose demands risked alienating other groups. The basic problem was that Villèle had to prove that a gradualist approach worked best for ultraroyalism, but his strategies were consistently undermined by his need also to accommodate far less patient ultraroyalists favoured by Artois.

Transition from Centre-Right to ultraroyalist government could be partly attributed to Villèle's skill in tempering ultraroyalism, but it was a combination of failed cabinet policies and unwise Liberal strategies that provided Villèle with his opportunity. In 1820–1 liberal revolt forced reactionary rulers in Spain, Naples and Piedmont to accept constitutional governments, leading the Holy Alliance of Austria, Russia and Prussia to meditate armed intervention at the Congress of Troppau in late 1820. Richelieu was no advocate of liberal revolution, but French geo-strategic interests ran against Count Klemens von Metternich's plan to send Austrian troops into Italy. Unfortunately for Richelieu, a French delegation at the Congress of Laybach in early 1821 failed to overcome Czar Alexander's backing of Metternich, and Austrian troops restored 'legitimacy' in Italy shortly thereafter. In a marriage of convenience they would soon regret, the French Left then joined with the extreme Right to attack the Richelieu government's 'impotence' in international relations.

Liberals calculated that by combining with ultraroyalists they could weaken the cabinet and thereby force Richelieu to look for support from the Left. Elections in November 1821 certainly indicated that the Centre-Right was in decline, but they also raised questions as to who might be the principal beneficiaries: fifty seats went to ultraroyalists, twenty to *ministériels* and fourteen to Liberals. Despite such portents, the Left again joined with the extreme Right in accusing the cabinet of sacrificing national interests in the opening address to the new parliamentary session, making Richelieu's position untenable.

Villèle had wisely distanced himself from attacks on Richelieu, cultivating a middle ground between the Centre-Right and the extreme wing of ultraroyalism. Thus it was to Villèle and Corbière that Louis XVIII turned for the formation of a new cabinet in December. Nevertheless, the difficulty of Villèle's position could be seen in that while he had the approval of Artois, he also had to work from a list provided by Richelieu. The resultant government saw power shift rightwards, with Villèle's relatively moderate wing of ultraroyalism in the dominant position. Respectively, Villèle, Corbière and Marshal Victor, Duke of Bellune, a Revolutionary and Imperial veteran who had followed Louis XVIII to Ghent in 1815, became Ministers of Finance, the Interior and War. The Marquis Gaspard de Clermont-Tonnerre, a centrist Peer much favoured by Louis XVIII, Count Charles-Ignace Peyronnet, a Bordelais lawyer, and the intensely devout Chevalier de la Foi leader Mathieu de Montmorency became Ministers of the Marine, Justice and Foreign Affairs.

Thereafter Villèle had to ward off endless challenges to his leadership by ultraroyalist rivals. He did possess assets in these struggles: pompous figures such as Chateaubriand were not necessarily popular with either Louis XVIII or Artois, while rivals such as Montmorency and Polignac were so 'pure' that their potential for forming a viable government was limited, despite their close relations with Artois. At the end of the day, however, Villèle's hold on power would be determined by his ability to achieve a very delicate balance between pleasing most ultraroyalists and not antagonizing the Centre-Right.

Villèle has gained praise from historians for the transparent practices he brought to French finance. Not only did his governments bring in annual surpluses, he also improved fiscal accountability through administrative reform and he instituted the practice of voting on ministry budgets item by item, rather than en bloc. This procedure gave Deputies the opportunity to exercise their right of approval over specific proposals, but such enhancement of parliamentary power would not have mattered much had Villèle succeeded in other aspects of his programme.

Villèle intended to control opinion so as to secure favourable elections, and he employed the usual means. An administrative purge begun under Richelieu in 1820 was immediately widened so as to remove all opponents of ultraroyalism, and in March 1822 the government expanded censorship.

Journalists who committed 'outrages' against the established faiths, attacked the principle of heredity, or mendaciously reported parliamentary or courtroom debates would be arrested, and a new 'law of tendency' would enable prosecutors to bring charges against journals for a series of articles whose 'spirit' tended to undermine public order, or respect for religion, royal authority and state institutions. Moreover, the government could re-establish preliminary censorship by simple royal ordinance outside parliamentary sessions, and court magistrates, rather than juries, would judge accused journalists.

In addition to repression, Villèle's agenda also featured measures designed to please theocratic members of the Chevaliers de la Foi. The Pantheon was restored to the Catholic Church, nineteen archbishops were appointed peers, and the ban on work on Sundays was rigorously enforced. With the appointment of Dennis-Luc de Frayssinous, bishop of Hermopolis, as Grand Master of the University in June, the government effectively delivered education to Catholic control, as the bishop gained powers to appoint teachers and determine programmes at the royal colleges. By April 1824 the right of rectors of the Academy to authorize primary school teachers would also be given to the bishops.

Despite such accommodation of the theocratic wing of ultraroyalism, Villèle could not be certain of his position until after the most important foreign policy initiative of the period: intervention in Spain. Revolt in Spain had begun in 1820 when liberals had forced their absolutist king to restore the constitution of 1812; thereafter the *constitutionnels* had held Ferdinand VII as a virtual prisoner at Madrid. A counter-revolt by extreme royalists in July 1822 had failed to liberate the king, but the *exaltados* had managed to set up a regency government at Seu d'Urgel and had gained control over parts of Aragon, Navarra and Galicia. Better yet, their exploits fixed the attention of the Holy Alliance upon Spain.

The possibility of the eastern powers meddling in Spain placed Villèle in a very awkward position. On the one hand, the British were opposed to intervention, viewing Iberia as their sphere of influence. On the other hand, Czar Alexander was eager to send troops. For his part, Metternich was all for restoring 'legitimate' monarchs, but, like Villèle, he was worried by the extension of Russian power that would be involved in such a development. Metternich also preferred not to antagonize the British and had plenty on his plate in subduing Italian revolutionaries, but he could not afford to alienate Alexander.

To forestall Russian intervention the French could invade Spain themselves, but the prospect of involvement gave Villèle nightmares. War was likely to prove expensive and he could not be certain as to the loyalty of the former Imperial army. Complicating matters further was that Metternich was leery of seeing the French return to Spain, and determined that they would not impose some sort of Charter, which could encourage liberals in Italy. Initially Villèle played for time by placing a cordon sanitaire on the Spanish border allegedly to keep out yellow fever, but in reality to establish a corps of observers.

Foreign Minister Montmorency badly wanted the French Bourbon monarchy to take part in the rescue of its Spanish counterpart. Thus he ignored cabinet instructions not to enter into discussions with the Holy Alliance as to whether they would back unilateral French action. Worse still, at the Congress of Verona of September to December 1822, Montmorency agreed that France would join the autocracies in sending hostile notes to the Spanish liberal government. Neither Villèle nor Louis XVIII wished to have their hands tied by such arrangements, and their subsequent tongue-lashing of Montmorency provoked his resignation on Christmas Day. From Villèle's point of view, the departure of a dangerous rival from the cabinet signified progress, but it did nothing to resolve the issue of what to do about Spain.

Into the breech stepped Chateaubriand. As the new Foreign Minister, he informed parliament on 28 December that war was inevitable, and subsequently he argued that intervention offered France an opportunity to regain great power status. Debates among the Deputies were tumultuous, leading to the expulsion of Manuel for allusions to 1792–3 and regicide in times of war. Most Liberal Deputies protested against the expulsion and boycotted the remainder of the session. Nevertheless, Chateaubriand smoothed the way for war by neutralizing the British through warnings of the greater danger of Russian intervention, and by keeping France free of any formal ties to the Holy Alliance.

In the event, the 'Spanish promenade' saw French forces rapidly overcome very little resistance. The campaign was led by Angoulême and began in early April 1823; by late September Ferdinand had been freed and the taking of the Trocadero fortress had given the Restoration its first significant military victory. There were some concerns over the way in which provisions had been supplied and Angoulême had little success in controlling Spanish ultraroyalists bent on revenge, but these were problems for the future.

In the meantime Villèle could exploit a swell of grateful patriotism by appointing a new batch of ultraroyalist Peers and calling a general election for late February and early March 1824. The results were devastating, as the

Left and Centre were reduced to a total of seventeen seats. In the long term, a massive triumph would actually exacerbate old problems for Villèle: the apparent destruction of the Left made ultraroyalism even more unruly, and the lengths to which he had gone to secure electoral victory had planted seeds for future defeat. Yet in the short term the electoral landslide of 1824 bore eloquent testimony to the success of his policies.

Massive rejection by the electorate also revealed the folly of previous Liberal dallying with revolution. To some extent revolt during the period of 1820 to 1823 was international, in that rebels shared a desire to overturn the regimes established by the Vienna Settlement of 1814–15. Beyond common aspirations, conspiratorial secret societies at times also combined to raise financial aid and share expertise as to how to organize disaffected groups. To conservatives, it seemed that revolts in Italy, Spain, Portugal, France and the Ottoman Empire must all be part of a coordinated onslaught against which all royalists must unite. In a sense, they were correct: revolutionary groups did see themselves as part of a universal crusade to advance liberty and national self-determination. There was, however, no truly united revolutionary front; the revolts were largely local affairs, rather than the product of international conspiracy. In truth, conservatives intentionally overstated the danger posed by the groups they confronted, making it difficult for the general public to distinguish between peaceful proponents of reform and agents of the violent revolutionary tradition. The resultant polarization served conservative interests very well.[2]

French historians have generally been inclined to focus on conspiratorial opposition in the 1820s and have frequently linked it to a long-term Jacobin republican tradition. In so much as they have recognized a Bonapartist component, they have usually viewed Bonapartism as an offshoot of Jacobinism. Conversely, P. Rosanvallon has recently placed emphasis on a liberal, as opposed to a Jacobin republican, tradition in the making of modern French politics. Neither approach, however, says much about the dynamic between neo-Jacobin insurrectionary movements and liberal legal resistance to state repression. How did they affect each other? Moreover, too much emphasis upon identifying ideological differences has tended to obscure how closely republicanism, Bonapartism and liberalism were bound.

Republicans, Bonapartists and liberals were prone to make divisively exclusive claims to the Revolutionary heritage after 1830, but ideological

[2] See J. Roberts, *The Mythology of Secret Societies* (London, 1972), pp. 300–46, and P. Pilbeam, 'Revolutionary movements in western Europe', in P. Pilbeam, ed., *Themes in Modern European History 1780–1830* (London, 1995), pp. 125–50.

differences were far less apparent during the Restoration, and the Liberal Opposition cultivated doctrinal ambiguity rather than rigidity. Where division arose lay in the means by which Liberals sought to combat political reaction, rather than in ideological differences. For a time, some Liberals resorted to insurrection, but revolt was generally viewed as a last resort, justified only when there were no other options to preserve national sovereignty. Some judged the point of no return to have arrived in 1820 and were proved wrong. Others stuck to a legal path, but they were no less part of Revolutionary tradition for the fact.[3]

The main conspiratorial group, the Carbonari, was an umbrella organization composed of various disaffected groups. One of the first tributaries was Joseph Rey's Union. Originally based in the Isère, the Union soon formed branches in neighbouring departments, made contacts with German liberals, and established a cell in Paris, recruiting Deputies such as Lafayette, Corcelles and Dupont de l'Eure. As long as legal means served Liberal purposes, the Union avoided insurrection, but Rey was alienated by the parliamentary exclusion of Grégoire.

During demonstrations in Paris against the 'Law of the Double Vote' in June 1820, the Union established contact with a group of retired and active army officers, including Colonels Charles Fabvier and Joseph-Augustin Caron, known as the Bazar Français. Added to the mix was a pseudo-masonic lodge, Les Amis de la Liberté, which consisted of perhaps a thousand students and *jeunes gens*. Their plans for insurrection were, however, soon uncovered by the authorities and the revolt scheduled for 19 August had to be aborted. The Chamber of Peers did not take a subsequent trial of seventy-five men seriously, and, while six minor figures were condemned to imprisonment, the principal organizers escaped retribution. Meanwhile a parallel project for Grenoble had also fizzled out, and Rey had taken flight to ultimate exile in London.[4]

In terms of numbers, a more significant contributor to the Carbonari was an organization known as the Chevaliers de la Liberté. Unlike the Union, the Chevaliers de la Liberté remained primarily provincial, and because so much of what we know about the Carbonari derives from memoir writers based in Paris, the Chevaliers remain largely anonymous. Even so, several points are clear. The Chevaliers initially sprang up in the west; in Brittany they were a reformulation of the federation of 1815. Local officials were made

[3] See E. Guillon, *Les complots militaires sous la Restauration* (Paris, 1895); Spitzer *Old Hatreds*, and A. Calmette, 'Les Carbonari en France sous la Restauration, 1821–1830', *La Révolution de 1848*, 9 (1912–13), pp. 401–17; 10 (1913–14), pp. 52–73, 117–38, 214–30.

[4] Neely, *Lafayette*, pp. 117–23, and Spitzer, *Old Hatreds*, pp. 212–19.

aware of this development by cavalcades that spirited Dunoyer, editor of the *Censeur*, and his lawyer Joseph Mérilhou from point to point in Brittany during a celebrated trial at Rennes in 1818. The chief orchestrators of these manoeuvres were Pierre Aubrée and René Losne-Rochelle, former *fédéré chefs* at Vitry.

It was protection that initially attracted Goyet of the Sarthe to Aubrée's group. Goyet needed an organization capable of countering the Chevaliers de la Foi, and a rendezvous was arranged between Aubrée and Goyet towards the end of 1819. Subsequently, the presence of armed men probably saved the lives of Lafayette and Constant during their voyage to the Sarthe in the autumn of 1820. Immediately after the departure of Constant, the Chevaliers de la Liberté were formed. It is probable that Goyet and Constant encouraged this development, but at this stage there was nothing conspiratorial about the organization. The initial corps of the Chevaliers de la Liberté consisted of the remnants of the federations of Brittany and the Maine, and numbers perhaps reached as high as 20,000.

Matters began to alter with affiliation to the Parisian Carbonari in May 1821, arranged by an agent of Lafayette. In the capital, leadership sprang from several groups. One was the Amis de la Liberté de la Presse, which continued to gather privately after Decazes shut down the association's public meetings in late 1819. This group then fused with the Union. At the heart of the combination were Deputies such as Lafayette, d'Argenson, Corcelles and Manuel. Ties were then established with the Amis de la Vérité and a second pseudo-masonic association of *jeunes gens*, the Amis de l'Armorique. The points of contact were two students: Charles Beslay *fils*, son of a Breton Liberal Deputy, and Nicolas Joubert. After the failed conspiracy of August 1820, the leadership role of students increased when Joubert and Pierre Dugied returned from hiding in Italy with knowledge of how Italian conspirators went about their business. From May 1821 the Carbonari network of secret cells, often cloaked under the cover of freemasonry, was rapidly built. Estimates of numbers range between 30,000 and 60,000, as cells were established in some sixty departments.[5]

Ultimately neither Constant nor Goyet transgressed into insurgency, unlike Lafayette. Moreover, it would appear that this division opened among the Chevaliers de la Liberté generally, as the Parisian *vente suprême* (head cell) found that some of their provincial allies were reluctant to engage in armed revolt. For example, a cell at Rennes wished only to provide protection to harassed Liberals. Local Chevaliers were, nevertheless, deeply

[5] Spitzer, *Old Hatreds*, pp. 219–66.

involved in a plot at Thouars (close to Saumur) timed to coincide with insurrection at Belfort in late December 1821. Loose lips sank ships in both regards and, although forces were mobilized, this merely led to massive arrests, while leaders such as Lafayette took flight without any real fighting having occurred.

Another attempt was made at Saumur in February 1822, but the town failed to respond to the appeals of General Jean-Baptiste Berton and his 150 men. Rennais Chevaliers sent two delegates to observe and report and, had rebellion become widespread, they would have joined, but it did not. Thus only the two delegates were arrested and others could return to wiser forms of resistance. Berton was not so fortunate, and shortly thereafter Colonel Caron was arrested for his plans to rescue the arrested Belfort conspirators. Caron was a victim of entrapment, but he shared the fate of Berton and both were executed in the autumn of 1822.[6]

There were perhaps another ten attempts at rebellion, but they were relatively minor and we need note only two. The first involved plans among officers at La Rochelle to join in the second attempt at Saumur. Several conspirators lost their courage, however, and turned informant. Ultimately four young sergeants took their knowledge of the principal organizers to the grave, but during the trials the public first learned of the vast extent of conspiratorial networks. At this point the revolutionary movement began to disintegrate, as figures such as Armand Carrel and Colonel Fabvier joined the *constitutionnels* in Spain. The final episode consisted of an attempt to subvert French troops as they crossed the Bidassoa River at the start of war with Spain in April 1823. Approximately 200 men dressed in French uniforms and flying the tricolour confronted the invading forces by singing the 'Marseillaise', but they were rapidly routed by cannon fire.

The majority of Liberal Deputies, including Constant, General Sébastien Foy, Casimir Perier and Girardin, did not conspire. Before we draw too sharp a distinction between them and the likes of Lafayette, d'Argenson, Manuel and the Alsatian industrialist Jacques Koechlin, however, we should note that there were two possible responses among those who stuck to legal means. One could break all ties with conspiratorial Deputies, or one could continue to associate with them in the Chamber. 'Legal' Liberals in fact did little to divorce themselves from their conspiring counterparts and,

[6] Guillon, *Complots*, pp. 175–211; R. Alexander, 'The Federations of 1815 and the continuity of anti-Bourbon personnel, 1789–1830', *Proceedings of the Annual Meeting of the Western Society for French History*, 17 (1990), pp. 290–1, and A. Bouton, 'Luttes dans l'ouest entre les chevaliers de la Foi et les chevaliers de la Liberté', *Revue des Travaux de l'Académie des Sciences Morales et Politiques*, 115, n. 2 (1962), pp. 1–13.

while they confined themselves to 'fair' means, they were willing to accept the results of successful 'foul' means. Even Guizot published brochures that, if they did not exculpate conspirators, certainly placed the onus of blame on the government. Guizot did not join the Carbonari when invited, but neither did he seek to prevent their undertakings. Casimir Perier was perhaps more scrupulous, but he, like Foy, several times rose to the defence of Carbonari Deputies in the Chamber, and joined in the ultimate act of solidarity when Manuel was expelled in 1823.[7]

Such solidarity facilitated government destruction of legal Liberal grass-roots organization. Attack was gradual, but central to its success was increasing public disinclination to respond to Liberal pleas for independence. In certain regards, Villèle simply built upon foundations laid by Decazes and Richelieu, but he was far more ruthless in pursuit of administrative despotism. The latter was the means by which he delivered ultraroyalism unprecedented power, as the majority of the electorate chose to follow government direction in the bipolar political world fostered by resort to revolution.

## PART TWO: ANATOMY OF DESPOTISM

In their massive histories of Restoration politics, Prosper Duvergier de Hauranne and Achille de Vaulabelle presented differing explanations of the crushing Liberal electoral defeat of 1824. For the former, the basic Liberal error lay in association with, or direct participation in, conspiracy. Duvergier did recognize the role of government corruption of the electoral process, but considered it a secondary factor, whereas Vaulabelle emphasized the executive's pursuit of despotism. Yet neither author recognized that despotism and conspiracy were complementary.

Because Villèle triumphed, it was easy to conclude that elections reflected the ascendency of the values he represented, but ultraroyalist victory was a product of means, not ends. Duvergier was correct in observing that Liberals had been defeated by absolutism, rather than counter-revolution. Liberals had, however, also played a part in the successful application of state despotism. By confirming their revolutionary image, they had surrendered their previous advantage in the wars of conspiracy theory. Charles Dunoyer, in a brochure published in the summer of 1824, chastised Liberals for abandoning public resistance in favour of covert 'operations'and he had a point: Liberals forfeited credibility by conducting themselves in one fashion

[7] Neely, *Lafayette*, pp. 169–73; Pouthas, *Guizot*, pp. 275–88, and Bourset, *Casimir Perier*, pp. 94–6.

publicly, and another privately. Mistrust of the Opposition, in turn, made repressive governmental actions appear reasonable to the public.

The progression of what ultimately became Villèle's system can be readily traced, beginning in 1820 when royalist governments commenced a sustained drive to control opinion. The de Serre press laws were rolled back, making anyone who criticized administrators vulnerable to charges of defamation, while removing judgement from juries. Similarly, inroads were made on Liberal ability to use the Chamber as a forum for expressing discontent. The violence of Liberal polemic led to the censorship of press reports, a process that culminated when the protest of the Left against Manuel's expulsion could not even be read in the Chamber.[8]

Although the major Parisian journals did survive repression, the departmental press was decimated. Local newspapers seldom had the resources to resist persistent harassment, and they collapsed as the government drained their supply of information through censorship, and repeatedly brought journalists and editors to trial. Under this onslaught the *Patriote* at Strasbourg, the *Echo* and *Journal libre* at Grenoble, the *Echo de l'Ouest* at Rennes, Goyet's *Propagateur de la Sarthe*, the *Journal du Cher* at Bourges, *La Tribune de la Gironde* at Bordeaux and the *Phocéen* at Marseilles were forced to cease publication, and at Périgueux the owner was induced to sell the *Bulletin du Département* to an old ultraroyalist émigré. A few Liberal journals, including the *Ami de la Charte* at Nantes and the *Indicateur* at Bordeaux, did survive, but overall the period was one of devastation.

At Grenoble, charges brought by a private party (a royalist spy) put an end to the *Echo*. At the heart of the affair was an article written by a Liberal notary who had exploited Montlivault's diatribes against Donnadieu for an analysis of the Didier revolt that was far from flattering for royalism. Worse still, Dr Reynaud had then published the article as a brochure and distributed 400 copies to workers and artisans. The key here for Choppin's replacement as prefect, Baron Charles Le Mercher de Longpré d'Haussez, was that Reynaud was a link between middle-class Liberals and the populace. This connection became obvious during the trial, when workers flooded the courtroom. More troubling still was that subscriptions were opened among worker corporations and the middle-class *cercle* Arribert to help Reynaud and the *Echo* editor cover court costs and fines. Liberals also undertook fund-raising drives at Romans, Bourgoin, Voiron, La Mure, Vizille and

8 Vaulabelle, *Histoire*, VI, 128–49, 161–8, 227–30, 262–72, Collins, *The Government and the Newspaper Press*, pp. 22–39, and C. Bellanger *et al.*, *Histoire générale de la presse française*, 4 vols. (Paris, 1969), II, pp. 149–59.

Valence. Nevertheless, the *Echo* always was a rather cheap production, and a single trial served to destroy it.

Thereafter the prefect focused his attention on the *Journal libre*. Despite having been elected to the *Chambre introuvable*, Baron d'Haussez was not a typical ultraroyalist in that he was no great advocate of counter-revolution, but he had little tolerance for those who criticized the state. D'Haussez therefore waged unrelenting war against the *Journal libre*, bringing the editors repeatedly before the courts throughout 1820 and 1821, and finally securing a fine of 2,000 francs against the journal in September 1821. That the *Journal libre* actually survived until February 1822 paid testimony to Liberal loyalty; by July 1821 d'Haussez had already reported that journals and brochures were rare in the countryside.[9]

Attack upon aggressive journals induced moderate newspapers such as the *Courrier du Bas-Rhin, L'Ami de la Charte* (at Nantes), the *Journal de la Meurthe* (at Nancy), and the *Journal de Toulouse* to soften or reverse support for the Left. For the local press government print commissions could prove an economic lifeline, and prefectoral pressure on mayors or communal councils to cancel subscriptions could prove lethal. Repeated pleas by journals in the Aube and Cher for permission to publish government acts were thus rejected, and the termination of subscriptions led to the collapse of two small Liberal papers in the Hautes-Pyrénées. In the Sarthe, after Goyet's *Propagateur* had been destroyed, prefects then concentrated on the local *Echo*, forcing the owner to drop Goyet as a contributor.[10]

Liberal Opposition had progressed by organizing publicly, and the local press had played a key part. With the advent of the second Richelieu ministry, however, came cabinet circulars instructing prefects to file monthly reports on local journals, reading circles and literary *cabinets*. Prefect Saint-Chamans seized on one such circular to advise that the 'revolutionary party' was deluging the Haute-Garonne with brochures designed to 'propagate poison', and recommended the passage of more forceful laws to prevent such 'culpable manoeuvres'. All the same, the laws in place were certainly rigorously enforced as the authorities seized banned brochures at six Toulousain cafés in May, and prohibited the import of liberal Spanish newspapers.[11]

[9] AN, F7 3679\6, 3–4 May 1820; F7 3794, 14 August 1821; F7 3795, 20 March 1823; F7 6745, 6 March, 27 May and 9 June 1820; F7 9667, 23 February, 12 March, 3 April and 12–26 July 1820 and documentation on the trials of the *Journal libre* from 2 December 1819 to 2 September 1821; BMUG, R8473, 31 December 1819, *and Journal libre*, 13–15 January and 5–8 February, 13, 20–29 April, 2 September and 30 November 1820.

[10] See A. Crémieux, *La censure en 1820 et en 1821* (Paris, 1912), pp. 70–170.

[11] AN, F7 9659, 17–27 May 1820; BB30 238, 18 May 1820, and ADHG, 6T3, 5 May 1820.

Judging by the response of the *Journal de Toulouse*, Opposition calls for rebellion served only to alienate moderates. Prominence previously given in the journal to reports from the Liberal press soon gave way to reliance on the *Drapeau blanc* and *Quotidienne*, and, upon the request of crown prosecutor general Gary, Vieusseux inserted biased accounts of Parisian riots that were unfavourable to Liberals. According to Gary, such reporting had a 'calming effect' because it destroyed exaggerations spread by private correspondence, and the cooperation of Vieusseux was all the more valuable in that the *Journal* was the departmental newspaper of choice, accounting, for example, for 57 of 107 subscriptions in the *arrondissement* of Villefranche.[12]

The harvest of insurrection was also apparent at Strasbourg. After a local trial of three officers for conspiracy, Silbermann, the new editor of the *Courrier du Bas-Rhin*, settled for sending contentious materials abroad to Baron Johann von Cotta's *Gazette d'Augsbourg*. Royalist spy Demougé thereafter attributed translation and forwarding of a speech by Humann to Silbermann and Ehrenfried Stoeber, a notary turned patriotic poet. In introducing the speech, Stoeber had exhorted Liberals not to retreat before the 'Jesuit onslaught' so troubling to 'Catholics of a Gallican tradition', but the result was a ban on the *Gazette*, the *Courrier des Pays-Bas* and the *Observateur Allemand*. Numerous other works were also seized at the frontier, and when a Liberal proprietor of a reading salon departed on a voyage, Demougé visited his wife to enquire as to her husband's movements. While he gained no information, the point had been made. The lawyer Louis Liechtenberger was fortunate that a crown prosecutor decided not to pursue him for a brochure appealing against the trial of Caron, but this was not a product of tolerance; the authorities wanted to concentrate on Jacques Koechlin and his more aggressive brochure on the Belfort conspiracy.[13]

The Strasbourg publisher Charles Heitz had produced a German translation of Koechlin's brochure and the resultant trial of Heitz brought him fifteen days of imprisonment and a fine of 320 francs. Moreover, seals were put on Heitz's press. Subsequently prefect Louis-René de Vaulchier du Deschaux, an extreme 'pure' tied to Artois since 1814 and a keen partisan of the *parti prêtre*, allowed Heitz to publish an almanac, a German bible, and several academic works, but permission was granted only after Heitz had promised to speak to Protestants at Wissembourg of the merits of Renouard

12 AN, BB30 192, 13 June 1820; ADHG, 6T3, 31 May 1820, and *Journal de Toulouse*, May generally, 14–21 June and 25 August 1820.

13 AN, BB30 240, 16 November 1822; BNUS, Ms. 1175, 26–8 July, 4–5 August, 18 September 1822, and Ms. 1178, undated note no. 353.

de Buissière. Heitz would fulfil his vow and contributed to Renouard's campaign in the election of 1824. Thus his licence was provisionally extended for six months.[14]

Although Liberals longed for a 'truly constitutional' organ, in February 1823 the *Courrier du Bas-Rhin* did manage to publish leaked reports on secret Chamber debates on the approaching war with Spain. As these reports were taken from the Parisian royalist press, Vaulchier could not prosecute Silbermann, but he then created the royalist *Journal du Bas-Rhin* to declare war on the *Courrier*. At least the *Courrier* survived. In the Isère, d'Haussez extended his onslaught against the Liberal press into reading rooms. After a Carbonari attempt at revolt at Grenoble in March 1821, the prefect ordered the disbanding of the *cercle* Arribert, and when Liberals sought to infiltrate the *cercle* Constant, d'Haussez ordered a purge.[15]

There was no Liberal newspaper in the Seine-Inférieure, so official attention in the summer of 1820 focused on points of distribution for Parisian journals and brochures. Police spies had ready access to *cabinets de lecture* and several were targeted for repeated searches. By late 1821, orders had come for a crackdown on unlicensed *casinos*. There followed instructions for information-gathering on the political inclinations of all printers and booksellers. As a final step, officials conducted a departmental survey concerning which newspapers were received at cafés. The survey revealed that the Parisian Liberal press was far more popular than its Parisian ultraroyalist rivals, but, then again, one could count eighteen cafés at Neufchâtel that received nothing but the *Journal de Rouen*. Some fifty-two cafés dispersed throughout the department were then selected to receive free subscriptions to the ultraroyalist press.[16]

That the *Journal de Rouen* was a prefectoral poodle could be seen in which Chamber speeches it published. Such selection, in turn, reflected a prefect willing to ensure profitability. For a couple of editions in February 1823, the owner Jacques Duval strayed from accustomed policies as growing alarm in the department over the prospect of war with Spain led him to publish the speeches of departmental Liberal Deputies, but after being summoned to the prefecture, Duval promised to be more careful in the future. By acting as a 'booster' for *ministériel* candidates thereafter, he ensured that

[14] AN, BB30 240, 13 September and 10 December 1822, 23 March 1823, and Leuilliot, *L'Alsace*, I, pp. 405–25.

[15] AN, F7 3795, 11 January 1822; F7 6696, 18 December 1822; ADBR, 3M19, 18 February 1822 and 15 February 1823; *Journal libre*, 7 August 1821, and Leuilliot, *L'Alsace*, I, pp. 395–7, 423.

[16] AN, BB30 238, 3 June – 11 July 1820; ADSM, 4M632, 19 November – 18 July 1822; 4M638, 27 May 1820 – 14 February 1823, and 4M643, 18 June 1820.

217 subscriptions would continue to be sent gratis to cafés throughout the department.[17]

For a brief period, Liberals did enjoy a voice in the *Nacelle*, a literary review rather than a political journal founded in December 1822. Edmond Corbière, a Breton previously involved in the riots at Brest, ran the *Nacelle* and while he could not legally address political questions directly, he certainly could come close. Satirical articles on the *mouche* (police spy) became a staple, and 'parasites' were defined as men who sold their opinions for a dinner (a reference to official banquets). Alongside such items came articles sympathizing with Spanish *constitutionnels*, and a fawning review of Emmanuel de Las Cases's *Memorial of Saint-Helena*. Predictably enough, the authorities had lodged charges against the *Nacelle* by 3 April 1823. Before it went down, however, the paper published lists of subscribers for a memorial silver sword for the National Guardsman Mercier, who had refused to arrest Manuel after the latter's parliamentary allusions to regicide. The publication of long lists of subscribers was an unwelcome reminder to officials of Liberal ability to organize, and it led to Corbière being sentenced to two years in prison.[18]

In a largely oral culture, attempts to command opinion naturally extended into the theatre. At Rouen Liberals were prone to dominate audience response, so that royalists were forced to remain silent. When officers of the Royal Guard objected, brawls ensued, but Liberal persistence was such that the theatre was largely their forum for expression.

Prefect Charles-Achille de Vanssay called in the appropriate authorities and presented them with a plan to rectify matters in March 1822. All leading officials would attend a performance of *The Deserter*, and should any Liberal prevent royalists from cheering, he would be arrested. The trap was, however, too obviously staged, so that Vanssay had to order the performance of a second play, *The Youth of Henri IV*. This time Liberals rose to the bait, leading to the trial of an obstreperous audience member who was duly sentenced to a month in prison and fined 100 francs. In October Vanssay could proudly report that he had also hooked the son of one of the richest merchants in the city, although, sadly, an appeal had reduced his imprisonment from four months to one.[19]

Similar scenes unfolded at Toulouse, where arrival of a Parisian actor gave occasion for a performance of *Sylla*. This was another Bonapartist play by

17 ADSM, 4M638, 22 October 1822, 14 February 1823, and 4M655, 17 February 1823.

18 See the *Nacelle*, 5 December 1822 – 21 June 1823.

19 AN, BB30 235, October–December 1822; ADSM, 1M175, February 1822 – August 1823, and 4M116, April–July 1823.

Jouy that the actor François-Joseph Talma had rendered a smash hit by miming Napoleon in performances in Paris from 1821 onwards. Students and Liberals at Toulouse noisily applauded untoward allusions, prompting the prefect to ban the play on 25 March 1822, and direct the actor to depart Toulouse. Two days later, royalists attended in force, causing fights and two arrests. On 28 March a royalist then demanded the singing of 'Henri IV', provoking brawls that spilled into the streets. Three more arrests followed, the theatre was closed, and public gatherings were prohibited. Far from sated, law students interrupted classes on the following day with cries of 'Vive la Charte!' and insulted professors who tried to restore decorum. Royalist students responded with cries of 'Vive le Roi!' and tumult erupted in the courtyard, requiring intervention by police and troops. In a final test of nerve on 31 March, 200 students and *jeunes gens* marched through the streets of Toulouse, until they were forcibly dispersed.

The leader of the march was Jean-Simon Tatareau, a half-pay officer who had been suspended from the law school for activities at the theatre in 1820. Officials blamed Liberals for encouraging agitation, and their conviction was not lessened when Romiguières successfully defended Tatareau in court. While the legal system thus proved disappointing, the Academic Council did at least ban Tatareau from courses for two years.

The troubles of March by no means marked the end of disturbances. Another theatre campaign launched in July led to the banishment of Tatareau from the department, but further skirmishes occurred throughout 1823 and 1824. Confronted by the effectiveness of royalist politics, and the failure of revolution, students and Liberals vented their spleen by attempting to bully royalists in public. Meanwhile the courts increasingly buttressed repression: a merchant was sentenced to five days' imprisonment for selling seditious stamps, a law student was given eight days for whistling while royalists applauded at the theatre, a worker received a month for yelling 'Vive l'Empereur!', and an art student was imprisoned for five months for defacing a portrait of Louis XVIII.[20]

In the Isère, d'Haussez sought control of public performance by terminating the banquets celebrating the defence of Grenoble in July 1815. That this had become increasingly aggressive could be seen in the lionizing of General François Ledru des Essarts, a former departmental commander whose royalism was suspect, and the protest against the prefect's crackdown

[20] AN, F7 3932, 18 March, 4–29 April 1822; F7 6692, 25 March 1822; F7 6769, 8 March 1822; F7 9659, 8 March 1822; BB30 245, 29 March, 2–23 April 1822; ADHG, 4M46, 9 April 1822; 6T3, 14–30 May 1822; BMT, LmC 4764, and J. Fourcassié, *Une ville à l'époque romantique, Toulouse* (Paris, 1953), pp. 119–26.

after a rebellion in March 1821. More provocatively still, in 1822 Liberals specifically designated seat number 18 at the banquet table for a fat individual who became the butt of ritualized insult. Thus in July 1823 d'Haussez posted notices banning the banquet and despatched troops to break up any meeting of more than twenty individuals. Despite the warnings, some 500 to 600 individuals had to take flight into a nearby forest.[21]

Cultural war was not waged simply through repression, as d'Haussez made much ado about commissioning the statue of the Chevalier Bayard that still adorns the place Saint-André. Although in certain regards rather ludicrous, the remains of the Chevalier having been 'miraculously' discovered while the statue was being made, subsequent ceremonies did at least honour a famous local figure. Conversely, a subscription for a monument to the 'martyrs of Quibéron' was overtly counter-revolutionary and had little to do with Dauphiny. Hence, while the Bayard subscription gained at least a lukewarm response, the 'martyrs of Quibéron' attracted virtually no public favour.[22]

Memorialization of the assassination of Berry did not achieve much in departments such as the Bas-Rhin, but in the Midi it became a vehicle for royalist mobilization in the form of subscriptions for a commemorative statue, and purchase of the chateau of Chambord for his widow and son. In June 1820 the municipal council of Toulouse donated 1,000 francs towards the statue. Smaller communities also contributed and 8,669 francs had been raised in the department by October 1823. Donations for the purchase of Chambord were also impressive and there were many, with the less fortunate giving sums as small as three francs.[23]

The government required willing agents in its pursuit of control over public opinion and, because the administration was a political tool, each major change in cabinet orientation required a purge. In March 1820 crown prosecutor general Baron Jean-Antoine Fouquet, long the target of ultra-royalist denunciations for alleged Bonapartism at Rouen, responded to a request from the Minister of Justice for reports on public opinion by complaining that 'espionage' was more suited to prefects. He then warned that local opinion was opposed to the laws being put forward by the government. The minister replied that it was well within his purview to direct Fouquet to

[21] AN, F7 3793, 18 July 1820; F7 3794, 7–8 July 1821; BB30 209 (Isère), 7 July 1823; ADI, 52M26, 4 July 1823; *Journal libre*, 8 July 1820 and 10 July 1821, and *Journal de Grenoble*, 8 July 1823.

[22] BMUG, R7906, 24 August 1822, 1–9 June 1823; *Journal de Grenoble*, 20 May 1820, 13 February 1823 and 23 November 1824, and baron d'Haussez, *Mémoires de Baron d'Haussez*, 2 vols. (Paris, 1896–7), I, p. 380.

[23] ADHG, 4M43 and 4M44.

monitor the Opposition, whereas Fouquet had no business commenting on cabinet policies. Fouquet then queried whether as a magistrate he forfeited the right to express opinions. The answer was obvious and subsequently Fouquet would be 'promoted' (after resigning) to an honorary post.[24]

The rate at which despotism advanced varied according to the nature of the department, or the character of the prefect. In the Isère, Liberals were given a first taste of what was to come during an election to replace Grégoire when d'Haussez threatened the tax receiver general with sacking if he did not rally prominently to the *ministériel* candidate. Given that voter registration depended on payment figures provided by the taxation administration, securing a reliably 'royal' agent was an important step for finagling lists. The receiver general complied, but a more scrupulous prefectoral councillor was dismissed.

According to d'Haussez, good government necessitated firm direction from the top and the removal of obstacles, especially officials appointed by the former prefect Choppin. Grenoble mayor Royer-Deloche was the first target and Liberals helped prepare the ground for his dismissal when law students shouted down cries of 'Long live the king!' with cries of 'Long live the Charter!' during a visit by Angoulême in early May 1820. D'Haussez immediately saw to the arrest of several students despite the reluctance of Royer and, indeed, Angoulême. The prefect had been threatening closure of the law school since April, but for the moment he settled for the expulsion of several students and concentrated on denouncing Royer to the Minister of the Interior.

D'Haussez was more immediately successful in seeing off Ledru des Essarts, though whether the general's transfer was due to failure to cooperate during the election of April or to allegations of conspiring with Carbonari agents is not clear. Serenades given to Ledru by Liberals in July did nothing to reduce d'Haussez's suspicions. Royer then compounded previous errors by allowing the municipal council to write a testimonial to the departing commander, while the *Journal libre* announced that Liberals had opened a subscription to purchase an honorary sword for Ledru. D'Haussez had no difficulty in convincing the government to order the removal of the testimonial and shortly thereafter Royer resigned.

Having established ascendancy among top officials, d'Haussez could then easily intimidate lesser civil servants. In a letter to another tax official, the prefect stated his anger that Liberals were circulating a petition based on information supplied by someone in the taxation bureau: 'I would have

[24] AN, BB30 238, 27 March – 5 April 1820.

grave reproaches for you if I thought you were responsible; I invite you to investigate which of your employees is responsible.' Thereafter mayors and justices of the peace were systematically directed to influence voters and mostly complied.[25]

The Richelieu cabinet liberally dispersed threats to its administrators, but there were limits to purge because the executive needed centrist support in the Chamber. Villèle was more disposed towards outright bullying. A notorious example of this occurred after an army captain had ignored orders from the Minister of War and publicly supported a Liberal candidate at Dijon in 1822. For his defiance of authority, the captain was incarcerated for a month, but he then petitioned the Chamber of Deputies against his punishment. The petition was ignored, and the captain was duly cashiered from the army, with loss of pension.

Such incidents did gain public notice, but voters increasingly accepted aggressive governmental practices. During the campaign of May 1822, the Liberal press published one of Villèle's circulars in which threats were anything but veiled, and Constant complemented the reports by pointing out the hypocrisy of Villèle's attacks on despotism in 1816. When parliament resumed, Chauvelin and Foy renewed the attack, but whatever good this might have done was immediately negated by press coverage of the Carbonari trial at La Rochelle.

Thereafter police operations became increasingly pervasive, helping to prepare the way for the elections of 1824. During the latter, Minister of Justice Peyronnet informed all crown prosecutors that 'the government confers public employment only so that it is served and seconded. If the civil servant refuses the services it expects of him, he betrays its confidence and voluntarily breaks the pact upon which his employment is based.' Officials had been reduced to subservience, and were all the more willing to further the cabinet's efforts to induce the same state among the electorate.[26]

Laws concerning voter registration allowed officials ample opportunity to secure government objectives. Lists were prepared by prefects and were not permanent, meaning that entirely new lists had to be composed for each election. For each new list prefects could demand all the required documents. In doing so, they could more or less invent new demands as they went along. Individuals with a grievance could lodge claims, but it was

[25] AN, F1C III Isère 4, 17 March 1820; F7 3792, 27 April 1820; F7 3793, 23 May 1820; F7 3679\6, 30 April, 3–4 May and 1, 13 and 20 July 1820; F7 6692, 21 May – 7 June 1820; F7 9667, 29 April and 5 July 1820; ADI, 8M4, 21 February 1824; 8M5, 28 July 1820; J514, 1 February 1824; *Journal libre*, 4–29 July 1820, and d'Haussez, *Mémoires*, I, pp. 321–3.

[26] See Duvergier de Hauranne, VI, 51–8, and Pilenco, *Les moeurs*, pp. 74–102 and 272–7.

the prefectoral council that initially evaluated such complaints. Thereafter the Council of State served as a court of appeal, but it was the government executive that appointed members of the Council. The king in his royal council rendered final decisions, and thus the entire process was utterly biased in favour of the cabinet. Moreover, initial prefectoral decisions remained binding as they were being adjudicated. Thus, even in the unlikely event that a claimant actually won his case, the previous prefectoral decision would have held till long after the election had been conducted.

Among many disreputable official manoeuvres were those of withholding the lists until the last minute, or seeking to make them as difficult to read as possible, thereby making verification problematic. Given that the lists were compiled from the current year's tax rolls, retarding distribution of the rolls served the same purpose. Former voters who found their taxes reduced below 300 francs had a material incentive not to complain, but even those who wished to act responsibly could find themselves confronted by a host of hindrances. For example, claims could be rejected because names on the tax rolls were not precisely the same as those on birth certificates – the slightest misspelling could become the pretext for rejection. Eliminating potentially hostile voters was, however, only half the story; to this was added a proclivity for the addition of royalist voters who previously had been well short of qualification.

Such practices increased dramatically from 1820 onwards and were systematized under Villèle. Exactly when prejudicial interpretation of the laws gave way to outright fraud varied from place to place, but as the Chamber became increasingly ultraroyalist, checks on cheating diminished. It was in the summer of 1820 that registration battles became the centre of electoral politics, and the impact of 'hardline' prefects could be seen in the struggles of Liberal electoral committees. At Marseilles, Liberal lawyers offered (without charge) to track down, assemble and present voter qualification documents, and in 1821 Goyet distributed brochures outlining how to force administrators to abide by the law. Yet there was no ultimate redress when petitions from disgruntled voters were either ignored by the Chamber of Deputies, or forwarded to the Council of State.[27]

Against this system, Liberal petitions gathered in the Isère foundered. The Opposition did manage to elect Camille Teissère in late April 1820, but d'Haussez could report that Teissère's margin of victory was less than that of Grégoire in 1819. D'Haussez had transferred the college to Vienne,

[27] See AN, F7 6767, dossier Bouches-du-Rhône, 23 August 1820, and Harpaz, *Constant et Goyet*, pp. 358–9, 410–33, 455, 680–2.

and official 'progress' could be seen in the fact that only 57.65 per cent (678 of 1,176) of registered voters actually participated, as compared to 77.37 per cent (1,002 of 1,295) in September 1819. By late May Liberals had presented a petition against exclusion of a voter to the Chamber; the petition was then referred to the Council of State. D'Haussez's response was to ask the director general of police for a list of those who had signed the petition. He showed particular interest in whether two professors at the Academy had signed, and their fates were thereby sealed.[28]

A broader front of Liberal legal action concerned creation of the new departmental college. As the *Journal libre* explained, the number of individuals in the colleges of the *arrondissements* would determine the number of voters in the departmental college. Large numbers in the departmental college would, in turn, reduce the percentage of noble voters. With such calculations in mind, Liberals launched a series of petitions. One set of petitions questioned the qualifications of fifteen (mostly noble) voters to vote. A second set of petitions was based on a comparison of d'Haussez's preliminary list of voters in late September 1820 with the list of September 1819. By this means a Liberal committee identified 260 individuals who had been dropped, and the petitioners argued that, given the length of time necessary to verify such a number of claims, these individuals should be reinscribed wholesale. In the case of the petition against fifteen royalists, the prefectoral council accepted one claim but rejected the others. The Liberal committee then had redress to the Council of State for both sets of petitions. The Council did not decide until July 1821, and then it rejected all claims.

D'Haussez was within his rights to drop electors who had not furnished adequate documentation, but there was little to stop him from ignoring inadequate royalist claims while directing officials to scrutinize the tax payments of Liberals. Documentation could conveniently go missing when sent by mayors to the prefecture. Officials could aid royalists in danger of being challenged, while sleeping Liberals could be left to lie.

For those willing to track down these manoeuvres, there were risks to be run. Supposedly concerned that men 'known for hatred of the government' were travelling the countryside not only 'to influence voters, but also to lead the population into excesses', the prefect warned Liberals that they would be arrested if found without a passport. After 1821 Liberals relented in their petitioning. They had for the time being given up, and this could be partly

[28] AN, F1C III Isère 4, 27 October 1820; F7 3679\6, electoral brochure of Alméras-Latour; F7 9667, 25 May 1820; ADI, 8M4, 26 April 1820; 8M5, 24–6 April 1820, and BMUG, 7453, 28 March, 20 and 29 April, and 6 May 1820.

attributed to threats made by the prefect. It should also be noted, however, that Liberals making legal arguments had less credibility after the Grenoble Carbonari revolt of March 1821. Sub-prefects at La-Tour-du-Pin and Vienne could then remove Liberal voters and add royalists with impunity.[29]

Practices designed to assure compliance within electoral colleges complemented the corruption of voter lists. As they stood before the voting urn, officials called out their vote and then handed their unfolded ballot to the college president so that he could read it prior to placing it in the urn. Such practices were not reserved for civil servants; anyone who wished to cast their influence publicly could do so. To combat these pressure tactics, Liberals demanded measures to ensure that the college bureau was prevented from watching the actual writing of the vote, and that ballots be burned immediately after counting. All the same, the bottom line was that voters did not insist on secrecy until the impact of the Carbonari revolt had worn off. When former Finance Minister Baron Louis sought to block the violation of secrecy of the ballot in Paris, the only reward he gained was removal from the Council of State, and there was no great public outcry. Claims by Jacques Laffitte that ultraroyalists were the true revolutionaries might have heralded future strategies, but they fell on infertile ground in 1822.[30]

Gerrymandering was another weapon in the government arsenal. In 1820 the Chamber had voted to redraw *arrondissement* college boundaries as part of the Law of the Double Vote and departmental councils, stacked with committed royalists, seldom posed difficulties for prefects who wished to redraw boundaries for partisan purposes. Selection of where colleges were to be held could also be based on calculations of how to reduce Liberal influence.[31]

At first glance, Saint-Chamans's proposals for the Haute-Garonne looked reasonable. For elections at the *arrondissement* level, Toulouse would choose two Deputies, whereas the less populous administrative *arrondissements* of Muret and Saint-Gaudens would be combined to form a single college. Nevertheless, below the surface of the prefect's recommendations lay partisan considerations: according to Saint-Chamans, if the electors of Saint-Gaudens were left to their own devices, they would favour the 'party of democracy'. Conversely, combining Saint-Gaudens with Muret

[29] The fate of the petitions can be traced in AN, F1C III Isère 4. See also F7 6740, 16 February 1824; ADI, 8M5, 4–5 October 1823, 2 and 24 February 1824; *Journal libre*, 23 September and 5–26 October 1820, and *Journal de Grenoble*, 26 October, 30 December 1820, and 28 July 1821.

[30] Duvergier de Hauranne, *Histoire*, VII, pp. 4–29, 38–50, 69, and Pilenco, *Les moeurs*, pp. 258–72.

[31] See Kent, *1827*, pp. 70–5.

would enhance the likelihood of gaining a *ministériel* Deputy. Furthermore, when the council proposed that elections be held at a central point for the two administrative *arrondissements*, this suggestion was ignored in favour of Muret, as far from Saint-Gaudens as feasible. For the Toulouse colleges, the southern canton was dominated by landowners and thus reliable, but the central canton was home to merchants and, therefore, the prefect attached other cantons best qualified to balance 'the most democratic canton'.[32]

D'Haussez also altered college boundaries in ways that made political but not topographical sense. Hence followers of the Liberal Charles Sapey had to apply to the prefect to switch the electoral colleges in which they voted, providing another opportunity to make life difficult. D'Haussez also transferred the colleges of Saint-Marcellin and La-Tour-du-Pin to Tullins and Crémieux, not because the latter were better equipped to accommodate voters, but because the former were considered Liberal bastions.[33]

The most striking development of the period was the extent to which the administration took on the role of political party. At Saint-Gaudens in 1821 the sub-prefect acted as campaign manager for Baron Puymaurin, keeping tabs on information supplied by a 'person of confidence' in each canton of the *arrondissement*. He soon learned that by late September Saint-Gaudens Liberals had begun circulating notices in favour of former mayor Durand, and that shortly thereafter a team of Liberals from Toulouse had commenced lobbying on behalf of Durand throughout the *arrondissement*. Liberals had distributed 600 copies of a brochure endorsing their candidate, and each Liberal voter had been sent a notice urging them to travel to Muret, where their costs would be reduced by the provision of meals and lodging funded by the Toulousain merchant Antoine Chaptive.

The mayor of Muret grew worried by developments during the first day of the college, and so the sub-prefect travelled from Saint-Gaudens to block 'the intrigues of the Liberal party'. Liberals hoped to deflect support from Puymaurin, if not towards Durand, at least to some other candidate so as to weaken royalist unity. This strategy, however, depended on the willingness of a moderate to run, and the sub-prefect therefore pressed Baron Marc-Bertrand Lassus de Camon, a Chevalier of the Legion of Honour and mayor of Montrejean, to grant him authorization to print a notice instructing his supporters to vote for Puymaurin. The notice was duly distributed among the voters, but Liberals continued to lobby inside and outside the assembly hall. To counter Liberal efforts, the sub-prefect employed 'all the influence

32 AN, F1C III Garonne (Haute-), 6, 6 March, 7–9 August 1820.

33 AN, F1C III Isère 4, 11 August 1820, and *Journal de Grenoble*, 12–14 February 1824.

of the administration', using civil servants to sway undecided voters. Shortly after his victory, Puymaurin directed the mayor of Muret to inform prefect Saint-Chamans of his gratitude.[34]

To appreciate fully how devastating the 'system' became under Villèle, we can turn to the Seine-Inférieure in 1824. In October 1823, Liberal activists had gathered at Rouen to discuss which candidates would contest which colleges. Once elections had been called, Liberals began the registration battle, circulating a brochure entitled *The Almanac of Electors*. At Rouen, the leaders of the Liberal committee, Henry Duhamel and the barrister Eugène Aroux, lodged claims for all of the colleges. Their efforts failed in 1824, but not for want of trying; they simply could not overcome a system wherein challenges to prefectoral decisions led to the Council of State appointed by Villèle.

Prefect Vanssay began the government's campaign by publishing a preliminary list in which only voters who had paid over 400 francs in taxes in 1823 were included. He thereby denied Liberals information as to voters who had paid between 300 and 400 francs, and we can deduce that there were many, given that the final count rose to 4,702 from the preliminary list of 2,307. As the lists were posted only on 16 January, and the elections were scheduled for late February, Vanssay greatly hindered Liberal efforts to identify potential voters. Not content with simply disrupting Opposition efforts, the administration used agents in each canton to mobilize royalists, collect and present documents for them, and urge them to scrutinize the lists for 'rogue' Liberal elements. Liberals could present their claims, but when information proved slightly inaccurate, no mention was made of it until the prefectoral council rejected them, leaving little time for correction. By way of contrast, incomplete royalist applications were, however, accepted on the basis of an oath.

'Men of confidence' helped royalist voters make travel arrangements, and ensured that they departed. They also sent the prefect and sub-prefects lists of confirmed and lukewarm royalists. Such lists were then collated, so that members of the two groups could be mixed at banquets hosted by officials during the college assemblies. Fourteen uncertain royalists thus found themselves seated among seven of the confirmed, dining at the home of the crown prosecutor general. Vanssay personally entertained 109 individuals between 24 and 26 February, and this was but one wave of such occasions.

34 AN, F1C III Garonne (Haute-) 7, 28 August 1821 and minutes of October 1821; ADHG, 2M24, 19–29 September and 3–12 October.

Stomachs were not always the way to a man's vote, but probabilities were enhanced in the voting halls. For the voters of each canton there was a royalist *surveillant* informed as to who was susceptible to Liberal 'intrigue'. Susceptible voters were paired with a 'mentor' who, if necessary, cast votes for shy rustics. Illiteracy was not, however, the reason for directing a court clerk and barrister to have their votes written by a 'mentor'; officials were taking no chances. Meanwhile, dispositions were taken to harass Liberal agents travelling in the department, and spies reported on each Liberal meeting. Thus Vanssay was informed of Liberal plans to force secrecy of the ballot, and instructed college presidents to prevent any such 'outrage'.

In the end, Vanssay secured the desired result; nine of ten seats went to *ministériels*. Vanssay had sent a circular to all voters, calling on them to reject 'our adversaries' and support candidates who 'would be close if necessary to sacrifice all for defence of the throne'. 'All' in this context was a not terribly cryptic reference to the Charter, although it could also be read to mean individual choice.[35]

In combination, the various steps taken by the Richelieu and Villèle ministries from 1820 onwards went a long way towards securing the smashing ultraroyalist triumph of 1824. Repression of dissent in the press and the theatre delivered a powerful blow to grassroots Liberal organization, and was complemented by a drive to establish state monopoly over what was brought to public attention through commemoration or celebration. Meanwhile purge and intimidation produced an administration largely willing to control elections by whatever means, legal or fraudulent, were deemed necessary by the cabinet. Villèle enhanced and coordinated practices introduced under Decazes and Richelieu and hence became the leading architect of state despotism. For all his accomplishments, however, Villèle also owed a great deal of his success to the actions of his Liberal opponents.

## PART THREE: THE ACHIEVEMENTS OF LIBERAL REVOLT

It took time for the impact of conspiracy to manifest itself fully. Initial abortive attempts at insurrection left much of the public incredulous and inclined to doubt the reports of a government already headed along the

[35] AN, F1C III Seine-Inférieure 4, 10 January, 11 February 1824; BB30 235, 6–8 May 1824; ADSM, 1M174, 18–22 October 1823; 3M158, 24 January – 24 February and 1 March 1824; 3M159, 10–14 February 1824; 3M160, 12 February 1824; 4M2684, 11 February 1824, and H. Putz, 'Les élections de 1824 en Seine-Inférieure. Action gouvernementale et propagande royaliste', *Annales de Normandie*, 5, n. 1 (1955), pp. 59–72.

path of reaction. Nevertheless, one can trace a steady decline in Liberal electoral fortunes that would accelerate as the extent of conspiracy was slowly revealed.

In the early summer of 1820 prospects appeared favourable as Liberal Deputies returned to ovations at Dijon, Rouen, Clermont, Aurillac, Rennes and Brest. Yet troubles to come could be seen in Brest, where demonstrations in favour of Deputy Guilhem led to the dissolution of the National Guard. More telling was the failure of a 'national subscription' to aid 'victims' of the law suspending individual liberty. The project started well, with radical and moderate Liberal Deputies signing a prospectus calling for the organization of subscriptions throughout the country, but almost immediately thereafter came legal proceedings against newspapers for publishing the prospectus. Recourse could then be had to brochures. In the Sarthe, Goyet set up subscription registers in several towns. The registers were placed with notaries, and subscriptions gathered pace until the police arrived, threatening arrest. Support also evaporated rapidly at Valence, once charges had been laid against two lawyers seeking subscribers.[36]

A second portent could be seen in harassment of Goyet after one of the Grand Elector's allies, Martial Sauquaire-Souligné, had involved himself in the riots in Paris during passage of the Law of the Double Vote. Goyet's papers were seized, and both men were brought to trial. Court procedures began prior to the elections of November and dragged on until March 1821, forcing Goyet repeatedly to depart from Mamers and disrupting his organizational efforts. Acquittal perhaps preserved Goyet's reputation for the moment, but that the stakes of opposition were rising was clear to everyone.[37]

In November, Opposition candidates barely held their own in the colleges of the *arrondissements*. Fifty of the latter were roughly divided between the Left and the Right, but return of the Deputies of the *Chambre introuvable* began. Liberal candidates, busily denying accusations, had lost credibility, as the *Constitutionnel* and *Courrier* lauded revolutions in Spain and the Italian states. Liberals were pleased to learn that they could win in the departmental colleges, but taking six of seventy-two seats was a small consolation for poor performance in the *arrondissements*. Worse still, the departmental colleges were already registering a trend which would become general:

[36] AN, F7 6769, folio Drôme, general report of February 1822; Duvergier de Hauranne, *Histoire*, VI, pp. 1–18; Alexander, *Bonapartism*, pp. 143–6; Crémieux, *La censure*, pp. 29–69, and Harpaz, *Constant et Goyet*, p. 291.

[37] Harpaz, *Constant et Goyet*, pp. 291–520, and Neely, 'Goyet', p. 332.

faced by aggressive candidates such as General François Lamarque and the possibility of revolution, royalists in centres such as Bayonne stampeded towards ultraroyalism.[38]

In the Haute-Garonne, Villèle was the principal beneficiary of growing voter preoccupation with order. While Gary was initially pushed as an official candidate, Richelieu soon reached an accord with Villèle and thus Gary stepped aside in favour of Baron Mathieu-Louis Hocquart, first president of the *cour royale*. Villèle's influence was further enhanced by his appointment as college president, but his speech was full of ultraroyalist reservation: institutions granted by the throne must not be used to overthrow it. Thereafter all three ultraroyalist candidates were elected comfortably and would follow Villèle's lead in the Chamber.

Prefect Saint-Chamans had been directed to detach Liberals 'of good faith' by exposing revolutionary intrigue and his task had not proved difficult. Although Liberals had disseminated 2,000 copies of speeches by Deputies such as Manuel, the brochures had produced the reverse of the desired effect. In July soundings had been taken on behalf of Durand, Chaptive, Lignières and General Pelet, but the response had not encouraged any of them to go forward. Officials thereafter reported that Liberals had not even bothered to coordinate their efforts.[39]

While royalists closed ranks, the Left began to splinter. Radicals in the Bas-Rhin seized the initiative with a banquet in honour of the department's Deputies and commenced festivities with serenades outside the homes of Turckheim, Brackenhoffer and Saglio on 25 September. The next day, 159 subscribers paid sixteen francs each for food, wine, coffee, a liqueur and music at the Hôtel Miroir. Deputies Turckheim and Brackenhoffer, however, either judged the banquet ill-timed, or had reservations over the organizers. Nor did Humann, Levrault and several other leading moderates participate.

Diminishing radical prospects could be seen in brochures published by Marchand. In the first he gave preference to Magnier-Grandprez and François-Joseph Rudler, a former Imperial war commissary, prefect and member of the Legislative Corps. By the second, Marchand had switched to an emphasis on discipline in Liberal ranks, warning against candidates

[38] On Bayonne, see AN, F7 6741, dossier Landes, 31 October 1820.

[39] AN, BB30 238, 15 April, 5–19 October, 6 and 11 November, and 9 December 1820; F1C III Garonne (Haute-), 6, 9 August 1820, minutes of 13–15 November 1820; F7 6740, dossier Haute-Garonne, 11 November 1820; F7 9659, 17 May, 17 June, 22 July, 8 August and 5 October 1820; ADHG, 2M24, 9 August 1820; 4M47, 27 September 1820, and *Journal de Toulouse*, September and October generally and 17 November 1820.

vulnerable to official influence, a barb aimed at Renouard de Buissière. Solidarity should be expressed by voting for Humann, and then Liberals could combine behind Magnier-Grandprez or Rudler. Electoral results, however, indicated that Marchand's warnings had gone unheeded: Humann, representing the Centre-Left, and Renouard, representing the Centre-Right, went through on the first ballot.[40]

In the Côte-d'Or, Liberals conducted themselves relatively wisely. At Dijon in early 1820 Carion had published Gabet's predictions of revolt should the electoral laws be revised, leading to the arrest of the author. Shortly thereafter came the arrival of Nicolas Séguier de Saint-Brisson, a prefect eager to terminate the Liberal press. Carion therefore accepted the Double Vote as a compromise. Proudhon, *doyen* of the law faculty, showed similar prudence when he convinced students not to contest calls of 'Long live the king!' with cries of 'Long live the Charter!' during Angoulême's visit in May. Clashes linked by the public to revolution were thus avoided, but Liberals tested the limits of toleration during the summer with boisterous serenades to Gabet during his trial, and to Deputies Hernoux and Chauvelin. When Chauvelin departed in July, he was accompanied by a show of force – some 150 marching men and women, a cavalcade, and about forty individuals in carriages. Next came Caumartin, also treated to Dijonnais serenades, and a banquet allegedly attended by 300 voters at Beaune. Fireworks followed the banquet and drew large crowds.

With elections to be contested in the autumn, Liberals then opened a subscription so that copies of the Charter could be distributed throughout the department. Ultimately, such efforts failed, but margins of defeat were not overwhelming. Given that Opposition candidates had been confronted by a royal letter to voters in support of *ministériels*, a college president championing candidates known for love of religion and legitimacy, and voter list finagling, prospects for future success in the departmental college could be considered favourable, provided that Liberals did not antagonize the electorate through civil disorder.[41]

Decline was more obvious in the Seine-Inférieure. In April 1820, before the riots in Paris, the Liberal Alexandre de Lameth had easily won a by-election. Lameth had been a Deputy to the Estates General, had emigrated during the Directory, had returned to serve Napoleon as prefect, had been

[40] AN, F1C III Rhin (Bas-), 3, 15 November 1820; F1C III Rhin (Bas-), 15, 26 September 1820; BN, NAF 20036, 3 September – 13 December 1820; BNUS, Ms. 1534, 22 and 27 September 1820; Ms. 1180, *Banquets . . . aux députés libéraux*, and Leuilliot, *L'Alsace*, I, pp. 282–92.

[41] Fizaine, *La vie*, pp. 176–213.

appointed to the Chamber of Peers in 1814, and then had been removed from the Peers in June 1815. His election thus clearly indicated a left-leaning electorate, although he certainly did not represent the sort of threat allegedly posed by Grégoire.

Thereafter Liberals made many voters rethink. In July and early August, Rouennais activists arranged serenades for departmental Deputies Abraham-Thomas Leseigneur, president of the tribunal of commerce at Saint-Valéry and a former member of the Chamber of Representatives of 1815, the wholesale merchants Bernard Cabanon (of Rouen) and Michel Delaroche (of Le Havre), and for two 'outsiders' – Casimir Perier and Jacques Laffitte. Crowds grew with each occasion, rising from 300 for Perier to 1,200 for Laffitte, and their threatening nature was made clear by the chanting of republican and Imperial battle cries. Then came news of the revolt in Paris. There were no serenades for Girardin in September, but by then it was too late. Liberals could be pleased with the election of the merchant Jean-Marie Duvergier de Hauranne *père*, who was then considered a moderate royalist, but the other three seats went to more decided royalists.[42]

In the renewal of autumn 1821, conspiracy loomed less large, although Opposition candidates were embarrassed by Cugnet de Montarlot's call for French revolution from the safety of Spain. Liberals in the Chamber had previously defended Cugnet while he was incarcerated in France. Accounts vary as to how well the Liberal vote held up, but the Right took roughly sixty of eighty-eight seats as ultraroyalism surpassed the Centre-Right. Liberal resolution to vote tactically in favour of Centrists came to little, and meanwhile four of their most left-leaning candidates went down to defeat.[43]

In the Haute-Garonne, Saint-Chamans received cabinet instructions as to which candidates to back. He should avoid extremists, including individuals who carried their royalism into the 'doctrines of opposition', but whether the latter description included Villèle was difficult to say. Villèle had by then left the cabinet, but Richelieu did not want a complete break. Hence Villèle, Limairac, Puymaurin, Hocquart and Armand-Joseph Saint-Félix de Maurémont were named college presidents; only the latter was not an outgoing Deputy, and he enjoyed the favour of both Villèle and the cabinet. The one outgoing Deputy opposed by the ministry was Castelbajac,

[42] AN, BB30 192, 17–26 April 1820; BB30 238, 13 August 1820; F1C III Seine-Inférieure 4, 25 April–16 November 1820; F1C III Seine-Inférieure 16, 1–31 August; ADSM, 1M174, 26 November 1820; 3M152, 24 June 1820, and 4M116, 1 September 1820 and 20 January 1821.

[43] Duvergier de Hauranne, *Histoire*, VI, 221–30, 324–43, 412–16, 439–70, and Vaulabelle, *Histoire*, V, 473–4.

but Saint-Chamans could not deliver the cabinet's wishes because Villèle would not cooperate.[44]

Liberal efforts looked weak, but they did at least put up a fight. At Villefranche Villèle romped home, distancing Chaptive by a count of 160 to 75. In Toulouse I, Castelbajac crushed the barrister Marie-Nicolas Ferradou by 243 to 95, and in Toulouse II Limairac defeated Cassaing by 237 to 174. At Muret, Puymaurin defeated Durand by 178 to 104, but as we have noted previously, the administration had been obliged to work hard to secure this result.[45]

Divisions among Liberals again came to the fore at Strasbourg, as organizers of a banquet for General Foy in the autumn of 1821 all hailed from the radical wing. Despite having helped secure Foy's attendance, Humann then withdrew because the organizers refused to invite Renouard. Nor did other Deputies attend; by taking a hard line, radicals weakened their position with moderates. Meanwhile Foy shied away from serenades complete with musicians of the former National Guard. When some young sparks suggested that the former Guardsmen strike up the 'Marseillaise', the request was sensibly denied, but cries of 'Down with the *droits réunis*' gave Mayor Kentzinger a pretext for assigning a heavy police presence thereafter.[46]

Due to budgetary concerns, Villèle held two parliamentary sessions in 1822; hence there were two renewal elections in that year. The first occurred in early May, in the aftermath of attempted revolt at Belfort and Saumur, but before the trial at La Rochelle began to take its toll.

In late February, Minister of the Interior Corbière had ordered a survey of public opinion, and reports had all pointed in the same direction. In the Hautes-Alpes, Cantal and Cher, Liberals attributed revolt to the work of madmen. In the Dordogne, the party of 'democratic ideas' fell back on claims of entrapment, and similar face-saving was apparent in the Haute-Loire. Such defensive posturing still retained some credibility, but prefects could report that 'former' Liberals in the Corrèze and Dordogne had reverted to royalism. In the Cher, Eure-et-Loire, Morbihan

[44] AN, BB30 238, 13 February, 31 March and 19 April 1821; F1C III Garonne (Haute-), 14, 10 April 1821; F7 3794, 25 January and 26 April 1821; F7 6692, 8 August and 20 December 1820; F7 9659, 30 April 1821; ADHG, 1M75, 6 June 1821; 2M24, 5 and 15–19 September 1821; 2M24, 4–30 July, 8 August and 11 September 1821; 6T1, 10 May and 2 July 1821, and 6T3, 21 April 1821.

[45] AN, F1C III Garonne (Haute-) 7, 28 August 1821 and electoral college minutes of October 1821; ADHG, 2M24, 23 October 1821.

[46] AN, BB30 260, 28 August 1821; F7 6719, 28–31 August 1821; F7 9693, 10–31 May 1820; BNUS, Ms. 1534, August 1821; Ms. 1180, 29 August 1821; BN, NAF 20036, 30 August and 12 September 1821, and *La vie en Alsace* (July 1934), pp. 163–5.

and Pyrénées-Orientales, Liberals were dismayed at the violence of the speeches of Deputies, especially those of Manuel.[47]

Under the circumstances, the Liberal vote held up well in May, but collapse of the Centre continued. In the provincial *arrondissement* colleges, ultraroyalists (who were now the official candidates) took thirty-two seats and twenty-three went to the Opposition. The provincial departmental colleges yielded twenty-four *ministériels* and nine Liberals. All told, the cabinet had improved its position by twenty-two seats. Liberals did take ten of the twelve seats in the Seine, and thus their position in the Chamber did not decline, but they were becoming highly reliant on the capital. Even Lyons wavered, as Corcelles lost while his followers rioted.[48]

In the Côte-d'Or, Liberals managed to swim against the tide. They had continued serenades until clashes between *jeunes gens* and the authorities in late 1821 gave Séguier the pretext to ban public gatherings. A *ministériel* brochure then set the tone for campaign strategy: royalists were committed to uphold the Charter, whereas Liberals openly lauded insurrection. Nevertheless, Liberal unity held as Chauvelin romped to victory at Beaune, and Hernoux succeeded comfortably at Dijon. At Semur, however, Caumartin's majority was a mere six votes. Worse still, ultraroyalists doubled the tallies of their Liberal rivals in the departmental college.[49]

Thereafter followed the executions of Caron and Berton, and a similar fate for the four sergeants of La Rochelle in September, and amidst startling revelations of widespread conspiracy the elections of November proved disastrous. Shifting expectations could be seen in campaign strategies. While the ultraroyalist press demanded exclusion of the 'impure', and the cabinet made few compromises with the Centre-Right in the nomination of college presidents, Liberals pleaded for Opposition unity. Of the eighty-six seats contested, Liberals took a grand total of six, thereby losing roughly thirty Deputies, including Constant.[50]

## THE BLURRING OF LEGAL AND ILLEGAL RESISTANCE

It was royalists who began the pattern of reaction, revolt and further reaction, but Liberals then contributed by responding to repressive legislation in ways that made them appear the aggressors in the political struggle and alienated the public. Radicals thought they saw an opportunity for

[47] Materials have been collated from the reports of 1823 in AN, F7 6767–72.

[48] Duvergier de Hauranne, *Histoire*, VI, pp. 4–11, and Vaulabelle, *Histoire*, VI, 161–8.

[49] Fizaine, *La vie*, pp. 215–43.

[50] Spitzer, *Old Hatreds*, pp. 119–97.

revolution where there was none, and the entire Opposition suffered in consequence.

When d'Haussez arrived in the Isère in early 1820, the *Journal libre* warned him not to listen to ultraroyalists, and happily reported that Liberals and royalists soon separated into opposite camps at the prefectoral investiture ball. D'Haussez immediately increased surveillance of 'enemies' and hired spies who ranged from Savoy to Vienne. Confronted by reaction, Liberals then had recourse to both conspiratorial and legal opposition, but the former negated the latter. In the aftermath of the attempted insurrection in Paris in August, departmental electors listened to Bishop Claude Simon's exhortations to combat revolution rather than pleas in the *Journal libre* not to forget liberty in November. Ultraroyalists Planelli and the mayor of Chandieu Félix Prunelle received, respectively, 192 and 158 votes, easily outdistancing Augustin Perier's 96.[51]

Thereafter legal Opposition focused on the campaign for voter list revision previously described. Among the organizers were Champollion, Perrin, Augustin Blanchet and Joseph Chanrion and the petitions were presented by a team of lawyers including Duchesne, Duport-Lavillette *fils*, Crépu and Félix Réal. Of these men, Champollion, Perrin, Crépu and Réal can definitely be identified as having been Carbonari. Whether the others were cannot be determined, but the entire group did remain closely associated for the remainder of the Restoration.

On 21 March 1821 Grenoble witnessed an attempt at revolt. Using rumours that Louis XVIII had abdicated as a pretext, a crowd of perhaps 600 led by Perrin and Renauldon *fils* besieged the prefecture. Tricolour ribbons were distributed and tricolour flags were raised, and it took several hours before d'Haussez and Lieutenant General Joseph Pamphile de Lacroix could convince the troops to clear the streets. D'Haussez and Pamphile then issued blood-curdling proclamations, put Grenoble in a state of siege, and ordered arrests. Yet no shots had been fired and a subsequent investigation mostly revealed the confusion of events. The authorities were unable to establish proof of conspiracy, and consequently repression was limited.

Enquiries did, nevertheless, reveal a great deal. Augustin Thévenet had started the rumour, Duport-Lavillette *fils* had announced the supposed abdication at the *cercle* Arribert, and ribbons had been distributed at Falcon's bookshop. Hughes Blanc and several professors had been prominent among the crowds, and Champollion and Ovide-Lallemand had been seen

[51] AN, F1C III Isère 4, electoral minutes of November 1820; *Journal libre*, 12 February, 7–11 March, 11 November 1820; *Journal de Grenoble*, 11 November 1820, and d'Haussez, *Mémoires*, 1, pp. 321–3.

conferring before the citadel where a tricolour was unfurled. All of these men were leading Liberal activists and it was little wonder that legal resistance in the form of petition campaigns soon lost credibility.[52]

Elsewhere, Constant was tarred with guilt by association, but it was a very close association. In late August 1820, he and Lafayette journeyed to the Sarthe. Each step of the way they were dogged by official hostility, and ultraroyalist aggression at Le Mans convinced Lafayette to beat a retreat. Constant travelled on to Saumur, where pitched brawls erupted as local Chevaliers de la Foi sought to disrupt Liberal banquets. Ultimately Constant defied threats of murder, but he departed with an escort of National Guardsmen.

Violence was not, however, the means by which ultraroyalism gained power. More revealing was cabinet reaction in August 1821 when the two extremes threatened to form public associations. A first initiative came from an ultraroyalist calling for association of all those who had 'legitimate' claims on lands seized during the Revolution. Pagès de l'Ariège then responded with a brochure calling for association of the owners of nationalized lands. Goyet immediately set about putting words into action, but the government wisely clamped down on both sides, using censorship to ensure that nothing more was said on the subject. Local organization was the greatest threat to official control, and misguided actions on the Right could spur dangerous initiatives on the Left.

By this stage the authorities were remorselessly tracking the movements of Deputies, and this carried over to local activists. Who in the Seine-Inférieure was to say whether the trips of Henry Duhamel to Nantes and Paris were simply business-related? Given the role of *jeunes gens* elsewhere, it would have been irresponsible not to have noted that Rouennais *jeunes gens* sent two delegates to a Liberal gathering in Paris in October, not to have investigated the role of the young clerks of the Bechet *cabinet de lecture* in disseminating seditious literature, and not to have kept watch on the boarding houses where significant numbers of them resided.

There undoubtedly was a great deal of opportunism in such monitoring, but the threatening serenades of the summer of 1820 had given the public good reason to view Liberal organization with scepticism. Hence when Deputies Girardin, Lameth, Cabanon, Bignon and Leseigneur gathered at Rouen for a round of dinners in late August and early September 1821, observers could only wonder. Girardin and Lameth then went on a tour

[52] AN, F7 3793, 2–3 July; F7 3679\6, 20 July 1820; AN, F7 9667, March–April 1821; BMUG, R4737; R7906; T3938, pp. 1–155; *Journal de Grenoble*, 24 March 1820; *Journal libre*, 22 and 27 March 1820, and D'Haussez, *Mémoires*, I, p. 325, 354–63.

of banquets at Bolbec, Le Havre, Saint-Valéry, Dieppe and then Rouen again, while police informants duly supplied lists of participants. There is in fact no evidence that the Deputies were doing anything illegal; they were simply consulting with their leading supporters. The point, however, is that all of this networking appeared sinister because Liberals were engaged in conspiracy elsewhere.[53]

After the returns of May 1822, Goyet was hopeful for the autumn, but then came revelations concerning Saumur. A Liberal who had played host to Constant in 1820 had committed suicide rather than face execution, Sauquaire-Souligné had also been involved in the rebellion, and General Berton had cited Constant as part of a planned provisional government. Attacking the leading prosecutor in the trial did Constant little electoral good; he went down to massive defeat in 1822. He could complain all he liked about intimidation, but he had done little to make ultraroyalist allegations of complicity implausible.[54]

Liberals also forfeited their strong position in the Bas-Rhin. Upon arrival in late April 1822, prefect Vaulchier soon established contact with Demougé, who duly hired seven spies. It remained nonetheless difficult to secure hard evidence of plotting and authorities in the Haut-Rhin badly over-played their hand in the Caron affair of early July 1822. While Colonel Caron certainly had tried to subvert troops in order to free Liberals accused of conspiracy at Belfort, official use of *agents provocateurs* gave credibility to Liberal claims of entrapment. The government therefore brought Caron before a military tribunal rather than risk civil trial, and the former officer was transferred to Strasbourg.[55]

Trial of the original Belfort conspirators overlapped proceedings against Caron. Crown prosecutors could present more damning evidence at Colmar, but the jury's verdict still constituted defeat for the government: of twenty-three individuals accused, nineteen were acquitted. The public remained sceptical of charges of widespread conspiracy, and hence when prosecution of Caron finally began on 18 September, attendance was restricted to a small number of officers.[56]

[53] AN, BB30 235, 24 March and 25 June – 9 October 1822; F7 6686, dossier 37, 17 September 1822; F7 6701, 1 July 1822; F7 6718, 29 August – 14 September 1822; F7 6772, 21 March 1822; ADSM, 1M174, dossier *réunions*, 18 March, 15–27 April, 5–13 June and 8–17 July, 1822.

[54] Schermerhorn, *Constant*, pp. 335–41, and Harpaz, *Constant et Goyet*, pp. 362–433, 588–93, 673–734.

[55] BCUL, Co 3712, July 1822; BNUS, Ms. 1175, 8 and 22 May, 4 October, 18–22 December 1822, and Leuilliot, *L'Alsace*, 1, pp. 346–69.

[56] BNUS, Ms. 1175, 13 June, 4–7, 25–30 August, 19 September – 11 October 1822, and F. Zickel-Koechlin, 'Souvenirs d'un contemporain sur les événements de 1816 à 1823 en Alsace', *Revue d'Alsace*, 1 (1850), pp. 118–32.

With the advantage of admissions made later, we now know that at least a handful of Strasbourg Liberals, most notably the lawyer Liechtenberger (part of Caron's defence team), Rudler, Alexandre Chastelain, retired Imperial war commissary, and Colonel Antoine Brack, were Carbonari agents. Demougé had suspicions of more extensive involvement, but he cast his net so widely that he and the authorities were unable to catch the real conspirators. Yet the key was that occasionally well-founded suspicion provided a pretext for harassment of individuals seeking to organize legal resistance.

Lawyers Liechtenberger and Philippe-Jacques Fargès-Méricourt offered their services free of charge to men accused of conspiracy, which struck Demougé as highly suggestive. Marchand was always high on the suspect list, and along with him came Jean-Guillaume Gravelotte, a former Imperial director of indirect tax collection who had helped fund the *Patriote*. All the same, the prime suspect was Schulmeister; it was natural that one spymaster should thus honour another. Schulmeister was in contact with Chastelain and Colonel Brack; moreover Schulmeister was friendly with Coulmann, who in turn was a childhood companion of Brack. Lest we become trapped in Demougé's web, we should, however, also note that allegations made against Stoeber, Levrault, Humann and Saglio were hardly credible.

Use of the term 'Carbonari' gradually declined in Demougé's reports as 'Liberal' returned to its rightful supremacy, and his spy network appears to have ceased operations, but Demougé remained valuable to the prefect. Knowing of Liberal connections – for example, that Humann consulted with Marchand and Anselme Marschal – was useful for blocking mobilizing efforts, and making surveillance of Schulmeister blithely obvious forced him to adopt a low profile. Vaulchier also used clergymen to determine the opinions of lawyers and lesser municipal employees, thereby learning the identity of leading Liberal activists at Wissembourg, Sélestat and Haguenau. All of this information would be put to good effect come the elections.[57]

The capstone of conspiracy was the Carbonari attempt to subvert French troops at the Bidassoa in early April 1823. Revolt again rapidly collapsed, but this act of folly cost Liberals their strongest political card – patriotism. To tempt the army in domestic battle was one thing; to call for rebellion at the start of a war was another. Few Liberals had gone this far, but when they departed the parliamentary session of 1823 in support of Manuel, they ensured their association with treason.[58]

57 This analysis is derived from the notes of Demougé's manuscripts in BNUS. See also AN, F1C III Rhin (Bas-) 15, 21 October 1822, 4 February and 8 March 1823.

58 Spitzer, *Old Hatreds*, pp. 197–209.

The expulsion of Manuel triggered the last major grassroots effort of the Left prior to the elections of 1824. Deputies gave the original impetus, but local activists directed activities thereafter. Copies of the protest of the Deputies of the Left were distributed hand to hand, and this gave rise to petitions protesting against the expulsion or opposing the war. Alongside the petitions came subscriptions for Manuel and Mercier.

Beslay *fils* commenced matters at Dinan, putting the Breton Liberal network into operation and extending it into Normandy. Attempts to convince chambers of commerce to send addresses against the war fizzled out, but alarm ran deep along the English Channel and several judges and civil servants did sign petitions against the war. At Tarbes and Tours, young barristers were particularly active, and National Guardsmen in many locations were sympathetic to Mercier. In the Haut-Rhin, the usual network of manufacturers was involved; at Lyons and Epinal the efforts of commercial clerks caught the attention of the authorities. Activity in the east often reached into the cafés and market places of the countryside.

At Rouen skirmishes commenced when a large number of National Guard officers endorsed a letter, published in the *Constitutionnel*, congratulating Mercier for his refusal to arrest Manuel. The Duhamel brothers (Henry, Thomas and Jean), all merchant-manufacturers, then opened a subscription to purchase an honorary gun for Mercier. According to the *Nacelle*, 2,804 individuals had signed by 6 April. Judging by official correspondence, the figure was probably accurate; subscriptions were set at ten centimes, and agents collected signatures in cafés, *auberges* and public squares. Officials were initially thrown into a quandary. Actions against the organizers might necessitate charges against subscribers, clearly an undesirable result, and alienation of the Guard would have been dangerous at a time when Royal Guardsmen were on their way to Spain. In the event, the solution was to destroy the *Nacelle*.[59]

The broader context for all of this activity was military mobilization, and hence the public closely linked Liberal efforts to attempts to sabotage the war effort. Wherever there was a garrison, seditious tracts were distributed, and one pamphlet, entitled 'An old soldier to the Army', echoed Liberal arguments in the Chamber: restoration of absolutism in Spain would lead to restoration of the *ancien régime* in France. Promotion based on merit

[59] AN, BB30 235, 29 March 1823; F7 6718, 5 March – 2 June 1823; ADSM, 1M174, 15 March – 1 April 1823; 1M175, 18 May 1822; 1M176, 26 March – 16 June 1823; 4M2684, 20 April 1823, and *La Nacelle*, 15 March – 6 April 1823.

would give way to noble privilege, and commoners could look forward to a steady diet of *coups de bâton*.[60]

Emotions ran high in the Haute-Garonne as Iberian conflict spilled over the Pyrenees. As elsewhere, Liberals encouraged desertion from the army, and in the *arrondissement* of Saint-Gaudens Spanish royalist refugees were repeatedly treated to public insult. Two lawyers, Jean-Augustin Laurent *fils* and Adolphe Martin, both sons of judges, were brought to trial at Toulouse for unflattering jokes about the king and Angoulême, but the authorities were unable to prove that Martin was a member of a secret cell. Absence of evidence did not, however, necessarily prove innocence; Martin was indeed a Carbonaro. So too were the notary Jean-Pierre Amilhau, a close friend of François-Bernard Boyer-Fonfrède, and the latter's nephew Henri Boyer-Fonfrède at Bordeaux. French officials spent long hours trying to establish that François-Bernard Boyer-Fonfrède was acting as a liaison between French Carbonari and Spanish liberals, but evidence remained sketchy.[61]

Preoccupied as they were by the Left, the police presumably had little time to file reports on Spanish royalists who found a haven in Toulouse in late 1822. Although thousands of refugees gained little sympathy from Toulousain merchants, the Spanish royalist leader Marquis de Mattaflorida received substantial aid from nobles, and used Toulouse as a base for refurbishing his *armée de la foi*. Villèle well knew of such efforts; indeed he arranged a government loan, enabling Spanish royalists to purchase supplies in November, well before war had been declared.

In the short term, Villèle managed the war to maximum benefit. Prior to the invasion Chateaubriand aligned with Villèle and, after they had been confronted by the extremism of Spanish ultraroyalists, the conquering Angoulême and his father Charles also drew closer to the cabinet leader. The ground was thus well prepared for an ultraroyalist electoral alliance.[62]

Bipolar politics reached a peak in the elections of 1824 because state despotism and ultraroyalism had fused. The process was not perfect, in that Villèle never did gain total control over ultraroyalism, but with the domestic spoils of victorious foreign war dancing in their heads, all 'pures'

[60] AN, BB30 235, 11 April 1823; F1C III Seine-Inférieure 16, 9 October 1823; F7 6772, 29 March 1823; ADSM, 1M162, 19 April – 10 May 1823, 1M175, 17 April 1823, and 4M632, 11–18 April 1823.

[61] AN, BB30 236, 25 April, 4–28 May 1822; BB30 245, 16 July, 24 September, 30 November, 14 December 1822 and 29 July 1823; F7 3932, 15–25 July 1822; F7 6686, 18 February and 2 October 1822; F7 6687, 26–31 July, 1 and 24 August, 28 September, and 15 October 1822, and F7 6692, 6 May and 5–23 July 1822.

[62] Fourcassié, *Villèle*, pp. 187–238.

were eager to associate with the cabinet. More importantly, Villèle was also able to capture virtually the entire political Centre, to which Liberals had forfeited any claim. Most telling, however, were the lengths to which the government went, even under such favourable circumstances, to secure the results it wanted.[63]

Liberal decimation in 1824 was almost total. A committee to coordinate efforts nationally was again set up in Paris, but as secretaries such as Charles de Rémusat soon discovered, there was little left of Liberal organization in the provinces. According to the young *doctrinaire*, local activists needed little by way of direction, but public opinion held Liberals in little regard. At Paris, Liberals were reduced to excluding Manuel from the ranks of candidates for the *arrondissements*, which enabled Constant, Casimir Perier and Foy to succeed. When Manuel did run for the departmental college, an ultraroyalist sweep ensued.[64]

If the Seine-Inférieure differed from other departments, it did so mostly in that Liberals fought the good fight; elsewhere Liberals were prone to throw in the towel. Even in the Haut-Rhin, Liberals were reduced to one Deputy. Perhaps, as in the Bas-Rhin, it was more difficult to cheat in the upper reaches of the *cens*; Koechlin won in the departmental college after being defeated at Altkirch by Louis-Antoine de Marchagny, who had prosecuted the four sergeants of La Rochelle![65]

In the Bas-Rhin, Vaulchier had long been preparing. While the more Liberal college of Strasbourg-*ville* had declined from 1822 by thirteen voters, the more conservative college of Saverne had grown by thirty. More important than list massaging, however, was use of the police to disrupt Liberal attempts to organize. Liberal brochures printed in German were seized, and when Schertz travelled to Saverne he found a guard posted outside his hotel and a *gendarme* who prevented him from speaking to voters. Fifty-eight government officials or employees were threatened with loss of employment, and similar pressure was applied to professors, notaries and anyone dependent on government contracts. Conversely, royalists could count on delivery to the college by diligence, lodging booked by the prefect, and a good deal of wining and dining. Before casting his vote, Humann told the college president General Pierre Castex, recently returned from Spain, that the entire electoral process had been vitiated.

[63] See Beck, *Legislators*, pp. 87–90.

[64] See Neely, *Lafayette*, pp. 231–64, and Rémusat, *Mémoires*, II, pp. 104–8.

[65] See H. Wahl, 'Les manifestations de l'opposition libérale et les complots militaires dans le Haut-Rhin sous la Restauration (1820–1824)', *Revue d'Alsace*, 92 (1953), p. 126.

The results were pleasing for Vaulchier. Strasbourg-*ville* returned Humann, but Renouard defeated Saglio at Wissembourg, Baron Louis Wangen de Géroldseck, a Strasbourg landowner, swept Saverne, and Baron Georges du Perreux, a miltary *intendant* and member of the Chevaliers de la Foi, took Sélestat. Better still, while the merchant Frédéric de Turckheim *fils* took one of the seats in the departmental college, the other fell to Castex. Yet prospects were not quite as bleak as they initially looked for Liberals. Compared to the rest of France, two of six seats was a victory, and resentment at the tactics employed by the prefect would provide future opportunities.[66]

By his standards, d'Haussez conducted elections in the Isère in a discreet fashion, and during the campaign he published articles in the *Journal de Grenoble* avowing respect for the Charter. Conspiracy had enabled d'Haussez to take the high ground, asking electors if they wanted the rewards of revolution apparent in Spain and Italy. Liberals had been conspicuously absent from victory celebrations; then again petitions against entry into the war had gained 300 signatures, and Liberals had subscribed to the purchase of a civic crown for Manuel. Ultraroyalists thus swept the elections.[67]

In her analysis of the Côte-d'Or, the historian S. Fizaine concluded that ultraroyalist victory resulted from despotism and not backlash against conspiracy. Under recently installed prefect Joseph d'Arbaud-Jouques, an émigré who had rallied to Napoleon during the Empire but refused to serve during the Hundred Days, purge and intimidation ensured that officials did as directed, and nocturnal student marches then gave cause in April 1823 for the further banning of unauthorized public gatherings, and deployment of troops at Dijon. Police surveillance of Liberals continued, leading to the arrest of three individuals for their part in plans to present Mercier with a medal. As the war with Spain reached its critical stage, cries of 'Long live the emperor!' echoed in both the *chef lieu* and the countryside, leading to a crackdown on *colporteurs*, and sinister predictions led to the suspension of Carion's journal in late November.

Just in case any voters were blind to the official message, troops were deployed at Semur and Beaune for the college assemblies. Liberals abstained en masse at Dijon and Semur; at the latter, a Liberal activist led some 120

[66] BNUS, Ms. 1182; *Courrier du Bas-Rhin*, 26–9 February 1824; Leuilliot, *L'Alsace*, I, pp. 428–45, and Ponteil, *Humann*, pp. 59–64.

[67] AN, F7 3795, 23 December 1823; F7 6718, 6 March – 29 April 1823; ADI, 8M4, electoral college minutes; BMUG, R7906, 21–3 December 1823; *Journal de Grenoble*, 8 August 1822, 5–12 April, 8 May and 30 October 1823, 24 January, 24–6 February and 2 March 1824.

voters in presenting a petition against the voter list, prior to walking out. The only place where Liberals fought was Beaune, where Chauvelin lost by 190 to 177 votes. Liberal abstention then extended into the departmental college and, when the ultraroyalist victor died, was repeated in August 1824. Upon the latter occasion, only 198 of 362 electors cast their vote on the final ballot. What better measure of Villèle's system?[68]

Fizaine was doubtless correct in the main: without despotism there would have been no ultraroyalist sweep of the Côte-d'Or. Yet evidence presented by Fizaine also demonstrates that Liberals worked to their own disadvantage. It was more good luck than wise planning that no attempt was made to raise revolt at Auxonne. Who could blame the authorities if police spies tracked the movements of leading Liberals? How could officials know that the men with whom Hernoux and Gabet continued to consort had now given up on revolution? How much better placed was the general public to make such distinctions?

In the Haute-Garonne the previously moderate *Journal de Toulouse* chose not to question prefectoral notices announcing that while the administration had the right to collect verifications for voters, it could do so for whom it pleased. Reflecting on the assassination of Berry, Vieussieux opined that it had been a consequence of 'detestable doctrines' championed by men who no longer sought revolution overtly, but instead covered their perfidy by spreading 'false alarms'. Happily, the true patriot would not be misled; France would choose the 'organs of its will' and reject the 'apologists of revolution'.[69]

Voters did indeed confirm their royalism, though not entirely in the way Villèle wished. At Villefranche turnout was low, but Villèle gained every vote. Gone were the days when Muret-Saint-Gaudens presented problems; Puymaurin gathered 243 of 247 votes. At Toulouse, however, the troublesome Castelbajac was returned with a vast majority, and in the departmental college a second fly, the Marquis Alexandre de Cambon, entered the ointment. Although he had served with Angoulême's forces in March 1815, Cambon was a moderate royalist. For Liberals, his election was a source of satisfaction and their pleasure would grow when Cambon began to attack Villèle in the Chamber. Otherwise, Liberal performance was dismal.[70]

Ultimately, the electoral landslide of 1824 was a product of three main factors. Administrative despotism and favourable public response to victory in war certainly were important. Nevertheless, the damage that Liberals had

[68] Fizaine, *La vie*, pp. 245–69. [69] *Journal de Toulouse*, 28 January and 6–13 February 1824.
[70] ADHG, 2M24, minutes of the elections of 1824, and Higgs, *Ultraroyalism*, pp. 93–5.

inflicted upon themselves should not be underestimated – revolutionary conspiracy had encouraged voters to accept government direction for want of a credible alternative.

## PART FOUR: THE CHARACTER OF LIBERAL OPPOSITION: 1820–1824

The secret societies that made up the Carbonari were a typically Liberal mix of republicanism, Bonapartism and liberalism. There were, of course, different shadings among the various groups. For example, in the *vente suprême*, students appear to have favoured republicanism, but constitutional monarchy and Bonapartism also had supporters. Thus the best the leadership could agree upon by way of alternative to the Bourbons was a parliamentary regime and a regency government for Napoleon II.

Although the Bonapartist element was doubtless designed to secure support within the army, one should not underestimate its broad appeal. After Napoleon's death in May 1821, even sceptics could see the virtues of tapping into popular Bonapartism, and while the tricolour was a powerful symbol, an embodiment was needed, hence the desperate search for a famous Imperial officer. But behind this was the attraction of Napoleon's name. When the refugees sought to subvert troops at the Bidassoa, they did so as the 'Council of the Regency of Napoleon II'.[71]

Doctrinal ambiguity could also be seen in the symbolism of revolt. Law students were partial to violets (a symbol of Napoleon's return in 1815) at Dijon. Despite the republican or Orleanist sentiments of the main agitators at Grenoble in March 1821, 'Long live the emperor!' was the favoured cry of the crowd. At Strasbourg a placard claimed that all of Italy had 'planted the flag of liberty' and concluded: 'Long live the constitution of 1791! Long live French soldiers! Long live the national colours.' Although law students donned republican *bonnets rouges*, in May 1823 Strasbourg authorities had to deal with a man who arrived from Nancy with a tricolour bouquet that included the Bonapartist violet.[72]

Some historians have described the Carbonari as middle-class and, hence, socially conservative because their strategy pivoted on military revolt rather

[71] Spitzer, *Old Hatreds*, pp. 273–80; Duvergier de Hauranne, *Histoire*, VI, 396–9; Guillon, *Complots*, pp. 251–91; Thureau-Dangin, *Le parti*, pp. 140–51, and Alexander, *Napoleon*, pp. 42–5, 150–7.

[72] AN, BB30 260, 7 April 1821; BB30 240, 25 February, 4–6 March and 21 May 1823; F7 9693, 17 December 1820, 23 January – 15 February, 27–8 March, 1–15 April 1821; BN, NAF 20036, 20 March – 27 April 1821; ADBR, 3M19, 27 November 1820 and 22 February 1821; BMUG, interrogations in R4737 and R7906; Leuilliot, *L'Alsace*, I, pp. 398–9, and Fizaine, *La vie*, p. 221.

than mass insurrection. The 'middle-class' description perhaps fits if we give it a very broad definition, as did contemporaries, but the Carbonari certainly were not simply 'bourgeois', and recruitment reached well below the level of the *cens*. Wage-earners and peasants do not appear to have played much of a role, but the Chevaliers de la Liberté, who spread from their original western base to departments such as the Côte-d'Or, followed the federative example of mixing middle-class leadership with a rank and file which included artisans, shopkeepers, commercial clerks and retired soldiers.[73]

The strategy of military revolt was based on the plausible appraisal of what was most likely to succeed. Spain provided the obvious model of military intervention, transforming despotism into a constitutional regime, but the Hundred Days also served as an example of revolution wherein the role of the military had been crucial, but there had also been national rallying and a parliamentary regime had resulted. Prosper Duvergier de Hauranne presumed that reliance on the generals would have led to military dictatorship, but Carbonari leaders such as Lafayette expected that an initial military action would be followed by popular insurrection.[74]

Few Restoration Liberals viewed the army as separate from civilian society. Pierre Aubrée, crucial in the formation of the Breton federation and its reconstitution as the Chevaliers, was a retired military officer, but he tended towards republicanism and was committed to constitutional government. Many Deputies, including Foy and Lafayette, were proud of their years of service, which they associated with defence of the *patrie* and the 'new France'. It was a great disappointment to Liberals to learn that the army would crush Spanish *constitutionnels*, and for a brief time they revealed their disillusionment. Nevertheless, thereafter they rapidly again positioned themselves as champions of the army.[75]

If appeal to the army constituted the most plausible option, it still misfired badly. Most officers and soldiers were no more inclined than civilians to involve themselves in harebrained plots. Nor did circumstance seem to warrant extreme action; France was not Spain, where genuine absolutism reigned, but the crown could seldom pay its troops. Moreover, the Saint-Cyr Law had reduced resentment. Problems remained regarding the organization of the reserve and General Latour-Maubourg's corruption of

[73] See Thureau-Dangin, *Le parti*, pp. 112–19; Spitzer, *Old Hatreds*, pp. 281–93; Fizaine, *La vie*, pp. 219–23; Wahl, 'Les manifestations', pp. 108–9, and Neely, *Lafayette*, pp. 168–9.

[74] Duvergier de Hauranne, *Histoire*, VI, 21–4; Neely, *Lafayette*, pp. 153 and 168, and Harpaz, *Constant et Goyet*, pp. 602–5, 698–700.

[75] Alexander, *Bonapartism*, pp. 271–2.

promotion in favour of inept but politically desirable officers. The latter policy was perhaps not quite so short-sighted, however, given that it went hand in hand with the removal of disloyal elements. At any event, Carbonari efforts to recruit high-profile officers were a resounding failure.[76]

What most characterized the Carbonari was the cosmopolitan nature of contemporary patriotism, a feature shared by the Liberal Opposition generally. Liberals were fired by the notion of global war for Liberty and there were many points of contact between leading French Liberals and European revolutionaries, Latin American republicans, and the growing problem known as the United States. If Metternich was prone to exaggerate conspiracy, he was not entirely off base about the networks extending from Paris and London.[77]

If we descend from high politics, we can see that cosmopolitanism extended more broadly. Toulousain Liberals did what they could to abet the Spanish *constitutionnels*, Grenoble Carbonari maintained contact with their Italian counterparts, and ties between Strasbourgois Liberals and German fellow travellers were close. From 1815 onwards Napoleon had cultivated an image of European liberal crusader, thereby aligning himself with the Revolutionary sense of mission, and Restoration Liberals saw themselves in much the same light. At times, the historian E. Guillon argues that the Bonapartist element within the Carbonari exalted military *gloire* rather than liberty, but the evidence he presents is unconvincing. Citing General Foy and the other leading officers/Deputies points only to the usual mix of Bonapartism, liberalism and republicanism. After all, when General Berton issued his address at Saumur he called soldiers to the 'standard of liberty'.[78]

Insurrection failed because the public did not judge rebellion as necessary or essentially defensive in character. Duvergier correctly asserted that divisions among Liberals in the Chamber were reflected in the nation generally, and at the local level there was a break between radical and moderate Liberals over conspiracy. When insurrection was triggered at Grenoble, Union members led it, while moderates remained uninvolved. In the Bas-Rhin, radicals Brack, Liechtenberger and Marchand took the illegal path, while the majority followed the legal strategies of Humann, Saglio and Turckheim.[79]

[76] D. Porch, *Army and Revolution, France 1815–1848* (London, 1974), pp. 1–33, and P. Savigear, 'Carbonarism and the French army, 1815–24', *History*, 54 (June 1969), pp. 198–211.

[77] Neely, *Lafayette*, pp. 148–75, 186–210, 231–67, and Spitzer, *Old Hatreds*, pp. 266–72.

[78] Guillon, *Complots*, pp. 56–62, 135–9, 185–6; Thureau-Dangin, *Le parti*, pp. 151–8, and Alexander, *Napoleon*, pp. 52–4, 63–74.

[79] Duvergier de Hauranne, *Histoire*, VI, p. 392, and Ribe, *L'opinion*, pp. 101–26, 306–7, 320–57.

Did social level separate moderates from radicals? The absence of Teissère and the Periers from the radical core in the Isère perhaps indicated reluctance on the part of notables, but against such evidence we must weigh the presence of the radical notables Bérenger, Augustin Blanchet and Renauldon *fils*. Ultimately wealth was less a factor than individual temperament.

Money matters, commercial or financial, often linked members of the Opposition. Among radicals, the Réals shared commercial interests with Bérenger and the Thévenets, and the Duport-Lavillettes did business with Sapey. The Réals were also connected to moderates such as Teissère, and Champollion received loans from the Periers. For that matter, the interests of the Periers brought them into economic relations with the entire political spectrum, although they appear untypical in the political heterogeneity of their liaisons. Economic relations often did form a fairly exclusive political link, but this was for the Opposition generally and did not separate moderates from radicals.[80]

Another point of contact came through education. The influence of Champollion and Berriat-Saint-Prix could be seen in loyalty shown them during the White Terror by former students Renauldon *fils*, Bérenger and Félix Réal. Officials viewed troublesome law students as a natural product of such educators, and ties of friendship were an important product of the educational system. Nevertheless, one must be careful here too: the abbé Antoine-Eugène de Genoude, a leading ultraroyalist journalist tied to Villèle, had been a school chum of Félix Réal.

Shared experience did, however, count for a lot. Bérenger, Rey, Réal, Sapey, Champollion, the Renauldons, the Duport-Lavillettes, Falcon and Perrin had all been punished for the choice they made in the Hundred Days. With ultraroyalism still very much alive and kicking, they were in a hurry to establish institutions capable of securing France from the extreme Right. For a time they were able to carry less radical figures such as Duchesne with them, leaving moderates behind, but when their methods failed, positions were reversed and they fell in line behind the proponents of legal means.

Wealth did not necessarily determine importance among Strasbourg Liberals, although this characteristic probably applied more to radicals than moderates. A subscription list for a banquet organized by radicals in 1820 reveals that 272 individuals were invited; 164 (62.84 per cent) of these men had the vote, and 97 (37.16 per cent) did not. Liberalism was similar at Dijon, where the key signifier was previous participation in the federation

[80] See Bourset, *Casimir*, pp. 58–85.

of 1815. Of twenty-five leading activists, twenty were former *fédérés*, of whom seven could not vote. At a banquet held for Liberal Deputies, about a quarter of the 210 places were occupied by non-voters.[81]

Leading moderates Turckheim, Brackenhoffer and Humann did not attend the Strasbourg banquet, but it is difficult to see any relation between wealth and attendance or non-attendance. Of those who feasted, ninety-three (61.18 per cent) had the vote; of those who did not seventy-one (65.14 per cent) had the vote. Attenders included fifteen *éligibles* who paid more than 1000 francs in taxes annually, and at least another sixteen participants were among the top 200 taxpayers in the department.

Contemporaries often identified Liberal Opposition with middle-class struggle against *ancien régime* elites. Academic debate over the relation between social status and political motivation has largely given way now to cultural analyses, with an implicit rejection of the argument that material interests determine political behaviour. For the Restoration, P. Pilbeam has argued against Marxist interpretation, although social analysis does remain integral to her work. On the whole, she rejects the stereotype that there was a direct connection between Liberalism and the middle classes.[82]

Departure from the narrow focus of historical materialism has enabled a more sophisticated evaluation of political motivation, but there is a danger that rejection of class-based analysis may push investigation to the opposite extreme, losing sight entirely of social and economic factors. If one drops the argument that material concerns were solely determinant, one can argue that Liberalism did have middle-class tendencies, although this was but one aspect of an Opposition in which ideological and cultural considerations also counted for a great deal.

Alsace was the best region for Liberal Opposition in France, and the Bas-Rhin produced a steady stream of Deputies who sat with the Centre-Left or Left of the Chamber. During the Restoration, Strasbourg and its hinterland suffered from commercial collapse as merchants clung to the hope that they could regain Imperial preferential treatment. In March 1817, Magnier-Grandprez pleaded in the Chamber for transit status and Rebeil and Metz joined him one year later, to no avail. Nor were the Deputies able to secure favourable tariff levels at a time when merchants in other regions

[81] Analysis of the Strasbourg banquet is based on BNUS, Ms. 1180, *Banquets . . . aux députés libéraux*, and the voter lists of 1819 in ADBR, 2M13. It is impossible to be certain as to eleven individuals and thus they have been removed from the calculation. On Dijon, see Alexander, *Bonapartism*, pp. 179–80.

[82] See Pilbeam, *1830*, especially pp. 1–12.

were bent on shutting out British textiles. Thus the commercial classes had much cause for discontent.[83]

The importance of commerce could be seen in voting lists. There were only a few large landowners in the department, and many of them were in fact Strasbourg bourgeois. Especially striking was the preponderance of the *arrondissement* of Strasbourg. In a first electoral list in 1819 it provided 483 voters; the three others combined amounted to only 213. Subsequent revision saw the *arrondissement* of Strasbourg add 102 voters, while the other three added only eight, bringing the respective totals to 585 and 221.

Within the electorate of the *arrondissement* of Strasbourg, middle-class domination was obvious. Alongside seventy-seven wholesale merchants were sixty-one merchants of a more middling order. Eighteen hotel owners could also be classed among the urban bourgeoisie. Thirty-three individuals were drawn from the liberal professions, although doubtless some of the thirty mayors or *adjoints* and fifty-five proprietors could make similar claims. Among the fifty-five proprietors, many were probably involved in commerce at some point, although fifty-six men listed as farmers probably were not. The other three *arrondissements* were less clearly urban, with higher percentages of landowners. Among the ninety for Sélestat, forty-five derived their income from the land, and this was probably also true of ten listed as government officials. For Saverne, among seventy voters one finds twenty-nine in the strictly landowning categories. For Wissembourg, fifteen of forty-six were in exclusively landowning categories, with six mayors or *adjoints*. All the same, the proportion of large-scale landowners and nobles was relatively small in the department.

Thus there were basic economic reasons why the Bas-Rhin and its *chef lieu* were not generally promising for ultraroyalist candidates. Tendencies did not preclude exceptions, as the results of 1824 demonstrated. Economic factors were not wholly decisive in vote-casting and, for that matter, the blending of material interests and politics occurred more readily in the Bas-Rhin than elsewhere. Yet it said a good deal that in the departmental college, where commerce was at its strongest, Humann could buck both the overwhelming national trend of 1824 and the particular inclination of departmental colleges to opt for right-wing candidates.

Unlike in the Bas-Rhin, ultraroyalism preponderated in the Haute-Garonne. In interpreting local politics, J. Fourcassié concluded that a largely pre-industrial economy meant that the middle class was too weak

[83] AN, F1C III Rhin (Bas-) 15, 9 December 1817; BNUS, Ms. 1176, 25 March and 19 May 1818; *Courrier du Bas-Rhin*, 16 March 1817, 1–15 April 1819, and G. Livet and F. Rapp, eds., *Histoire de Strasbourg* (Toulouse, 1987), pp. 285–90.

Table 3.1. *Voter occupation (Haute-Garonne)*

| Category | Number of voters | Percentage of electorate |
|---|---|---|
| Proprietors | 615 | 42.15 |
| Government and military officials or administrators | 340 | 23.30 |
| Business (commerce, finance or industry) | 299 | 20.49 |
| Liberal professions | 192 | 13.16 |
| Clergy | 13 | 0.89 |

to overcome noble domination. Whether politics can be linked so readily to class remains, however, to be pondered. Towards this end, one can turn to lists of voter preference compiled by the administration beginning in June 1820.[84]

The lists reveal certain points concerning which social groups were most receptive to Liberal Opposition, but one must proceed with caution in deriving conclusions. While the lists do cite '*professions et emplois*', these must be taken as rough indicators only. Almost all citations give us one occupation only, when many individuals could have claimed several. Nevertheless most of the citations are reasonably precise and the lists do provide useful information that can be regarded as suggestive rather than definitive. For the department as a whole, the '*professions et emplois*' of 1,459 voters have been identified. They can be divided into the categories set out in table 3.1. In terms of perceived voting preference, these categories yield the figures set out in table 3.2.

Upon first glance, some of the figures are puzzling, given descriptive accounts of voter preference. These anomalies are, however, largely explained by the imprecision of certain citations. Especially in the *arrondissements* of Villefranche, Muret and Saint-Gaudens, a high proportion of royalist landowners possessing the franchise were appointed mayors, *adjoints* and councillors. Thus the proportion of royalist proprietors is doubtless underrepresented. Nevertheless, it is apparent that one could not assume that a landowner was automatically royalist; 291 of them were thought to be Liberal. Similar caution should be exercised when pondering the 'business' category. Clearly, many such individuals were royalist and here too we can note that at least some royalist merchants went into the 'government'

[84] See Fourcassié, *Toulouse*, pp. 112–26. The following calculations are derived from the lists in AN, F1C III Garonne (Haute-) 6, *Travail demandé*.

Table 3.2. *Occupational voting (Haute-Garonne)*

| Category | Royalist voters | Liberal voters |
|---|---|---|
| Proprietors | 324 (52.68%) | 291 (47.32%) |
| Government and military officials or administrators | 259 (76.18%) | 81 (23.82%) |
| Business (commerce, finance or industry) | 126 (42.14%) | 173 (57.86%) |
| Liberal professions | 117 (60.94%) | 75 (39.06%) |
| Clergy | 12 (92.31%) | 1 (7.69%) |

category. When all is said and done, however, the outstanding point is that the one group perceived to be Liberal in majority was that of business.

Descriptive reports also pointed to the liberal professions as particularly receptive to the Opposition, but the figures belie this. Several points can be made here. Members of the professions attracted particular attention, either because their positions had a public quality (lawyers, judges and educators) or because they were thought to exercise an exceptional degree of influence (doctors of medicine and especially notaries) over their clientele. For these reasons, officials perhaps over-reacted to examples of Opposition among this group. Many members of the liberal professions did not, however, have the vote, but were thought to be influential. It is tempting to suspect that such individuals were more inclined to Liberalism than those who held the vote, especially when one considers the problems experienced with the law and medical schools. Such thoughts may also have given rise to misperceptions about the present, if not the future.

An 'Observations' column in the lists also reveals which Liberals were thought to be 'influential', and detailed cross-referencing with other sources indicates that the citations were largely accurate. In the forefront throughout the department were wholesale merchants, members of the bar and, especially in the countryside, notaries – another indication of Liberalism's middle-class tendency. Yet there were important exceptions: Malaret, Picot de Lapeyrousse and Tauriac were nobles. Moreover, the fact that Malaret, Picot, Amadée de Tauriac and the solicitor Jacques Malafosse could move in certain royalist circles was probably instrumental in Liberal support given to Cambon in March 1824. This strategy, based largely on resistance to ultraroyalist 'exclusion', would be repeated in the future.[85]

[85] See Higgs, *Ultraroyalism*, pp. 94–5.

Liberals frequently expressed hostility towards formal privilege, and at times their rhetoric could sound like an attack on the nobility as a class. No ground was to be given over equality before the law, and no barriers were to be erected in the pursuit of office. Imagery could also enter the fray: Liberals preferred republican 'simplicity', to royalist ostentatious display. The greatest exemplar of 'republican simplicity' was, however, the Marquis de Lafayette, a reminder that not all nobles fitted the stereotype. Many of the most prominent Liberal Deputies, Voyer d'Argenson, de Corcelles and de Girardin among them, in fact had blue blood coursing through their veins. Thus while Goyet frequently railed against aristocracy, in 1821 he could speak of a Sarthois candidate as a 'noble constitutional aristocrat, zealous friend of the Charter' and a man of 'merit'. The target of Liberal criticism was the part of the nobility that wanted a return to *ancien régime* privilege, not the group as a whole.[86]

Social tensions did spill into the political domain in debates over the franchise. Ultraroyalists, for example, were determined to eliminate what they considered the undue influence of 'middle-class' elements at the lower ends of the *cens*. By such means the power of large-scale landowners, among whom nobles were plentiful, would be enhanced, and thus ultraroyalists viewed inclusion of the *patente* in the *cens* with scepticism because this fell on commerce and industry.

Even a fleeting glance at the differing results of elections held at the *arrondissement* and departmental levels reveals that ultraroyalists knew what they were doing. Matters could vary regionally; in the Aube large-scale landowners joined men of commerce in supporting 'Liberal doctrines', and in the Haut-Rhin the combination of Protestantism and industrialism meant that Liberal influence was deeply engrained in the countryside. Anywhere one looks, the issue of nationalized lands played a major part in the extent of the Opposition; where distribution had become widespread, as in the Drôme, Isère or Côte-d'Or, unfettered ultraroyalism could prove dangerous to its exponents. In departments such as the Sarthe and Mayenne, Liberalism found its base among small or middle-scale landowners. Elsewhere, however, as in Brittany or the Vendée, Liberalism was largely restricted to towns and cities. Nevertheless, for France generally, the rule of thumb that the higher the land-based *cens*, the greater the royalism, held true.[87]

[86] On republican austerity, see Neely, *Lafayette*, pp. 79–81; see also Harpaz, *Constant et Goyet*, p. 681.

[87] Opposition to noble privilege was particularly apparent in reaction to the Barthélemy proposal; see Harpaz, *L'école*, pp. 103–6. For the departments mentioned, see the reports of 1823 in AN, F7 6767–72.

Opposition was generally stronger in urban areas, where a much higher percentage of voters were involved in commerce and industry. This was soon apparent in cities such as Paris, Lyons, Rouen, Brest and Strasbourg, and it would become progressively more manifest in Marseilles and Bordeaux. Contacts between urban metropolis and hinterland could be important, although such contacts should not be related obsessively to economics; religious affiliation or family ties could also provide a fillip to political organization. Furthermore, matters could vary dramatically from *arrondissement* to *arrondissement* and village to village. It was not contact with Le Mans or Mamers that gave owners of nationalized land in the Sarthe their penchant for voting Liberal.

At the end of the day, when their policies and strategies were in line with broad public opinion, Liberals could make inroads virtually anywhere in France. In 1827 the *arrondissements* of Besançon and Baume both yielded Liberal victories in the Doubs. The former was more urban in character, with a higher proportion of merchants and *patente* holders, and yielded a Liberal victory on the first ballot. The latter was largely rural, with a higher percentage of landowners, and gave victory to a Liberal on the third ballot. Similarly, analysis of a voter preference list for the Pas-de-Calais reveals that 55.7 per cent of landowners or farmers were considered Liberal, as compared to 75.2 per cent of manufacturers, merchants or bankers. As Pilbeam concludes: 'Wealth and social position were not the sole determinants of a man's politics', but middle-class elements did tend towards Liberalism.

Analysis thus reveals that the Liberal Opposition defies simplistic categorization. Even the Carbonari was not part of a solely republican tradition. The conspiratorial societies did indicate a fissure in the ranks of Liberalism, but this was over means, not ends, and in doctrinal terms the Carbonari shared the ambiguous mix of republicanism, Bonapartism and liberalism typical of the Opposition. They also wrapped themselves in a mantle of patriotism that envisaged France as a fount of world progress, and this too was typical of Liberalism. In social terms, while the Opposition did have middle-class tendencies, it was by no means exclusively middle-class in its following or its objectives. It claimed to be national and drew support from a broad range of social levels and economic categories. In a country where economic interests divided along regional lines at least as much as social ones, no group with aspirations to represent the nation could afford to tie itself too closely to narrow economic interests.

In its political and social heterogeneity the Liberal Opposition possessed a certain modern character. Battles with ultraroyalism and state despotism forced Liberals to appeal to a diverse range of interests inside and outside the electorate, and this necessitated acting as a mediator among those interests. Hence Liberals searched for broad, common values and avoided potentially divisive clarity. Ability to compromise was crucial to Liberal fortunes and the consequences of insurrection provided a strong reminder of this basic point.

## SILVER LININGS

The departure of insurrection left behind a more astute Opposition. From 1824 onwards, battle would be waged from a defensive posture, and aggression would become associated with royalism. Moreover, a 'first past the post' system had obscured the fact that Liberals still retained a significant base, although at times this was mainly apparent in abstention. What was missing was local organization and here the crucial point was not that government agents had stopped Schertz from going about his work; it was that the administration could adopt such tactics and not suffer significant voter backlash.

Liberals would return to the path pioneered by Goyet, who endlessly preached the message of legal resistance, and became increasingly critical of the provocative speeches of Deputies such as Corcelles. One looks in vain, however, for recognition that Lafayette was legal resistance's worst enemy. Goyet did not take part in conspiracy, but he knew what the general and the local Carbonari were playing at. Goyet finally retired from politics after 1822. While it may be that he at last gave in to persecution, it seems more likely that his departure was attributable to disillusionment with the Liberal Deputies for whom he had fought.[88]

The essence of previous Liberal progress had come from provincials such as the 'Grand Elector'. Goyet, in fact, disliked the epithet because it obscured the role of organization through networks of local associations. He viewed himself as a conduit between the departments and Paris, and here it must be emphasized how much Liberal initiative sprang from local sources. When in 1819 the *Renommé* set about improving Liberal fortunes, it published a long description by Goyet of how to network at the departmental level, and then coordinate nationally. When in 1822 censorship limited the press, Pagès wrote a brochure on organization based on Goyet's writings and advice. Pagès was at the centre of the Parisian Liberal press, just as

[88] See Harpaz, *Constant et Goyet*, 588–93, 602–14, 636–9, 655–9.

Constant was at the centre of every legal organization of Liberal Deputies, but it was Goyet who repeatedly hectored Constant in 1821 to impress on his fellow Deputies the necessity of rejecting conspiracy: 'Those who wish the ends wish the means. I would say to those who have not wanted the means that they have not wanted the ends.'[89]

[89] *Ibid.*, pp. 620–1, 631, 655–69 and 694.

4

# *Back on track: from March 1824 to January 1828*

## PART ONE: PARADISE LOST

Most historians have interpreted the election of the *Chambre retrouvée* in February–March 1824 as a watershed, but the exact nature of this turning point in Restoration politics needs further clarification. Ultraroyalist triumph was due partly to the opportunities presented by Liberal rebellion, and due partly to the deployment of executive despotism. Under Villèle, there was no longer any place for ultraroyalist attack on the centralization of power, because the latter had become crucial to ultraroyalist ascendancy. This fusion of state despotism and ultraroyalism, however, meant that the latter became increasingly dependent upon the control of government. Independent organization at the grassroots level did not entirely disappear, but it was significantly weakened.[1]

Conversely, Liberal Opposition steadily recovered. In part, recovery could be attributed to ultraroyalist overconfidence. Moderate by the standards of the extreme Right, Villèle was nonetheless an ultraroyalist and he put forward a steady stream of legislation that consistently favoured the interests of the former privileged orders. Meanwhile Liberals maintained their posture as representatives of the nation, and they profited as association with patriotism returned to them, while alarm over counter-revolution rose.

In the first session of the new parliament, Villèle tabled two closely related bills. The first proposed indemnification of émigrés whose lands had been confiscated during the Revolution. Indemnification would be funded by a second proposal: conversion on the rates of government bonds from 5 to 3 per cent. The latter measure would have saved the state roughly 28 million francs per year, which could be used for the compensation of émigrés.

[1] For general background, see Bertier de Sauvigny, *Restoration*, pp. 365–404; Jardin and Tudesq, *Restoration*, pp. 47–57, 60–6; Waresquiel and Yvert, *Restauration*, pp. 361–404, and V. Beach; *Charles X of France* (Boulder, 1971), pp. 213–52.

The bills produced a backlash among bondholders, however, and many émigrés were themselves uncomfortable with the prospect of profiting by the losses of small bondholders. Moreover, with an eye towards supplanting Villèle, Chateaubriand encouraged a revolt among the Peers, torpedoing the conversion bill in June. Louis XVIII had put great stock in the bill, and for his treachery Chateaubriand was dismissed from his position as Foreign Minister. The post went to Baron Damas, who left direction to Villèle. The dismissal of Chateaubriand was one of the last significant acts of the ailing king, who was succeeded by Artois as Charles X in September.

Villèle pressed on and in April 1825 secured the passage of an indemnification bill that fixed the total sum owed at 988 million francs, to be paid in 3 per cent bonds. Ultimately 630 million francs would be disbursed to roughly 700,000 claimants. In the long run, the owners of nationalized lands benefited as the value of their properties rose, but the short-term impact of the indemnity was to exacerbate insecurity over nationalized lands generally. Had not most of the lands been taken from the Catholic Church?

Liberals interpreted the indemnification as an attack upon the Revolution, and meanwhile the extreme Right demanded restitution of all 'stolen properties'. Villèle had himself taken the latter position early in the Restoration, and it was easy for Liberals to depict his alleged moderation as a stalking horse for further reactionary plans. Such arguments were then buttressed when the government decided to retire some 250 army officers who had not seen active service since 1823. Almost all of them were Imperial veterans, giving the left the opportunity to attack the government for ingratitude.

The session of 1825 heightened alarm over ties between Church and state already stimulated by the appointment of Frayssinous as Minister of Religious Affairs and Education. The reopening of convents was more significant than the 'Sacrilege Law' of April, but the latter had greater symbolic import because it provided for the death penalty for profanation of sacred vessels. Ultimately, parliament placed so many conditions on the definition of the crime that the law was never actually enforced, but speeches had clearly revealed that many ultraroyalists viewed the state as a vehicle for implementing their version of God's will.

Anticlericalism was further inflamed by the coronation of May 1825, in which Charles prostrated himself before a cardinal. Louis XVIII had not had a coronation and thus had avoided feudal ceremonial replete with religious sanctification of royal rule, but Charles X showed no such discretion. Thereafter, his inclinations were again on display during the Papal Jubilee of February–May 1826 when, along with the rest of the court, Charles fell to his knees before the archbishop of Paris during an expiation ceremony for the death of Louis XVI. That Charles had donned a velvet mourning cloak, while the bishops wore velvet robes, was tailor-made for allegations that the king had fallen under the sway of clerical intrigue.[2]

The following year brought a second embarrassment for the cabinet, when Villèle's *droit d'aînesse* (right of the eldest) bill was defeated in April. The bill was designed to strengthen the nobility by allowing families that paid over 1,000 francs in taxes to give the eldest son a disproportionate amount of family inheritance and entail family estates. In essence, it constituted regression towards primogeniture and was rejected by the Peers as an attack upon the principle of equality in the Civil Code. Not for the last time, Villèle had reason to regret the large number of Peers inherited from the Imperial Senate, or created during the Decazes era.

Each time a bill was retired, public approval was registered by an illumination, leading Villèle to conclude that further measures were necessary to curb expressions of opinion that were obviously influencing the Peers. He laid blame for his setbacks upon the press, and hence Peyronnet proposed the Law of 'Justice and Love' in December 1826. Peyronnet's bill would have increased stamp duties on publishing, imposed preliminary censorship on brochures, and made fines for press infractions sufficient (3,000 francs for the slightest irregularity) to eliminate criticism rapidly. Moreover, ownership of periodicals would have to be declared, so that owners, in addition to editors, could be punished for infractions. Once again the Peers rejected the bill in April 1827 amidst public celebrations.

When members of the Parisian National Guard shouted 'Long live freedom of the press' and 'Down with the Jesuits' in a royal review, the result was dissolution of the Guard in late April. To deal with the recalcitrant Peers, Villèle then persuaded Charles X to nominate seventy-six new ones, and he also decided to call for general elections in November, hoping to shore up an eroding position in the lower house.

As in 1824, the government could hope to ride the wave of a military victory when a combined Franco-Russo-British fleet destroyed the Ottoman navy at Navarino on 20 October, thereby taking a major step towards securing Greek independence. Yet the latter cause was a sword that cut both ways. Liberals had been the first advocates of Greek independence and, indeed, the former Carbonaro Fabvier had led Greek forces in defence of Athens. Nevertheless, royalists were also attracted, seeing in the cause a Christian crusade. For Villèle, involvement reversed the previously neutral

[2] See Kroen, *Politics and Theater*, pp. 116–21, and Waquet, *Les fêtes royales*, pp. 109–19 and 132–3.

foreign policy that he preferred, but he judged it necessary to prevent the Russians and British from dictating a peace settlement that would have taken no account of French interests in the Levant. The chief domestic consequence of philhellenism, however, was to foster a tactical alliance between Liberals and dissident right-wing elements that spelled doom for Villèle's government in November.

For Liberals, divide and rule was the only viable strategy, but this could not be deployed if they remained in isolation due to revolutionary associations. Avowals of loyal opposition therefore became the order of the day, and as ultraroyalist radicalism became manifest, Liberals charged their opponents with revolutionary intent. Ultraroyalist dismissal of national sovereignty could easily be construed as disrespect for the Charter and the institutions based upon it.

Sources of royalist division will be explored in detail shortly, but for now they can be reduced to certain broad lines. Religious controversy, in the form of allegations of Jesuit conspiracy, served Liberal interests by shifting association with covert political organization to the Right. Ultimately more important, however, was that Villèle simply could not control a splendid variety of royalist factions, each with its own demands.

Villèle's methods had brought ultraroyalism to power, but his response to dissent, royalist or Liberal, was to silence it. Hence the period saw repeated trials not just of Liberal journals, but also of the dissident royalist press. In both Chambers a Counter-Opposition of the Right developed as the coalition of 1824 unravelled. To the left of the government (but actually the Centre-Right of the political spectrum) emerged a block nominally led by Chateaubriand and known as the Agier defection. To the right of Villèle could be seen two blocks: theocratic members of the Chevaliers de la Foi led by Ferdinand de Bertier, and the Pointe, a generally hard-line group of parliamentarians led in obstinate but personally ambitious inconsistency by Count François La Bourdonnaye, an extremist mostly known for his bloodlust during the White Terror.

Royalist division provided opportunities for Liberals to form tactical alliances. Liberal complaints during the verification of elections in 1824 gained little, but even at this stage several royalists expressed misgivings over prefectoral influence. Such complaints were an important portent as gradually an increasing number of royalists found that Villèle's government worked against anyone who was critical.

Recovery for the Left also came by way of initiatives aimed at rebuilding public association, especially grassroots organization of support for the war of Greek independence. Along similar lines, reactivation of Liberal networks could also be seen in the national coordination of a subscription campaign in favour of the widow of General Foy in late 1825 and early 1826.

Villèle's position depended on delivering reforms desired by the king, but he found himself repeatedly blocked as dissident ultraroyalists combined in the Chamber of Peers with members appointed during the Decazes and Richelieu cabinets. Rebellion also grew in the Chamber of Deputies, although the lower house always passed the cabinet's bills. What was essential, however, was that opposition to Villèle fused in an attack on executive despotism. Two crucial steps in this process came simultaneously during the parliamentary session of 1827. The first lay in rejection of the Peyronnet press law, which would have transferred press trials from the royal courts to a body largely controlled by the executive. The second occurred when the two Chambers combined to rewrite a government proposal to reform jury and voter lists and transferred adjudication of claims against prefectoral decisions, when they involved political rights, from the Council of State to the *cours royales*. Backlash against the executive was also apparent in new rules regulating prefectoral preparation of the lists.

The reforms of May 1827 greatly facilitated the work of two associations formed to combat administrative cheating in the summer of 1827. The first of these, the 'Society of Friends of the Free Press' was drawn partly from the Left and partly from the Counter-Opposition of the Right, principally the Agier defection. The second, the Aide-toi le Ciel t'aidera (God helps those who help themselves) society, was wholly Liberal. While the contribution of the 'Friends' lay mostly in brochure writing, the Aide-toi tapped into the old network of local Liberal committees, who saw to the actual registration of voters. Liberal success in November 1827 was not solely attributable to such efforts, but an increase in the electorate from 70,000 to 89,000 played a part.

The election of 1827 ushered in what can be interpreted as the final phase of the Restoration, and for that reason it has received a fair measure of attention. Too often, however, conclusions have been drawn without paying adequate attention to the Decazes era. Contrast with the elections of 1824 is insufficient, because in 1824 politics had been polarized by Liberal insurrection. By 1827 a more complex dynamic was at play. Villèle led a *ministériel* party that enjoyed the usual support of the administration, but opposition came from two fronts: Liberals and the Counter-Opposition of the Right.

Despite the obvious ideological differences among them, the various Opposition groups formed an electoral coalition and adorned themselves with the title *constitutionnels.* The term itself has given rise to a certain amount of confusion among historians who have assumed that it was tantamount to Liberal. In most cases it was, but certainly not in all. Crucial to the outcome of electoral campaigning was that the grip of administrative despotism was considerably weakened. Liberals could claim some credit for this, in that for three years they had reverted to the themes of legal liberty developed in the Decazes era, but the Agier defection also played a vital role by encouraging the judges of the *cours royales* to force prefects to abide by the law in voter list formation.

Registration success would not have mattered had the electorate been unwilling to break free of administrative control, but in this regard coalition provided further benefits for the Left. Because royalist members of the Counter-Opposition joined with Liberals, the administration tempered its zeal for practices such as violation of secrecy of the ballot. Moreover, by entering into coalition with Liberals, the Counter-Opposition effectively legitimised the Left as a viable option for moderates.

Liberals always had been the chief beneficiaries of an electorate willing to vote according to its own lights, rather than the wishes of the cabinet. Better yet, Liberal organization at the local level was vastly superior to that of the Counter-Opposition of the Right and a major challenge to an administration hampered by the rule of law. Thus Liberals recaptured the advantage in local organization, although it would take time to undo years of fraud. The results of November spoke for themselves: Liberals and *ministériels* held roughly 180 seats each, while the remainder were divided in roughly equal numbers between the Agier defection and the extreme Right. Matters were in flux because the balance of power was obscured by fragmentation within the Chamber, but by January 1828 France had a new government.

## PART TWO: THE ERRORS OF ULTRAROYALISM

Liberal fortunes touched bottom as the *Chambre retrouvée* began verification procedures. That a certain grassroots base remained could be seen in petitions attacking administrative malpractice in the previous elections. From Dijon came a protest of 150 voters, but to Girardin's demand for an enquiry, an ultraroyalist Deputy responded that voter lists were the purview solely of the administration. Casimir Perier replied that by allowing free voting to be replaced by cabinet direction, the Chamber was submitting to a system that threatened its own independence. Such arguments were of little avail; with a single exception, the ultraroyalist majority voted the order of the day on each petition.

The exception was the crown prosecutor general of the Creuse, who confirmed Liberal charges where his department was concerned. In the short term this was a small matter, but it did point to a certain uneasiness to which Liberals could appeal. Once the session had begun, Foy and Royer-Collard returned to the issue of fraud, with the latter proposing that control over the lists should be transferred to 'independent magistrates'. Even at this stage tactical alliances had begun over certain bills, and the appeal to break administrative control began to make its way. By the summer, La Bourdonnaye was accusing the cabinet of using the *fonds secrets* (for police operations) for electoral corruption, and he linked this practice to Villèle's desire for 'slavery' – a term he repeated seven times amidst tumult. All the same, few ultraroyalists agreed with Girardin that the speech should be published.[3]

The position of the government appeared unassailable, especially after passage of the Seven-Year Law extended the duration of the current Chamber and eliminated annual renewal. Liberals vowed they would not sit for more than five years, and some of the emergent Counter-Opposition of the Right joined in voting against the proposal. More revealing, however, was that Villèle could easily pass a measure that clearly altered the Charter. Gone was the sound and fury of 1820, as discussion moved on to which articles of the Charter were fundamental, and which were simply 'regulatory'. Nevertheless, one wonders whether this law was not a political error, given that it removed an argument for caution among the majority. Immediately after passage, a former Villèlist Deputy proposed yet another bill to force Deputies to submit to re-election should they be appointed to government service. The motion was defeated, but this indication of interest in parliamentary independence on the Right was an ominous sign of things to come.[4]

Prior to each session, Villèle was presented with a list of proposals that the king wanted passed. Given Charles was himself the leading ultraroyalist, this did not bode well for the gradualist approach favoured by Villèle. Worse still, Charles and several ultraroyalists, including Sosthènes de La Rochefoucauld, had visions of shifting legislative prerogative from parliament to the Council of State. Such intent could be discerned in commissioning the redecoration of the chambers of the Council of State, recently moved to the Louvre, in 1825–7. The message of the commissions was that

[3] Duvergier de Hauranne, *Histoire*, VII, pp. 537–42, VIII, pp. 1–25, 50–4.

[4] J. Crauffon, *La Chambre des Députés sous la Restauration, son recrutement et son organisation* (Paris, 1908), pp. 105–32, and Girard, 'La réélection', p. 232.

the sovereign lawmaker was the king himself, and frequent depictions of Moses suggested strongly that the origins of royal sovereignty were divine.

For Villèle, such projects were dangerous because they risked reopening the question of where ultimate sovereignty truly resided. Unlike utopian ultraroyalist theorists such as Viscount Louis de Bonald, a keen advocate of restoring lands appropriated from the Church during the Revolution, Villèle was well aware of the potential consequences of simply shunting aside the political role of the public in such an abrupt fashion. Moreover, Villèle's strongest suit lay in his ability to manipulate elections; this would no longer be significant if the constitutional role of parliament was seriously downgraded. The path he took still consisted of state despotism, but it was subtler in that it followed the Napoleonic formula of at least appearing to consult opinion through maintenance of an allegedly freely elected body of legislators.

A closely related problem was that the king was fond of figures, Bertier and Polignac among them, who were more 'pure' than Villèle. Royal favour, or the hope of gaining it, encouraged the fissiparous qualities of ultraroyalism. While Villèle had managed to cobble together an ultraroyalist electoral *union sacrée* in 1824, the very success of that coalition carried the seeds of its downfall. There was much blind ambition at play, but more destructive were ideological zealotry and a fierce independence that made discipline virtually impossible.[5]

Villèle led the main ultraroyalist block, with aid from Corbière, Peyronnet and Frayssinous. This was the *ministériel* party, united by patronage, clan loyalty, and recognition of Villèle's accomplishments. After February, Villèle could count on better than 200 supporters in the Chamber, but he also had to worry about Deputies migrating to other ultraroyalist camps.[6]

An important division could be seen in the Chevaliers de la Foi. Liberal resort to insurrection in 1820 had reinvigorated the Chevaliers, although their local base had shifted towards religious institutions, as the National Guard became a Liberal bastion. Villèle enjoyed the support of the majority of Chevaliers and this was crucial, given that there were roughly 120 Chevaliers in the Chamber of Deputies. Yet one wonders whether Villèle was not the death of the Chevaliers. Certainly his relations with founders

[5] D. Wisner, 'Law, legislative politics and royal patronage in the Bourbon Restoration: the commission to decorate the *conseil d'état* chambers, 1825–1827', *French History*, 12, n. 2 (1998), pp. 149–71, and J. Ribner, *Broken Tablets. The Cult of the Law in French Art from David to Delacroix* (Berkeley and Oxford, 1993), pp. 50–69.

[6] Vaulabelle, *Histoire*, v, pp. 325–8, vi, pp. 186–227, 230–47, 272–8, vii, pp. 24–72.

such as Bertier, Montmorency and Polignac were frayed, especially after he forced Montmorency out of the cabinet prior to the invasion of Spain, and then sacked Bertier from the Council of State in the summer of 1824. Personal rivalries were thus involved, but differences also stemmed from the theocratic tendencies of the founders. Villèle was willing to enhance the social influence of the Catholic Church, but his penchant for despotism was royal, not clerical, and his relations with theocratic writers such as Bonald and Lammenais could be venomous.[7]

Worse still, Villèle's methods were essentially those of Decazes – using the state apparatus as a political party. Villèle rapidly jettisoned notions of decentralization of power, whereas Bertier and Montmorency had built the Chevaliers upon opposition to the centralized state. Villèle had brought ultraroyalism to power, and hence most 'pures' were willing to follow him, but his strategies sapped any organization (including the Chevaliers) that purported to be independent of state control. Ultimately the relationship between Villèle and the theocratic wing of ultraroyalism was fratricidal: while Villèle accommodated the theocratic Chevaliers at certain points, and thereby gained the hostility of other groups, he could never appease them sufficiently to secure loyal support.

It did not help that Chevaliers appointed to leading administrative positions undermined Villèle's cultivation of a moderate image. Under a new prefect of the Isère, Jules de Calvière, the *Journal de Grenoble* became provocative after the elections of 1824. Calvière was an old émigré who had served in the counter-revolutionary army of the princes of Condé in the 1790s and been elected to the *Chambre introuvable* in 1815. Under his tutelage the *Journal de Grenoble* criticized Liberals for constantly referring to public opinion, and opined that Louis XVI had erred in listening to public appeals when he recalled the *parlements*, when he allied with the Americans in their War of Independence, and especially when he recalled Necker and the Estates General. To consult a people with more imagination than judgement was to open the door to 'irredeemable stupidities'. Equally striking was that in referring to an ultraroyalist pamphlet, the *Journal* agreed that the Chambers and the courts were 'secondary powers' in relation to the royal will. All in all, Calvière and the *Journal* provided fine examples of the ultraroyalist proclivity for forgetting and learning nothing.[8]

At times the theocratic element of the Chevaliers could merge with the ultraroyalist faction known as the Pointe. They shared a desire for rapid advance towards their versions of the *ancien régime*, and determination to

[7] Bertier de Sauvigny, *Le Comte*, pp. 302–420.

[8] See the *Journal de Grenoble*, 23 November 1824.

escape from Villèle's control. Nevertheless, they were uneasy bedfellows, given that La Bourdonnaye was even less attracted to clerical rule than Villèle. La Bourdonnaye's aggression in the Chamber made him a leading figure of the Pointe, but he was consistent only in making life miserable for the cabinet. Ultimately, the primary role of these factions was to destabilize the government. Thus one finds repeated instances of theocratic Chevaliers such as Bertier, or members of the Pointe such as Duke Edouard de Fitz-James (one of the earliest recruits to the Chevaliers), combining with the Left to attack proposed legislation.

The Agier defection was even more troublesome for Villèle. François-Marie Agier and his group had close ties to the judiciary, particularly Antoine-Mathieu Séguier and the *cour royale* of Paris, and they also possessed Chateaubriand as their champion and mouthpiece. Chateaubriand was redoubtable because he carried the *Journal des débats* into opposition, and moved it dramatically to the left. There were perhaps ideological reasons for this progression in that Chateaubriand was a natural champion of freedom of the press. He also liked to pose as a founder of constitutional monarchy based on his writings early in the Restoration. There was a kernel of truth to such claims, but it was mostly for tactical reasons that Liberals at this point chose to overlook the criticisms of *De la monarchie selon la Charte* made by Constant in 1816. Once he had moved into opposition to Villèle, Chateaubriand was lionized by the Left and this alliance was furthered by Chateaubriand's following Lord George Byron's lead in championing Greek independence. Here lay the heart of the matter: Chateaubriand was well situated to bring royalists back from the extremes not just of the Pointe, but also of Villèle. Nothing suited his individualism better than to combat despotism, and prefects soon reported that while the *Constitutionnel* and *Courrier Français* were bad, the *Journal des débats* was worse, but any shift of royalists towards the left was bound to benefit Liberals.

As a leading member, Chateaubriand could also mobilize opposition within the Peers. It was natural enough that Peers appointed prior to the advent of ultraroyalist rule should attempt to moderate aggressive governmental proposals, and the Peers were particularly susceptible to warnings against clerical domination, but it was Chateaubriand who could swing the balance in the upper house by appealing to conservatives.[9]

Part of the problem for the cabinet was that, in accommodating one faction, it was apt to incur the wrath of others. Villèle's attempt to appease

[9] Vaulabelle, *Histoire*, VII, pp. 24–58, 95–131, 204–18, and Duvergier de Hauranne, *Histoire*, VII, pp. 526–95, VIII, pp. 59–71, 174–300, 469–99.

theocratic Chevaliers with the Sacrilege Law more or less ensured the permanent hostility of the Agier defection. Moreover, attempts at accommodation in the lower house were apt to produce troubles in the upper.

The 'defection' of a sizeable portion of the judiciary was largely due to alarm over rising clericalism, but it also resulted partly from resentment at playing second fiddle to the civil administration. Judges were expected to contribute to Villèle's system, but it was the prefects who were in command of implementing policy.

Decazes had employed the same system, and during the 'liberal experiment' Liberals had attacked it by advocating the division of power and judicial independence of the executive. Once insurrection began, however, Liberals had forfeited whatever good will they had thereby gained. Especially corrosive had been the crossfire that developed in trials as crown prosecutors sought to discredit Deputies. Some presiding magistrates had joined in, and Liberals had responded by castigating the judiciary as a political tool. Calls by Constant to put crown prosecutors on trial in the Chamber of Deputies had done little to improve relations, and even Guizot had entered the fray, asking judges to act with integrity – the implication being that they were not doing so.[10]

In pondering the performance of the judiciary in the trials of the Carbonari, one has to wonder whether Liberal criticisms were justified, let alone *politique*. Lawyers could certainly push their attacks on the government to great lengths, and, given the number of acquittals, judges could not have been very effective in imposing on juries. It said a great deal that the Caron affair, where entrapment was involved, was transferred to a military tribunal. On the whole, the trials of the Carbonari appear far less unjust than earlier sad mockeries such as the Fualdès affair. A key figure in the latter had been the Toulousain barrister Romiguières, who also led the defence of the *transfuges* (refugees) of the Bidassoa in 1824. Romiguières focused his attack solely on the executive, and thereby secured remarkably light sentences.[11]

In the trials that dotted the period after 1824, barristers of the Liberal press made a point of appealing to the judiciary as a bastion of enlightenment. They did not always succeed, but results were far better than one might have expected. In the absence of any study, one can only speculate as to what extent judicial attitudes were based on material interest. All the same, one can note that legislation enabling the executive to remove

[10] Duvergier de Hauranne, *Histoire*, VII, pp. 39–50, 72–90, 92–128.

[11] AN, F7 3796, 12 and 22 May, 3 and 19 July 1824; ADHG, 1M75, 26 May 1824, and Spitzer, *Old Hatreds*, pp. 197–200.

mentally or physically 'infirm' judges could be interpreted as a step towards abolishing life tenure entirely; such was the construction Deputies of both the Left and the extreme Right put on the bill prior to its passage in 1824.[12]

One of the most ardent defenders of freedom of the press was, of course, Chateaubriand, and his connection to the Agier defection was much to the advantage of the *Journal des débats* when it was hauled before the *cour royale* of Paris, presided by Séguier. By January 1827 Charles X was so infuriated with the performance of the judges in press trials that he ostentatiously snubbed Séguier and the entire bench during court ceremonies. Central to this growing antagonism was the issue of Church–state relations, but before we turn to religion as a source of division, we should note one other consequence of the 'revolt of the judges'.[13]

A means by which the government sought to prevent public criticism was the *caisse d'amortissement*, which Sosthènes de La Rochefoucauld used to buy shares in Opposition newspapers. Once a majority had been gained and effective ownership secured, the head editor would then be forced to change direction or simply resign. At least seven royalist journals, among them the *Drapeau blanc*, the *Gazette de France* and the *Journal de Paris*, were obtained by such stealthy manoeuvres, and the Liberal journal the *Tablettes* was induced to shut down operations entirely after the indebted owner had decided to sell rather than remain in prison.

This form of creeping despotism was soon denounced in the *Courrier Français*, forcing the agents of the *caisse* to stoop to duplicity and virtual blackmail to secure shares. Moreover, when the *Quotidienne* was targeted as an organ of the extreme Right (and de Bertier), ultraroyalists realized that their ability to express discontent was just as vulnerable as that of Liberals. The *Journal des débats* duly sounded royalist alarm; the *Quotidienne* took the *caisse* to trial, and the affair turned into a scandal as the *cour royale* rendered a verdict highly critical of underhand government tactics.

For Liberals this affair meant that for a time they had allies over the issue of press freedom in the *Journal des débats*, the *Quotidienne* and the *Aristarque*. To acquire the latter, La Bourdonnaye also had to have redress to the courts, and a second judicial verdict again chastised the government, leading to the collapse of the *caisse*. Meanwhile the barrister Mérilhou played on the decision over the *Quotidienne* to laud the independence of the judiciary, which helped secure acquittal of the *Courrier* from state

[12] Vaulabelle, *Histoire*, VII, pp. 61–5.

[13] See Collins, *Government*, pp. 36–52.

prosecution. The Liberal press, of course, applauded the verdict, but so too did the journals of the Counter-Opposition of the Right, and this was a resounding chorus for the judges to listen to in the summer of 1824.[14]

Freedom of the press became closely intertwined with the most contentious of issues: theocracy. At times politics defies ideological, if not rational, analysis – among those brought to trial for press offences was the leading ultramontane, Lammenais, for his attacks on the Gallican Frayssinous. Thus the government found itself in the position of prosecuting Liberal journals for their onslaught on clericalism, while also trying to restrain clericalism's most ardent proponent.[15]

Liberal alarm over clerical influence originated early in the Restoration and there was nothing novel about the issue when it rose to the fore with debate over the Sacrilege Law. Liberal journals, especially the *Constitutionnel*, had long found 'exposing' clerical turpitude popular with their readership. There was an element of gutter journalism involved, but Liberal preoccupation with the clergy also reflected genuine fear of the influence of *père* Jean-Baptiste Rauzan and his followers. Rauzan considered any constitution a 'regicide', and, encouraged by state backing, too many missionaries approached re-Catholicization in the spirit of *reconquista*.

Thus there were good reasons why the term 'Inquisition' became popular after Manuel deployed it in the Chamber. Meanwhile Adolphe Thiers was writing articles in the *Constitutionnel* underlining government support for Spanish fanaticism. Subsequently published as *Les Pyrénées et le Midi de la France*, Thiers' work developed themes reminiscent of Edward Gibbon. In late 1822 Thiers journeyed to Grenoble and Marseilles, where he found a spirit of independence that he linked to commerce and industry. Thereafter, as he travelled towards, and into, Spain, he increasingly emphasized the impact of 'priest-ridden' society – indolence, poverty and crime. Although the priestly caste was not redoubtable on its own, it was powerful by means of a covert influence that was spreading from Spain to France, and was already well established at Toulouse.[16]

If the broad issue of clerical domination was familiar, the form it took had some novelty as Liberals launched an onslaught on what came to be known as 'Jesuit conspiracy'. There are a number of ways to approach this development. One can, for example, note that there were not many Jesuits in France. One can also note that in their fulminations against

[14] Duvergier de Hauranne, *Histoire*, VII, pp. 513–16, 593–606, VIII, pp. 35–48, 87–95.

[15] *Ibid.*, VII, pp. 445–8, 476–9.

[16] A. Thiers, *Les Pyrénées et le Midi de la France, pendant les mois de novembre et décembre 1822* (Paris, 1823).

the 'Congregation', Liberals were often wide of the mark because most congregations were engaged in non-political activities, although charity never was entirely innocent of local politics. A problem with such approaches, however, is that they risk throwing the baby out with the bath water. Catholic institutions played a major part in the organization of ultraroyalism and, in return, ultraroyalist government favoured the interests of the Catholic Church.

There was a remarkable parallel in the way both Left and Right fell back on allegations during their hours of peril. That the public could be receptive was repeatedly demonstrated, and one can conclude that the public had a predisposition towards conspiracy theory, but one should not overlook the substance upon which reaction was based. Jesuits were not the problem; theocracy was. If the public had any doubts about this, all it had to do was refer to the writings of Lammenais. Thereafter it could read the speeches of Bertier or Bonald in the Chambers as it pondered the legislation passed by the *Chambre retrouvée*.[17]

When Liberals referred to 'Jesuitism' they did not have a single Catholic order in mind. Since the revelations of Madier de Montjau in 1820, they had reason to suspect the existence of a powerful secret society and they knew that its connections to the Church were close. If in their charges against the *parti prêtre* Liberals targeted the religious dimensions of this mysterious association, they were not totally off the mark. Ties between Montmorency, Bertier and Polignac and the charitable congregations were close, and the latter two Chevaliers always had the ear of the king. None of which is to say that all religious congregations were Chevalier-inspired. Within the congregations there were clerics who did distinguish between spiritual and temporal struggles, but many did not, and often the same clergymen distinguished by their 'good works' did battle for ultraroyalism at election time.

After their own conspiratorial dabbling, Liberals well knew how little the public cared for secret societies. Moreover, much of their strategy pivoted on assuring the public of their dynastic loyalty, so direct attack on the monarch was to be avoided. Thus they resorted to insinuating that the good king was subject to bad influences. Many such allegations were far-fetched, but innuendo had an advantage in that its imprecision could be used to target anyone suspect, while loosely associating all suspects. Villèle, for example, could be associated with theocratic elements even when he

[17] The mythical aspects of 'Jesuit conspiracy' are analysed in G. Cubitt, *The Jesuit Myth* (Oxford, 1993), pp. 1–104.

was, very loosely, restraining them. Similarly, it did not matter whether Gallicans such as Frayssinous were just as wedded to close Church–state ties as certain ultramontanes; when divisions among these groups arose, they were there to be exploited.

For Liberals, an attack launched by the ultraroyalist Count François de Montloisier on Jesuit conspiracy was a godsend. Much was confused in Montloisier's denunciations, but there was no doubting his royalism. What gave some substance to his allegations was that he took up where Madier had left off – on the track of the Chevaliers. Into this pursuit Montloisier wove the element of Jesuit conspiracy. Jesuits conjured ultramontanism, and therefore Montloisier called in Gallicanism to the rescue. Gallicanism, in turn, had many advocates among judges who considered themselves heirs of *parlementaires* who had fought for the expulsion of the Society of Jesus in the first place.

Montloisier's strategy was to expose intrigue to public scrutiny; thus he not only published brochures and articles in the *Drapeau blanc*, he also carried his case into the courts and then to the Peers. Liberals lionized him because such 'revelations' re-enforced their allusions to dark powers behind the throne. It was also useful that the Jesuits were associated with ultramontanism, which meant that religious controversy could be linked to patriotism. Just as the Carbonari could be portrayed as an international conspiracy, so too could ultramontanism. If such considerations absorbed public attention, so much the better, because memories of Liberal conspiracy would duly fade.

All these threads were interwoven in trials of the *Courrier*, the *Constitutionnel* and the *Journal des débats* in the autumn of 1825. Charges were based on the argument that in attacking the official state religion journalists were undermining the stability of the regime. As usual, Liberal lawyers turned proceedings into a showcase for polemic, but this time they made a point of expressing reverence for king and dynasty. They also appealed to Gallican tradition, to underline their own religious 'sincerity'. It did not hurt that the Society of Jesus was not in fact legally constituted; in other words, if they really were back in France, the Napoleonic Concordat and the expulsion of the 1680s were being ignored.

Trial verdicts were not a complete triumph for the Opposition, but a combination of lenient sentences and complete acquittals constituted a major setback for crown prosecutors in late November. Matters worsened in 1826 when Frayssinous admitted that Jesuits were indeed running seminaries in France. His aim had been to put the issue into perspective: there were not many Jesuits and they went about their educational work as individuals, not as part of an order. Nevertheless, the mere revelation of Jesuit presence was perfectly fitted for sensationalism.

By 1826 at least some ultraroyalists of the Piet salon had decided that if the judges could not be relied on, the Chamber of Deputies should be used to silence critics. Thus the head editor of the Liberal *Journal de Commerce* was brought before the Deputies for having criticized the *droit d'aînesse* as representing private, rather than national, interests. The Liberal lawyer Félix Barthe's defence of the right to criticize the Chamber did not prevent the latter from sentencing the editor to a month of imprisonment, but newspapers of both the Right and Left lashed out at this decision.

That Villèle's position was declining became further evident when the *cour royale* of Paris determined that investigation of Montloisier's charges was beyond its competence, but gave its opinion that Jesuits had no legal right to be in France. Given that this occurred during the jubilee of 1826, marked by countless Catholic processions and the archbishop of Besançon's public launching of the 'Association for propagation of the faith', it was very easy to place an apocalyptic interpretation on Montloisier's allegations. Beneath the smoke there was, however, some fire; the 'Association' was initially presided over by Montmorency and subsequently by Bertier. Nor was it coincidental that it was at this stage that the Chevaliers ceased as an organization; by picking up the trail left by Madier, Montloisier had made continuation risky.

Cabinet response to the 'revolt of the judges' was a series of measures designed to restore control. The first was the Peyronnet Press Law. The bill threatened to cripple both the independent press and the entire publishing industry. For this reason it triggered 252 opposing petitions by booksellers and publishers across the country. Also ominous was that trial of press offences was to be shifted from the courts to a new body selected by the executive. Although judges were to be included, this was a clear warning to the judiciary.[18]

Public attention focused on stormy debates in the Chamber of Deputies. Among those who were opposed were Agier, La Bourdonnaye, Bertier and the Deputies of the Left. More significant trouble in the upper house had already been apparent in January, when the Peers voted to recommend Montloisier's petition for further investigation. Thereafter battle over the

[18] M. Maget-Dedominici, 'La "loi de justice et d'amour" ou la liberté de la presse? Etude d'un mouvement oppositionnel en France (1826–27)', *Schweizerische Zeitschrift für Geschichte*, 40, n. 1 (1990), pp. 1–28, and D. Rader, *The Journalists and the July Revolution in France* (The Hague, 1973), pp. 13–15.

press law was hotly waged, but the result was obviously going to be rejection, so the bill was retired.[19]

Equally significant was the fate of the bill concerning jury and voter lists. The initial proposal was to eliminate from jury duty all men who did not qualify for the *cens*. Those who possessed the vote thus could expect more arduous jury obligations. Government intentions were partly political in that the cabinet thought that jury duty might disincline Liberals from claiming their voting rights, whereas royalists would act more responsibly. There were also technical reasons for altering the jury lists, although the cabinet had been indifferent to such concerns in the past. Whatever the ultimate motivation might have been, the proposal opened a Pandora's box. Because jury members and voter lists were compiled together, alteration in the regulations for one meant alterations for the other.

Chamber amendments significantly reduced the powers of prefects in drawing up the lists. Lists would be compiled according to a specific schedule: the process would begin on 1 August and an initial list must be posted on 15 August; claims of rectification could then be made until 1 September, whereupon the lists would be closed. In the event of an election, rectification would begin upon parliamentary dissolution and continue until five days prior to the convening of the college. Prefects must publish changes every ten days in this period. Lists would be posted in every commune, in an accessible place so that they could actually be read, and every mayor would have a second copy available to anyone upon request. Furthermore, the lists were to be considered permanent, in the sense that prefects could not remove former voters without providing just cause. If the voter decided to contest the prefectoral decision, removal would be suspended until the appeal had been heard. The final change to the government proposal was crucial, although it was in fact merely a confirmation of previous law. By the terms of article 6 of the Lainé Law, appeals against prefectoral decisions were to be judged by the *cours royales* if they concerned political or civil rights, whereas matters related to the *cens* and political domicile were to be judged by the Council of State.[20]

With hindsight we can see that this division of adjudication was momentous, because it had the potential to break the executive's monopoly of the composition of voter lists, but it does not appear that this point had been grasped prior to 1827. The historian S. Kent also overlooked it,

[19] Vaulabelle, *Histoire*, VII, pp. 266–95.

[20] Duvergier de Hauranne, *Histoire*, IX, pp. 139–47, 212–26, and Kent, *1827*, pp. 18–31.

but he did underline that discussion of the lists recharged the Opposition for battle. The *Constitutionnel*, for example, immediately began drawing attention to the possible consequences of the new regulations for the preparation of voter and jury lists in the law of 2 May 1827, and appealed for voter registration drives.

Looking at the legislation alone, however, does not fully explain why events unfolded as they did. In effect, the hazy wording of the legislation left the courts with an opportunity to determine their own purview in judging claims. How did one define what constituted civil or political rights? Liberal lawyers seized on this possibility by appealing to judicial pride in their own competence, and thereafter many courts would take a highly interventionist line in regard to appeals, surprising prefects and ministers alike.[21]

For the first time since 1791, magistrates began to judge decisions made by the administration, admittedly in a restricted field. More as a product of daily political combat than any calculated plan, parliament had moved towards division of powers; the executive, no more able to foretell the future than historians, had allowed this by miscalculation. The bill, after all, could have been withdrawn, although this would have risked even more strident opposition in the next session. The irony was that Liberals would be the first to profit from the new scenario, very much to the disadvantage of the many ultraroyalists who had voted for the amended bill. In combining with Liberals to clip the means by which Villèle had established control, ultraroyalists had unwittingly cut the ground from under ultraroyalist government. Matters now were partly out of the control of the administration, and this made 1827 very different from 1824.

The call for general elections in November has long aroused curiosity. Given the Seven-Year Law, the *Chambre retrouvée* could perhaps have been extended until 1831 and, while opposition was growing in the lower house, the government still held a clear majority. Moreover, resistance in the upper house could have been addressed by creating a large batch of loyalist Peers. The latter did not have to come from the Chamber of Deputies, and this procedure certainly did not necessitate a call for general elections. Why then the fateful decision?

For Villèle, power depended on securing legislation desired by the king, but he was increasingly handcuffed by ultraroyalist dissension. From reports in the provinces, and the results of recent by-elections, Villèle knew that Liberals were recovering and he calculated that limited Liberal success

[21] Kent, *1827*, pp. 18–32.

would shore up ultraroyalist unity. Where Villèle erred lay in underestimating the impact of the new registration laws, but then again even Liberals were astonished when the returns of November 1827 rolled in. Guizot on 18 November forecast a house with eighty Liberals, forty to fifty members of the Counter-Opposition of the Right, and, therefore, a clear *ministériel* majority. Between the elections of the *arrondissements* and departmental colleges, Rémusat did not do much better, predicting ten to twelve more seats for Liberals. Surprise was also in order for members of the Counter-Opposition of the Right.[22]

Liberals had adroitly exploited ultraroyalist divisions that ultimately stemmed from a refusal to accept Villèle's version of despotism. Religious controversy was frequently at the heart of such divisions. Liberals were not overly scrupulous in their allegations of clerical conspiracy, but their claims possessed credibility due to genuine alarm over the theocratic tendencies of certain leading ultraroyalists, state policies that consistently heightened the influence and resources of the Catholic Church, and the seeming inclinations of the king himself. In seeking to put a lid on criticism of his social and religious policies, Villèle only exacerbated tensions within the Right. The Left thus found new allies on the Right and they strengthened such ties through the defence of freedom of expression and appeals to judicial independence. In reaction to the draconian Peyronnet Press Laws, dissident elements in the two Chambers combined to rewrite an apparently innocuous bill on voter and jury lists. In doing so they, in many cases unwittingly, dealt a mortal blow to Villèle's system.

## PART THREE: LIBERAL RESTORATION

Initially treated to derision in the *Chambre retrouvée*, the handful of Liberal Deputies claimed to be the true representatives of public opinion. This assertion was an obvious rhetorical gambit, but it gained force as disenchantment with the government set in. The cabinet enjoyed a remarkably short 'honeymoon' period after the Spanish promenade. Although Ferdinand VII was not as bloodthirsty as his own pack of ultraroyalists, French lobbying for amnesty and some form of constitutional power-sharing was futile. Worse still, Ferdinand soon turned to the Holy Alliance for support. Thus Villèle's government began to look like a pawn of either Iberian fanaticism or the Holy Alliance, and neither reflected well on the French throne.

[22] *Ibid.*, pp. 31–58.

France gained few economic benefits from the intervention, as the British ensured there would be no South American spinoffs. Customs reductions proved elusive as Spain continued its downward economic spiral, and against such meagre returns had to be measured costs. Given the Spanish propensity for anarchy, a large number of French troops had to be maintained on the peninsula for years to come. Meanwhile, financing of the war came under scrutiny: investigations began to uncover the dubious role of the banker Gabriel Ouvrard in supply, and a War Ministry that was either scandalously inept or simply criminal. Villèle was caught in that his government could either stonewall or place blame on Angoulême or the Duke of Bellune, beloved in extreme ultraroyalist quarters. Stonewalling was the order of the day, but its impact was corrosive.[23]

Having sought to block the war, Liberals then lamented decommissioning and demobilization upon every possible occasion. While Casimir Perier criticized expenditure in Spain, he often stepped to the podium warning against decline in army morale and calling for involvement in Greece. Political expedience could descend into inconsistency, but it was effective.[24]

Judging by prefectoral reports, Liberal recovery in the provinces was slow in 1825. The distribution of speeches against the indemnity law was reported at several points in March, but petitions calling on Charles to form a new government as part of his coronation inspired little enthusiasm in May. Nevertheless, a visit by Casimir Perier became a pretext for Liberal rallying in the Isère in July. A cortege of fifteen carriages and students on horseback met the Liberal leader of the Chamber, and in the evening there were serenades for Casimir outside the windows of the Teissère residence. Grenoblois expressed their approval by leaving candles on the window ledge overnight. At Vizille, the public were treated to a fireworks display. Liberal ability to rival the state in the distribution of charity was then demonstrated by donations to local *hospices* and an organization for orphans, and gifts of 200 francs to each worker corporation at Grenoble. Serenades for Foy at Bordeaux, and demonstrations on behalf of Lafayette, fresh from his triumphal tour of America, thus appear to have been part of a broad pattern.[25]

[23] Duvergier de Hauranne, *Histoire*, VIII, pp. 28–33, 147–62, 261–7, 305–31, 362–6, IX, pp. 2–25, and O. Woolf, *Ouvrard* (New York, 1962), pp. 151–85.

[24] Holroyd, 'The Bourbon army', pp. 529–52; Porch, *Army*, pp. 17–44, and Bourset, *Casimir*, pp. 98–104.

[25] See AN, F7, 6770, dossier Mayenne, 23 March 1825; F7 6771, Saône-et-Loire, 25 March 1825; F7 6772, Seine, 26 March 1825, ADI, 5J32, 10 July 1825; BMUG, R7380, 10 July 1825; Bourset, *Casimir*, pp. 109, 136–7, and Duvergier de Hauranne, *Histoire*, VIII, pp. 391–2.

The first clear sign of organizational renewal came with the death of Foy in late November 1825. In the eyes of much of the public, the general was a great patriot. That he left little by way of inheritance to his family did not diminish his stature, and Liberals exploited sympathy through a massive funeral procession in Paris and a national subscription campaign. While perhaps 30,000 attended the funeral, it was the subscription campaign that served to rally the troops. According to Duvergier, the sum of a million francs was raised within six months.

In the Seine-Inférieure, subscriptions were opened at Rouen, Darnétal, Dieppe, Le Havre, Bolbec and Elbeuf. Manufacturers gathered donations among National Guardsmen, and even the clergy felt obliged to hold funeral services in the churches of Saint-Ouen and Saint-Vivien. The latter raised official alarm because Saint-Vivien was located in 'one of the most popular quarters, which holds the greatest number of industrial establishments', but the service proved orderly. When asked in 1827 to chart public opinion, several prefects pointed to the Foy subscription campaign as marking the turning point in the decline of royalism.[26]

With no elections in the offing, other modes of organization became more important. Partly because they had avoided Carbonari association, masonic societies continued at Strasbourg. Royalists were convinced that the lodges were Liberal political associations and such suspicions were only confirmed when in December 1825 the 'Loyal Hearts' lodge conducted funeral commemorations in honour of Foy, and their 'venerable' Stoeber published 'General Foy in Alsace', an account of the tour of 1821 which cast Bourbon rule in an unfavourable light by highlighting state repression.

While Constant attracted attention with a funeral oration published in the Parisian *Courrier*, Frédéric de Turckheim announced a subscription to build a monument to the general. Proceeds from sales of Stoeber's pamphlet were donated to the subscriptions, and the lodge collected funds more generally. Within a week 5,543 francs had been subscribed and, as a portent of their future alliance, Stoeber sent Chateaubriand copies of his brochure, all but one of which were in turn gallantly delivered to Countess Foy. Shortly thereafter, Stoeber began German translations of Chateaubriand's major works.[27]

[26] On the Seine-Inférieure, see AN, F7 6719, 7–15 December 1825. See also, F7 6767, folio Ardèche, 12 January 1826; F7 6768, Doubs, 12 March 1827; F7 6769, Gard, 12 December 1825; F7 6770, Meuse, 4 December 1825; F7 6771, Rhône, 7 December 1825; F7 6772, Var, 14 July 1827, and Vendée, 23 July 1827; Duvergier de Hauranne, *Histoire*, VIII, pp. 414–18, and Ben-Amos, *Funerals*, pp. 89–90.

[27] BCUL, Co 1028, Jouy to Constant, December 1825; BNUS, Ms. 121 121, *Loge des Coeurs fidèles;* letter of Stoeber to Chateaubriand in *La Vie en Alsace*, 7 (July 1934), p. 166, and the *Courrier du Bas-Rhin*, 8–13 December 1825.

Liberal support for the Greeks carried major domestic political benefits. It was a useful way to recover from the disaster of 1823 by demanding an aggressive foreign policy, and it provided a cause for public organization, thereby recharging old networks. It also consolidated the alliance with Chateaubriand and, most importantly of all, it fostered division within royalism.

When the Parisian Philhellenic Committee was created in 1824, it had a mixed political hue, although most royalists came by way of the Agier defection. Nevertheless, Liberals formed the majority of the original twenty, and thereafter the Committee swung increasingly to the Left with the addition of figures such as General Etienne Gérard, Constant and Las Cases, Napoleon's memorialist. The organization was not overtly partisan, but it did give Villèle's leading enemies an opportunity to place themselves in the public spotlight. It was not until July 1827 that the government finally decided to reverse its policy of non-involvement, and even then this appeared a matter of grudgingly following the lead of Russia and Britain. In the meantime, Liberal Deputies had wasted few occasions to castigate official foreign policy, and this could be contrasted to the enormous sums raised by the Committee on behalf of Greece. For the year 1826, subscriptions reached the impressive amount of 1,232,891 francs.

Aiding the Greeks could be viewed as a blow against despotism or as a Christian mission, but one way or another it legitimated revolution. More dangerously, philhellenism enabled Liberals to escape isolation. Prefects could see the danger, but could not prevent royalists from discovering that not all Liberals were evil. In the Seine-Inférieure, enquiries into the 'morality' of philhellenic societies at Elbeuf and Le Havre gained huffy responses that members were 'highly esteemed' royalists.[28]

In April 1826 the fall of Missolonghi produced a wave of sympathy. As well as fêting a French colonel for his service to the Greek army, Strasbourg masons joined in the campaign to support the struggling rebel government by sending their donations to the philhellenic association in Paris. Most Strasbourg donations, however, went to a banker in Geneva to whom Schertz forwarded 5,676 francs between December 1826 and June 1828. Gradually the movement expanded beyond Liberal circles, as the *Courrier du Bas-Rhin* published articles portraying the cause as that of all

[28] AN, F7 6772, folio Var, 3 January 1828; F7 6722, dossier 22, 31 July 1826; ADSM, 1M174, 13 June 1826, and M.-P. Macia-Widemann, 'Le Comité philhellénique et la politique intérieure française (1824–1829)', *Revue de la Société d'Histoire de la Restauration et de la Monarchie Constitutionnelle*, 5 (1991), pp. 27–41.

Christianity, and Protestant pastors and Catholic priests joined in organizing collections at the village level.[29]

Similar connections were made at Toulouse. Prefect Antoine Leclerc de Juigné hesitated when the director of the city theatre asked permission to stage a benefit performance for the Greeks, but he found nothing offensive in the programme and therefore consented. Much to Juigné's satisfaction, Liberals were unable to fill the hall despite giving away tickets, but sympathy for the Greeks did lead to the formation of a local philhellenic society headed most notably by Cambon (a member of the Agier defection) and Malaret (a Liberal). Not long thereafter forty-six volunteers departed Toulouse for Greece.[30]

More national Liberal organization could be seen in April 1826 when the proposed *droit d'aînesse* stimulated a campaign that saw sixty-one petitions against the bill presented to the Chambers. At Rouen Liberal Henry Duhamel organized the city's petition. At Le Havre the chamber of commerce supported the local petition, unlike in 1823 when it had not associated itself with petitions against war with Spain, and, according to the sub-prefect, many who signed were known for their 'devotion' to the throne. At Elbeuf, Mayor Georges-Paul Petou, a manufacturer, reported that satisfaction at the retirement of the bill had been general, but that this was not a product of partisan politics: loyal royalists joined in the 'illumination'. Meanwhile an ultraroyalist Deputy, Baron Auguste-Louis de Saint-Chamans, warned the cabinet that its policies were facilitating Liberal recovery by sowing royalist division. Similar tidings came from prefects, many of whom reported that Liberal concentration on religious controversy was having a major impact on opinion.[31]

Liberals again seized the initiative in mobilization against the Peyronnet Press Laws. Because it was a major publishing centre, response in Strasbourg was especially strong. In January 1827 Turckheim presented the Chamber with a petition from 100 print workers, and followed this with a second from just about everyone else connected to the publishing industry – publishers, booksellers, reading room proprietors, paper manufacturers and bookbinders. While they were couched in economic terms, the petitions contained a political sub-text: Bourbon government was incompetent

[29] BNUS, Ms. 121 121, *Loge des Coeurs fidèles;* Ms. 1535, 10 January – 16 August 1828; *Courrier du Bas-Rhin*, 1–17 January, and 17 August 1828; Leuilliot, *L'Alsace*, I, pp. 454–8, III, pp. 248–60.

[30] AN, F7 6722, 27 June 1826, and Fourcassié, *Toulouse*, p. 163.

[31] AN, F7 6768, folio Côte-d'Or, 1 September 1826; F7 6770, Haute-Marne, 8 April 1826; F7 6771, Rhône, 22 June 1825 – 8 December 1826; ADSM, 1M174, 11 April 1826; 4M2684, 21 February 1825, and 4M116, 23 March 1826.

in economic management because it favoured noble landowners and the Catholic clergy. When the government retired its proposals, 'illuminations' for Deputies Turckheim and Humann were held on the nights of 20 and 21 April, but the crowds that gathered outside the office of the *Journal du Bas-Rhin*, which had supported the Peyronnet proposal, were more impressive. The crowds dispersed without doing material damage, but they had made clear the rising hatred of Jesuits.[32]

In addition to such signs of Liberal recovery, Villèle also had to ponder a series of by-elections in 1827. These had seen victories for Lafayette at Meaux, Bignon at Rouen, Laffitte at Bayonne, André Dupin *aîné* at Mamers and Gabriel Laisné de Villevêque at Orleans. Also worth consideration was the possibility that some previously royalist Deputies might be considering a migration beyond the confines of 'defection'. Petou, mayor of Elbeuf, had been an official candidate in 1824, but by the spring of 1827 he was receiving Liberal serenades.[33]

The cabinet had begun to weigh the merits of a call for general elections early in 1827 and hence circulars were despatched asking prefects to report on public opinion. Very different from the survey of 1822 was a strong sense of stability; no prefect expressed concern about revolt. There was, however, a high degree of anxiety over the press, particularly the divisive impact of the *Journal des débats* and the *Quotidienne* on royalism. From all corners came reports of 'defection', especially over clerical influence. This shift of opinion could reach into the nobility in the Doubs, Ille-et-Vilaine and Bouches-du-Rhône, and could ignite antagonism in the army. Most striking was its impact among the judiciary: prefects cited the magistrates as figures of Opposition in the Moselle, Meurthe, Doubs, Nord, Mayenne, Ille-et-Vilaine, Finistère, Haute-Garonne, Gironde, Vienne, Haut-Rhin, Rhône and Somme.[34]

Passage of the electoral Law of 2 May soon triggered extensive grassroots reactivation. The initial impetus is generally credited to two sources – the Society of Friends of the Press, and the Aide-toi le Ciel t'aidera society. The former remains somewhat mysterious, perhaps because its existence was short and its organizational development small. A report by the Paris prefect of police listed a large number of Deputies, Peers and leading journalists of the two Oppositions as having formed the Society. Much of the report was confused, but it did point in directions largely confirmed by

[32] BCUL, Co 4557, *cahier* of the chamber of commerce; Ponteil, *Humann*, p. 68, and Leuilliot, *L'Alsace*, I, pp. 462–5.

[33] AN, F7 6720, 18 and 24 March 1827, and Kent, *1827*, pp. 36–7.

[34] This information has been culled from the résumés of March–April 1827 in AN, F7 6767.

other sources and we can note that Liberals such as Laffitte, Alexandre Méchin, Constant, Perier and Count Auxonne-Marie de Thiard combined with Counter-Opposition figures such Agier, Baron Jean-Guillaume Hyde de Neuville and Charles Cottu. Also present was a similarly mixed combination of writers of the main Opposition newspapers – Achille de Salvandy, Abel-François Villemain, Etienne and Pagès.

The Aide-toi was formed about a month later, towards the middle of August. The idea appears to have come from the young cadres of the *Globe*, but the Aide-toi from its start had a rather mixed composition of *doctrinaires* such as Rémusat and Louis Guizard and more left-leaning figures such as François Mignet, Nicolas Joubert, Barthe and Odilon Barrot. Shortly thereafter this corps was joined by a band of young proto-republicans – Jules Bastide, Auguste Blanqui, Godefroy Cavaignac, Etienne Cabet and Ulysse Trélat. Guizot accepted presidency of the association and it set up at the offices of the *Globe*.

The 'Society' and the Aide-toi both launched massive brochure campaigns, but it would appear that the former group had the greater impact in this regard. Salvandy, 'friend' of Chateaubriand and contributor to the *Journal des débats*, was especially prolific, attacking the government with a devastating mixture of wit, sarcasm and spite in a series of fifteen brochures. Because they thought royalists were more likely to listen to a Society that included Chateaubriand and Salvandy, the authorities were more worried by the 'Friends' than the Aide-toi. Moreover, the 'Friends' were first in the field, and in greater volume.

The vital contribution of the Aide-toi was to provide a specifically Liberal base to which local committees could write as contacts with some thirty-five departmental committees were established. The Society was not alone, however, in performing this function: the *Constitutionnel*, the *Courrier*, and the *Journal des débats* also supplied information as to registration, and charted progress in the departments on the basis of supplemental lists. By August, the *Constitutionnel* was averaging three articles per week on registration, and had a running column of questions and answers designed to advise barristers on arcane technicalities. Still, several prefects noted that brochures were more suitable for mobilization in the countryside and had more enduring value, and the manuals of the Aide-toi were undoubtedly superior, especially for barristers making rapid reference.

How novel were the activities of 1827? The content of Aide-toi brochures was unoriginal: warnings of the return of the *dîme*, the restoration of seigniorial obligations, and the loss of nationalized lands had begun in 1814. Brochures on registration had commenced in 1817 and had become more sophisticated in 1820 when creation of departmental colleges had encouraged Liberal committees to engage themselves more fully in registration wars. In 1820 and 1824 Liberals had fought not just to register voters, but also to remove unqualified royalists. Liberals were thus well aware of how prefects had corrupted lists prior to 1827, but as the petitions at Grenoble had demonstrated, the electoral regime had left few means for remedy. What was useful about the brochures and newspaper articles of 1827 was that they pointed to the enormous potential of the Law of 2 May.[35]

Coordination at the national level did take a significant step forward in 1827, as the Aide-toi renewed the initiatives begun by the electoral wing of the Amis de la Presse in 1819. The key to success, however, lay in the reactivation of local committees. This explains why it was the Aide-toi that progressed beyond publication: whereas the politically mixed 'Friends' had no grassroots base, the Aide-toi could tap into an older network. If there was anything new about the composition of the registration committees, prefects failed to notice; in fact officials reported that membership was familiar from past organizations.[36]

At Rennes five of the seven departmental committee members had been *fédérés*, including future Deputies Thomas Jollivet and the lawyer Louis Bernard de Rennes, who had led the local Opposition since 1815. At Dijon, the key figure was Hernoux; at Bordeaux Henri Boyer-Fonfrède, hardly a neophyte, took the lead. At Rouen, the barristers Eugène Aroux and Jean-Baptiste Thil, and the merchant-manufacturer Louis Adeline led the registration campaign; they had all acquired experience of such activities long before 1827. In Paris, the prefect of police underlined the continuity that reached back to 1816 – the mechanisms and personnel were basically the same.[37]

Liberals in the Isère threw themselves into the fray as committees at Vienne, Saint-Marcellin and La-Tour-du-Pin fought to alter lists and succeeded in many cases. For the department as a whole, a coordinating committee was established at Grenoble with Teissère and Duchesne presiding. The Grenoble committee was, in turn, in contact with the Parisian society, perhaps through Rémusat, but the advent of the Aide-toi was of limited significance because the methods it employed were long familiar.[38]

[35] Pouthas, *Guizot*, pp. 369–80, and Kent, *1827*, pp. 81–156.

[36] Pouthas, *Guizot*, pp. 369–80; Kent, *1827*, pp. 81–106, and Huard, *La naissance*, pp. 49–50.

[37] AN F7 6769, folio Gironde, 2 July 1827, 19 September 1827; F7 6772, folio Seine, 7 September 1827; F1C III, Seine-Inférieure 5, 1 September 1827, and Alexander, *Bonapartism*, pp. 152–3, 182–3.

[38] ADI, J551, 25 March 1827; BMUG, R90630, 10–18 November 1827.

The impact of Liberal organization was heightened by the fact that it was not met by corresponding enthusiasm among royalists. On the one hand, ultraroyalist leadership had previously come from the administration, but the latter was aggressively attacked and, for a time, neutralized, by the 'Friends'. The call of the latter was for voter 'independence', and hence ultraroyalists responded poorly to initial prefectoral efforts to mobilize registration. On the other hand, the Counter-Opposition had little by way of local organization, and prefects reported Liberal registration committees only. Visits by figures such as Cottu, a member of the *cour royale* of Paris and a partisan of the Agier defection, to destinations such as Bordeaux, were different from those of leading Liberals. Cottu did not meet with groups of political activists; rather, he dined nightly with magistrates. By such means was the 'revolt of the judges' encouraged.

In the Haute-Garonne, Liberals spent the summer of 1827 launching registration campaigns. By July Juigné had decided to mobilize a counter-offensive, but Liberal organization was more extensive, based on a committee of barristers who travelled in the countryside, soliciting votes and distributing brochures. By the time the final supplementary lists had been published in mid-October, 227 new voters had been added, and 223 former voters had been removed. Nevertheless, the prefectoral council had rejected a significant number of claims, and battle was far from over.[39]

The role of the judiciary became crucial when Villèle called for elections on 5 November and within a fortnight Juigné found himself testifying before the *cour royale* in a series of disputes. The court had first to rule over its own competence, which gave Romiguières occasion to flatter the non-partisan character of the judges. Whether the judicial decision in favour of their own competence was so very disinterested could, however, be questioned. Presiding over the case was Hocquart, who had joined Cambon in the Agier defection, and two of the judges, Noel Solomiac and Baron Joseph Podenas, were part of the Liberal electoral committee! Nevertheless, the court did not uniformly favour Liberal claims. An attempt by crown prosecutor Raimond Bastoulh and Juigné to have the decision over competence removed to the Council of State was blocked by Romiguières, but the judges then proceeded cautiously, restricting themselves to questions of registration procedure. Liberals won the majority of decisions, but time constraints meant that this involved only a handful of cases.[40]

[39] AN, F7 6769, 9 July, 2 August and 4 September 1827, and *Journal de Toulouse*, 16 October 1827.

[40] AN, F7 6769, 7 December 1827, and *Journal de Toulouse*, 15–17 November 1827.

Prefects began urging the reconsideration of judicial fixity of tenure after the implications of the new electoral law became apparent. According to the prefect of the Eure-et-Loire, the rights that the courts attributed to themselves in electoral registration encouraged infringement of administrative authority. 'Independence' broke the unity of power in Restoration government, and should be rectified immediately. When the Rouennais Liberal barrister Thil appealed to the *cour royale* to take a liberal view of its competence in electoral jurisdiction, he criticized the administration for using all possible means to avoid having their acts scrutinized by an 'independent body'. Worse still, the press covered these cases in detail, giving prefects further cause to squirm. At Rouen, a new literary journal, the *Neustrien*, gave the case extensive coverage and thereby gained praise from a Liberal reader because 'the nation' had its eyes on officials who stepped beyond the bounds of the law.

Theories of government are one thing and practice another. Thil lost his case, which meant that a host of claims over dubious decisions by prefect Vanssay went to the Council of State, where they were duly rejected. Certain courts, at Paris, Lyons and Limoges, did take an aggressive position over their rights to judge electoral registration conflicts, but others did not. It thus would take time for the impact of the law of 2 May to come into full effect, but the old system of administrative despotism had suffered a heavy blow.[41]

Assessing the relation of registration to electoral results is not a simple matter. Over the six weeks between publication of the initial and final lists, the electorate rose from 70,000 to 88,000, an increase of roughly one-quarter. The rise was not uniform; it varied by department and doubtless bore relation to the enthusiasm of local committees. Here, however, we must keep in mind that committees also occupied themselves with removing unqualified royalists. At Epinal the prefect found himself confronted by Liberal demands for the removal of fifty royalists; he agreed to twenty-one and would subsequently regret not having removed the rest.

Assessment is further complicated by the fact that prefects launched their own registration drives. Response was limited during the summer, but it does appear that in certain departments there was significant rallying during the campaign. Moreover, some royalists drew back from Opposition when they heard of Liberal triumphs in adjacent departments, and this retreat became even more pronounced when the departmental colleges met.

[41] AN, F1C III Seine-Inférieure 5, 30 October – 17 December 1827; F7 6769, folio Eure-et-Loire, 6 October 1827, Gironde, 16–31 August 1827; 6772, Var, 1 September 1827 and Vendée, 23 July 1827, and *Neustrien*, 12–20 November 1827.

All the same, we should not race to the opposite conclusion. Even where prefects waged successful registration battles, they uniformly recognized that Liberals had dramatically improved their positions.

The electorate had decreased from roughly 110,000 in 1820 to 102,000 in 1822, to 99,000 in 1824, to 70,000 on 15 August 1827. The official explanation was that numbers had diminished due to reductions in direct taxes. The recovery of the electorate to 95,000 by October 1829 was, however, unaccompanied by tax increase. Nor did increase reflect economic growth; France had lurched into economic depression in 1825. In truth, the decline of the electorate had resulted from fraud.[42]

Registration committees did not win all battles. At Niort resentment against prefect Léonard de Roussy de Sales had been stimulated in 1824 by the removal of 263 voters, including the incumbent Deputy. Liberals had lodged protests, but the impossibility of overcoming fraud had been made apparent by the subsequent appointment of the prefect to the Council of State. By 1827 the son of the former Deputy had formed a registration committee that presented claims on behalf of prospective voters and queried the inscription of royalists. The prefect, however, ignored claims made by third parties, and recourse to the crown prosecutor merely led to charges being sent to the Council of State. In this case, registration failures did not matter much, as the Liberal Maughin won at Niort, while Agier triumphed at Parthenay.[43]

A. Spitzer has found that changing results in the Doubs cannot be attributed solely to alterations in the electorate, although slight shifts could mean a great deal. Given the narrow Liberal victory at Baume, new voters were probably crucial in swinging the balance, but by far the majority of Opposition votes came from individuals who had supported ultraroyalism in 1824. So a shift in general public opinion was the primary factor, a point re-enforced by an increase in voter turnout – this time there was enthusiasm on the part of the Opposition. Both leading ultraroyalist candidates suffered from the backlash against the Forest Code of May 1827, and the fact that a petition from the print industry against the Peyronnet Press Law had had to be presented by Casimir Perier. On the Opposition side, victory at Besançon fell to a Liberal barrister who had entered into a 'public alliance' with a moderate royalist, enabling the latter to gain election subsequently in the departmental college. By such means moderate Liberals were able to cut out two extreme ultraroyalists, and part of this agreement involved no

42 See Kent, *1827*, pp. 58–62.

43 R., Charbonneau, 'Les élections de 1827 dans les Deux-Sèvres', *Bulletin de la Société Historique et Scientifique des Deux-Sèvres*, 51, n. 10 (1956), pp. 234–9.

'illuminations' at Besançon between the colleges of the *arrondissements* and the department.[44]

Elsewhere, change in the composition of the electorate was greater and probably more significant. Ultimately one could conduct such investigations in every college and still be left with a measure of uncertainty, because one cannot know how individuals actually voted. Shifting opinion and registration were both important, but certainly Opposition success would have been greatly reduced had the electorate remained as constituted in the initial lists of 15 August.

During the summer Liberals had engaged in registration wars as though they were in the midst of a campaign, and they were encouraged to do so by Liberal luminaries who fanned out into the countryside. Constant devoted a journey covering the Bas-Rhin, the Haut-Rhin and Saône-et-Loire to co-ordinating Liberal efforts, and in the Saône-et-Loire, Constant, Thiard and Maughin conferred with local activists over which candidates would contest which colleges. At Bar-le-Duc, Etienne was already campaigning in early September, joining his local supporters. In the Ardèche, Chauvelin consulted with local Liberals in August, after which the prefect could predict that Madier de Montjau would contest the college at Privas, and François Boissy d'Anglas that of Tournon. In the Auvergne, the Lafayettes encouraged Liberal enthusiasm, with George travelling to Brioude to meet with Liberals of the Haute-Loire. Dupin travelled in the Massif Central, whereas Ternaux was to be found in the Haute-Vienne.

In Normandy, rallying the troops fell to Dupont de l'Eure and Baron Bignon. Matters commenced in early September with a banquet at Elbeuf where Petou made his conversion public. There followed feasting at Rouen, attended by the same three figures and some 200 Liberals. Unlike in the past, there were no demonstrations, and serenades were discouraged. In the following week, Duke Victor de Broglie, a *doctrinaire* Peer, joined Dupont, Bignon and 215 Liberals from all points of the department of the Eure for a banquet close to Bernay.[45]

Thus Liberal committees were purring, and once the campaign officially began another feature became apparent. Given the destruction of electoral prospects in the early 1820s, one might have expected rupture between moderates and radicals. If anything, however, the two wings drew closer. There was a significant exception at Strasbourg, which will be discussed

44 Spitzer, 'The elections', 153–75, and C. Weiss, *Journal, 1823–1833* (Besançon, 1981), pp. 99–109.

45 AN, F7 6767, folio Ardèche, 1 September 1827; F7 6769, Eure, 12 September 1827; F7 6770, Haute-Loire, 18 August 1827, Meuse, 9 September 1827; F7 6771, Haut-Rhin, 7 September 1827, Saône-et-Loire, 31 October 1827, and F7 6701, reports of 29 August – 7 September 1827.

later, but more the norm when radical and moderate Liberals could not agree was the transaction. Such had been the case in a by-election at Vervins in April 1826, where Count Horace Sébastiani, an Imperial general, gained the supporters of Laffitte on the second ballot, thus ensuring victory.

When it came to registration, moderates and radicals combined. In part this resulted from the radical recognition that they had erred; hence pursuit of liberty through legal means proved rigorous. Corcelles at Lyons followed the lead set by Augustin Perier, and Liberals in the Rhône made a point of reassuring royalists that they had no revolutionary intentions. At the personal level, reconciliation also appears to have been typical. Casimir Perier, no friend of revolt in the early 1820s, thereafter struck up amicable relations with Champollion *le jeune* and, during his tour of the Isère in 1825 decided to employ Jean-Baptiste Froussard as tutor for his children. Neither Champollion nor Froussard could be considered moderates.[46]

Liberals also demonstrated unity in supporting candidates thought to have the widest voting appeal. In the Isère, this amounted to backing Augustin Perier in three *arrondissements*, and the judge Michoud in the fourth. For a time Duchesne and Sapey showed an inclination to run, but after warnings from Augustin Blanchet they retired from the field. The triple candidature of Perier pointed to the development of a degree of party discipline that could supersede local attachments. Moreover, the fact that three *arrondissements* had the same candidate meant that Perier's chief agents coordinated their efforts closely with Liberals throughout the department and thus became a nexus. The Perier team was also in contact with supporters of Jean Michoud, and thus the fourth college.[47]

Liberals were also becoming sophisticated in canvassing. Prior to the assembly at Tullins (for the college of Saint-Marcellin), Liberals led by a notary had taken a poll of voters by canton. Knowing how close the contest was, a group of Liberals purposely misled the administration as to their voting intentions. Thus misguided, the sub-prefect did not exert sufficient pressure on royalists and eleven qualified electors failed to attend the college. Furthermore, the notary had also collected information as to whether support for Perier was based on his personal qualities or loyalty to the Opposition. This 'survey' indicated that if Perier opted for some other seat after victory, it would be unlikely that a subsequent election would produce an Opposition Deputy. There was some casuistry in the argument, motivated by desire to have a Perier as a representative, but the

[46] AN F7 6771, dossier Rhône, 8 December 1827; Duvergier de Hauranne, *Histoire*, VIII, pp. 431–8, IX, 276–7, and Bourset, *Casimir*, pp. 136–7, 146 and 164.

[47] BMUG, N2442, 18–21 November 1827, and N1730, 13–14 November 1827.

fact that the notary could present numbers to substantiate it illustrated a remarkable degree of preparation.[48]

Desire to defeat Villèle could carry over into electoral pacts with members of the Agier defection and, in certain cases, members of the Pointe. Deputies and journalists in Paris took the first steps towards a national alliance strategy, and by 9 November combined initial lists of some 286 candidates had been published in the *Journal des débats*, the *Courrier* and the *Constitutionnel*. Nevertheless, there could be no specific orders given to local committees as to whom to support. The Deputies and journalists in Paris tried to take the departmental council into consideration when composing the initial lists, and the summer registration campaign had given a fair indication of the leading local exponents of Opposition. In fact, many candidates had been determined by late August. Moreover, the initial lists left room for local committees to recommend 164 candidates, who were added to the lists by 21 November. Even so, it would appear that the main effect of the Parisian initiative was to give a boost to the strategy of coalition, rather than to specify candidates.

Coalition took a variety of forms, and in many departments there was no alliance because the Left did not need one. Where Liberals and the Counter-Opposition both had strong candidates, recourse could be made to transaction. In certain departments there was, however, full alliance wherein royalists would support one Liberal candidate in return for Liberals performing the same service for a candidate of the Right.

At Toulouse, the combination of Cambon and Malaret in the philhellenic society reflected increasingly close ties in parliament between Liberals and the Agier defection. The alliance was first broadcast in the *Journal des débats*, in the form of support for the Liberals Joseph Viguerie, a merchant-banker, and Romiguières, and the Agier defection's Alexandre de Cambon and his brother the Marquis Auguste de Cambon. The Parisian initiative was then adjusted to suit local realities and it was the *Journal de Toulouse* that announced the actual Opposition slate: Hocquart, Joseph Cassaing and the Cambons. That coordination was thorough could be seen in the parallel announcement of 'alliance' slates for election to college bureaux.[49]

Ultraroyalist errors had played an important part in Liberal recovery, but one should not underestimate the positive steps that the Left had taken between 1824 and 1827. In essence, Liberals had regained the ground lost after 1820. The death of Foy had provided a first opportunity to re-establish

48 AN, F1C III Isère 4, minutes of the electoral college at Tullins, 16 November 1827, and BMUG, R90630, 26 November 1827.

49 *Journal de Toulouse*, 13–17 November 1827.

local networks. Support for Greek independence had then furthered the process and, better yet, had enabled Liberals to break out of the isolation that had followed the Carbonari revolts. Opposition momentum had been evident in the by-elections of early 1827 and thereafter the law of 2 May had provided an incentive to renew voter registration battles that could now actually be won. There was, in fact, little that was original in the work of the Aide-toi, although national coordination did advance, partly due to the efforts of Liberal luminaries travelling in the provinces. What was essential, however, was that the grassroots organization built between 1817 and 1820 had been renewed and extended.

## PART FOUR: THE CHARACTER OF LIBERAL OPPOSITION: 1824–1827

Given their decimation in 1824, the fact that the Left had become the largest voting block in the Chamber by December 1827 constituted a remarkable recovery, and this has led to much consideration of what had changed in the interim. In general, historians have put forward two complementary lines of explanation. The first is comprised of what can be considered negative factors: ultraroyalist overconfidence produced excesses that Liberals exploited. The second line of explanation is that the Liberal Opposition changed after 1824. The most influential proponent of the latter interpretation was the historian Thureau-Dangin, who, however, argued that Liberal change was a matter of form only. Throughout their fifteen years of opposition, Liberals failed in what was a litmus test for the author – loyalty to the dynasty – but their seeming moderation was effective, and gave them the support they eventually used to destroy the regime.

Thureau-Dangin did have a point; the image of the Opposition became less threatening as the minority of Liberals who had conspired rejoined the majority who stuck rigorously to legal means. Thus perception of the Opposition gradually shifted, as the public increasingly associated Liberals with legal resistance rather than armed insurrection. Even so, the employment of legal means of opposition was hardly something new for Liberals in 1824. What changed was that Liberals returned to the mode of opposition that they had employed during the Decazes era. In doing so, they regained the support base apparent in 1819.

For the wrong reasons, Thureau-Dangin was correct in arguing that an altered image did not constitute new ideological convictions. The Liberal Opposition had always manifested certain republican and Bonapartist tendencies and, although they were muted during the period under consideration, such inclinations could still be seen in one of the more striking events of 1824 to 1825 – Lafayette's triumphal tour of the United States. Coinciding roughly with the statement of the Monroe doctrine, Lafayette's tour served a certain purpose for the Republic, but more striking for our concerns was the way in which it was used in France.

That the intention was one of propaganda could be seen in the presence of Auguste Levasseur, the 'official biographer'. Levasseur and Lafayette's son George sent packets of American newspaper reports to Pagès in Paris, and Pagès, in turn, arranged their distribution to journals such as the *Constitutionnel* and the *Courrier*. Nevertheless, reporting was erratic, and thus Pagès and the Lafayette family decided that censorship should be circumvented through the publication of a book. In 1825 Pierre-Jean Béranger wrote a poem on the tour and this inspired a contest for verse on the subject. Contestants submitted their compositions to a selection committee that included Laffitte, Foy and the lawyer Mérilhou, and several poems were then published.

Much of this propaganda was implicitly republican in character. Accounts of Lafayette's contribution to the American Revolution, Lafayette's speeches during the tour, and praise of American liberties and institutions were all intended to present an unfavourable contrast with a France still troubled by *ancien régime* privilege. None of this, however, produced a significant republican movement prior to the July Monarchy; indeed, Lafayette counselled moderation among his followers upon his return. Moreover, one of the more significant themes of the literature was that America had provided a better model of revolution because the American version had been free of violent, disorderly excesses.[50]

If republican tendencies could thus still be seen, so too could Bonapartism. Napoleon's ghost continued to stalk Alsace. Busts of the emperor openly hawked in market places, and cheap manuscripts purporting that he had escaped from Saint Helena, were but two examples. The behaviour of certain notables in the Haut-Rhin fostered the suspicion that Liberals were behind flourishing popular Bonapartism, but a more plausible explanation was that no market had to be created by the foreign merchants who supplied it. Aggressive placards at moments of crisis were one thing, furniture, pottery, engravings, jewellery and pipes were another. The problem for the regime was that while Bonapartism could not be repressed, neither could it be safely embraced.[51]

[50] S. Neely, 'The politics of liberty in the old world and the new: Lafayette's return to America in 1824', *Journal of the Early Republic*, 6 (Summer 1986), pp. 151–71.

[51] P. Leuilliot, 'L'Opposition Libérale en Alsace à la fin de la Restauration', in *Deux siècles d'Alsace française* (Strasbourg, 1948), pp. 308–10.

Lingering republicanism and Bonapartism did reveal that alternatives to Bourbon rule had not been forgotten, but Thureau-Dangin's depiction of Liberals as hypocrites was based on an inappropriate emphasis on dynastic loyalty. The issue of the ruling house was secondary to Liberals. More important were questions of the relation of the monarchy to counter-revolution, and the willingness of the monarch to abide by the Charter. Whenever Charles X gave public recognition that the Charter was fundamental, Liberal testimonials of loyalty gushed. If this did not endure, it was because Charles's counter-revolutionary proclivities were never long absent. Liberals learned to live with the Double Vote, but they would fight the complete destruction of national sovereignty. If acceptance of despotism was the test of loyalty, Liberals were disloyal but, then again, they always had been.

Thureau-Dangin attributed the altered image partly to a younger generation of Liberals. They brought enthusiasm and knowledge of organization gained from an apprenticeship in the Carbonari, and thus they revivified the Opposition by launching new initiatives such as the Aide-toi. As evidence Thureau-Dangin pointed to the *Globe*, suggesting that liberalism among students could be attributed to this source. More recently, historians A. Spitzer and J.-J. Goblot have amplified the theme of the younger generation by exploring the series of ideas associated with it, and the web of contacts connecting its leading figures, but evaluating the impact of generational differences remains difficult.[52]

One cannot view the 'cohort of 1820' as politically distinctive, given that they repeated the divisions they claimed to rise above. Many political traditions would in fact reach back and claim the younger generation as their own. Socialism could certainly do so, given the presence of Pierre Leroux, Armand Bazard, Victor Cousin and Prosper Enfantin. Among proto-republicans were Cavaignac, Trélat and Hippolyte Carnot. Conversely, members of the Aide-toi such as Rémusat and Duvergier reflected the liberal influence of the *doctrinaires*. Nor was Bonapartism foreign to the younger generation; as Spitzer has concluded, youthful politics tended to reflect the ambivalence of the Opposition as a whole.[53]

One has to wonder whether the *Globe* was as important as scholars have at times maintained. Rémusat and Paul Dubois did provide a striking

[52] Thureau-Dangin, *Le parti*, pp. 217–64; Spitzer, *The French Generation*, and J.-J. Goblot, *La jeune France libérale. Le Globe et son groupe littéraire 1824–1830* (Paris, 1995).

[53] See G. Weill, 'L'idée républicaine en France pendant la Restauration', *Revue d'Histoire Moderne*, 2 (1927), pp. 331–48; Pouthas, *Guizot*, pp. 369–80; E. Newman, 'Republicanism during the Bourbon Restoration in France, 1814 – 1830' (Ph.D. dissertation, University of Chicago, 1969), pp. 257–315, and A. Spitzer, 'La république souterraine', in F. Furet and M. Ozouf, eds., *Le siècle de l'avènement républicain* (Paris, 1993), pp. 358–69.

orientation; moderation, even in religious controversy, was preached, alongside legal opposition. The difference was partly a matter of tone: gone was the stridency of the past. According to the *Globe*, the younger generation was free of the animosities of the Revolutionary and Imperial epochs, and better able to view matters from a dispassionate perspective.

For his part, Thureau-Dangin did recognize that there was more to the world of journalism than the *Globe* by giving consideration to two men who did not fit the moderate stereotype – Thiers and François Mignet. Both contributed more than their share to the anticlericalism of, respectively, the *Constitutionnel* and the *Courrier*, and Thiers was particularly fascinated by Bonapartism. Nor did these two young writers follow the *doctrinaire* liberal line of Guizot; they viewed the Revolution as a block and did not divorce Jacobinism from it, although they condemned the excesses of the Terror.[54]

This is not to say that the generational divide held no meaning; one runs across too many royalist lamentations not to think that it had some veracity. Baron Prosper de Barante was probably correct in speculating that voters recently come of age showed a greater disposition towards independence. Charles Dupin's *Forces productives et commerciales de la France*, published in 1827, argued precisely this, and the *Globe* naturally dedicated an entire issue to reviewing his 'findings'. Given that ballots were burned, there is no conclusive way to test such propositions. Nevertheless, there was a tendency which saw Opposition ranks replenish themselves more easily than royalism, and one suspects that rebellion against what Spitzer has termed the 'attempt to resacrilize the education system' had a good deal to do with it. Typically, prefects attributed the defection of young voters to frequent praise directed at them by the press, but in the provinces this meant the *Courrier* and the *Constitutionnel*. While the *Globe* had 900 subscribers towards the end of 1827, the *Constitutionnel* had 20,000.[55]

What was most significant about the construct of generation was its rhetorical utility. Liberals in 1824 did need to put a fresh face on Opposition. Deputies ranging from Casimir Perier to Lafayette had frequently appealed to youth before and after 1820, but suddenly the younger generation became associated with legal means of opposition. If proclamation of this in the *Globe* was unctuous, it was better than the threatening behaviour that

[54] Thureau-Dangin, *Le parti*, pp. 202–17; Spitzer, *The French Generation of 1820* (Princeton, 1987), pp. 66–9 and 97–128, and J. P. T. Bury and R. P. Tombs, *Thiers 1797–1877; A Political Life* (London, 1986), pp. 6–16.

[55] See AN, F7 6767, folio Aisne, November 1827, Hautes-Alpes, 4 September, 1827; F7 6768, Dordogne, 28 August 1827; F7 6771, Hautes-Pyrénées, 14 July 1827; Barante, *Souvenirs*, III, pp. 435–6; C. Dupin, *Forces productives et commerciales de la France* (Paris, 1827), and Goblot, *La jeune France*, p. 74.

had characterized the previous contributions of the younger generation to Liberal Opposition.

Youthful, particularly student, support for the Left had been apparent from the federations of 1815 onwards. Young men had always been more inclined to confront authority directly, but when their vigour was harnessed to the legal approach, they became a more valuable asset, whether in terms of organizational 'legwork', or the resolution required to force the government to test the limits of the law. A strong sense of inevitable victory could also undermine royalist confidence, producing defeatism over future prospects.

In the end, however, the image as designed by the *Globe* had a great deal of myth to it. The 'older generation' – men such as Goyet, Constant and Pagès – had many of the attributes which the younger generation claimed: belief in the rule of law and desire for gradual, progressive change. Having experienced the excesses of idealism, the 'older generation' took a pragmatic view that at times made it cautious, but also made it willing to compromise through alliances that in the end secured its objectives. In this sense, the Restoration Opposition possessed political virtues that were lost in the early 1830s, recaptured in the 1840s and then lost again immediately following the Revolution of February 1848. All generations shared in this failure to adhere to the means that brought positive change.

## LIBERAL POLITICAL CULTURE

Liberals claimed that they represented the nation, whereas ultraroyalists were 'anti-national'. Given the nature of the franchise, there were limits to the legitimacy of such claims. Both sides did, however, pay close attention to public opinion, and concern was not restricted to the electorate. France was not in constant turmoil, but certain issues smouldered constantly. Several of these issues were politically partisan, and they concerned far more than the electorate. Liberals harped on them, and ultraroyalists ensured that they would not be resolved until 1830.

Napoleon had not blazed a new path when he returned in 1815 warning against the pretensions of the former First and Second Estates. Ultraroyalists had themselves raised the issues of nationalized lands, restoration of the *dîme* and seigneurial obligations; moreover, their words and actions had provoked doubt over their acceptance of religious freedom and civil equality. It was these issues that made Napoleon's Flight possible, and they did not end with the advent of the Second Restoration. The alliance of *blouse* and frock coat became most obvious in 1830, but it was not so very different from what had been apparent in 1815. Ultraroyalists also had a certain popular constituency that in certain circumstances they would deploy. Nevertheless, it would be a mistake to deduce that mass royalism held anything like the potential for alliance between the Left and the masses. The years 1815 and 1830 both pointed to an obvious conclusion, as did the consequence of Allied non-intervention in 1830.

Early in the Second Restoration, Liberals had little choice but to accept the regime, and many sincerely hoped that it would develop into a genuine constitutional monarchy. As crisis returned in 1819, Liberal insistence on national sovereignty led them to shift their appeal beyond the confines of the political elite. All of the rhetoric deployed in the petition campaign against revision of the Lainé Law reflected the broad following Liberals held in the general population.

Officials had long reported that Liberal victories triggered celebrations that included the disenfranchised, and the events in the Isère surrounding the election of Grégoire were but one example of a widespread phenomenon. Officials also noted the attendance of non-voters at Liberal banquets, serenades and speeches. Villèle had set the precedent for public demonstrations in 1816, but in Liberal hands it was much more redoubtable. Some 600 people gathered at Rennes in May 1817 to cheer Dunoyer during his trial; 2,000 or so cheered Marchand after his acquittal at Strasbourg in 1820. Crowds attending Liberal celebrations of the defence of Grenoble were in the thousands; similar numbers could be seen at Lyons in 1821 when supporters of Corcelles followed their banquet with fireworks. The ties between Liberals such as Guilhem and the populace were obvious during the anticlerical riots at Brest; some 2,000 people participated in the latter in 1819 and one rather doubts that the majority of 500 Liberal banqueters honouring Guilhem held the vote in 1820. Crowds attending serenades of Liberal Deputies at Rouen in the summer of 1820 were also estimated in the thousands.

When Liberals wished, they could mobilize mass support. After they realized in the mid-1820s that using crowds for intimidation only confirmed royalist allegations of conspiracy, and thereby destroyed electoral prospects, Liberals were more cautious over such means. All the same, this did not necessarily mean that they were afraid of mass gatherings – the funerals of Foy and Manuel, and the events surrounding the tours of Constant and Lafayette in the late 1820s, demonstrated quite the opposite.

The reasons why middle- and upper-class Liberals had a mass following were diverse. Most Liberals were open to at least a limited expansion of the franchise, which explains why much of the Dijonnais Liberal leadership was actually disenfranchised. Goyet was typical of radical Liberals in believing that the 'people' had learned to reason over politics, which they followed closely. This did not make him a democrat in the full sense of the term, but he put none of the bounds on 'reason' associated with the *doctrinaires*, and when he spoke admiringly of the 'intermediary classes' he meant small property holders, not the groups we associate with the bourgeoisie.

Ultimately, however, the alliance of *blouse* and frock coat sprang from ultraroyalism, which presented Liberals with issues and values that transcended social origins. Liberals directed much invective towards the Catholic Church; nevertheless, they were neither anti-Catholic nor opposed to the Church as an institution. Liberals opposed clerical privilege and resisted theocracy, and they were determined to defend freedom of opinion by blocking attempts to reduce the civil rights of non-Catholics. For these reasons, Protestant groups, whether in Alsace, the Seine-Inférieure, the Drôme or the Gard, were almost uniformly drawn to the Opposition by a desire to ensure religious liberty.

Liberal objections to clerical domination were cultural, in that Catholicism identified itself with a set of values defined in opposition to the ideas or values associated with the Revolution. Thus the Church became closely associated with ultraroyalism. Early in the Restoration there was relatively little opposition to state efforts to revivify the Catholic Church, but the increasingly dogmatic and invasive character of rejuvenated Catholicism changed matters. All social groups were touched by fulminations against the ownership of nationalized lands, theatres, dancing, card-playing or carnival, and everyone was vulnerable to the humiliation of refusal to grant Christian burial. The basic message of the ritualized Catholic auto-da-fé was that those who did not accept Church control were not to be tolerated.

Most prefects were alert to the dangers of extremism, and officials, at least until 1824, sought to temper aggression. Yet for the following three years restraint was relaxed, enabling zealotry to do crown and altar severe harm. In one notorious episode, the archbishop of Rouen threatened the excommunication of parents who failed to have children baptised within eight days of birth. Equally troubling was that he referred favourably to the practice of publicly posting lists of individuals who had not attended communion on Easter Sunday, and therefore had Christian burial withheld from them, and that he directed priests to keep registers of 'illegitimate' marriages.[56]

[56] Lyons, 'Fires of expiation', pp. 240–66, and R. Eude, 'Un archevêque de Rouen au XIXe siècle: le Cardinal-Prince de Croy (1824–1844)', *Précis Analytique des Travaux de l'Académie de Rouen, 1951–3* (1955), pp. 230–9.

While patriotism had been the central cultural value linking elite and lower-class demonstrations at Rouen prior to the war with Spain, anticlericalism surged to the fore in 1825. Once again *charivari* in the streets against a mission was accompanied by the demand for *Tartuffe* in the theatre. With its emphasis on religious hypocrisy, *Tartuffe* surpassed *Sylla* and *Sicilian Vespers* as the favoured piece to demonstrate opposition. Tumult at Rouen was just the first episode in a wave of some forty-one such incidents in twenty-three departments between 1825 and 1829. The Liberal press played a major role not just in reporting the incidents, but also in instigating them, and meanwhile Liberals saw to the publication of hundreds of thousands of cheap copies of *Tartuffe*. This were designed to encourage readers, and listeners, to apply Molière's attack on clerical hypocrisy to the contemporary scene, and the missions served to ensure that such reflections went well beyond the electorate. While middle-class Liberals could coordinate such modes of protest, they were not, however, simply pulling lower-class strings; the essence lay in shared values.

What was different in 1825 was the extent to which former royalists joined in calling for *Tartuffe*. This transformation partly reflected divisions among royalists over the theocratic inclinations of ultraroyalism, but it was also true that Liberals had learned the lesson of adopting a defensive posture. Another anticlerical outburst at Brest, lasting from September 1826 to March 1827, illustrated these points. Here too, *charivari* against a mission and a demand for *Tartuffe* were combined, and meanwhile requests by the prefect that missionaries temper their zeal gained little. The theatre director did, however, follow instructions not to allow the performance of Molière's play, and the various forces of law and order were marshalled to prevent disruption of mission ceremonies. In response a mannequin of a leading missionary was hung, pamphlets summarizing laws against the Jesuits were distributed, songs and seditious placards were circulated, and stink bombs were exploded in churches. Meanwhile protests against the banning of *Tartuffe* went on each night for two weeks at the theatre, and the same figures could be seen alternating between the two scenes of conflict. Matters reached a crescendo on 12 October when troops entered and an eruption of violence led to fourteen arrests.

In their defence of the accused, Liberal lawyers attributed disorder to the missionaries and the officials who had resorted to undue force against a public that was legally expressing its opinion. The *Constitutionnel* put forward similar arguments and, indeed, legal arguments were distributed among the population in pamphlets. With the mission over, permission to stage *Tartuffe* was granted, whereupon the public made a point of honouring the accused when they were freed during appeal procedures. Thereafter the accused were treated to a series of banquets and balls. In the trial defence, Liberal lawyers went out of their way to appeal to the judges to defend not just the public but also the Charter from the aggression of clerical conspiracy.

The mixed social nature of dissent was again apparent. Sheer numbers, with crowds in the thousands, point to the popular component. Use of *charivari*, with the mockery of authority, the hanging of effigies, rude songs and chanting, and tossing stink bombs, were perhaps popular in nature, but middle-class students and *jeunes gens* were also practised in such tactics. Cane-tapping at the theatre was a hallmark of the latter groups; balls and banquets for the accused were certainly not popular in nature, and neither was the distribution of pamphlets outlining the history of laws against Jesuits. In short, then, *Tartuffe* incidents were popular only in the sense that they included a variety of social groups and demonstrated the ways in which Liberal Opposition could reach beyond the electorate.[57]

Under ultraroyalist government, the Church made steady progress towards the monopoly of education, troops played an increasingly important part in mission ceremonies, and civil officials were forced to attend missions until parts of the judiciary began to baulk. Fear thus focused on theocracy, and this would become the centrepiece of Liberal Opposition. Even so, it was clerical will towards social control that produced an anticlerical backlash.[58]

Most clergymen were probably reluctant to engage in the drive for domination. From the commencement of the Restoration, one can trace a desire to moderate extremism, and by the mid-1820s the Church itself was divided over unbridled clericalism. The latter internal war sprang from the recognition that zealotry could produce 'irreligion', weakening the faith rather than strengthening it. Making this crossfire more lethal still were battles between Gallicanism and ultramontanism. Both could be theocratic, but Gallicanism drew back well before the ultramontane Lammenais, 'the most systematic and prestigious' theoretician of theocracy, underwent his conversion to religious liberty. By the late 1820s, however, it was too late for moderates to prevent extremists from doing great harm to the Church generally.[59]

There were several reasons why clergymen were rarely associated with Liberal Opposition. On the one hand, whereas no politician could impose

57 Kroen, *Politics and Theater*, pp. 216–84.
58 Le Gallo, 'L'anticléricalisme', pp. 115–20.
59 Rémond, *L'anticléricalisme*, pp. 61–121.

conformity on nobles, the means to impose discipline on the clergy were many. Any association with Napoleon or the Revolutionary constitutional clergy was a great disadvantage for an aspiring clergyman during the Restoration, and just as reports on clergymen who had supported Napoleon during the Hundred Days were collected during the White Terror, so too would Archbishop Clermont-Tonnere purge former *constitutionnels* in the Haute-Garonne in the early 1820s. In this regard, clergymen shared the vulnerability of civil servants and tended to act in a similar fashion.

On the other hand, all certainly was not craven conformity and there is no denying the depth of religiosity underlying rejuvenated Catholicism. Few Restoration *dévots* would have followed Lammenais completely in concluding that the king should take his instructions from Rome, but inclination to draw a line between temporal and spiritual governance was weak among figures such as Bonald and Bertier. Ultraroyalist government distinguished itself by the extent to which it strengthened the influence of the Catholic Church and, thereby, took France in a theocratic direction. Not surprisingly, the clergy responded not simply as a buttress of royalism, but often as its most fervent political activists.

Liberal response to the privileged position allotted to the Catholic Church could at times be extreme, and was frequently unscrupulous. Given that religion had entered the political domain, and vice versa, this was to be expected. Clerical domination would become the central political question of the 1820s, permeating issues such as the Loveday affair of 1821–2. As Dubouchage noted of Liberals in the Drôme, however, even the handful of radicals who denounced the clergy continued to practise their religion.[60]

Clericalism, particularly in its ultramontane form, ran up against patriotism. One could see this clash when the liberal Peer Jean-Denis Lanjuinais questioned proposed laws to reduce the state regulation of Catholic women's associations in 1822 by appealing to the sovereignty of French law, and when General Foy warned against divisive forces undermining national unity through the creation of two 'younger generations' by clerical invasion of the French University.

Worse still for the regime and its supporters, ultraroyalism and the dynasty were linked to foreign intervention. Liberals took pains to twin their advocacy of the liberties of 1789 with praise for the army as a source of national achievement, and when they wished to prick ultraroyalism, this was precisely the tack they took. More insidiously, while attacking despotism,

[60] On the Loveday affair, see C. Ford, 'Private lives and public order in Restoration France: the seduction of Emily Loveday', *American Historical Review*, 99 n. 1 (1994), pp. 21–43.

they often treated the period of 1789 to 1815 as a block, and reference to the glories of the military was the means by which they achieved this unity. The historian S. Mellon has a point in underlining a liberal desire to separate 1789 from the Terror, but in politics seeming inconsistencies do not always matter. In both the *Patriote de '89* of the Hundred Days and the *Minerve* of the Decazes 'experiment', one can find the Opposition press arguing that while no one wished to defend the 'crimes' of the Terror, still the Convention did enable the 'new' France to survive the onslaught of the old order.[61]

The most able practitioner of having one's cake and eating it too was Napoleon, and Liberals derived much benefit from the interpretation he placed on his historical role. After occupation, Bonaparte and the army gained in popularity, and with the emperor locked away on Saint Helena, even Liberals could see the advantages of making themselves the spokesmen of patriotism. In doing so, as the general and Deputy Lamarque pointed out, Liberals found a common ground and confirmed a mass following. It was the combination of opposition and patriotism that made the poems and songs of Béranger so dangerous to the regime, and it was in his guise as general that Lafayette was best placed to link the Opposition to a 'global' battle with reaction, and provide an appeal to the disenfranchised.[62]

Popular Bonapartism was prone to mushroom at times of constitutional crisis – an indication that antagonism to the regime superseded class boundaries. Among differing groups it manifested itself in varying ways – actors miming the emperor in plays, merchants hawking plaster busts or engravings, or fencing masters singing songs of the 'good old days'. The rise of popular Bonapartism has often been linked to Romanticism, but Honoré de Balzac, Victor Hugo and Stendhal (Henri Beyle) came to the game rather late. Their audience was not to be found among the peasant majority, and in tapping into Bonapartism they were conforming rather than innovating. Romanticism did play its part in middle- or upper-class Bonapartism, but this had long been apparent in Liberal reading rooms.[63]

There is no mistaking the vital role of army veterans in spreading the cult of the emperor. The historian J. Vidalenc has argued that the active

[61] Mellon, *The Political Uses;* Thureau-Dangin, *Le parti*, pp. 57–77, and Harpaz, *L'école*, pp. 42–3, 93–7, 223–33, 242–8.

[62] See S. Neely, 'Lafayette: the soldier of two worlds', in L. Kramer, ed., *The French-American Connection: 200 Years of Cultural and Intellectual Interaction* (Chapel Hill, N.C., 1994), pp. 6–19, and Rémusat, *Mémoires*, II, pp. 12–13.

[63] See J. Lucas-Dubreton, *Le culte de Napoléon, 1815–1848* (Paris, 1960), pp. 49–298; Ménager, *Les Napoléon*, pp. 15–83; J. Vidalenc, *Les demi-solde: étude d'une catégorie sociale* (Paris, 1955); Day-Hickman, *Napoleonic Art*, and Alexander *Napoleon*, pp. 117–34, 147–63.

resistance of the legendary half-pay officer has been overestimated, but perhaps the operative word here is 'active'. Sources at the local level give a powerful impression that authorities had good reason to fear the influence of the *demi-solde*, and retired or half-pay officers did play a major part in the attempted revolts of the early 1820s. Opposition was not, however, necessarily a matter of taking up arms; more corrosive efforts took place in the bars and cafés where official harassment could make social lions of veterans. At the very least, in countless places their presence could stimulate contrasts captured by Géricault's drawing of a Swiss Guard and an impoverished French veteran. At Le Havre, in response to the expulsion of Manuel in 1823, Liberals seized on the performance of a play to heckle a character named La Bourdonnaye and the arrival of Swiss Guards then ensured that fights would spill over into the streets.

Liberals such as Corcelles knew that when they presented petitions for the banishment of foreign troops they consolidated the alliance between middle-class voters and a populace smitten with Bonapartism in places such as Lyons. Perhaps the most arresting account of this connection came from the prefect of the Meuse when he reported in 1822 that for the past couple of years Liberals had taken to holding dinners and public dances on 15 August. Whether visiting Deputies such as Etienne actually took part in celebrating Saint Napoleon day is questionable, but the timing of their arrival at several villages was striking.[64]

Experience in the army tended to act as a unifier. Historians have placed great emphasis on draft-dodging and desertion as forms of resistance against oppressive Revolutionary and Imperial regimes, but what needs to be emphasized is how rapidly the image of Napoleon as ogre disappeared when peasants were confronted by Allied occupation. Veterans fortunate enough to return to their villages had better tales to tell than the local draft-dodger, and much of the veteran's swagger lay in identification with the 'little corporal'. Better yet, it was now the veteran, whose courage and patriotism could not be contested, who was the resister.

## THE REWARDS OF RETURN TO LEGAL OPPOSITION

Turning away from revolt made for closer relations between the two wings of the Left after 1824. There were differences, apparent in Humann's support

[64] See the reports of 1822–3 in AN, F7 6770, dossier Meuse, and 6772, dossier Seine; J. Legoy, 'Un espace révolutionnaire: le théâtre du Havre, 1789–1850', in *Révolutions et mouvements révolutionnaires en Normandie. Actes du XXIe Congrès des sociétés historiques et archéologiques de Normandie tenus au Havre du 24 au 29 octobre 1989* (Le Havre, 1990), pp. 280–1, and Ribe, *L'opinion*, pp. 90–101, 194, 397–407.

of Villèle's plan to convert government bonds which Casimir Perier and Girardin attacked, but on the whole the embattled few drew together. A reduction in numbers had advantages in terms of discipline; parliamentary speeches reveal that the Deputies divided fields of expertise. Perier, whose domains were finance and military affairs, spoke 178 times between 1824 and 1828. Discipline was also apparent in what was not said at untimely moments as ultraroyalists ripped into each other.

Officials repeatedly reported that local Liberals in salons and cafés replicated the moderation of Deputies in the Chamber. Predictably, this was attributed to the *comité directeur*, but no Parisian prodding was required for local activists to recognize that the best strategy for promoting royalist division was to drive a wedge between those who saw no need for the separation of Church and state and those who did. From Toulouse, the prefect reported that royalists were amused by coins depicting Charles X as a Jesuit. While royalists were thus engaged in internecine warfare, Liberals reconstituted their base.[65]

Such developments were facilitated by a change in Liberal comportment. Salon talk was full of speculation, but a prudent distance was maintained from the subject of revolution. Liberals spoke respectfully of the king, although they did lament Jesuit influence. While brochures usually targeted cabinet ministers or clerics, at times they could be directed at local officials. In 1826, for instance, the mayor of Boulogne (in the Haute-Garonne) found himself denounced in a brochure by some eighty of his fellow townsmen. Local rivalry doubtless lay behind much of the criticism, but prefect Juigné saw in it something that Villèle also noted: Liberals were employing an old ultraroyalist tactic of attacking the central government by championing municipal liberties.[66]

According to officials in the Isère, in the summer and autumn of 1824 Liberals tempered their behaviour so as to regain influence and they focused on philanthropic societies devoted to aiding the poor. Liberal agents directed the societies and most of the 1,800 or so who joined in Grenoble were becoming dangerously habituated to following the Liberal lead. Whether the associations actually reflected any great threat to the monarchy can be questioned, but it was certainly true that Liberals Augustin Perier, Bérenger and Félix Réal were heavily involved in such projects.[67]

65 AN, F7 6769, general report of March 1826 and 2 June 1827; F7 3797, 1 April 1826 ADHG, 4M47, 11 March 1825.

66 AN, F7 3797, 1 April and 24 May 1826; F7 6769, 20 December 1825, general report of March, 2 May, 31 December 1826, 29 January, 2 June, 27 July, and 2–9 August 1827.

67 AN, BB30 209 (Isère), 31 July 1824; F7 6687, dossier 30, 19 November 1824; BMUG, N1684, 11 June 1825 and 28 March 1827; N1782, 16 November 1827 and 24 August 1828.

In 1827 Liberals built on traditions established earlier in the decade. Just two days before the date for the closure of the electoral list revision, the Grenoble Liberal committee published a petition to the prefect. While most of the petition dealt with the number of individuals who had lost the vote since 1824, potentially more fruitful were arguments concerning the interpretation of the laws governing revision. The petition started from the premise that jury duty was a collective responsibility and that every qualified member had an interest in extending the list so as to distribute the burden as widely as possible. From this premise the committee derived the conclusion that third parties (individuals already on the list) should have the right to make claims concerning interested parties (individuals who were qualified but not listed). This interpretation was then buttressed with quotations from legislation and an argument that the relevant legislation did not directly preclude the right of third parties to make claims. Furthermore, in decisions reached in the early 1820s, the Council of State had tacitly accepted the right of third parties to make claims.

The tone of the document served Liberal interests by cultivating an image of respect for the law, but the seemingly narrow argument over the rights of third parties also had broad political implications. If this right were recognized, the committee's ability to organize opposition would be greatly enhanced because it could then undertake much of the work required to assemble and present the documentary proofs of qualification, thereby securing the gratitude of voters.[68]

The reward for the registration efforts was triple election for Augustin Perier and success for Michoud at Crémieux in November. In congratulating Perier, the twelve-man Liberal committee for the *arrondissement* of Saint-Marcellin cited the qualities they saw in their candidate – independence from the seductions of power and attachment to public liberties. They then described what they expected: a courageous 'fight to defend what remains of our constitutional institutions', to 'reconquer those [rights] which fraud has taken from us', and to 'obtain those [rights] which we lack and which France has long claimed as a consequence of our representative government'. While such language was defensive in form, the content was precisely what Liberals had maintained under Decazes.

In response to congratulatory letters, Perier stressed respect for legality and loyalty to both king and constitution. Subsequently he would develop this line in a Chamber speech defending his department from attacks by

[68] See AN F1C III Isère 5, *Pétitions à Monsieur le baron de Calvière*, and the minutes of the electoral college at Tullins for 17–18 November 1827 in ADI, 8M4.

d'Haussez. In the Isère, 'where all rose in the name of liberty, but where all inclined towards the letter of the law, one knew how to fulfil one's political duties with constancy and reclaim rights with a measured firmness which would not transgress legal order and to the contrary would assure its maintenance'.[69]

Opposition effectively shifted from the Left to the Centre-Left in the Isère, but in the Bas-Rhin the reverse occurred and for a time this transition threatened to reopen the division in Liberal ranks. Because the shift in orientation was confined within emphasis on legal modes of resistance, however, no great fissure resulted.

Matters commenced in March 1827 when prefect Claude Esmangart de Feynes decided to take action to preclude the possibility that Benjamin Constant might shift his political base to Alsace. Esmangart had good reason for suspicion. In Chamber debates Constant had questioned whether Bishop Frayssinous might not have a conflict of interests in acting as both Minister of Education and of Ecclesiastical Affairs. Would he not use his direction of education to lead Protestants to what he considered the 'greatest happiness in this world or beyond'? Did this not explain why Catholics were favoured at the Academy in Strasbourg? Moreover, was this not typical of a government that excluded Protestants from the municipal council?[70]

In articles published shortly thereafter in the departmental *Journal*, Esmangart contradicted Constant's assertions, detailing appointments. He also remarked that the *Courrier du Bas-Rhin* had not reported Constant's speech, and alleged that this was because local Protestants were embarrassed by its inaccuracies. Esmangart's 'spin' was questionable. Although Protestants were not being cut entirely out of the administration, they were being reduced proportionately. Yet it was not the practice of Protestant leaders to court controversy and Turckheim, president of the Consistory, did not enter the fray. Moreover, Silbermann, editor of the *Courrier*, and moderate Liberals generally were uncomfortable with Constant's confrontational approach and it would appear that Esmangart had the better of this initial clash.[71]

Further trouble was nevertheless brewing as Silbermann began to show some spine in attacking the Peyronnet Press Law: 'The harder and the more

[69] BMUG, R90630. [70] AN, F7 6771, 23 March 1827, and F7 6767, 23 March 1827.

[71] AN, F7 6719, 23 and 30 May 1827; V. Glachant, *Benjamin Constant sous l'oeil du guet* (Paris, 1906), pp. 356–60, and M. Richard, 'La bourgeoisie protestante de Strasbourg à l'époque de Benjamin Constant', in *Autour des 'Trois Glorieuses' en 1830: Strasbourg, l'Alsace et la liberté* (Strasbourg, 1981), pp. 158–9.

offensive the weight placed on the press, the greater the hope for a striking justice when the day of publicity arrives.' Shortly thereafter, discussion of new electoral registration laws gave further evidence of local interest in Constant. In debates over the latter legislation, Deputy Humann irritated local radical Liberals by questioning Opposition proposals for amendments, whereas two petitions for revision written by Charles Marchand were presented to the Chamber by Constant.[72]

Rupture between Humann and local radical Liberals had long been in the offing, but it was not until Humann supported Villèle over the conversion of government bonds that a clear break had occurred. Esmangart concluded that royalism could only benefit by such Liberal internecine warring, and he saw in Constant's arrival in the Bas-Rhin in August an opportunity to promote division. For their part, radical Liberals had long pressed Constant to represent Alsace. They were especially attracted by his being Protestant and able to speak German, and the fact that Constant's personal relations with Humann were decidedly chilly.[73]

Thus it was the radical core that organized Constant's August tour of the Bas-Rhin, arranging meetings with local activists along the route. At Bischwiller musicians and young men on horseback, joined by peasants, accompanied the Deputy. At Strasbourg, along with the usual serenades, came a floating barge adorned with an orchestra. From the balcony of the Hôtel de l'Esprit, Constant covered all political bases: 'Long live the Charter!'; 'Long live civil and religious liberties!'; 'Long live freedom of the press!'; 'Long live Alsatian commerce!'; 'Long live the merchants of Strasbourg!'; and 'Long live Alsatian youth!' All this was, of course, contrived, but even hostile witnesses agreed that the Deputy was sincerely moved. Constant was notorious for his love of acclaim and official estimates put crowd numbers at 3,000.[74]

The main event, on 2 October, was the first major banquet since 1821. It was initially planned as a show of unity and Humann and Turckheim were invited to join Constant at the table of honour, but the Deputies of the Bas-Rhin had qualms. Turckheim sought a compromise: he would subscribe to the banquet, but did not wish to be associated with Constant as a beneficiary of the subscription. Shortly thereafter Humann drew the

[72] AN, F1C III Bas-Rhin 3, 12 April and 19 August 1826; BCUL, Co 1352, 14 February 1827; Ponteil, *Humann*, p. 68, and Leuilliot, *L'Alsace*, I, pp. 300–1, 464–6, 478–9.

[73] BNUS, Ms. 1534, 30 June 1827; BCUL, Co 1326, 3 May 1826; Leuilliot, *L'Alsace*, I, pp. 451–4, 467–72; Ponteil, *Humann*, pp. 26–68, and Coulmann, *Réminiscences*, II, pp. 91–2.

[74] ADBR, 3M19, 6–21 August 1827; Glachant, *Constant*, pp. 375–90, and Leuilliot, *L'Alsace*, I, pp. 473–7.

same line, but went on to explain that he and Constant did not have the same conception of 'legal liberty', opining that thirst for popularity was dangerous for the independence of a Deputy.

It is difficult to believe that the banquet organizers had not foreseen such a response, but they chose not to relent. In a verbal discussion Turckheim apparently accepted the original terms. Humann was contacted by writing. According to the radicals, the idea was not to show preference to any particular line of constitutional opposition, but to demonstrate that Deputies who supported civil and religious liberties would always have firm backing. Humann stood his ground, and Turckheim then rethought his position and decided he too would abstain. Rupture was now complete.[75]

Battle would not, however, be waged on just two fronts, as Esmangart re-entered the fray with a report in the departmental *Journal* stating that only three members of 'high commerce' had deigned to attend the banquet. Among the 154 original subscribers, only 104 participated, and 80 of these were from the 'inferior' classes – butchers, bakers and hatters. He then wrote a second article questioning Constant's integrity during the Hundred Days. Irritated, Constant wrote to Coulmann that if Esmangart wanted war, he would have it.

In fact Constant needed to deliver only one blow, which came in the form of a pamphlet entitled 'Letter to Mr Esmangart . . . by a Sausage-maker of Strasbourg'. Printed in Paris and posted in thousands to Alsace, the 'Letter' combined saucy irony with a shrewd calculation of which groups constituted the majority of voters. The humble 'sausage-maker' reminded the prefect that bakers, artisans, tavern-keepers, and small-scale merchants played an important role in feeding and clothing the upper classes. They sometimes also even loaned money to '*grands seigneurs*', a reference to Esmangart's indebtedness that was cheeky coming from Constant. More important, however, was the blow directed as much at Humann as the prefect. While Esmangart may have had the better of Constant over religion in May, he would have the worst of this socio-economic dispute.

Silbermann challenged the prefect's account of the banquet, but he chose to fence-sit over the choice between Humann and Constant for Strasbourg-*ville*. The latter confrontation was then clouded further when the *Journal des débats* announced that the *constitutionnel* candidates in the Bas-Rhin were Humann for Strasbourg-*ville* and Turckheim and Michel Saglio *fils* for the departmental college. Thus the contest was shaping up as a battle

[75] BNUS, Ms. 1534, *Banquets aux députés libéraux*, 7–27 September 1827; ADBR, 3M19, 26 September – 5 October 1827; Glachant, *Constant*, pp. 391–406, and Leuilliot, *L'Alsace*, 1, 473–7.

between the *doctrinaires* (Royer-Collard was a patron of Humann) and the Left. Angered, Schertz wanted to put d'Argenson forward in the departmental college, but Constant directed Coulmann to mobilize support behind Turckheim.

The results of the elections were not a disaster for the prefect. In the rural colleges three *ministériels* were returned. Nevertheless, provoking division at Strasbourg backfired as Constant defeated Humann, whom the prefect supported, by 124 votes to 108. In the departmental college, both Saglio and Turckheim won on the first ballot, with the official candidate receiving a paltry thirty votes. From the standpoint of royalism, the exchange of Constant for Humann represented a shift from an increasingly amenable centrist to a leading opponent. Worse still, their magnetic new colleague would soon pull Saglio and Turckheim towards the Left.[76]

Liberal progress was even more pronounced elsewhere, and as the returns of the colleges of the *arrondissements* arrived in November, it was apparent that Villèle was in deep trouble. During the interval prior to the elections in the departmental colleges, however, rioting returned to Paris. Liberals charged government forces with provoking disorder, and it appears likely that the police did intentionally allow rioting to take on threatening dimensions before moving in. The prefect of police was well aware that Liberals had more to lose than the government and, indeed, he had been disappointed by the absence of fully fledged revolt at the Manuel funeral during the previous summer. Due to the presence of proto-republican *jeunes gens* the latter ceremonial had been far more ominous, and therefore promising, than the respects paid to Foy.[77]

Renewed violence played a part in *ministériel* recovery in the departmental colleges, as royalists had second thoughts about division, and what emerged in December was a very fine balance. The Left had roughly 180 seats, as did Villèle's *ministériels.* Thus the Agier defection and the Pointe held a balance of power, but they were roughly equal and were headed in opposite directions. It would take a month before Charles X finally recognized the necessity of replacing Villèle. Ultraroyalism, at least for the moment, would not hold unchecked power. This was just as well, as Corbière and Villèle had initiated one last refinement prior to their departures. Previously

[76] BN, NAF 24914, 22 October 1827; ADBR, 3M19, 16 October 1827; 15MII 9, 14 November 1827; Coulmann, *Réminiscences*, II, pp. 101–2, 178–82; Glachant, *Constant*, pp. 377–413; Ponteil, *Humann*, pp. 69–70, and Leuilliot, *L'Alsace*, I, pp. 480–1.

[77] AN, F7 6772, folio Seine, 19 September 1827; Duvergier de Hauranne, *Histoire*, IX, pp. 300–20; Vaulabelle, *Histoire*, VII, pp. 306–31, and Ben-Amos, *Funerals*, p. 91.

prefects had been directed to predict voting; in 1827 they were asked to report on how individuals had voted.[78]

With Villèle defeated, the Liberal Opposition need no longer be quite so constrained in their rhetoric, but they also knew that they had failed to exploit fully the possibilities presented by voter response to legal opposition in November. The Liberal press made great play of police brutality in the Parisian riots, but was more than a little reticent over the resort to barricades. Similarly, when Louis Cauchois-Lemaire published a brochure in December more or less calling on the Duke of Orleans to lead a revolt, Opposition journals either criticized or ignored it. Lafayette, the voice of moderation, treated it as a joke. Meanwhile reports from the provinces indicated that the brochure was useful for the recovery of royalist unity, which was why the *Gazette de France* published extracts. The lesson was obvious.[79]

[78] Duvergier de Hauranne, *Histoire*, IX, pp. 356–82; Vaulabelle, *Histoire*, VII, 345–6, and Kent, *1827*, pp. 130–83.

[79] AN, F7 6767, folio Ardèche, 2 January 1828; F7 6770, Loire, 11 January 1828; Duvergier de Hauranne, *Histoire*, IX, pp. 336–55, 382–4, and Rader, *Journalists*, pp. 38–41.

5

# *Towards victory?: from January 1828 to July 1830*

## PART ONE: HARVESTING 1827

The final years of the Restoration saw Liberals confront two royalist governments. The first was largely Centre-Right in political orientation and was led by Viscount Jean-Baptiste Martignac, a former Bordelais lawyer who had been elected Deputy in 1825 and thereafter had staunchly supported Villèle. Martignac had not to that point established himself as a major political figure and he was not officially appointed as *premier ministre*, but his oratorical skills in parliament soon established him as the leader of the cabinet. The second royalist government, appointed in August 1829, was very much ultraroyalist in character and was led by Jules de Polignac. During both ministries Liberal strength grew, registered in by-elections under Martignac and in the general election of July 1830 under Polignac, and thus there was a consistent underlining theme to these years.

Faced by the possibility of a Liberal majority in 1820, royalists had passed the Law of the Double Vote, and this alteration of the electoral regime had helped secure domination for the next seven years. The Law of 2 May 1827 had then reduced administrative fraud, thereby contributing to Liberal recovery and again raising the spectre of an Opposition majority. Latent in this scenario was the potential conflict that had always lurked in the Charter. Accommodating the representative element of the constitution posed little concern as long as parliament was suitably royalist, but what would happen if voters chose to elect an Opposition majority?[1]

When the new parliament first met in January 1828, Liberals and the Agier defection launched an assault on the former government to distance Martignac from Villèle and drive the latter permanently from office. Debate over the response to the throne speech led to an address labelling

[1] For general background, see Bertier de Sauvigny, *Restoration*, pp. 405–39; Jardin and Tudesq, *Restoration*, pp. 66–9, 93–7; Waresquiel and Yvert, *Restauration*, pp. 407–54, and Beach, *Charles X*, pp. 253–340.

the previous government a 'deplorable system', and thereafter Liberals and the Agier group fired off charges of treason. Clashes between Count Guillaume-Isadore de Montbel, a member of the Chevaliers de la Foi and mayor of Toulouse since January 1826, and Agier were venomous, but Montbel managed to rally former Villèlists in a defence to which members of the Pointe, led by La Bourdonnaye, rallied.

More significant was damage inflicted on Villèle's methods during verification procedures. With support from the Agier defection and cabinet neutrality amounting to tacit acceptance, Liberals put forward petitions of complaint against all the essential ingredients of despotism. Not all petitions gained redress, as the Deputies opted for a rule of thumb which led to reversals only when it appeared that the extent of corruption of voter lists was greater than a candidate's margin of victory. Even so, six elections, including all five in the Vosges, were annulled. This step, and incriminating revelations concerning the prefect of the Lot, Saint-Félix de Maurémont, led several other Deputies to resign rather than risk further investigation.

Better yet, the Chamber established a committee that investigated corruption in twenty-four departments. Thus Liberals found an opportunity to roast Director of the Post Vaulchier for violation of private correspondence. Puymaurin rose in Vaulchier's defence, arguing that interception of correspondence was necessary to protect France from the agents of revolution, but such arguments no longer carried much resonance and it was only the king's intervention that prevented Martignac from sacking an embarrassing reminder of Villèle. Prior to the committee's report, three prefects were dismissed, and fifteen were transferred to other departments. Ultimately, only twelve were found to have committed 'errors'.

By the stage at which committee decisions were reached, the Opposition was less interested in pressing the cabinet, but d'Haussez did come in for tongue-lashing by Augustin Perier when he sought to defend Vanssay from an assault launched by three Liberals of the Seine-Inférieure. De Pina, a Chevalier de la Foi and former mayor of Grenoble, duly countered with an attack on the 'dangerous federation' known as the 'consultative electoral committee' of the Isère. This attempt to link Liberal organization to conspiracy drew fire from Bérenger de la Drôme, who refocused attention on the administration by reporting that mayors in the first *arrondissement* of the Isère had believed themselves obliged to threaten mass resignation should any of them be sacked after the elections of November. Below the verbal thunder, an important precedent had been established: not only could judges reverse prefectoral decisions, the Chamber also could inflict punishment for systematic illegality.

Parliament again tightened the rules of list compilation. Particularly significant was that 'third parties', provided they were enfranchised, could challenge prefectoral decisions and would not need notarized approval from directly interested parties. In other words, electoral committees could act on behalf of potential voters who did not wish to go to the trouble of initiating actions themselves. This made the monitoring of lists far easier. Several prefects, Vanssay among them, had in 1827 refused to recognize claims that were not notarized.

The Law of 2 July 1828 made registration lists permanent, so that while they could be revised voters need not go through the process of registration unless prefects specifically excluded them. Regulations established exact schedules for the entire registration process, including provisions that the prefectoral council must make its decisions regarding claims within five days of registration. Rectification lists must be published at fifteen-day intervals, and definitive closure of the list must occur on 12 October. All claims must be adjudicated within eight days of the publication of final lists. Liberals and the Agier group also pressed to enhance judicial authority in the composition of lists, with Bérenger de la Drôme arguing that the administration should be stripped entirely of its role, but a government compromise proposal that all contested prefectoral decisions should go before the courts then gained passage.[2]

A measure of the decline of despotism was a subsequent increase in the electorate. By 1 October 1828 numbers had increased by 5,000 to 93,000; one year later 98,000 had the vote. Caution, however, has to govern conclusions drawn from expansion. Between November 1827 and June–July 1830, the electorate of the Haute-Garonne increased by 200 voters. This probably contributed to a reduction in ultraroyalist majorities, but in 1830 it did not yield a single Liberal Deputy. Over the same time span in the Isère, the electorate increased by a grand total of two voters, but Liberals took the majority of seats in 1830. Thus the key to list battles was not simply the addition of Liberal supporters; it also entailed the removal of unqualified royalists.

More telling of where ultraroyalism stood without Villèle's system were the results of eighty-one by-elections held between May 1828 and January 1830. Because the Opposition had made a policy of running its strongest candidates wherever battle was apt to be close in 1827, a disproportionate number of Liberal candidates had been elected in several colleges. Hence a

[2] See AN, F1C III Seine-Inférieure 5, 3 August – 3 September 1827; ADI, 14M5, *Pétition . . . à Messieurs les Membres de la Chambre des Députés*; Duvergier de Hauranne, *Histoire*, IX, pp. 399–424, 504–23, and Vaulabelle, *Histoire*, VII, pp. 413–35.

high percentage of the by-elections of 1828 were in colleges previously won by the Left. One should not, therefore, make too much of the fact that the Left gained thirty-six of forty-two seats contested in May; more impressive was that prior to 1830 the Left improved its position in the Chamber by twenty-four seats. Virtually all of this was achieved under the Martignac ministry – a clear indication of where the electorate was headed before the appointment of the Polignac cabinet.[3]

Politics was byzantine under Martignac. Relations between the cabinet and Villèle were awkward, especially given the wrecking inclinations of the Villèlist *Gazette de France*. Nevertheless, the new government did not constitute a decisive break from the old, and while Martignac was happy to see Villèle sidelined, he could not ignore Charles X, who showered Montbel with praise for his defence of Villèle. Movement away from the former government could be seen in the suppression of the position of *directeur* of police, but Martignac (at the Interior), Count André-Jean de Chabrol de Crouzel (Minister of the Marine), Frayssinous (Minister of Ecclesiastical Affairs and Public Instruction), and Count Pierre-Laurent de Saint-Cricq (Minister of Commerce and Manufacturing) had all served under Villèle in various capacities. By the autumn of 1828, failure to make more than token change in the Council of State or administration had made accommodation with the Left difficult; yet former Villèlists formed the base of the *ministériel* block upon which the cabinet counted in the Chambers.

To succeed, Martignac needed to hold the Right and simultaneously appeal to the Agier defection and moderate Liberals. While theoretically possible, such a balancing act was extremely difficult. In February 1828, amidst the attack on Villèle, Chabrol and Frayssinous resigned, and a limited peace with Chateaubriand was gained by the replacement of Chabrol with Hyde de Neuville.

Although he did not deem the cabinet post sufficient for himself, Chateaubriand did agree to represent the government as ambassador in Rome. Dislike of Chateaubriand ran high at court, however, and few members of the administration viewed the judiciary fondly. Thus ties with the Agier defection were tenuous. Further complicating matters was the fact that, as Liberals went from strength to strength in by-elections, the need for the cabinet to reach further left increased, but even limited overtures to the Left strained the patience of Charles X, and royal dissatisfaction eroded Martignac's ability to hold the Right. Martignac thus had limited

[3] Kent, *1827*, pp. 60–2, 187–8, and Duvergier de Hauranne, *Histoire*, IX, pp. 467–92.

options, and at times his government appeared to be an exercise in dodging an inevitable lethal blow.

The most controversial measure of 1828 was the ordinance of 16 June ordering the closure of *petits séminaires* run by religious orders that were not legally established in France. The seminaries were not devoted to preparing priests; they taught lay Catholics and many were run by Jesuits. Much of the theocratic Right interpreted the ordinance as appeasement of Liberals in league with Satan, but the ordinance could also be seen as a step towards healing divisions among royalists by the removal of the stigma of Jesuit conspiracy. Yet the latter objective proved elusive as Anne-Antoine de Clermont-Tonnerre led a revolt among the bishops from his base at Toulouse. Although the new cabinet minister, Jean-François Feutrier, bishop of Beauvais, stood relatively firm over what was, after all, a challenge to crown authority, doubts over clerical influence continued.[4]

If controversies over the Jesuits were largely symbolic, more substantive changes were made concerning education. The first step came by way of the division of Ecclesiastical Affairs and Public Instruction back into two separate ministries. Jean-François Lefebvre de Vatimesnil replaced Frayssinous as Grand Master of the University, and Liberals gradually returned to a *université* freed of clerical domination. Better yet, an ordinance of 21 April 1828 restored the authorization of teachers to rectors, and placed the supervision of schools under new local committees. Unfortunately for the cabinet, however, closure of the *petits séminaires* led many bishops to refuse to appoint clergymen to the new supervisory councils, disrupting the entire process. For Liberals the revolt of the bishops meant that progress was fragile, and they watched zealously for any signs of weakening government resolve.[5]

Signs were mixed in press legislation passed in mid-July. On the one hand, preliminary censorship, the law of tendency, and the right of the government to impose censorship by simple ordinance outside parliamentary sessions were all removed. On the other hand, literary journals would join the political press in having to pay a surety bond and rates were increased, as were fines for infractions. Thus Liberals criticized certain provisions, but the new laws did lead to rapid press expansion.[6]

The issue that brought the fall of Martignac was a proposal in February 1829 to make local government elective. Such a development of

4 Duvergier de Hauranne, *Histoire*, IX, pp. 393–4, X, pp. 1–51; Vaulabelle, *Histoire*, VII, pp. 447–64, and Rader, *Journalists*, pp. 74–88.

5 Duvergier de Hauranne, *Histoire*, IX, pp. 388–99, 495–504, and Gildea, *Education*, pp. 37–9.

6 Collins, *Government*, pp. 54–5, and Rader, *Journalists*, pp. 17–35, 52–6.

representative government had long been a Liberal objective but, as proposed, the government bill would have entrenched the Right by means of a franchise significantly narrower than that for national elections. Conversely, Liberal counter-proposals would have expanded the electorate beyond the national franchise. Behind a government proposal designed perhaps to entice Liberals, but calibrated to favour ultraroyalists, stood Charles X; Martignac could go no further than what was offered. Thus when Martignac was obliged to retire the bill, Charles X had his pretext for putting an end to compromise, and the fate of the cabinet was sealed.

The appointment of the Polignac cabinet on 8 August 1829 commenced the second major crisis of the Second Restoration. Polignac (Foreign Minister), La Bourdonnaye (Minister of the Interior), and General Louis-Auguste de Bourmont (Minister of War), notorious for his desertion of Napoleon three days prior to Waterloo, composed an unholy trinity for the Left, and Montbel (who gained the recombined posts of Ecclesiastical Affairs and Public Instruction) and d'Haussez (Minister of the Marine) were not much better. Initially royalist unity appeared to shatter, as former Villèlists warred with the theocratic former Chevaliers in the cabinet. When La Bourdonnaye left the cabinet in November, principally because he was not able to make himself *premier ministre*, splintering appeared to progress further. Nevertheless, Liberals viewed such squabbles as no more than family feuds, and the rallying of all ultraroyalists in July 1830 proved that they were correct in the main.

Liberals and royalists alike saw in the cabinet a first step towards coup d'état, by which they meant violation of the representative element of the Charter, and there were signs of reaction analogous to Liberal response to the Double Vote. A tour by Lafayette through the Auvergne, Dauphiny and the Rhône became a parade of defiance, but even at this juncture Liberals avoided the errors of 1820. Although much invective was unleashed, it was directed specifically at the cabinet and twinned with avowals of loyalty to a deceived king. Liberals' fears of coup d'état had much to do with their penchant for conspiracy theory and, given that the new cabinet was partly the work of a palace intrigue in which Bertier was involved, such suspicions were natural. Polignac, however, entered government with naïve expectations that tempers would calm in time. That he had no specific programme does not appear to have troubled him unduly.[7]

The royal address at the opening of parliament on 2 March 1830 was ominous, suggesting that Opposition Deputies had failed to 'understand'

[7] See Bertier de Sauvigny, *Le Comte*, pp. 445–64.

the will of the king. In preparing responses, the committees of the Chambers debated fiercely over whether they should take a compliant or defiant line. The Peers adopted a submissive posture, while the Deputies responded in measured but firm terms that the ministry was ill chosen. The reply of the lower house could have been much stronger, but the Left wisely bowed to their moderate allies and the result was the address of the 221 Deputies, composed of Liberals and the Agier defection. In essence the address called on the king to remove a government that could not find a majority in the lower house.

Thus the issue of cabinet responsibility surged forward. Louis XVIII had maintained the first Richelieu cabinet in 1815–16 despite ultraroyalist domination in the Chamber. Whether a majority had been clearly hostile to the cabinet had been, however, an open question and the cabinet had been able to cobble together majorities and pass legislation. After the fall of the *Chambre introuvable*, subsequent governments had at least been capable of finding a majority in the Chamber. Thereafter the convention of choosing cabinets with claims to represent the majority had strengthened with the second resignation of Richelieu, and Villèle's call for elections in 1827.

It was this convention that Charles challenged, but in doing so he raised a broader issue: did the king have the right to appoint a government to which the majority was obviously antagonistic? The question was thorny because it issued from a basic contradiction in the constitution. The lower house could refuse the budget, and thus cut off the fiscal lifeline of any government, but the Deputies had no means to reject a cabinet beyond the unappealing prospect of bringing all government to a halt. At one short remove from this problem was the question that would not go away: in the event of impasse between the royal will and that of the nation as manifest in its elected representatives, where did ultimate sovereignty lie?

The question was so clearly posed that moderates, generally inclined to avoid confrontation, took the lead in forcing the issue. Times had changed, as Lafayette and Constant acted with what was, for them, discretion, while Royer-Collard, Félix Faure and the Marquis of Cordoue played key roles in assuring Opposition alliance did not waver. Parliament was prorogued on 19 March, and matters simmered.[8]

After much pondering, on 16 May king and cabinet decided to dissolve parliament and hold elections in late June and early July. To prepare for the campaign, Polignac brought into the cabinet two veterans of despotism – Peyronnet at the Interior, and Baron Guillaume Capelle, a former prefect

[8] Duvergier de Hauranne, *Histoire*, x, pp. 414–54, and Vaulabelle, *Histoire*, viii, pp. 68–93.

of the Seine-et-Oise reputed to be a master chef when it came to 'cooking' elections, at the newly created Ministry of Public Works. Return to Villèle's 'system' could also be seen in the reappointment of prefects Saint-Félix de Maurémont and Calvière, both disgraced in 1828 for electoral misconduct in 1827. In the meantime, press trials brought severe punishment for the editors responsible for the *National* and the *Globe*, for speculation over a possible fall of the dynasty. Moreover, these trials were but part of a much broader assault on the Liberal press.

In 1824 Villèle had exploited intervention in Spain, and in 1830 royalists could hope for similar rewards from successful foreign policy. Martignac's Foreign Minister, Count Pierre-Louis de La Ferronays, had committed troops to armed mediation between the Greeks and the Ottoman Empire in Morea, enabling France to play a major role in the securing of Greek independence in 1829. Thereafter Polignac had decided in January 1830 to send an expeditionary force under Bourmont to Algiers after a diplomatic incident in which the Dey struck a French official. Designed to enhance royal prestige, the expedition seized Algiers on 5 July. News reached France on 9 July, but by then the elections were largely over.

There was less than usual by way of active campaigning by the Opposition in June, but, then again, there was little need, due to determination to return the 221, and the extent of previous organization. Moreover, given the grim economic circumstances of the winter of 1830, officials were keeping a hopeful watch for anything that might be construed as insurrectionary intent. Materials for conflagration were not lacking, but the campaign was conducted with a discipline that left more than one prefect expecting the worst. Despite intense pressure applied by the administration and the Catholic Church, the electorate duly delivered a verdict on royal policy that could hardly have been more devastating for cabinet and king.

## PART TWO: DESPOTISM IN DECLINE

In 1828 Martignac sought to woo the Centre. For a brief period encompassing the by-elections of May, administrative intervention in elections was negligible, but it is unclear whether this constituted cabinet policy, or disarray among officials as parliament took up the question of prefectoral illegalities. One way or another, the results were not good for royalist candidates, and prefects soon returned to organizing campaigns for *ministériels*.

A similar pattern had unfolded in March over another proposal to force Deputies to submit to re-election if appointed to government office. This time the bill passed the lower house by a margin of eleven votes; while the cabinet remained neutral, the Pointe joined former Villèlists in opposition. When the bill reached the upper house, however, Baron Pasquier led the attack against it. Infused by Villèle's Peers of 1827, the upper house was now well to the right of the Deputies, and the bill was easily defeated.[9]

As in the Decazes era, cabinet attempts to build bridges on the basis of educational policies showed initial promise and then foundered. With official backing, mutual schools again mushroomed in the provinces as the ministry responded to Liberal demands by allotting 100,000 francs in the budget for funding. For a time, official approval encouraged royalists to participate, and subscriptions to the Parisian 'Society for Encouragement of Elementary Education' skyrocketed. Nevertheless, hostility among the bishops remained and ultraroyalists fought 'encouragement' every step of the way in the Chambers. Although mutual schools flourished, they remained a partisan issue.

On 13 February 1829, a new Toulousain Liberal journal, the *France Méridionale*, reported the origin of a new educational society that would encourage the formation of mutual schools throughout the Haute-Garonne. Notable among subscribers was prefect Emmanuel Camus du Martroy, an Imperial veteran who had chosen not to serve Bonaparte in 1815, but the founding members and elected administration of the society were all Liberals. High enrolment assured success, and the Maison Cibiel was soon stretched to full capacity, so that plans were made for a second school. All the same, mutual schools thereafter remained strictly a Liberal affair, and it was no coincidence that when Toulousain Liberals gathered prior to the election of June 1830, they did so in the building that also served as home to the mutual school.[10]

Under Martignac, legislative olive branches were accompanied by administrative behaviour designed to detach moderate from radical Liberals. In some cases, prefects appointed prior to 1828 could not adjust to viewing Liberals of any stripe as anything other than latter-day Jacobins, and thus Jacques-Etienne de La Grange-Gourdon de Floriac, an irascible ultraroyalist who had served in the émigré army of the princes of Condé, was 'promoted' from the prefecture of the Aisne to the Council of State in November 1828. At times lesser officials were also slow to grasp that Villèle's system was no longer in place; in the Oise in January 1829 the prefect had to prevent a sub-prefect from forcibly blocking a Liberal preliminary poll. Nevertheless, most prefects were more willing to pursue the broad policy

[9] Girard, 'La réélection', pp. 232–40.

[10] *France Méridionale*, 13 January, 13–23 February, 18 March, 1–10 May 1829, and Tronchet, *L'enseignement mutuel*, III, pp. 83–143.

outlines apparent in cabinet circulars. At Toulouse, invitations secured the return of Liberals to prefectoral balls, and at Foix this sign of reconciliation occurred in March 1829 for the first time in four years.[11]

Several prefects wrote reports encouraging the strategy of division, noting when the moderate voting of *constitutionnel* Deputies disappointed more left-leaning Liberals. From Lyons came reports distinguishing the moderate Antoine Jars, a merchant and former mayor during the Hundred Days who, however, was described as certainly loyal to the dynasty, from the radical Jean Couderc, also a merchant and the son of a Deputy to the Constituent Assembly of 1789. More informative were reports in January 1829 from Macon of a rift between the radical Count Thiard and the moderate Jean-Pierre Moyne-Petiot, a lawyer based at Chalon-sur-Saône. Thiard had upbraided Moyne for voting for the government's press law, and when Thiard's supporters refused to attend a banquet for Moyne at Chalon, moderates asked the prefect to grace the proceedings. The prefect demurred, but he reported that Moyne would sit in the Centre-Left in the forthcoming session, with the implication that he would not be obdurate in his opposition. For a cabinet in search of a majority, such information was vital.[12]

Banquets posed a test for several prefects. The successor to Vanssay in the Seine-Inférieure found himself confronted by invitations to banquets at Elbeuf and Rouen in October and November 1828 respectively. While the first included all the Deputies of the department and was moderate in character, the latter was radical, given plans to include Bignon, Dupont de l'Eure and d'Argenson. Wisely, the prefect consulted the Minister of the Interior, and then declined both invitations. So too did the crown prosecutor general and the Lieutenant General, whereas lesser officials were left to decide for themselves. Such a solution was typical of the middle course pursued by the Martignac ministry, but its long-term effect was to continue the reversal of the previous isolation of Liberals.[13]

In the Loire in January 1829, the prefect grasped the nettle of aligning with moderates by joining the mayor of Saint-Etienne in backing a moderate Liberal candidate on the second ballot of a by-election. The only alternative was an ultraroyalist, at a time when voters were reacting against clerical opposition to the ordinances of 16 June. The prefect could not, however,

[11] AN, F7 6767, folio Aisne; see also Ariège, 5 March 1829, and F7 6771, Oise, 7 January 1829.

[12] AN, F7 6767, Aveyron, 16 July 1828, Bouches-du-Rhône, 27 May 1829; F7 6771, Rhône, 5 January 1829, and Saône-et-Loire.

[13] AN, F7 6718, 6–15 October 1828; *Neustrien*, 1 October – 3 November 1828, and *Journal de Rouen*, 13 October – 7 November 1828.

risk too public an endorsement, and he was relieved when Liberals agreed to forgo their usual victory banquet.

In what was to prove a singular departure, prefect d'Arros attended a banquet for the radical Liberal Etienne at Bar-le-Duc in November 1828, after extracting promises as to who would attend and what would be said. By way of explanation to Martignac, d'Arros argued that his actions were the best way for the government to gain influence. His attendance incited criticism even in the *ministériel Moniteur*, however, and this experiment would not be repeated. It was perhaps a coincidence that d'Arros was dismissed under the Polignac cabinet, but one doubts it.[14]

The cabinet wished to assess public opinion in the summer of 1828, and prefects were therefore directed to conduct another survey. Reports gave a complex picture, but certain themes could be extracted. The administration had received a battering in the first half of 1828, and several prefects referred to despondency among their charges, and a spirit of independence creeping into local and departmental councils. Such 'independence' came partly from the Right, especially in clashes between local officials and the clergy, and religious issues also carried 'insubordination' into the departmental general councils.

Initially the ordinance of 16 June provoked seemingly major divisions in regions associated with strong Catholic religiosity – parts of Brittany and Normandy, departments such as the Doubs and the Jura, and, especially, the Midi. Nevertheless, most departments accepted the ordinances readily enough, and reports of satisfaction far outnumbered accounts of discontent. The problem with the measures was not that they were especially unpopular; it was that defiance of them played into the hands of the Opposition.[15]

Prefects uniformly reported growing alarm over the influence of the Liberal press, but, then again, the administration knew no greater enemy. More significant was confirmation that Liberals worked by legal means; revolutionary agitation was nowhere to be found. Liberals were now a more difficult foe because moderate conduct enabled them to spread their doctrines. Loyalty to the crown was still pervasive, but most prefects took care to associate this with loyalty to France's 'new institutions'.[16]

It was in this context of administrative uncertainty over the future that the cabinet began to ponder whether to make departmental and local councils

[14] AN, F7 6770, Loire, 25 January 1829, Meuse, 19 November 1828, and F7 6767, Ardèche, 2 January 1829.

[15] AN, F7 6767, Ardèche, July–October 1828; Ariège, July–November 1828; Bouches-du-Rhône, July 1828 – May 1829, and F7 6772, Somme, July–November 1828.

[16] These conclusions derive from the résumés for June–August 1828 in AN, F7 6767.

elective. From the provinces, however, came waves of prefectoral alarm. Foremost was concern that the administration might in the future have to share power with local bodies: such a division of authority would entail a significant loss of patronage disposal – a potentially lethal blow for royalism. A closely related refrain was that desire for democracy was again stalking the land. The spectre of democracy could be seen in the 'spirit of independence' presently invading councils, and it would only grow if given justification by notions of representation. Moreover the 'zeal' of current members was sapped by the knowledge that few of them could expect to be elected. According to one prefect, if the crown gave way, it could expect democrats to challenge all sources of authority, leading inevitably to a republic. If change had to come, let it be by royal ordinance rather than legislative enactment, so that notions of national representation played less part in the process.[17]

Critics of the centralization of power saw matters differently, and the issue of whether to make local councils elective sparked a response in the departmental press that was highly revealing of grassroots Liberalism. At Rouen, the centrist *Neustrien* and the more radical *Journal* (under new Liberal ownership) responded in ways that differed in nuance, but were basically similar. The *Journal* criticized government proposals because they 'left the Napoleonic system almost entirely intact', leaving prefects with excessive powers. Furthermore, franchises should be broad enough to prevent councils from falling under the control of 'narrow coteries'. The *Neustrien* was more cautious, opining that the laws of 1790 had brought anarchy; nevertheless it did argue that a *cens* could be safely set at 100 francs. The *Neustrien* was also looking for real power for elective councils, which should appoint police commissioners and forest guards. Those who paid taxes should decide how revenues were spent.[18]

In parliament, battle boiled down to a cabinet proposal which would have restricted the franchise to numbers (roughly 31,400) well below the national franchise, and a counter-proposal in the Chamber which would have been more generous (roughly 157,000). If the latter proposal fell well short of what grassroots Liberalism wanted, this was because Deputies were more cognizant of the need to compromise with a vulnerable cabinet – a visit by Polignac to Paris had provided clues of what might be in the offing.

The cabinet's proposal in fact bore close resemblance to ultraroyalist proposals made back in 1815–16. The Right had since evolved, however,

[17] Ibid., Allier, 4 May 1829, Ariège, 4 May 1829, Aube, 6 January and 1 April 1829, and F7 6769, Eure-et-Loire, 8 May 1829.

[18] *Journal de Rouen*, 10–12 February 1829, and *Neustrien*, 13–25 February 1829.

and most ultraroyalists were now wedded to the centralization of power. Moreover, what the Right most wanted was to expose the futility of seeking to reach accommodation with the Centre-Left. Thus ultraroyalists played the role of wrecking agent throughout the parliamentary debates, and in the end they achieved what they wanted when Charles X directed the cabinet to withdraw the bill and appointed the Polignac cabinet in August 1829.[19]

In domestic politics an attempt to crack down on the press and the cabinet's conduct of the elections of 1830 were the two key aspects of government under Polignac. The former will be discussed in the final section of this chapter; here we will settle for discussing the nature of the government's electoral campaign.

For ultraroyalists, the central issue was whether the royal will would be followed. Charles X saw matters in this light, and royal intervention in the elections was direct. Much has been made of the king's address to the electorate, but it was hardly unprecedented; Louis XVIII had made similar addresses several times. In 1816 ultraroyalists had tried to divorce the royal from the ministerial will in the minds of voters, and Liberals followed suit in 1830, but few were duped by such fictions. Nor was there anything very exceptional about the government campaign. Rhetoric was apocalyptic, but no more so than in 1820. The clergy played a major role in organizing the vote, but there was nothing new in this.

In the Isère, prefect Antoine Finot directed officials to spare no effort to turn out the vote. After the elections he then filed extensive reports on the conduct of his subordinates, and, given the electoral results, his assessments were surprisingly favourable. Almost all salaried officials had openly campaigned for government candidates, and while non-salaried officials, primarily mayors and *adjoints*, had been less enthusiastic, support had been far from negligible. The main problem was that independent voters had fallen under the sway of Liberal lawyers and notaries.[20]

At Toulouse in April the *France Méridionale* warned that local ultraroyalism was again organizing: 'the committees of these messieurs . . . who determined the elevation of Villèle alongside the bloody corpse of Ramel, reunite their men'. Though overstated, this was correct in the main. Despite his distaste for the cabinet, Villèle accepted the post of president of the departmental electoral college, and joined with the prefect in fostering 'royalist' unity.[21]

[19] Duvergier de Hauranne, *Histoire*, x, pp. 63–174.
[20] AN, F1C III Isère 5, 26–8 June and 24 July 1830.
[21] *France Méridionale*, 13 April 1830, and Villèle, *Mémoires*, v, pp. 422–53.

At the colleges, ultraroyalists harried *constitutionnels*, labelling them Jacobins, and d'Aldéguier, as college president for the *arrondissement* of Toulouse, ostentatiously arranged seating so as to violate the secrecy of the ballot. At Muret, measures designed to protect the secrecy demanded by an Opposition voter were accepted on the first day, but then removed when it came to voting for the Deputy, and similar alterations occurred at Villefranche. Amidst all of this manoeuvring, one development pleased the *France Méridionale*: prior to the departmental college assembly the prefect had sent out notices calling on royalists to conduct a preliminary poll. Thus the legitimacy of preliminary polls had now been recognized 'by the administration itself'.[22]

Elsewhere officials acted with more restraint. The events of 1827 and 1828 had revealed that administrators could be punished for illegal actions should they not be on the winning side, and prefect Finot therefore stayed within the letter of the law in the Isère. Although violation of the secrecy of the ballot was systematic in the Haute-Garonne, the president of the departmental college of the Gard recognized that such tactics were now largely discredited, and thus he gained expressions of gratitude from an Opposition wise enough to shout 'Long live the king!' while saluting integrity.

Liberal moderation ensured that alliance with the Agier group held, although some 'defectors' such as Hocquart doubled back into the ultraroyalist camp. The Agier alliance, in turn, helped to ensure that the judiciary, for the most part, continued to insist upon the legal registration of voters. There was some wavering, but this simply slowed Liberal progress while the gains made since 1827 remained in registration lists.

At Toulouse, Liberals provided a bureau of free consultation composed of barristers, leading merchants, and the staff of the *France Méridionale*. When several mayors failed to verify tax statements, the newspaper informed readers that officials had no right to question the purpose of document requests. Any prospective voter confronting obstruction should contact the Liberal bureau, and claimants who wished to appeal to the royal court could do so free of cost. By 5 June, 378 claims had been lodged at the prefecture. Prefect Camus had, however, ruled not to accept individuals who could have registered prior to September 1829, and thus changes were reduced to ninety-four new voters inscribed and twenty-six removed.[23]

The prefect's decision would be appealed, and the *France Méridionale* optimistically forecast that the judiciary would act in an enlightened fashion.

[22] *France Méridionale*, 5–29 June and 3–30 July 1830.
[23] *Ibid.*, 27 February, 22–9 May, 1–8 June 1830.

After all, the courts had redressed twenty-one illegalities in September 1829. Liberal lawyers did win several individual cases, but the major issue of registration prior to September was lost in a session presided over by Hocquart. As both the *Journal* and *France Méridionale* noted, this put the Toulousain court in opposition to the decisions of most of the other royal courts. Indeed, a Liberal committee of the Seine-Inférieure was given little cause for complaint by the *cour royale*; hence the judges were lauded at a Liberal gathering prior to the departmental college.[24]

Voter registration was fiercely contested in the Isère, where the prefectoral council accepted forty-one claims, but rejected seventy-six. Ninety claims were then brought before the *cour royale*. The Liberal committee had organized a network of agents who operated in each canton and most communes, and they had established a fund so that claimants could put forward their demands, even when they knew the prefect was likely to reject them, necessitating recourse to the courts. Here too, a key consideration sprang from the question over rights that had not been renewed during the period specified for annual list revision. Because a ministerial circular stated that individuals who had not renewed during the previous annual registration period would not be allowed to vote, royalists for whom this applied did not register claims during the immediate pre-election list revision process. Conversely, knowing this ministerial decision would be contested, Liberals registered during the immediate pre-election revision to cover the eventuality of a favourable judicial verdict.

Recognizing the danger, Finot ordered officials to scour taxation lists seeking royalists in this position. Only twenty-six agreed to go forward, however, partly because royalists were confused by a prefect admonishing them to register claims he intended to reject, knowing there would be more Liberals making such claims. Worse yet, by the final pre-election registration day, not all the necessary documents had been assembled, necessitating that a royalist committee register that 'several' individuals planned to make claims, without even naming them.

Confirmation of the administration's declining position came in the rulings of the courts: prefectoral decisions were reversed in seventy-four of ninety challenges. The judges ruled that claims presented by third parties with a simple signature from the interested parties were valid, although the signatures had not been notarized. They accepted that eight individuals should have been taxed as bankers rather than merchants (thus paying

[24] AN, F1C III, Seine-Inférieure 5, 9 June 1830; *Journal de Rouen*, 17 and 29 May, 11–12 July 1830, and *France Méridionale*, 18–29 May and 10 June 1830.

higher *patente* rates) and that this error was the responsibility of the administration rather than the taxpayer. They also ruled that the voting rights of thirty-three individuals could not be denied, despite the fact that their eligibility had expired during the annual registration period. Worse still, the claims of twenty-six royalists in the same position were thrown out because of the irregularities previously admitted by Finot himself. In a long report Finot asked the Minister of the Interior to consider whether the decisions of the judges constituted an attack on administrative authority.[25]

Attempts by the Polignac cabinet to resurrect Villèle's system thus largely failed. Although ultraroyalists closed ranks, punishment for previous electoral irregularities in 1828 thereafter led prefects to act more cautiously. Practices such as violation of the secrecy of the ballot reappeared in some departments, but were less widespread than in the past because the electorate was less disposed to accept such means of control and intimidation. Efforts by the Martignac government to woo the Centre-Left had further undermined allegations that Liberals were bent on revolution and, although the judges proved relatively less receptive to Opposition arguments than in 1827–8, Liberal gains in voter registration continued. Polarization did regain some moderates for the Right, but this was far from sufficient to overcome Liberal advances.

## PART THREE: FROM STRENGTH TO STRENGTH

Press expansion was vital to Liberal progress, and came by several routes. Veteran publishers such as Carion at Dijon returned to levels of direct commentary not seen since the Decazes era, while in the Seine-Inférieure Edmond Corbière took over the *Journal du Havre* and made it a fully political paper. At Troyes, criticism by the *Journal de l'Aube* was nothing new in 1829, but the journal's ability to trouble officials had certainly increased. Similar remarks could be made at Orleans concerning the *Journal du Loiret*, given new teeth by several young journalists. At Chaumont, the *Courrier de la Haute-Marne* rediscovered a critical voice and thereby stimulated desire for subscriptions among rural municipal councils. At Caen, the *Journal du Calvados* had lapsed into political silence since 1821, but it was now transformed into the *Pilote* to guide readers hostile to the government. In some cases, formerly moderate editors took a sharper approach to prevent being outflanked by the creation of a more left-leaning journal. For example,

[25] AN, F1C III Isère 5, 26 June, 4 and 20–4 July 1830. See also the petition *A Messieurs composant la cour royale de Grenoble* in the same carton and ADI, 7M2, 19 June 1830.

at Rennes the editor of the departmental journal agreed to publish political articles and thereby gained subscriptions already established for a proposed radical journal that Liberals duly cancelled.[26]

In some departments criticism of local government was an entirely new experience. In the Creuse, the prefect dismissed the advent of the *Album* at Aubusson as inconsequential in January 1829, but by March 1830 he was reporting that the *Album* was a significant source of trouble. A similar pattern unfolded concerning the *Aviso* at Toulon; initially described as having little influence, by January the journal was considered a major problem. In the Oise, the *Pandore* stated its intention to watch over the administration, and at Amiens *The Sentinelle Picarde* also began its existence by declaring it would monitor local government. Meanwhile Liberal journals also sprang up in the Pas-de-Calais, the Basses-Pyrénées, the Deux-Sèvres, the Yonne and the Haute-Vienne.[27]

At Lyons, Liberals already possessed the redoubtable *Précurseur*, founded in August 1826. Linking itself to 1789 in its original prospectus, the journal stated its intention to oppose a king who sought absolute power, an aristocracy blinded by its pretensions, an illiberal and intolerant clergy, and a political system wherein the powers of government ministers were illusory, the judiciary possessed no independence, and elections were not free. Starting with a base of 1,000 subscribers, the *Précurseur* soon established a readership throughout the south and east of France and greatly troubled the authorities.

In several instances the coexistence of moderate and radical Liberal journals emerged. At Bourges, radicals considered the *Journal du Cher* too moderate, and so they embarked on the *Revue mensuelle du département du Cher*, and at Metz the *Courrier de la Moselle* rapidly surpassed the departmental *Journal* in vehemence. At Lyons the *Journal du Commerce* was less impressive than the *Précurseur*, but it did share the 'liberal opinions' of the latter.

The backing of Liberal committees could sustain opposition in the face of prefectoral hostility. In the Nord, the Opposition was represented by the *Mémorial de la Scarpe*, the *Feuille de Valenciennes* and, most importantly, the *Echo du Nord.* Liberals could do little about six months' imprisonment when the editor of the *Echo* went too far, but they did raise 3,000 francs to pay his fine. At Marseilles, an aggressive prefect managed to convert the *Echo*

26 AN, F7 6767, Aube, 26 November 1829; F7 6770, Loiret, 5 October 1829, Haute-Marne, 4 June 1828; F7 6776, Ille-et-Vilaine, 28 November and 12 December 1829.

27 AN, F7 6768, Creuse, 23 January, 9 October and 16 November 1829, 10 March 1830; F7 6771, Oise, 7 January 1829, and F7 6772, Somme, 9 February 1829, Var, 30 September 1829 and 9 January 1830.

*Provençal* to an organ of 'royalism', but this required some 10,000 francs for the purchase of subscriptions. The removal of printing commissions did not, however, transform the *Sémiphore*, leading the prefect to commence legal harassment. Yet continued Liberal control of the redoubtable *Nouveau Phocéen* meant that public opinion was 'no longer what it used to be'. At Bordeaux, the *Mémorial* took a line similar to that of the *Journal des débats*, while the *Indicateur* approximated the Parisian *Courrier* and *Constitutionnel.* Worst of all was the *Propagateur*, which, in the hands of Henri Boyer-Fonfrède and Etienne Arago, possessed a radicalism which would make Thiers' *National* appear a poor cousin in 1830.[28]

At Rouen the *Neustrien* traded its former literary confines for political journalism in late August 1828; its initial tendency was *constitutionnel*, but sympathetic to the Martignac cabinet. More striking was change in the *Journal de Rouen*, purchased by two young Liberals who hired Auguste-Théodore Visinet, a Rouennais who practised law at the Parisian bar, as head editor. Visinet took the *Journal* well to the left of the *Neustrien*, and in its first edition under the new ownership, on 1 August 1828, the *Journal* announced its intention to report on local government. Thus Rouen was similar to Toulouse, where the *Journal* inched leftwards to find readers the *France Méridionale* left behind.[29]

Not all new ventures were fully fledged political newspapers; many were literary journals that pushed the limits of legal restrictions. Few published daily, and many were probably ephemeral. The *Omnibus* of the Eure, for example, launched its attacks on the administration on a monthly basis only, and the *Indicateur* appeared but once a week at Besançon. Collectively, however, all these changes marked an important transition.[30]

We can gain some appreciation of the import of this expansion of the local press by looking at the *France Méridionale*, founded at Toulouse on 2 December 1828. Like the Parisian *Globe*, the *France Méridionale* presented itself as the organ of a younger generation. Published by Jean Hénault, the newspaper was largely based on the contributions of newcomers to the political scene. One of the more aggressive was Charles Bart, born in 1799, and while Arnaud-Laurent Dupin, Adolphe Cazes and Jean Gasc

[28] See J. Popkin, 'Un grand journal de province à l'époque de la Révolution de 1830: Le *Précurseur de Lyon*, 1826–1834', in M. Biard *et al.*, eds., *Hommages à Jean-Paul Bertaud* (Paris, 2002), pp. 185–6, and Popkin, *Press*, pp. 82–6; AN, F7 6767; Bouches-du-Rhône, 27 May and 10 December 1829; F7 6768, Cher, 8 July 1829, Calvados, 15 April and 6 December 1829; F7 6769, 13 July, 13 August 1829; F7 6770, Moselle, 16 March, 20 August and 2 December 1829, and F7 6771, Nord, 1 October 1828, 2 January 1829, Rhône, 5 January 1829.

[29] *Neustrien*, 29 August 1828, and *Journal de Rouen*, 1 September, 1828.

[30] AN, F7 6768, Doubs, 6 February 1830, and F7 6769, Eure, 15 November 1829.

were older, none of them had previously made much of a mark. The latter two were lawyers, and ties to the bar could also be seen in aid given to the journal by the barristers Jean Vacquier and Adolphe Martin. All the same, the *France Méridionale* was not entirely dewy-eyed. The young journalists had a mentor in Pagès, who gave advice and direction while providing contacts with the Parisian press.

The new Liberal organ provided consistency to local Opposition, as it welded previously disparate concerns into a sustained critique. As part of this process the *France Méridionale* systematically linked national and local politics and gradually something resembling a party platform emerged. An early grievance with the Martignac ministry was that it did not thoroughly purge Villèle's appointees. The journal believed that public scrutiny would force progress, however, and thus in July 1829 it provided a revealing discussion of the departmental budget. In this, large sums spent on the palace of justice and subventions granted to Clermont-Tonnerre, the vicars general, the canons and seminaries were contrasted with neglect of public education and inadequate expenditure on road-building.[31]

A difference between the *France Méridionale* and Vieussieux's *Journal* was that whereas the latter printed the archbishop's outbursts without commentary, the former was less disposed to turn the other cheek. Clermont-Tonnerre's defiance of the ordinance of 16 June 1828 ordering the closure of Jesuit seminaries provided ample opportunity. At one level, the *France Méridionale's* criticism of Clermont-Tonnerre was a simple matter of demanding due recognition of the royal prerogative; nothing could have been more divisive for royalists. Nevertheless, the Liberal press was deeply interested in associating ultraroyalism with their *bête noire*. Thus speculation on a trip by the abbé Jean-Joseph Berger to Paris served to raise images of back-room intrigue involving more than the clergy. Upon Berger's return, the *France Méridionale* quickly linked a suspicious meeting to the Congregation. As all good Liberals knew, the Congregation was an ultraroyalist secret society that specialized in covertly directing government in favour of clerical domination, against the wishes of the nation.[32]

With considerable relief the *France Méridionale* subsequently reported that a seminary at Saint-Gaudens had been ordered to close in January 1829 after illegally reopening. Yet the long arm of Clermont-Tonnerre was again in evidence shortly thereafter, when he convoked an assembly to

[31] *France Méridionale*, 2–20 December 1828, 3 January, 5–18 February, 6–18 March, 10–17 April, 17 May, 12 June and 19–30 July 1829.

[32] AN, F7 6769, 11 January 1829; *Journal de Toulouse*, 20 February 1828, and *France Méridionale*, 2–6 December 1828, 6 January 1829.

found a lending bank which would seek a lower-class clientele. Because leading officials, Deputies and notables attended the meeting, the *France Méridionale* sounded the alarm over what looked to be a drive to reinvigorate royalist–clerical patronage, and a second initiative, to found a *mont-de-piété* (charitable pawn shop), attracted similar scepticism. It was bad enough that Viscount MacCarthy, Count Montbel, the abbé Berger and several of the vicars general headed the project; it was even worse that the regulations of the founding society stated that borrowers must provide testimonials as to their morality. According to the journal, such regulations surely meant that the borrower would have to share the religious and political opinions of the lender, which, given the presence of Montbel and the vicars general, must mean belonging to the Congregation.[33]

Foreign affairs also received novel commentary when the commemoration of victory in Spain was begun at Toulouse in September 1828, with the Duchess of Berry placing the first stone of a monument honouring the army of Spain and the dauphin. The *France Méridionale* saw little gold in such glitter: intervention had brought anarchy and religious despotism to Spain, and ruin to merchants engaged in trade beyond the Pyrenees.[34]

Although the war with Spain was thus denigrated, criticism did not extend to the army, and the first edition of the newspaper contained an advertisement for a poem entitled 'Napoleon in Egypt'. Advertising such a work did not necessarily indicate Bonapartism, and the newspaper certainly had little favourable to say about the Napoleonic administrative model, but what was one to make of a review lauding elegant verse 'worthy of its subject and the hero of Egypt and Italy'? In April 1829 an article in which scorn was poured upon Toulousains who had hailed Wellington upon his victory fifteen years before was equally worthy of reflection.

The *France Méridionale* was well aware that struggle against ultraroyalism was far from over in the Midi. Journalists must write with prose carefully attuned to the sensibilities of their readership, otherwise moderate royalists would pay heed to the likes of Montbel, but at which point liberty became licence was a prickly issue. For example, in December 1828 the newspaper published a letter questioning whether it had a right to 'impose candidates on electors'. The response of the journal was firm, but also measured: voters could see the candidates for themselves and would judge accordingly, but they were unfamiliar with new cabinet strategies of not appointing *ministériels* as presidents of electoral colleges, while encouraging candidates

33 *France Méridionale*, 13–24 January 1829.

34 AN, F7 6769, 15 October 1828, and *France Méridionale*, 2–27 December 1828, 15–27 January, 7–11 February, 6 March, 15 April, 23 June and 12 July 1829.

capable of splitting the *constitutionnel* vote. It was therefore necessary to point out that the president was a friend of the official candidate, who was also the choice of ultraroyalists.

According to the *France Méridionale*, within the Liberal press no one spoke of the king with anything but 'respect and loyalty' and no writer attacked the doctrines of constitutional monarchy. If the Martignac cabinet was criticized, this was because it reflected the previous Chamber and not the current one. Thus the press deserved praise for performing its function responsibly, not official harassment.

Freedom of expression was vital because publicity could expose corrupt practices. That such exposure was a source of power could be seen when the sub-prefect of Muret wrote a letter to the *France Méridionale* explaining that his *cens* had been evaluated inaccurately in the previous year due to honest error, that he had not voted in the departmental elections, and that in August 1828 he had written to have the matter rectified. The journal's reply was finely calibrated. One might give the sub-prefect the benefit of the doubt in regard to the inflated *cens*, but it was, after all, he who had submitted the inaccurate information. Furthermore, in the previous election at Muret, the sub-prefect had violated the secrecy of the ballot. If he had not voted in the departmental college, perhaps this was because there were Liberal electors ready to bring him to trial? At any event, the sub-prefect's letter did demonstrate that he felt a need other than that of pleasing his superiors – public esteem. His letter thereby illustrated 'the benefits of publicity'.[35]

Royalists were less certain of the benefits of such exposure, and they also feared that the annual revision of voter lists would encourage the formation of permanent Liberal committees. Their fears were borne out in many departments, but registration battles were just one of many means by which Liberals sought to stimulate political commitment.

In the Isère in 1828 the previous multiple elections of Perier and the death of Michoud left three places vacant in the Deputation, and thus the other *arrondissements* remained hives of activity after Perier had opted for Grenoble. At the same time, voter registration kept the Liberal committee at Grenoble busy. In response to a prefectoral reply to their earlier petition, the committee wrote a second that cited several works of jurisprudence on the rights of third parties in list revision, and was more specific in claims. First it noted eight voters added by the prefect late in the campaign of 1827

[35] *France Méridionale*, 2–16 December 1828, 29–31 January, 16 February, 2 March, 10 April, 31 May, 7 June, and 10–12 July 1829.

so that it was impossible to verify their qualifications prior to closure of the list. Then seven individuals were listed who, when challenged at the electoral college, admitted they had not paid sufficient taxes and retired. Finally, another nine individuals, including the prefect, were charged with having voted illegally.

Times were changing. A new cabinet was in place, and Liberals now had Augustin Perier as a spokesman in the Chamber. Prefect Calvière therefore softened his position, conceding that eight individuals would have to be removed. A problem remained, however, in that several decisions hinged on when information had been submitted, concerning which the prefect's word could either be accepted or not. Moreover, in a printed response to the prefect's arguments, the committee could raise further questions, for which conclusions could not be drawn unless the prefect made available all the evidence in his possession. Thus Liberals decided to contest matters before the Council of State, where they broadened their attack by charging that the prefect had acted illegally by refusing to accept claims presented by third parties.[36]

The committee also decided to send a petition to the Chamber, where debate had begun over revising the electoral laws. At first a litany of misdeeds was presented. In his first list published in August 1827, Calvière had reduced the number of voters to 496 from the previous 1,264 of 1824. Not surprisingly, those still on the list had concluded that they would not have to resubmit their proofs and, although notices had subsequently stated otherwise, confusion had led many to fail to provide their documents. On the first day of the elections, the prefect had then refused to allow them to vote. Far from taking such a hard line with royalists, however, he had included many who were unqualified. Furthermore, officials had been threatened with the loss of their posts, had been directed to influence other voters, and had been ordered to ensure that all could see for whom they were voting.

Recommendations flowed naturally from complaints. Any voter should have the right to demand list revisions. To simplify procedures, contested decisions should be judged by nearby civil tribunals rather than the Council of State. To prevent fraud, electors should not have to reverify their rights unless other electors made claims against them. Prefects should not be allowed to add new voters in the month preceding college assembly, and should be obliged to keep exact registers concerning

[36] AN, F1C III Isère 5, 28 March – 30 April 1828 and *Pétitions à Monsieur le baron*; see also BMUG, R90671, 5 March 1828.

qualification documents. Thus local Liberals adumbrated many of the reforms that shortly thereafter were put into legislation.[37]

Not all departments sprouted revision committees, and not all were as aggressive as that of the Isère, but the main point had been gained by 1829: under Martignac prefects were more scrupulous. In departments where cheating had gone on blithely in 1827, this was rectified in 1828. For instance, in the Nord some 375 voters (including a royalist Deputy) were removed from the 'inaccurate' list of 1827 and some 425 new voters were added. Thereafter only sixteen claims went before the *cour royale*, demonstrating an administrative change of ways, and thus what some prefects termed Liberal 'Inquisition' diminished.[38]

Inquisition did not, however, decline in other matters, due to knowledge that the cabinet planned to reform local government, and particularly worrisome for officials was the Marchais proposal launched by the secretary of the Aide-toi. So that parliament might be better 'informed' of the state of local government, André Marchais proposed the collection of information on current officials, concerning whether their positions reflected local standing, or whether they had been chosen for partisan reasons. Were mayors absentees living elsewhere, so that *adjoints* or justices of the peace actually performed the work? Were communal lands well administered, and did the clergy exercise undue influence in civil government?

Even the staid *Moniteur* howled against this 'exercise in defamation', to which newspapers such as the *Journal de Rouen* replied by publishing the Marchais circular, so that readers could 'judge for themselves'. Not all departments experienced 'enquiries', but many Liberal committees did swing into action, and their network of sub-committees enabled them to send agents into the communes of rural France. In the opinion of the prefect of the Hérault, moderates were taken aback and, according to the prefect of the Moselle, activists grew weary of the amount of work imposed on them. Nevertheless, wherever Liberals went, they left a trail of rising expectations.[39]

[37] ADI, 14M5, *Pétition . . . à Messieurs les Membres de la Chambre des Députés.*

[38] AN, F7 6767, Ardèche, 28 January 1829, Aube, 12 October 1829, résumé of Haut-Rhin, June 1828, résumé of Moselle, August 1828; F7 6769, Eure, 25 December 1828, Ille-et-Vilaine, 8 December 1829; F7 6770, Loire, 27 October 1829, Moselle, 23 December 1828; and F7 6771, Nord, 1 December 1828 and 2 January 1829.

[39] AN, F7 6767, Aisne, December 1828 – March 1829; F7 6768, Dordogne, 23 April 1829; F7 6769, Eure-et-Loire, 10 February 1829, Gironde, 31 December 1828, Hérault, 24 January 1829; F7 6770, Haute-Loire, 6 May 1829, Manche, 6 December 1828, Haute-Marne, 4 June 1828, Moselle, 16 March 1829; F7 6771, Saône-et-Loire, 8 October and 1 November 1828; and F7 6772, folio Vendée, 3 April 1829. See also *Journal de Rouen*, 13 December 1828.

Some committees applied direct pressure over appointments. In the Ille-et-Vilaine, residents of a rural commune petitioned the prefect on behalf of a specific replacement when the post of mayor fell vacant, and in a second instance, thirty-two delegates of another commune, urged on by the departmental Liberal committee, presented their request personally. Elsewhere, a more typical practice was for municipal councillors to refuse to convene, preventing the necessary quorum for business to be conducted. To overcome such obstruction, the prefect of the Vaucluse had to write a threatening letter reminding councillors in a village close to Avignon that the choice of mayor was his alone.[40]

According to the *France Méridionale*, the remedy for bad government lay in extending the representative system to the local level, but such a prescription could present administrators with all sorts of unappealing complications. Shortly after his arrival, prefect Camus was called on to choose a new list of the Toulousain 'notables of commerce', and the chamber of commerce proposed to present him with a list previously composed by Juigné, to which forty merchants of the chamber's choosing would be added. According to the *France Méridionale*, however, a problem with this procedure was that Juigné had ignored those who paid the most in *patente* taxes (the leading merchants) and included individuals who did not even pay the tax. To hammer home the point, the journal presented tables of *patente* payments, and in his correspondence with Martignac, Camus largely agreed.

When the new list was finally produced, the *France Méridionale* commented that the prefect had generally selected well, but that matters could be improved by the resignation of illegally included members. The good news was that the tribunal of commerce would be elective in the future, but five of the nine current members should resign immediately, and the president of the tribunal should convoke elections without delay.

Matters then took a nasty turn in May 1828 when the cabinet ordered Camus to reverse his initial decision by reintegrating the thirty-one individuals dropped from Juigné's list. When the assembly of merchant notables was finally convened, the Liberal Chaptive protested against the 'illegal' composition of the assembly and demanded that the protest be placed in the official minutes. He and twenty-five other merchants then walked out. A motion for the protest to be read out loud was then rejected, and the Liberal Cassaing's request that mention of the protest be made in the minutes was also denied. Thereafter the assembly began constituting itself

[40] AN, F7 6767, Aisne, general report of April 1828; F7 6769, Drôme, 2 September 1829; F7 6770, Ille-et-Vilaine, 6 September 1829; F7 6771, Saône-et-Loire, 8 October and 1 November 1828; and F7 6772, Vaucluse, 8 January and 16 February 1829.

through voting, but when called on, Cassaing announced he must abstain and departed. Cassaing was a former judge and president of the chamber of commerce, and his actions made a strong impression, leading another seventeen merchants to exit. Given that eight notables had abstained from even attending, the assembly was reduced from ninety-four to a rump of forty-two, well below a quorum.[41]

The revolt of the merchant notables occurred when parliament was debating the issue of whether local councils should be made elective, and the *France Méridionale* made a point of linking the two issues by emphasizing the common theme of representative government. Thus, Martignac's withdrawal of the proposal to change the laws of local government provoked widespread anger, partly because it was directly connected to a host of battles being waged at the local level.[42]

While Liberals posed new challenges to the government, they also refined old practices. By 1828 political banquets were, of course, a familiar phenomenon. As before, Deputies returning from Paris or visiting from other departments could provide an opportunity, whereas a banquet held without the presence of a Deputy incited commentary at Angoulême. At a time of shifting allegiance, however, banquets played an important part in competition to attract new supporters. Some former royalists were drifting, and banquets were a means of attaching voters. The procedure was simple enough – a committee would send invitations to voters, asking them to subscribe to a festivity honouring certain Deputies. The choice of Deputies made political orientation obvious, as did the composition of the committee issuing invitations. Banquet attendance did not necessarily equate to a vote cast, but it was taken as a sign of allegiance.[43]

Radical Liberals were the most enthusiastic banqueters. Royalists had little to counter this device other than gatherings at the prefecture, which the Villèle era had discredited, and at times royalist *constitutionnels* and moderate Liberals also hesitated. When radicals at Moulins sought to pair Victor de Tracy with a moderate, the latter refused to participate, and a similar process unfolded at Caen in December 1828, negating radical attempts at 'fusion'. To woo moderates, radicals had to give up ostentatious defiance and avow loyalty to the dynasty. Those who did not, at a banquet

41 AN, F7 6769, 11 January 1829, and *France Méridionale*, 13 December 1828, 30 March, 10–13 April, 3–22 May 1829.

42 *France Méridionale*, 30 December 1828 and 21 July 1829.

43 AN, F7 6767, Aube, 26 November – 28 December 1829; F7 6768, Charente, 2 January 1829; F7 6769, Eure-et-Loire, 10 January 1829; F7 6771, Nord, 2 January 1829, Orne, 13–20 October 1828, Rhône, 29 August – 22 September 1829, and F7 6772, Seine-et-Marne, 8 October 1828.

for André Dupin close to Saint-Pons (in the Hérault), came in for a lecture from Dupin on the folly of publicly supporting republicanism.

Compromise was not hypocritical; most radicals knew that a change of dynasty was not highly desired by voters. Nevertheless, drawing moderates into combination with radicals produced moderates with more backbone when it came to supporting grassroots initiatives. More insidious, from a prefectoral point of view, was the mutual honouring between Deputies and supporters at banquets. At times this was overt, as when voters of the Ardennes expressed their satisfaction with Laurent Cunin-Gridaine for having fulfilled his mandate. When Deputies, in turn, went so far as to avow that they represented the local team of supporters, official disdain knew no bounds.[44]

In the session of 1828, much invective was directed at the Opposition because in by-elections in Paris Liberals gathered to conduct preliminary polls, complete with candidates presenting their credentials to a gathering of over a thousand. As the term suggested, preliminary polls were conducted prior to the elections and gave voters an opportunity to choose which candidates they would support. Martignac joined in the parliamentary attack and, as usual, the bogey of Jacobinism was trotted out. Yet there was nothing novel about a preliminary poll. The historian S. Kent found evidence of nineteen departmental Liberal 'caucuses' in 1827, and we have found the procedure employed as early as 1817 at Dijon. What does appear to have been distinctive about the Parisian poll was that some candidates presented their testimonials personally. Despite its bluster, the cabinet settled for banning the practice in public buildings, so that Liberals met in private premises, which posed no great obstacle.[45]

'Professions of faith' complemented preliminary polls and were a refinement of the patriotic oath, which had begun in 1818 as a means of providing voters with a broad outline of principles. One does find examples of 'professions' prior to 1827, usually in the form of handbills distributed to voters at the college, but they are relatively rare. After 1827, however, the practice became more widespread, and the press made 'professions' highly public. They also became increasingly detailed and specific, thus heightening the degree of commitment. Many of the 'professions' contained a promise not to accept a government appointment or promotion without submitting to re-election and, although frontal assault on state patronage was mainly associated with radicals, the press lionized the moderate Félix Faure when he

[44] AN, F7 6767, Allier, 14 November 1828, Ardennes, 31 July 1828; F7 6768, Calvados, 21 December – 2 January 1828, and F7 6769, Hérault, 9 December 1828.

[45] See Duvergier de Hauranne, *Histoire*, IX, pp. 467–74.

refused promotion in the judiciary. By 1830 many royalists felt compelled to make 'professions', though these tended to be very short on substance.[46]

How these components worked in combination could be seen in the Seine-Inférieure in 1828. Having gained election at both Rouen and Les Andelys (in the Eure) in 1827, Bignon opted for the latter, knowing the former was a safe Opposition seat. More than six weeks before the resultant by-election, a Liberal committee called a meeting and sent invitations to all registered voters. Some 700 to 800 attended, presenting their letters of invitation as they entered. To commence proceedings, a letter from Bignon was read out. He had consulted with the other Deputies of the Seine-Inférieure prior to choosing, and hence there was no discontent among the voters. Thereafter the barrister Aroux informed the assembly of a petition concerning the false inscription of royalists in the *arrondissement* of Dieppe in 1827 and invited voters to read and sign the petition.

Prior to determining who would run as the *constitutionnel* candidate, the assembly voted that candidates must promise not to accept government office or promotion. The committee then presented three candidates, but invited voters to propose alternatives. Each of the three proposed candidates took their oath and then presented their professions. Thereafter, immediately prior to the college assembly, Liberals gathered again to select their candidate, and the other two gave way to Louis Martin, a Rouennais merchant, after he emerged from voting as the favourite. On 26 April Martin trounced his royalist opponent on the first ballot.[47]

The appointment of the Polignac cabinet led Liberals to add a new weapon to their arsenal when the former *fédéré* and Deputy Charles Beslay *père* launched an association based on the refusal to pay taxes should the government 'violate the Charter'. The prospectus of the Breton Association was published in several Parisian and departmental journals in September, and shortly thereafter crown prosecutors laid charges against them.[48]

The idea of tax revolt had in fact been rumbling about with regard to several issues. For example, prior to the government of 8 August, Liberals had circulated proposals to refuse to pay taxes until the departmental councils were revamped. The idea had been given national prominence in the *Constitutionnel*, and in the Eure-et-Loire the Deputy François Isambert, a lawyer

[46] *Ibid.*, *Histoire*, IX, pp. 459–74.

[47] AN, F1C III Seine-Inférieure 5, reports of 9 March – 20 April and the college minutes; ADSM, 1M174, dossier *réunions*, 8 March 1828, and *Journal de Rouen*, 12 November 1828.

[48] D. Rader, 'The Breton association and the press: propaganda for "legal resistance" before the July Revolution', *French Historical Studies* 2, n. 1 (1961), pp. 64–82, Pilbeam, *1830*, pp. 32–3, and Bourset, *Casimir*, p. 179.

who had gained notoriety by defending members of the Carbonari, had drawn up petitions threatening a tax revolt. Liberal sub-committees had then circulated petitions in the *arrondissements*. Nor was Beslay's proposal unique; on 14 August the Liberal committee of Angers also published a pamphlet explicitly threatening a tax revolt should any attempt be made to suppress France's new institutions. At Rouen on 17 August, the *Journal* argued that if the cabinet tried to circumvent the Charter by ruling by ordinance, the duty of citizens would be refusal to pay taxes.[49]

According to the historian C. Pouthas, the organization of regional Associations based on the Breton model did not attract much response until the Aide-toi took up the idea. Pouthas does not give much by way of evidence, but his point would seem to be supported by a report by the prefect of the Côtes-du-Nord that Beslay had drawn up his proposal with the intention of disconcerting the new cabinet, rather than propagating an association that in fact did not exist. The latter point was pivotal to government prosecution of the press, but whether an association had actually been founded at Rennes prior to publication remains a mystery. Whatever the case, rapid government action in laying charges against the press slowed initial development. At this point it would appear that the Aide-toi did encourage local Liberal committees to proceed.[50]

Towards the end of 1829 regional Associations spread rapidly in number. Expansion could partly be attributed to coverage in newspapers such as the *Journal* at Dijon, the *Courrier de la Moselle* at Metz, the *Revue mensuelle du Cher* at Bourges, the *Sentinelle des Deux-Sèvres* at Niort, the *Nouveau Phocéen* at Marseilles, and the *Indicateur* at Bordeaux, and endorsement by Liberal Deputies, including moderates Casimir Perier, Ternaux and Duvergier *père*, was also important. Constant advocated using taxation to ensure responsible government in a letter in the *Courrier Français*, which Silbermann also published in the *Courrier du Bas-Rhin*, and Duchesne and the Liberal committee ensured that an Association was established throughout the Isère.[51]

Roughly 500 joined in the Nord, whereas 1,000 signatures were gained at Brest alone, due primarily to the influence of Deputy Guilhem. Elsewhere response was muted; while three Deputies signed at Bourg-en-Bresse, only sixty voters had joined them as of 22 January 1830. Official reports indicated that by 22 December the local Association had gained 200 supporters at

49 AN, F7 6769, Eure-et-Loire, 10 June 1829, and F7 6770, Loire, 3 and 29 April 1829, Maine-et-Loire, 31 August 1829.

50 Pouthas *Guizot*, pp. 395–9, and O. Barrot, *Mémoires posthumes*, 4 vols. (Paris, 1875–6), 1, pp. 79–81.

51 Materials on the Associations can be found in AN, F7 6776.

Strasbourg, but that it was not expected to gain much backing outside the *chef lieu*. At Toulouse, the *France Méridionale* printed a notice of the foundation of the Parisian Association and petitions were duly hawked about, but the prefect reported that few signed.[52]

In Normandy, the *Journal du Havre* and Martin Laffitte, a local merchant, were the first promoters of an Association. The *Journal de Rouen* more or less courted legal charges by publishing the Breton Association's prospectus on 13 September, and then stoutly defended the principle of refusal while awaiting its trial on 20 November. Nevertheless, Rouennais Liberals did not proceed to form an Association until 28 October, several weeks after their counterparts had done so at Le Havre, and after a lead had been set by Deputies such as Dupont de l'Eure. Thereafter recruiting began in the cantons. Signature collection ended when the Chambers were summoned, because the main purpose of the Associations had always been to force the convening of parliament. Liberals had been alarmed that the cabinet would seek to rule by ordinance, and hence the act of the Normandy Association proposed tax refusal should the government seek to collect taxes based on ordinance rather than legislation.[53]

In the meantime, the Associations had demonstrated that Liberals had learned from the early 1820s. They were conceived as a defensive response: not a word was breathed about refusal prior to illegal government action. Nor was there any suggestion of resort to force; the whole direction of the movement went towards legal resistance. Thus in October 1829 Casimir Perier could be found at a banquet of sixty Liberals at Joigny, toasting an association and emphasizing that the Charter stated that for taxes to be legal, they must first have the consent of the Chamber. Furthermore, it was difficult to portray the Associations as conspiratorial; they were intentionally public and when the question of whether they constituted subversion went before the courts in press trials, the crown's position was not given much by way of judicial backing. By that stage politics had moved on, but the idea of tax revolt had been widely disseminated and was in readiness should occasion warrant.

Taken in sum, organizational advances between 1827 and 1830 were substantial as Liberals built upon foundations established under Decazes. Gains made in the local press enabled Liberals to surpass the levels of publicity they had achieved by 1820, and by training their guns on issues of local

52 See the folio in *ibid.*, and F7 6769, 29 October 1829. See also ADHG, 6T3, 10 May 1830, and *France Méridionale*, 26–30 January and 2 February 1830.

53 AN, F7 6776, dossier 34, 29 October – 26 November 1829, and *Journal de Rouen*, 13 September – 26 November 1829.

government, Liberals had put officials under a great deal of pressure, seriously eroding administrative influence. Initiatives such as the Marchais proposal had also broadened the field of battle, complementing ongoing struggles over voter registration as Liberals continued their championing of the 'representative principle'. At the same time refinements in the use of banquets, the development of practices such as the 'profession of faith' and preliminary polls, and organizations such as the Associations against tax payment had heightened activism and deepened politicization. While the Liberal Opposition may not have been a political party in the full, modern sense of the term, it had certainly made marked progress in this direction as its activities became virtually permanent.

## PART FOUR: UNITE AND RULE: DISCERNING LIBERAL CHARACTER

It is logical to assume that rapid expansion in any group should produce at least some change in its nature. Analysing the character of the Liberal Opposition during the period under consideration is, however, complicated by the tendency of the moderate Centre-Left and radical Left to position themselves in terms of circumstance. Moreover, the fact that victory in 1827 had been built on coalition with parts of the Right further muddies the waters.

For the Opposition, the central question was whether the Centre-Left and Left, roughly equal in size, would remain united along broad policy lines. In the *Chambre retrouvée* this had not been difficult, but Martignac thereafter posed a different set of problems. From the standpoint of unity, there were two identifiable phases during the brief span of the government. The first lasted from the naming of the cabinet until the parliamentary session of 1829, a period wherein legislation and certain royalist overtures to the Centre-Left suggested the possibility of driving a wedge between the two blocks. Thereafter, however, the limits of accommodation became apparent to the Centre-Left, while part of the Left realized that intransigence might lead to a complete loss of influence.

According to Thureau-Dangin, the ultimate condemnation of the Opposition lay in the fact that the Centre-Left did not break with the Left and rally fully to Martignac. It is true that the Centre-Left worked towards Liberal unity, and that moderates took the lead in opposition to the cabinet's proposal for elective councils. All the same, Thureau-Dangin's perspective left him blind to what actually bound Liberal Opposition – that the Restoration consisted of more than the dynasty. At times Opposition could amount to little more than partisan politics, but the tussle over local government was not a case in point, and in other regards the cabinet did find support for its bills. Furthermore, when it came to influence through unity, Thureau-Dangin had the relationship in reverse. The main difference between 1819–20 and 1827–30 was that in the latter period the Left moved towards the Centre-Left.[54]

Beginning in January 1828, Liberal Deputies gathered as a single block in a building on the Rue Grange-Batelière. Meetings could draw anywhere from 100 to 150 Deputies, and a steering committee represented all nuances within the Opposition. It was here that broad policy was formulated. A small group of radicals briefly attempted to establish an alternative, but this failed and the practice of meeting as a single block continued in subsequent sessions.

The threat of fragmentation reached its apogee when part of the Left joined with the extreme Right in attacking the press laws of 1828. Although the legislation had much to recommend it, the Parisian *Courrier* insisted on partisan opposition, dragging an embarrassed Constant along in tow. Nevertheless, only part of the Left took this course, and the legislation passed easily. The desire of moderates to temper pursuit of Villèle, so as to draw the cabinet to the left, also irritated radicals. While a group of radical Liberals led by Guillaume Labbey de Pompières fought to have Villèle brought to trial, moderates took the view that sufficient damage had been inflicted by the discussions of a commission set up to investigate whether a trial was justified.

It would appear that during the autumn of 1828 the cabinet made overtures to the Centre-Left, represented by Casimir Perier and Sébastiani. Whether such 'soundings' were made in good faith is questionable, given that the king was already pushing for the inclusion of Polignac in the cabinet, but one way or another, Liberal demands for four cabinet posts and twelve peerages were hardly feasible for Martignac. Indeed the main consequence of the discussion was that part of the Left became convinced that they must moderate their demands in order to avoid alienating the Centre-Left. Such an evaluation of the dangers of isolation was astute; the loss of ties with figures such as Casimir Perier would have altered the balance in the Chamber and jeopardized the recent gains that provided the base for Liberal victory in the future.[55]

Ultimately, simply dragging out proceedings served to distance Villèle. Moreover, educational reforms and measures against Jesuit seminaries held

[54] Thureau-Dangin, *Le parti*, pp. 392–452. [55] See Bourset, *Casimir*, pp. 171–7.

an appeal for both parts of the Left, and thus tactical considerations overrode impatience. Relations were at times strained, as Constant fought the extreme-left abbé Dominique de Pradt in a bitter press battle, and Béranger ignored requests not to publish provocative verse, but unity largely held until the fall of the cabinet. For this reason, three radical Liberals, de Pradt (in 1828), Voyer d'Argenson and Chauvelin (both in 1829), grew restless and resigned their seats.[56]

Old habits were not confined to Deputies. Below the moderate leadership of Augustin Perier and Faure in the Isère, there were less patient elements. Among this circle were Blanc and Froussard, by then in charge of the education of Casimir Perier's children in Paris. In May 1828 Froussard began to take an interest in an old acquaintance of Blanc, the Robespierrist arch-conspirator Philip Buonarroti. Froussard had managed to obtain several volumes of the *Conspiracy of Equals* and, while promising to send a copy to Blanc, he expressed a fear that the old man would not be able to complete his labours for lack of financial support.

One of Froussard's roles appears to have been to aid needy radicals. Grenoblois Liberals responded well to such appeals, making donations to a subscription for Rey when he was allowed to return from exile. By June 1830 they were also contributing to a subscription for Buonarroti organized by Froussard and another Carbonaro, Charles Teste. Moreover, Teste and Froussard were writing regulations for a new 'masonic' society that had been requested by Blanc. There was irony in a secretary of Casimir Perier organizing aid for a man whose work was to be the handbook of violent revolution during the July Monarchy, but this appears less astonishing when one takes the character of Restoration Opposition into account. Matters would change after July 1830, but before then the Opposition was characterized by the willingness of differing groups to work together.[57]

An example of ongoing collaboration could be seen in Lafayette's tour through the Isère in August 1829. While family ties perhaps provide the explanation for the assiduous efforts of the Perier clan, it was also true that unrelated moderates vied with radicals in heaping honours on Lafayette. At Grenoble Lafayette was presented with a civic crown, and then fêted with a parade and banquet. Whether any of this was truly seditious was open to interpretation, though allusions to republicanism were plentiful.[58]

[56] Duvergier de Hauranne, *Histoire*, IX, pp. 483–6, 537–91, 625–8, X, pp. 299–309, and Vaulabelle, *Histoire*, VII, pp. 441–6, 455–60, VIII, 1–24.

[57] BMUG, N2136.

[58] AN, F7 3798, 13, 17 and 19 August 1829; BMUG, R90576 and R9513, 16 August 1829.

In the midst of Lafayette's tour, news arrived of the appointment of the Polignac ministry, which partly accounted for intemperate speeches. Perhaps wishing to make up for recent laxity, prefect Finot then dismissed the mayor and first *adjoint* at Vizille for taking part in the festivities. Augustin Perier's rejoinder was to send an article to the Lyonnais *Précurseur* deploring this disgrace of officials who surely had the right to honour a famous champion of liberty. Matters simmered down shortly thereafter, however, as Liberals refrained from provocative outbursts.[59]

One of the keys to future success was that Liberals maintained ties with moderate royalist allies. The most important of the latter, the Agier defection, had grown as a result of the elections of 1827, and its denunciations of Villèle's 'system' had secured the conversion of several former ultraroyalists, such as the Marquis of Cordoue. By 1828 the Agier defection constituted a block of roughly thirty Deputies who effectively represented the Centre-Right.

Where Liberals were weak, they threw their support behind Agier affiliates. Villefranche had long been a rotten borough for Villèle and there was little chance for a Liberal candidate in February 1828, so alliance with Hocquart was renewed. Hocquart's victory thereafter pivoted on the inability of his rivals to reach a transaction. The role of the administration in arranging such agreements had never been overlooked under Villèle, but on this occasion the authorities were slow to act. Moreover, none of the main candidates, Hocquart, Saint-Félix de Maurémont (currently under investigation for his electoral malpractices as prefect of the Lot) and Robert Morier de Mourvilles, a wealthy local ultraroyalist landowner, were named president of the college. After the second ballot, Hocquart had the lead but was well short of a majority. Hasty attempts by the sub-prefect and Villèlists prior to the third ballot almost saved the day, but the absence of a formal arrangement meant that not all of Saint-Félix's supporters shifted to Morier. The result was the narrowest of victories for the candidate whom most ultraroyalists wanted to defeat.

According to the *Journal de Toulouse* the final count produced ecstatic cries of 'Long live the king!', but a report by three ultraroyalists that voters had been outraged was closer to the truth. Liberals had envenomed relations between the two ultraroyalist candidates through rumour-mongering and had then blocked two voters by challenging their qualifications. The election of Hocquart thus was a triumph for Liberal tactics, but it also illustrated the basic weaknesses that necessitated alliance.[60]

59 BMUG, R90630.

60 AN, F1C III, Garonne (Haute-) 7, 'Observations', and report of the college president; ADHG, 2M24, college minutes of 25 February 1828, and *Journal de Toulouse*, 28 February 1828.

Moderation in the realm of political action was, therefore, crucial to maintaining solidarity among the Liberal Opposition as a whole, and securing alliance with moderate royalists. Moderation, in turn, revealed a willingness to compromise. These pronounced characteristics of pragmatic moderation and compromise have not, however, received due attention from historians, who have generally tended to concentrate on potentially divisive differing ideological components of the Opposition – liberalism, Bonapartism and republicanism. There is a certain amount of logic to such approaches in that they help to reveal the long-term development of the three components over the course of the nineteenth century, but such perspectives should not obscure the essential point that clarification of ideological differences occurred only after the Revolution of 1830. In other words, future divisions should not be read back on a Restoration Liberal Opposition that was characterized by a painstaking search for unity.

It was not that Liberals were muddle-headed over ideology; the threat posed by ultraroyalism meant that they could not afford the luxury of doctrinal squabbling. How far Liberals actually intended to go in their objective of advancing 'the representative principle of the Charter' was a question that they had little interest in answering accurately. One can perhaps find answers to such questions if one narrows one's scope to the writings of individual thinkers, but even here matters become exceedingly complicated if one compares, for example, Constant's constitutional theories to his actions and speeches as a politician. Despite the liberalism of his classic works, as a politician Constant was quite capable of flirting with Bonapartism and at times his speeches indicated more than a little sympathy for the democratic aspirations usually associated with republicanism. Moreover, the Opposition's collective doctrinal ambiguity can render conclusions drawn from a handful of political theorists highly misleading.[61]

A great deal of misrepresentation has resulted from confusion of Liberals with the *doctrinaires*. Whereas the *doctrinaires* wished to strike a balance between national and royal sovereignty, Liberals clearly and consistently placed priority on ensuring national sovereignty. Most Liberals did want constitutional monarchy, but national sovereignty was their fundamental principle and monarchy was secondary.[62]

From 1820 until 1830, *doctrinaires* and Liberals drew closer, with Guizot shifting more rapidly than Royer-Collard and Broglie. Given the current circumstances, *doctrinaires* placed emphasis on representative government,

[61] See A.-J. Tudesq, *La démocratie en France depuis 1815* (Paris, 1971), pp. 29–35.

[62] See E. Cappadocia, 'The Liberals and Madame de Staël in 1818', in R. Herr and H. Parker, eds., *Essays presented to Louis Gottschalk* (Durham, N.C., 1965), pp. 182–98.

which was what they had in common with Liberals. Indeed, Guizot travelled surprisingly far to the left prior to the Revolution of 1830 and began to mix with Foy, Constant, Voyer d'Argenson and Lafayette. It was these connections, and the backing of a local Liberal committee, that secured Guizot election at Lisieux in early 1830. Under other circumstances, however, *doctrinaire* emphasis on royal authority would reveal the limits of their championing of national sovereignty, and how they differed from Liberals.[63]

It has often been demonstrated that no party or movement that was specifically republican existed during the Restoration, but the same point can be made concerning the other Liberal components – Bonapartist or liberal. There were coteries of all three elements, but none of them were dominant within the Liberal Opposition. Nor can one find a doctrinal basis for the Opposition in the writings, thought or action of any one central political figure – at most Constant, Casimir Perier, Foy, Manuel, d'Argenson, Dupont de l'Eure or Lafayette represented tendencies which, in turn, were frequently readjusted to suit specific circumstance.[64]

If we leave aside the search for doctrinal clarity, we begin to see a group that takes on a modern political hue. Modern parties or movements, if they are to succeed, are based on alliances that, from an ideological perspective, are compromises in the pejorative sense of the term. Nevertheless, compromise is essential in politics. Analysts seeking, say, the origins of republicanism, have often treated Liberal pursuit of coalition, opportunism, gradualism and timely obfuscation as negative characteristics because they indicate an absence of doctrinal purity or commitment, but they were all crucial to Liberal success.

Liberals gained their name by their repeated reference to the liberties of 1789 as their touchstone. Yet association with 1789 was by no means monopolized by Liberals; a very similar rhetoric had returned to Bonapartism in the crisis of 1813–15. Try as she might to separate liberalism from Bonapartism, de Staël could not do so and, under the urging of Goyet, Constant curbed his inclination to distance himself from the Imperial despot. Constant did so because he wished to be elected. The message from the electorate and the broader Liberal following was not to draw too clear a line between liberalism and Bonapartism.[65]

[63] See Pouthas, *Guizot*, pp. 472–7, and Rosanvallon, *Le moment*, especially pp. 11–31.

[64] Among works on liberal writers, see Jardin, *Histoire*, 1–304; Girard, *Les libéraux*, pp. 1–125, and B. Fontana, *Benjamin Constant and the Post-Revolutionary Mind* (New Haven and London, 1991).

[65] Thureau-Dangin considered liberal Bonapartism a flaw; see his *Le parti*, pp. 14–32, 57–77, 91–106, and Harpaz, *L'école*, pp. 157–63.

Bonapartism fitted comfortably within the Opposition because it replicated the protean qualities of its originator. Bonapartism did stand for a cluster of loosely associated ideas and values, but during the Restoration it was characterized by ambiguity and a more than healthy dose of opportunism. On the one hand, Bonapartism had an authoritarian tendency that at points linked it to both extreme Jacobinism and ultraroyalism. Among Napoleon's legacies was centralization of power in pursuit of national unity, and anyone actually in government could be tempted by this tradition. On the other hand, the Hundred Days had brought about an alliance between Napoleon and liberals, something that the deposed emperor then cultivated with propaganda written at Saint Helena. Thus former authoritarian Bonapartists could view liberty anew, especially when confronted by the possibility of no longer holding power. Bonapartism of the Left flourished during the Second Restoration, and it was parliamentary government that took hold within Bonapartism. It was for this reason that figures such as Clausel, Lamarque, Méchin and Girardin could play such a major role in the Opposition; those who voted for them did so without visions of dictatorship dancing in their heads.[66]

In the same way, republicans learned to temper old inclinations. They too had a stake in 1789 which linked them to liberals and Bonapartists, and whatever their thoughts about the superiority of 1792, they also knew to what the First Republic had led. Pragmatism derived from previous failure characterized the group whom the historian E. Newman has termed 'gradualist republicans' – individuals such as d'Argenson, Lafayette and Joseph Rey were willing to settle for progressive enlargement of the franchise while throwing themselves into mass education. Such long-term strategies were sensible, given the realities of contemporary politics, and they also provided common ground with liberals and Bonapartists. Initiatives such as mutual schools attracted Liberals because they were a practical way of putting one's effort where one's ideals were. Better yet, they entailed leaving the search for doctrinal purity to ultraroyalism.[67]

The pragmatic character of the Opposition could be seen in the emphasis that Constant placed on securing unity through compromise and moderate behaviour in the Bas-Rhin, where he started from a difficult position, having unseated Humann in 1827. He did have a devoted core of radicals, but relations with moderate Liberal Deputies Turckheim and Saglio were not going to be easy. Crucial to Constant's subsequent success was that he

[66] See Bluche, *Bonapartisme*, pp. 95–204, and Alexander, *Napoleon*, pp. 36–45.

[67] See Newman, 'Republicanism', Pilbeam, *Republicanism*, pp. 60–94, and Neely, *Lafayette*, pp. 39, 69 and 58.

was a great constituency man. Immediately after his election, he solicited information on Alsatian interests and did not complain when deluged with petitions, brochures and long letters. In the summers of 1828 and 1829, Constant returned to the department to meet with a 'constitutional committee' to plan strategy for the coming parliamentary sessions, and when he was uncertain as to how to broach a subject in budgetary debates, he could turn for advice to his Alsatian correspondents – Coulmann, Louis Schertz and Jean-François Walter.[68]

One of the first matters to be put on a proper footing was Constant's relationship with Silbermann. Schertz wanted to create a rival journal, but such an action might have made conflict with moderate Liberals permanent, and a better alternative came by way of the poet Ehrenfried Stoeber acting as intermediary. By 9 December 1827 Stoeber could report that Constant would have his speeches and articles published in the *Courrier du Bas-Rhin.* In return, when Silbermann wished to have an article reach a wider audience, Constant would use his contacts to secure publication in a Parisian journal.[69]

Relations with Turckheim and Saglio would not be so easily settled, and Schertz was convinced that neither of them could be relied upon because in the past they had combined with Humann in making too many 'concessions to the administration'. How matters would unfold only gradually clarified during the Chamber sessions of 1828. Constant, who had been asked to take up the cudgels so as to avoid fratricide within the Deputation of the Haut-Rhin, played a major role in attacking the prefect of the other Alsatian department. Significantly, Saglio supported him, and even Turckheim lashed out against the 'deplorable system' of the previous government. Nevertheless when the two Centre-Left Deputies put forward a claim to the Minister of Justice they did not ask Constant to join. Furthermore, it was Constant who had to search out his colleagues concerning economic petitions they were about to put before the Chamber.[70]

There was a raft of petitions ranging from demands that an end be put to restrictions on transit of colonial goods through the interior, to plans to improve transportation along the Rhine. Moderates and radicals were essentially in agreement as to objectives, and thus the three Liberal Deputies

68 BN, NAF 24914, 26 July, 13 November 1828, 27 October and 30 November 1829; Constant to Stoeber in *La vie en Alsace* (July 1934), p. 167, and Coulmann, *Réminiscences*, II, p. 112.

69 BN, NAF 24914, 26 July 1828 and 27 October 1829; BCUL, Co 1327; Co 1330; Co 1370, Co 1975; Co 1976; letters from Constant to Stoeber, 18 May, 1 July, 2 August 1828 in *La vie en Alsace* (July 1934), pp. 166–8, and Coulmann, *Réminiscences*, II, pp. 113–14.

70 BNUS, Ms. 1534, 29 May 1828, and BCUL, Co 1327–30.

combined while speaking in the Chamber. In the event, their efforts came to nothing as the issues were deferred to the next year, but the ice between Constant and his colleagues thawed: Constant was assigned the task of contacting the Minister of Commerce to forward the petitions and open negotiations over customs tariffs.[71]

Encouraged by the concessions made by the Martignac cabinet, Liberals decided upon a show of loyalty during the journey of Charles X to Alsace in September 1828, and Coulmann pressed Constant to take part in a banquet offered to the king at Strasbourg. Constant did so and Charles was pleased by the protestations of affection he received. The king, however, concluded that he could do whatever he liked in the future and still count on avowals of loyalty prevailing. He thus misconstrued support for Martignac's reforms as unqualified royalism.[72]

Immediately thereafter local radical Liberals organized another Constant tour of Alsace, concluding with a Strasbourg banquet wherein Turckheim and Saglio joined Constant at the head table. Toasts were suitably mixed: along with Foy and Manuel (radical icons), Girardin and Jordan (moderates) were commemorated, and toasts to religious liberty and 'our future municipal institutions' were balanced by toasts to the king and the judiciary. Thereafter Constant made a point of praising his two colleagues for their defence of religious liberty, emphasizing common ground among all parties in attendance.[73]

By the parliamentary session of 1829, it was Constant who took the lead in the Deputation's exasperatingly futile demands for economic reform. Meanwhile tempers flared even more in debates over local government. In the previous year, Turckheim had charged that centralization was killing local patriotism, which needed representation to flourish, and in 1829 Constant played a major role in the Chamber debates, pushing for a more liberal franchise than the government was willing to grant.[74]

How far Silbermann had travelled could be read in the reaction of the Strasbourg *Courrier* to the announcement of the cabinet of 8 August:

[71] BN, NAF 20037, 22 June 1828; NAF 24914, 1 February 1828; BNUS, Ms. 1534, 16 and 29 May 1828; Ms. 113 441; BCUL, Co 1328–30; Co 3756; Co 1401; Co 2010; Co 4600; Constant to Stoeber in *La vie en Alsace* (July 1934), pp. 167–8; *Courrier du Bas-Rhin*, 1 June, 20–2 July 1828, and Leuilliot, *L'Alsace*, I, pp. 495–7.

[72] BN, NAF 24914, 28 August 1828; *Courrier du Bas-Rhin*, 10 February, 20 April, 9–16 September 1828, and Leuilliot, *L'Alsace*, I, pp. 497–505.

[73] ADBR, 3M19, 9 October 1828; BCUL, Co 3748, invitation to Constant, October 1828; *Courrier du Bas-Rhin*, 9–19 October and 2 November 1828, and Coulmann, *Réminiscences*, II, p. 105.

[74] BN, NAF 24914, 24–5 May 1829; BCUL, Co 1422; Co 3379; Co 1966; Co 1967; Co 1975; Co 4546; Co 3935; Co 4551; Co 1972; Co 4554; *Courrier du Bas-Rhin*, 1–6 January 1829, and Leuilliot, *L'Alsace*, I, pp. 507–11.

'We again fall under the yoke of Jesuitism and despotism!' Apocalyptic as this was, it did not herald an ill-considered response to royal provocation. Caution was, for example, apparent in the radical's invitation to the guest of honour at the banquet of 1829: 'The *constitutionnels*, certain as to their political character, invite Benjamin Constant to a Strasbourgeois family fête to present him, with Saglio and de Turckheim, to the people.' Moreover, the Liberal committee wished that no speech be given; now was not the time for Constant to bare his fangs. Nevertheless, arrangements to 'introduce the Deputies to the people' were less modest. There were two floating barges, each with thirty musicians illuminated by 1,200 Chinese lanterns, for the serenades. Crowds, estimated by the prefect at 2,000 to 3,000, but by the *Courrier* at 10,000, then gave the customary cries. They were encouraged by the lawyer Liechtenberger from the balcony of the hotel, prior to the arrival of Saglio and Turckheim on either side of Constant.

Unity was the order of the days following. Constant was again given star billing when presented with a silver vase, a gift from 256 subscribers. The three Deputies subsequently dined together, with a small group of electors; the contrast with previous years was striking. Esmangart lamented the change in Turckheim and especially Saglio, who was Catholic and owed much of his monetary and political fortune to Humann. The latter had, however, departed Strasbourg the day prior to the banquet.[75]

Thus, despite attempts by Martignac to divide the Left, Liberal unity held. Better yet, the willingness of Liberal moderates to compromise helped to sustain ties with the Agier defection. The Opposition was therefore well prepared to confront the more direct challenge posed by the king's appointment of the Polignac cabinet.

## TOWARDS HIGH NOON

Politics in the second half of 1829 consisted of a battle for public opinion. Most of this struggle was conducted in the press, and here differences from 1820 came further to light. The ultraroyalist press immediately reverted to the extremes that had accompanied the assassination of Berry. Initially the Liberal press responded in kind, but then it wisely drew back and, while the Right openly called for a constitutional coup d'état, the Left did not espouse revolution.

[75] AN, F7 6771, 5 September 1829; BN, NAF 24914, 2 October 1829; BCUL, Co 2050; Co 2013; Co 2015; Co 1976–7; Lafayette to Stoeber, 13 October 1829 in *La vie en Alsace* (August 1934), p. 192, and Leuilliot, *L'Alsace*, I, pp. 465, 509–15.

The *France Méridionale* reacted to the appointment of the new ministry by printing La Bourdonnaye's bloodthirsty call for increasing the number of executions during debates over the law of amnesty in November 1815. More troubling for the journal than matters of personnel, however, were questions of what such a cabinet meant for the political system. The ministry could expect no cooperation from the majority of the Chamber; how then could it function? Doubtless it would like to change the electoral laws so as to produce a compliant house, but such a measure would necessitate summoning the current Chamber. Rumours circulated that the crown would resort to article 14 of the Charter and rule by ordinance, but article 14 could only be invoked when the security of France was endangered, whereas France was at peace. Thus the cabinet could expect to govern only by breaking the law, and illegal means were natural to the men of the White Terror, as a recounting of the murder of Ramel demonstrated.[76]

When a coup d'état did not immediately ensue, a measure of calm returned. Even so, the journal dismissed government avowals of respect for the Charter; the cabinet had backed away from direct confrontation, but a creeping assault on the constitution could be expected. Suspicion did not thereafter abate; in late September the *France Méridionale* attacked royalists who were pondering the use of article 14. A constitutional monarchy was one in which the powers of the monarchy and its ministers were limited by the 'fundamental law' (the Charter). Dictatorship would be illegitimate because the nation possessed inalienable liberties consecrated in the Charter, but given the nature of ultraroyalism, the public must be constantly vigilant against any erosion of the nation's liberties.[77]

The trial of journals that had published the prospectus of the Breton Association commenced a broad governmental attack. Several convictions ensured that Liberal enmity would be bitter, and one could note a tempering of polemic in the later stages of 1829, but, by and large, the judiciary did defend the free press. Journals at Rouen, Boulogne and Metz were completely acquitted. In Paris, the *Journal de Commerce* and the *Courrier* were both fined, but punishment was based on a verdict that one could not suppose that the cabinet would violate the Charter, not that resistance to such violation would be illegal.

While newspapers such as the *Constitutionnel* grew cautious, the founding of several new journals recharged Liberal batteries. The *National*, led

[76] *France Méridionale*, 13–25 August 1829.

[77] AN, F7 6769, 29 October 1829, and *France Méridionale*, 20–9 August, 3–29 September, 13 October, 14 November, 5 December 1829, 16–23 March and 27 April 1830.

by Thiers, Mignet and Armand Carrel, became the most famous, but there was a bevy of others. The *Temps*, directed by Guizot, took a line of legal resistance designed to encourage Liberal unity in the Chamber, whereas a revamped *Journal de Paris* and the *Tribune des départements* joined the *National* and the *Globe* in speculating about the possible fall of the dynasty. Under Armand Marrast, *La Jeune France* was frankly republican and, consequently, short-lived.[78]

Rapid and relatively radical expansion in the press illustrated the conundrum faced by the cabinet: existing laws allowed Liberals to continue pleading their case. The government therefore had two options: it could seek to revise laws to its own advantage, or it could invoke article 14. Recourse to the latter was frequently advised in the ultraroyalist press, but it was attendant with danger. Villèle, who had paid attention to reports from the provinces, was well apprised of the risks of tampering with the Charter so egregiously. Polignac and Charles perhaps were less cognizant, but they did search for a parliament that would do their bidding.

The main front of battle shifted when the cabinet announced the convocation of the Chambers. Fears of an immediate coup receded further, leading to more provocative journalism as the *National* and the *Globe* rehearsed analogies to the fate of the Stuart dynasty. Two trials thus resulted in March, this time leading to the convictions of the editors responsible for the *National* and the *Globe.* Allusions to king and dynasty would have to be framed very carefully, but aggressive attacks on the government continued.[79]

Meanwhile, government attempts to bully the provincial press increased. Charges were brought against Hénault, the editor responsible for the *France Méridionale*, and the journalist Dupin for attributing Polignac's appointment to British influence. Acting in defence, Vacquier tried to turn the trial into an attack on the government, but the difference between judges at Toulouse and their counterparts elsewhere began to show. Each defendant was condemned to three months in prison, 300 francs in fines and court costs. While awaiting an appeal, the journal limited itself to praising judges of the *cour royale* in Paris. In the appeal of 14 January 1830, however, Vacquier extended unfavourable observations to Villèle and Montbel, and predicted the imminent fall of the ministry. This brought forth an explosion from crown prosecutor Raimond Bastoulh and was unlikely to

78 AN, F7 6770, Moselle, 10 March 1830, and Rader, *Journalists*, pp. 106–51.

79 Collins, *Government*, pp. 55–8; Bury and Tombs, *Thiers*, 18–28, Goblot, *La France*, 547–54, and Rader, *Journalists*, pp. 168–85.

please the presiding judge Hocquart, both of whom as Deputies supported Polignac.[80]

In March the *France Méridionale* was again indicted for printing the article 'France and the Bourbons', originally published in the *Globe.* The accusation – provocation to capital crimes – was grave, and the trial was fractious. The journal itself kept silent, while following trials of the *National*, the *Globe*, and the *Journal de Commerce.* In late April, however, it did print extensive coverage of the ongoing appeal of its first case; matters had taken a vindictive course and the crown prosecutor had described employees of the *France Méridionale* as the dregs of society. For once the journal let down its guard and replied in kind.

The second case demonstrated intent to destroy the *France Méridionale*, as Hénault was condemned to six months in prison and an unprecedented 6,000 francs fine. Further charges were then brought for comments on the crown prosecutor in the appeal case. Against this onslaught, Liberals opened a subscription, and thereafter the journal printed letters from young lawyer/journalists inviting the government to charge them for their part in the article on the crown prosecutor. Through such collective acts of defiance the stakes were raised, and meanwhile in poured letters approving the subscription.[81]

It took courage for the journalists of the *France Méridionale* to soldier on; at Besançon the editor of the *Impartial* was sentenced to a month in prison for simply pointing out that the clergy were seeking to influence voters. Conversely, recourse to the courts failed the prefect of the Calvados in an attempt to destroy the *Pilote*, and acquittal only made the *Journal de Rouen* more ferocious in attacks on the government that took a back seat to no Parisian journal.[82]

Prior to the elections of November 1820, the Opposition had been deprived of its voice; in 1830, the Opposition retained its ability to address the public. Perhaps this amounted to a loss of nerve on the part of the cabinet, but the circumstances of 1830 were different. In 1820 parliament had itself provided the means of repression following the assassination of Berry; in 1830 royalism found no such pretext. Thus the Opposition continued to enjoy the benefits gained by the press law of 1828. Crucial to this was the unwillingness of most of the courts to see the rule of law flouted by the

80 AN, F7 6769, 29 October 1829; *France Méridionale*, 28 November, 3–31 December 1829 and 14 January 1830.

81 *France Méridionale*, 10 December 1829, 12 January, 2–30 March, 1–29 April, 1–20 May, 3–8 June 1830.

82 AN F7 6768, Calvados, 6 December 1829 and 21 January 1830; Duvergier de Hauranne, *Histoire*, x, pp. 388–409, and Weiss, *Journal, 1823–33*, p. 154.

state. Hence censorship could only be applied by royal ordinance, a dangerous recourse unless given sufficient cause. That the judiciary ruled as it did, effectively demonstrated that no such cause existed.

The press at times pushed matters, but the Opposition continued along the path of legal liberty. Given the harshness of the winter of 1829–30, such restraint required discipline. For their part, officials were on the watch for insurrection as popular Bonapartism, particularly interest in the Duke of Reichstadt, again surged. At Le Havre, Corbière blasted authorities for threatening merchants who displayed images of Napoleon, and suggested depictions of 'Bourmont at Waterloo' might sell well. At the other end of the political spectrum, a mysterious epidemic of fires in Normandy, lasting from February to July 1830, gave hope to the ultraroyalist press that fears of conspiracy could again be fanned.[83]

Liberals were, however, just as concerned as ultraroyalists by the potential consequences of insurrection; memories of 1827 remained fresh. Liberals therefore rallied to administrative drives to provide basic necessities for the poor. From the Ardennes came grateful official reports that Liberal manufacturers continued to employ their workers despite absence of demand for their products. In the Isère prefect Finot could announce road-construction projects in February, but the demands of some 5,000 indigents at Grenoble alone went well beyond the resources of the *bureau de bienfaisance*, necessitating further reliance upon Liberal aid. In the Bas-Rhin, Esmangart ordered the creation of cantonal charity committees, and the *comité de secours* at Strasbourg, aided by the masonic lodges and *casinos*, distributed soup, bread, wood and coal to the impoverished.[84]

For the Opposition, caution maximized their chances of victory. At the time of the address of the 221, Faure drew attention with a speech warning of danger for the monarchy if the Polignac cabinet remained. Thereafter he and Cordoue played crucial roles in holding together the *constitutionnel* coalition of Liberals and Agier defection. That two such moderates played a decisive part in charting the course that challenged the crown spoke volumes.[85]

Meanwhile Constant and Humann took differing paths to the same destination. Humann initially hoped for a centre-right combination, including Villèle, which might yet breach the gap between king and Deputies. Constant sought the opposite and in the secret Chamber committee

[83] See J. Merriman, 'The Norman fires of 1830: incendiaries and fear in rural France', *French Historical Studies*, 9, n. 3 (1976), pp. 451–66, and Rader, *Journalists*, pp. 186–201.

[84] AN, F7 6767, Ardennes, 10 January 1830; F7 6769, 8 December 1827; F7 3798, 12 May 1829, and *Journal de Grenoble*, 12–19 January and 9 February 1830.

[85] Vaulabelle, *Histoire*, VIII, pp. 75–93.

meeting of 15 March he stated: 'The duty of all Frenchmen is to resist all that which is contrary to the Charter.' Nevertheless, both Constant and Humann joined in the address of the 221 Deputies.

Much attention was focused on the 221, and the Aide-toi sent 'directions' to the provinces that the Deputies should be given public receptions upon return to their constituencies. It seems unlikely, however, that only young activists in the capital were inspired by the obvious. Judging by debates over toasts at a massive banquet for the 221 in Paris, in which Odilon Barrot wisely overruled Godefroy Cavaignac concerning moderation, the young radicals of the Aide-toi had little to do with the strategies that brought victory in the provinces. Barrot's speech was firm, warning that government force would be met with force, but it continued the theme of dynastic loyalty and thereby reflected the wishes of the eighty Deputies in attendance.[86]

In the departments, there was little disturbance as Liberals marshalled their forces. All the Deputies of the Seine-Inférieure had voted for the address, and hence they were met by groups of electors expressing satisfaction. At Strasbourg Turckheim and Saglio were also greeted with serenades. After receiving a serenade close to Tournon, Cordoue set the tone for the campaign by declaring loyalty to Charles X, but also to his brother's Charter.

Once the actual campaign began, the Opposition went about its work in discreet fashion. From the provinces came a steady stream of official reports remarking on Liberal avoidance of anything that might be seen as provocative. In the Aube, Liberals reached their decisions 'in silence'; there were no public meetings, no rumours circulating in cafés, and there was complete submission to law. In the Charente, Liberals had become 'reserved and prudent'. In the Creuse, Liberals held to their opinions, but a 'moderate instinct' seemed to attach them to order. In the Haute-Loire, Liberals made a point of not compromising themselves by agitating the masses. In the other Lafayette bastion, the Seine-et-Marne, Liberals were all the more effective in that they had shorn themselves of 'the brutality of previous epochs', exercising exceptional prudence.[87]

A prefect manufactured the one potentially serious incident of the campaign. Plans for a cavalcade to greet two Liberal members of the 221 were banned at Angers, so Liberals travelled to the outskirts of the city, intending

[86] Duvergier de Hauranne, *Histoire*, x, pp. 414–95; Pouthas, *Guizot*, pp. 433–9, and Barrot, *Mémoires*, i, pp. 86–92.

[87] AN, F7 6767, Aube, 31 March 1830; F7 6768, Charente, 28 November 1830; Creuse, 10 March 1830; F7 6770, Haute-Loire, 6 May 1829 and 12 March 1830; F7 6772, Seine-et-Marne, 5 January and 8 March 1830. See also F7 6768, Côtes-du-Nord, 12 March 1830; F7 6769, Eure, 15 November 1829, Ille-et-Vilaine, 12 March 1830; F7 6770, Loire, 27 October 1829.

to form a procession behind their candidates as they entered the city. As they returned to the city gates, they found themselves blocked by troops. Fortunately, the mayor interceded and the candidates agreed to enter alone, with no parade.[88]

Maximization of prospects could also be seen in the careful selection of candidates. In the Isère, a setback had been suffered at Crémieux in April 1828 when Teissère had failed to deliver his followers to Duchesne, despite the Perier team's negotiation of transactions. Moreover, the moderate Liberal tendencies of voters had been illustrated at Vienne, where Faure had easily overcome the more radical Français de Nantes. Given that Français had enjoyed backing from Lafitte and Dupont de l'Eure, Faure's victory bore testimony to the wisdom of not pushing too far to the left in this college.

At La-Tour-du-Pin (the college having been transferred back from Crémieux) in 1830, Cordoue comfortably dislodged the incumbent royalist Meffray, and at Vienne Faure defeated the *ministériel* candidate by 176 to 17! In their post-election analyses, officials emphasized Opposition discipline. At La-Tour-du-Pin, both Teissère and Duchesne had stood aside in favour of Cordoue and, according to the sub-prefect, selection of Cordoue had demonstrated to what extent Liberal strategy had become based on anti-ultraroyalist coalition. Cordoue was a noble and a devout Catholic, and these two qualities would have been liabilities had Liberals been less determined. Finot interpreted the selection of Cordoue as part of a strategy of displaying less hostility towards the administration in order to counter attempts to play on fears of radicalism.[89]

In the Haute-Garonne, Liberals sought to make the best of a bad situation by wooing moderates, but this time there was no ultraroyalist disunity in a campaign supervised by Villèle. The *France Méridionale* and the *Journal de Toulouse* both backed an alliance slate of Joseph Viguerie, Malaret and the two Cambons, but, unlike the *Journal*, the *France Méridionale* voiced preferences: Viguerie was 'well qualified to defend the interests of commerce and industry', and Malaret was a 'true friend of constitutional monarchy'. When the Liberal Cazeing-Lafont entered the lists at Muret, however, the *France Méridionale* withheld recommendation for the sake of unity; the Agier defection's Alexandre de Cambon stood a better chance of winning.[90]

88 AN, F7 6741, Haut-Rhin, 21–9 June, 4–7 July 1830, and Duvergier de Hauranne, *Histoire*, x, pp. 507–9.

89 AN, F1C III Isère 5, 26 June 1830; BMUG, N1942, 25 March and 2 May 1828; N2043, 12 January 1828; N2198, 28 March and 1 April 1828; N2442, 8 February 1828; R90622, 7 April 1828.

90 *France Méridionale*, 19 January, 21–3 March, 5–24 June, and 3 July 1830, and *Journal de Toulouse*, 7–14 June and 2 July 1830.

Previous ultraroyalist majorities were reduced in the *arrondissements*, but not a single alliance candidate succeeded. While Malaret managed 45.23 per cent of the vote in Toulouse II, and Alexandre de Cambon 40.06 per cent at Muret, Viguerie gained only 33.73 per cent in Toulouse I, and Auguste de Cambon 33.06 per cent at Villefranche. Worse still, in the departmental college Auguste de Cambon and Malaret fell far short of the required majority.[91]

Conversely, unity favoured the Opposition in the Bas-Rhin. Saglio concentrated on the third *arrondissement*, where the college had been shifted to Haguenau. Turckheim again ran in the departmental college, but twice had to announce in the *Courrier du Bas-Rhin* that he was not running for Strasbourg-*ville*. The latter was reserved for Constant, so much so that Humann let it be known that he would run in the second *arrondissement*, where the college would now be held in the sleepy burg of Benfeld. Esmangart sought to stir up trouble by informing electors that he was uncertain as to whether Humann had joined the 221, forcing Humann to publish a letter clarifying the issue. Furthermore, to assure the voters of Benfeld, Humann published a letter avowing he would continue to 'defend the constitution', which Silbermann interpreted as a 'profession of faith'. With four of the six contests settled, two remained. Liberals fixed on two local figures of long-standing Opposition – Baron Rudler and Mathieu-Faviers. Rudler, preferred by the radicals, would run in Saverne and, in case of defeat, he would also run in the departmental college.

Voting came to a satisfactory conclusion for Liberals of both radical and moderate stripe. Saglio won comfortably; Constant collected 201 votes, while the prefect's manoeuvre produced 68 for Turckheim, and Humann 'triumphed' by collecting slightly better than one-quarter of the votes cast for Constant. The sole disappointment came when Wangen de Géroldseck defeated Rudler, which the *Courrier* attributed to 'tricks'. Even so, this defeat was largely rectified in the departmental college when Turckheim (on the first ballot) and Rudler (on the second) were elected. Thus unity among Liberals yielded five of six available seats.[92]

Even after victory there was little demonstration in the Isère, which was just as well, given the deployment of troops in the streets of Grenoble. Perier was determined that Liberals would not compromise their triumph, and

[91] AN, F7 6640, 4 July 1830; ADHG, 2M24, college minutes of 23 June and 4 July 1830, and *France Méridionale*, 6 July 1830.

[92] BN, NAF 24914, 28 May 1830; ADBR, 2M20, college minutes of 23–4 June and 3–4 July 1830; BCUL, Co 1208; Co 1489; *Courrier du Bas-Rhin*, 3–25 June 1830; Leuilliot, *L'Alsace*, I, pp. 523–6; Ponteil, *Humann*, pp. 73–5 and Félix Ponteil, *L'opposition politique à Strasbourg sous la monarchie de juillet (1830–48)* (Paris, 1932), pp. 26–7, 41–2, and Coulmann, *Réminiscences*, III, pp. 194–8.

scrupulously legal behaviour stood in stark contrast to events at Montauban, where thirty to forty ultraroyalist thugs threatened the *constitutionnel* candidate after his election. At Le Havre, the election of Duvergier *père* gave rise to cries of 'Down with the Jesuits!' in the streets, but did not spark disorder. In the Haut-Rhin, Liberal celebrations at Altkirch and Munster included parades, banquets and fireworks that attracted large crowds, but the authorities reported that all of this was conducted in 'good order'.[93]

A striking feature of the campaign was the way in which the Liberal press approached the expedition to Algiers. By and large the expedition gained little commentary. There were exceptions: the *National* took a partisan line and the *Journal de Rouen* argued that the objective justified neither the costs nor the hazards of the expedition. Then again, taking such an initiative without consultation with parliament did illustrate the limits of royal understanding of representative government; even Villèle had cleared the path for war in 1823 with discussion in the Chambers.

Towards the end of the electoral campaign the expedition did gain some remarkably neutral coverage. Completely ignoring a military venture could prove dangerous, especially if it proved successful. All the same, reporting was almost entirely bereft of commentary, a sign that the lesson of Spain, when the Liberal press had been full of dire foreboding and been proved wrong, had been learned. Coverage in the *France Méridionale* amounted to little more than a technical evaluation of the difficulties likely to be encountered. Fortunately, reports of victory arrived after the elections of the *arrondissements*, and then interest began to break out. Only on 13 July, however, after the departmental colleges had voted, did commentary commence, and then it was to announce that the returning glorious army would be presented with 'the fruits of our peaceful combat . . . a sage liberty established, all our new institutions consolidated'.[94]

## END GAME

That 202 of the 221 were returned had great symbolic import; after all, the ultraroyalist press and government had specifically targeted them. Conversely, 80 of the 181 who had voted against the address lost their seats. Several other points also merit underlining. The Liberal Opposition had

[93] AN, F7 6741, Haut-Rhin, 21–9 June, 4–7 July 1830; F7 6769, 23 July 1830; *Journal de Grenoble*, 24 June 1830; P. Barral, *Les Perier dans l'Isère au XIXe siècle d'après leur correspondance familiale* (Paris, 1964), pp. 111–12, and J. Vidalenc, *Le département de l'Eure sous la monarchie constitutionnelle* (Paris, 1952), pp. 156–7.

[94] *France Méridionale*, 27 February, 4–25 March, 24 April, 8–13 May, 12–29 June, 3–17 July 1830.

won a clear majority; there was no longer any need for alliance with the Centre-Right. Taken as a whole, the Opposition held 274 seats, compared to 143 for the *ministériel* block. As usual Opposition strength derived from the *arrondissements*, but *constitutionnels* had also taken seventy-five seats in the departmental colleges, whereas eighty-four had gone to official candidates. Liberals had finally achieved what had seemed in the offing in 1819, before insurrection and despotism had intervened.[95]

By calling for elections, Charles X had appealed to the French elite in his struggle with the Opposition. Since the fall of Villèle, an increasing number of prefects had called for the government to take a firm line, but the majority had specified that governmental actions must be confined within the limits of what the Charter would allow. While they were pouring over electoral prospects, Peyronnet, Capelle and Polignac could not have missed this refrain. Where public opinion stood was clear, but it remained to be seen what ultraroyalism would make of an electoral Valmy.

[95] Duvergier de Hauranne, *Histoire*, x, pp. 487–527.

6

# *Aftermath: Liberal Opposition and the July Revolution*

The July Revolution has been given less attention than those of 1789 and 1848, partly because it did not yield striking democratic progress, and partly because it did not bring a major transformation in the social system. The Revolution was, however, effective in establishing its limited objectives. Until recently, it has been treated largely as a Parisian rather than French affair, but such an interpretation has ignored the point that Parisian revolt required provincial approval to become revolution.

Two crucial elements allowed the July Revolution to proceed. The first consisted of public opinion generally, and in this regard the Liberal Opposition played a vital role by providing an elite leadership that possessed mass support. A second factor lay in the army's response to revolt. One can perhaps argue that the army had become so professional that it was incapable of acting in partisan fashion in a civil conflict, but such 'neutrality' was in fact tantamount to sealing the fate of the regime. Save for the King's Guard, by 2 August forces concentrated near Saint-Cloud had been reduced by desertion to roughly 1,350 men, and virtually all garrisons in a fifty-mile radius had declared for the Revolution, rendering royalist plans to continue the fight south of the Loire unfeasible.[1]

Most of the public perceived resistance as defensive in character. Charles X and the cabinet had been given clear warning by the elections of June–July, but chose to ignore this by issuing the ordinances of 25 July. The ordinances restored preliminary press censorship, dissolved the new parliament before it had even met, and revamped the electoral regime. Change in the latter was drastic. The *arrondissement* colleges would be reduced to proposing candidates, while the departmental colleges would elect 258 Deputies. Moreover, the influence of commercial and industrial groups would be diminished by the removal of the *patente* tax from evaluations of the *cens*.

[1] See Pilbeam, 'The "Three Glorious Days"', pp. 831–2; Porch, *Army*, pp. 34–8 and R. Price, 'The French army and the Revolution of 1830', *European Studies Review*, 3, n. 3 (1973), pp. 243–67.

Thus the crown was asserting a right to alter parliament in whatever manner it chose, effectively nullifying any notion of contract between throne and nation. While royal objectives were much the same as in the Law of the Double Vote, the latter had been voted in parliament, whereas the ordinances were a clear violation of division of powers. The regime had effectively fulfilled Liberal warnings of a coup d'état and was the obvious aggressor.

Battle was short. Serious fighting occurred in Paris, where barricades went up on the night of 27 July and some 12,000 troops of the line under Marshal Auguste de Marmont, notorious among Parisians for his defection to the Allies in April 1814, sought to overcome a revolutionary crowd of at least 8,000. Many of the soldiers and lower-ranking officers, however, fraternized with the rebels, and former members of the Parisian National Guard, abolished in 1827, joined in the resistance. Betrayal of the regime by a significant proportion of the forces of order turned the tide of battle and by the morning of 29 July Marmont was already in retreat, having lost control of Paris. Roughly 800 insurgents and 200 troops died during the *trois glorieuses* (days of fighting).

By 2 August Charles X had decided to abdicate in favour of his grandson the Duke of Bordeaux, prior to departing for his final exile. There was little choice, given the rapidity with which provincial France had aligned with a Parisian provisional government. Thereafter a rump parliament of 252 Deputies and 114 Peers rejected Bordeaux and established a new constitutional monarchy under the Duke of Orleans. By 9 August Louis-Philippe I had become king of the French, thereby establishing the principle of national sovereignty.

Although Liberals played a fundamental part in the Revolution and its settlement, neither constituted a complete success for them. In considering why this was, this chapter will investigate the Liberal response to the Revolution, and then discuss the impact of July and its aftermath on the Opposition. As we will see, unity in power proved no easier for Liberals than it had for ultraroyalists under Villèle. Clarification along ideological lines inevitably entailed new contestation and reformulations of political division, but it was not ideological difference that turned an initially promising regime into a conservative one by 1835. Liberals who were disappointed by the Revolutionary settlement committed a fundamental error in thinking that change in July 1830 had been achieved simply by the application of force.

If the July Monarchy was not all that it might have been, it nonetheless did constitute a decisive step forward from the Restoration. Among the continental powers, France had re-established its position as progressive and independent. Better yet, a model for change, based on a Revolutionary tradition of persuasion and legal organization, had been established. This model was the great Liberal contribution, although many failed to recognize its true nature.

## RESISTANCE IN PARIS AND THE PROVINCES

The July Revolution was political in its origins. France was in the midst of a depression that produced great suffering among the lower classes and created alarm within the elite, but prior to the Revolution the economy had begun to improve, a trend apparent in increased employment in the capital. More to the point, official reports in the winter and spring of 1829–30 had made clear that there was virtually no linkage of economic grievance and political agitation in the provinces prior to the issuing of the royal ordinances.[2]

When the ordinances were issued, only their draconian nature took anyone by surprise. The first acts of resistance came from the press as journalists such as Thiers and Rémusat defied orders to cease publication. Moreover, most of the publishing trade (including some 5,000 print workers) heartily disliked the regime. Thus the first instances of violence occurred when government forces arrived to impound or break printing presses. On 27 July print workers joined with artisans in crowds that began to erect barricades and insurrection began.

Several points concerning the *trois glorieuses* bear remark. It is probable that artisans hoped that a new regime would improve their economic plight, but this does not mean that economic factors motivated revolt. The regime was despised in Parisian *quartiers* for much the same reasons as elsewhere – because it represented noble privilege, clerical domination and defeat. Royalism had found few supporters among Parisian workers in 1815, and matters had not changed over the following fifteen years.[3]

What was revolutionary in 1830 was that constitutional struggle had created a circumstance wherein insurrection could successfully come forward. Similar attempts had been made in 1820 and 1827, but crowd actions were

[2] AN, F7 6767, Aisne, 21 October 1829, Ardèche, 2 October 1829, Ardennes, 10 January and 8 February 1830, Aube, 28 December 1829–31 March 1830; F7 6769, Drôme, 1 March 1830; F7 6770, Meuse, 14 November 1829; F7 6771, Orne, 28 February 1830, Rhône, 17 March 1830, Sarthe, 1 March 1830; F7 6772, Somme, 3 November 1829 and 9 January 1830. See also P. Gonnet, 'Esquisse de la crise économique en France de 1827 à 1832', *Revue d'Histoire Economique et Sociale*, 33 (1955), pp. 249–92; Pilbeam *1830*, pp. 37–59; and D. Pinkney, *The French Revolution of 1830* (Princeton, 1972), pp. 65–72.

[3] Pinkney, *1830*, pp. 52–108, 143–80.

routinely crushed if they did not have the support of middle-class elements. In the case of 1830, support could be seen in the closure of shops and industries, and the participation of students, National Guardsmen, the Parisian Liberal electoral committee and its supporters, and former Napoleonic officers. It was against this broad base that military intervention collapsed.

Etienne Cabet's subsequent charge that the revolution was 'stolen' from the people tells less than half the truth if the people are defined exclusively as proto-proletarians. Cabet himself used the term 'patriots' and, given that his tract was dedicated to the voters of Dijon, we can safely assume that he did not have only workers in mind. Furthermore, there would have been no change of regime had Deputies not defied Polignac, had journalists not called for resistance to the ordinances, had the National Guard and Parisian electors not moved into the vacuum of power created by the withdrawal of troops, and had the Deputies not turned Parisian revolt into national revolution by creating an alternative government.[4]

Historians have made much of the reluctance of the roughly thirty Opposition Deputies in Paris at the start of the *trois glorieuses* to join in armed resistance, as though their hesitation represented middle-class timidity. Yet any other behaviour would have been irresponsible. The Deputies had started the process of resistance, but had done so along legal lines. The intervention of the crowd then changed the nature of resistance, but this could be seen as either a disruption or the furthering of the process. Certain Liberals, including Pierre Audry de Puyraveau, Bernard de Rennes and François Maughin, concluded that the Deputies should join in armed revolt and pushed for the creation of a provisional government, whereas Deputies such as Guizot and Perier were predisposed to think solely in terms of tax revolt. Liberal newspapers, including the *National*, also initially confined themselves to calls for tax revolt. All the experience of the past fifteen years pointed to the dangers of armed insurgency – Allied intervention on the one hand, and, on the other, the way in which crowd violence had benefited political reaction in the 1820s. One way or another, the Deputies did intend to resist, although in the heat of rapidly unfolding events they, for a time, disagreed as to the means of resistance.

Foreign intervention did not in the event occur, but this outcome had more to do with the efficacy of Orleanist diplomacy than the possibility of France withstanding another Allied assault. That domestic revolt would not trigger international war was, of course, hardly apparent in July, but the

[4] E. Cabet, *Révolution de 1830 et situation présente* (Paris, 1833); Vaulabelle, *Histoire*, VIII, pp. 219–31, 234–51, 272–94; Pilbeam, *1830*, pp. 60–7; Girard, *La garde*, 159–64, and Newman, 'The blouse', pp. 26–59.

risks of repeating the experiences of 1815–16 certainly were. In pondering the July Revolution in the long term, one also has to wonder whether the Deputies were not correct in fearing the impact of insurrection. Armed insurgency did hasten change, but whether it extended or restricted the dimensions of change is another question.[5]

All told, there was little violence in the provinces. A major exception occurred at Nantes, where troops fired on a group of 150 men attacking barracks in search of arms. Thirteen were killed and fifty-two seriously injured in the resultant fighting, before a royalist general led his troops out of the city in a futile search for support among Vendean peasants. Elsewhere, in cities such as Arras, Le Havre, Rouen, Lille, Caen, Bordeaux and Lyons, Liberal newspapers ignored the ordinances, provoking scenes similar to those in Paris, but bloodshed was averted and a wait and watch compromise was tacitly agreed upon by local officials and leaders of the Opposition.[6]

Transition of power proceeded at varying rates, and in centres such as Metz, Dijon, Beaune and Chalon-sur-Seine it preceded knowledge of the final outcome in the capital. At Rouen, resistance developed immediately upon the arrival of news of the royal ordinances. The *Journal de Rouen* continued to publish, as 'patriots' gathered outside the office to block the use of force. Liberal leaders, including Deputies, met close to the *Journal*'s office and despatched two emissaries to Paris to establish contact with the leaders of the Parisian resistance; meanwhile 300 National Guardsmen patrolled the streets. Officials wisely temporized, until the process of handing power over to Liberals began on 31 July with news of the success of the revolt in Paris. Thereafter some 600 'patriots' were sent to Paris, joining similar forces from Le Havre.[7]

At Besançon authorities removed the *drapeau blanc* from the city hall on 1 August, but crowd pressure was necessary before the tricolour was hoisted on the day following. Until such events in the provinces are systematically studied, it will be difficult to say conclusively whether such crowds were simply popular in nature. At Toulouse, Grenoble, Strasbourg and Rouen, however, middle-class elements were part of the crowds from the very

[5] Pinkney, *1830*, pp. 180–95; Pilbeam, *1830*, pp. 64–6; Pouthas, *Guizot*, pp. 440–51; Bourset, *Casimir*, pp. 183–99, and H. Collingham, *The July Monarchy* (London, 1988), pp. 6–22.

[6] Except where noted, the following is drawn from AN, F7 6771, Nord, 29 July 1830, Rhône, 29 July 1830; Pinkney, *1830*, pp. 196–226; Pilbeam, *1830*, pp. 60–79; Rader, *Journalists*, pp. 260–5; Lévêque, *Une société*, pp. 486–9; Alexander, *Bonapartism*, pp. 153–4 and 183–4, Legoy, 'Un espace', pp. 281–2, and Popkin, *Press*, 86–7.

[7] *Journal de Rouen* and *Neustrien*, 28 July – 3 August 1830.

beginning. At Le Havre and Nantes revolt began at the theatre, a social milieu not exactly foreign to the middle classes.[8]

The most striking feature of the revolution in the provinces was how little resistance the authorities offered to challenges to the regime. News of the ordinances reached Grenoble on 27 July and drew huge crowds into the streets. The subsequent absence of newspapers and official correspondence tested the mettle of both sides, but crowds contented themselves with awaiting couriers. Crowds at Brest made officials think twice about plans to prevent the distribution of arms among National Guardsmen, and at Lyons a combination of the Guard, huge crowds and troops of the line also checked official initiative. At Bordeaux, the royalist *Mémorial* printed the ordinances while piously hoping that a government that had 'compromised the future of France' would respect the Charter. In places such as Bar-sur-Aube, Besançon, Lille, Limoges and Rouen, official reluctance was more or less confirmed by judges condemning the ordinances as illegal.

Hesitation was also attributable to the presence of Liberal committees, which rapidly provided an alternative to which power could be transferred. News that fighting had begun in Paris did not reach Grenoble until 1 August. Prefect Finot then defused a potential riot by agreeing to create a provisional municipal government led by three members of the Liberal electoral committee – Penet, Teissère and Rivier. Rumours of the creation of a provisional government in Paris arrived the day after, leading to demands for the formation of a new National Guard, and so Finot gave permission for the provisional municipal government to reorganize the Guard. On 3 August confirmation of the existence of the Parisian provisional government arrived, along with a tricolour flag. The latter was raised at the prefecture and tricolour flags and hatbands suddenly appeared in profusion.[9]

At Strasbourg the transition of power was also smooth. On 25 July the *Courrier du Bas-Rhin* refused to print the ordinances and ceased publishing, but prefect Esmangart posted government notices in the streets. While the populace remained calm, agitation among artillery officers soon spread throughout the garrison. During this uncertain period, groups of voters gathered to discuss how to respond to the apparent crisis. On 31 July Silbermann began publishing again, noting reports in the Parisian press of disturbances, urging calm, and calling on the government to return to the rule of law. On 1 August word arrived by courier of the provisional government in Paris and the lawyer George-Frédéric Schützenberger rode

[8] Weiss, *Journal, 1823–33*, pp. 158–64.

[9] BMUG, R9513 and *Journal de Grenoble*, 3–21 August 1830.

through the streets proclaiming the downfall of the monarchy. It was concern over the garrison, however, that led Esmangart to order the formation of a new National Guard. Mayor Kentzinger, the sole leading official who wanted to resist change forcibly, was a potential source of trouble, but Esmangart shunted him aside by authorizing a provisional municipal government. Like Finot in the Isère, Esmangart had been a very loyal servant of the Bourbon regime and he was no friend of Liberals, but he wisely gave ground to the public consensus surrounding him.[10]

Matters were more complicated at Toulouse. Although the *France Méridionale* evaded orders not to publish on 29 July, it then lapsed into silence until 4 August. Conversely the *Journal de Toulouse* published an edition on 2 August by agreeing to print the ordinances. Information consisted primarily of government orders, but the newspaper included a report in which reference was made to an address signed by Parisian journalists. While the address was not described as a protest, reporting that government action was pending gave the point away. It was also apparent that there was a crisis in Paris and Bordeaux, and that communications with Rouen and Lyons had been cut. No disorders had arisen at Toulouse, but on 1 August a deputation of notables had visited prefect Camus, offering to form a National Guard. Camus had refused approval, saying he already possessed the means necessary to maintain order.

Events then accelerated. By 1 August a copy of the *Messager* had slipped through, bringing news of bloodshed in Paris. On the morning of 2 August, a traveller then announced the formation of the provisional government in Paris. These fragments of information initially produced stupor, but when the prefect issued an aggressive notice on 2 August, he set off a revolt. Signed by most leading officials, the notice was read publicly at the city hall by an *adjoint*, and elsewhere by officials accompanied by troops. 'Factions' had taken control of Paris and were trying to use the post to drag the rest of France into revolt, but troops remained loyal, and provincial France would repulse the titles claimed by the revolutionaries.

Attempts to organize counter-revolution proved even less successful than in March 1815. The procession reading the notice soon attracted large crowds chanting 'Long live the Charter!' and by nightfall 3,000 Toulousains were marching through the streets. On the morning of 3 August the prefect met with a delegation of 'citizens', including several members of the *France Méridionale*, and Camus was warned of the necessity of no longer

[10] *Courrier du Bas-Rhin*, 31 July – 31 August, 28–30 September 1830; P. Leuilliot, 'L'Alsace et la révolution de 1830', *La Vie en Alsace* (1929), pp. 73–94, and Ponteil, *L'opposition*, pp. 45–64 and 932–4.

holding back news from Paris. Large crowds had collected in the faubourgs Saint-Etienne and Saint-Cyprien, and 'men of all classes' had taken to the streets, destroying Bourbon icons. By early afternoon tricolour flags had been unfurled from windows at the Capitole. Troops were then deployed and their 'prudent attitude' helped to prevent violent clashes as journalists from the *France Méridionale* circulated among the crowd, advising patience.

Events took a dangerous turn in the late afternoon, when Camus ordered a brigade of gendarmes to remove a tricolour guarded by law students in the Place du Capitole and a small-scale riot ensued. Arrival of a proclamation by the Duke of Orleans, however, then put an end to official resistance; the group of 'citizens' again went to the prefect and Camus finally ordered the creation of a provisional municipal commission. Installed at midnight, the commission immediately set about organizing a new National Guard, while the prefect hastily departed.[11]

Liberals were well placed to ensure that little by way of a power vacuum existed. On 5 August, officers of the National Guard at Besançon forced the prefect to depart, prior to convincing the municipal government to resign. An 'Assembly' of 100 notables then elected a commission of twelve Liberals, which duly announced its support of the provisional government. Thus direction was given to the crowds, which reduced violence, while leading towards coherent objectives. At Grenoble the Liberal municipal council also sent a letter to the provisional government giving full allegiance.

Radical Liberal strength at Strasbourg was apparent in the municipal commission; among the nine members were Liechtenberger, the merchant Louis Kob, Schützenberger, the manufacturer Jean-Michel Schweighauser, Steiner and Walter. The commission maintained order, and Guardsmen dispersed a crowd bent on tearing down a mission cross that had been placed outside the cathedral, but there could be little doubt as to the news for which Liberals were hoping. When it came on 1 August by way of a proclamation in favour of the Duke of Orleans co-signed by Constant, a Liberal pharmacist provided the Guard with two tricolour flags he had kept in hiding since 1815. A letter from Turckheim in Paris was also reassuring: Russian and British ambassadors had stated that no intervention would be forthcoming, and Deputies in the Chamber would guarantee national needs through an accepted, not a granted, Charter.

On 5 August the *France Méridionale* could report 'perfect calm' at Toulouse, and meanwhile a pattern of revolution similar to that of Toulouse

[11] *Journal de Toulouse*, 28 July and 2 August 1830; *France Méridionale*, 29 July, 4 – 10 August 1830, and R. Aminzade, *Class, Politics and Early Industrial Capitalism: A Study of Mid-Nineteenth-Century Toulouse, France* (Albany, N.Y., 1981), pp. 100–1.

had unfolded at Saint-Gaudens. Here agitation created by the authorities withholding information had led to the recreation of the National Guard, which, in turn, had ensured that the transfer of authority by the sub-prefect was conducted amidst scenes of joy, but not vengeance.

One could afford to be magnanimous as power shifted in a desirable direction. Opposition takeover was apparent in the provisional municipal commissions: at Toulouse, Joseph Viguerie, the bankers Duffé and François Sans, the merchants Authier and Cassaing, the barristers Gasc and Bernard-Antoine Tajan and proprietor Zéphirin Picot de Lapeyrousse were all long-standing Liberals. Similar transitions were conducted at Villefranche and Muret on 4 August, and shortly thereafter at Saint-Gaudens.[12]

Inevitably, revolution brought iconographic destruction and at times it was necessary to protect unpopular figures. The temptation for a historian is to assemble examples of violent confrontation when discussing revolution; but such an approach gives a misleading impression. Except for the fighting in Nantes and Paris, and subsequent turmoil beginning on 15 August at Nîmes, transition between regimes was remarkably bloodless.[13]

In some provincial centres riots occurred, but most crowds simply demonstrated. At Besançon a statue of the counter-revolutionary conspirator General Charles Pichegru was dismembered, and the head paraded in the streets. This was a potent symbolic act, and well designed to make authorities think. Besançon was also the scene of attacks on the office of the administration of the *droits réunis.* In this case, crowds were repulsed, but elsewhere, as at Bordeaux, tax offices were ransacked. Mission crosses were another lightning rod for discontent; seminaries were attacked at Chalôns and Nancy, and clergymen had to beat a hasty retreat from several towns. In the Ariège, peasants angered by battles over forest rights attacked chateaux, but this was part of a struggle that preceded the Revolution and did not originate from it. When all is said and done, however, violence was extraordinarily limited. Carrying the head of a statue was not quite the 'real thing', and this episode nicely captured how little was required to bring down a tottering regime.[14]

## LIBERALS AND THE JULY SETTLEMENT

In terms of ends, the Revolution was largely a success for Liberals. Basic revision of the Charter was conducted between 4 and 7 August, so as to

[12] ADHG, 1M98, 4 August 1830, and *France Méridionale*, 4–14 August 1830.

[13] See Fitzpatrick, *Catholic Royalism*, pp. 97–104.

[14] See P. Sahlins, *Forest Rites. The War of the Demoiselles in Nineteenth-Century France* (Cambridge, Mass., and London, 1994).

preclude republicanism, Bonapartism or support for Charles X and his immediate family from exercising influence. Haste fostered compromise because rapid Chamber approval required advancing broadly accepted proposals unlikely to provoke division and extend the process. Thus the Chamber Commission took a middle position between Auguste Bérard's initial proposition (which represented radical Liberalism), and the more conservative proposals of Guizot and Broglie. Not all matters could be addressed so rapidly, however, and hence trial by jury for press infractions, organization of the National Guard, electoral laws and reorganization of primary education were reserved for future revision. That the Commission's approach succeeded could be seen in broad acceptance: 219 Deputies voted in favour, and only 33 against. Among Parisian journals, the *National*, the *Courrier*, the *Temps* and *the Journal des débats* registered general satisfaction; only the *Constitutionnel* expressed strong reservations.[15]

Because the constitution of the July Monarchy was simply a revision of the Bourbon Charter, inclination to link the two regimes has been strong among historians. Nevertheless, changes were of a systemic nature, and the political practices of the two periods differed greatly. The Liberal Opposition wanted constitutional monarchy founded upon the principle of national sovereignty. Republicanism had few adherents in 1830 and waving a red flag to the rest of Europe made little sense; when Lafayette conceded these points, he simply recognized the obvious. Bonapartism held more appeal, but lacked a viable candidate. Liberals thus turned to the solution that divided them least – Thiers' formula for the Third Republic applied as much to the Orleanist dynasty.[16]

The July Monarchy did establish genuine constitutional monarchy. While the exact nature of relations between parliament and throne would evolve, certain parameters were fixed. In the revised Charter both Chambers gained the formal right to initiate legislation, and rights of petition were strengthened. Louis-Philippe sought to govern as well as reign, which could lead to problems with his cabinets, but his cabinets were chosen to reflect majority opinion in the Chamber of Deputies. Furthermore, while figures such as Perier and Guizot would subsequently prove adept at 'working' the electoral system through patronage, they did not resort to fraud.

Division of power in terms of the judiciary presents a more subtle transition. The executive appointed judges in both regimes, but the independence of the judiciary from the executive was strengthened under the July Monarchy. After the purge of 1816, fixity of tenure had been more or less

[15] Pouthas, *Guizot*, pp. 451–72.

[16] Pinkney, *1830*, pp. 46–52; Newman, 'Republicanism', pp. 284–315; Lucas-Dubreton, *Le culte*, 272–80, and Bluche, *Bonapartisme*, pp. 207–12.

respected during the Restoration, but the purview of the judiciary had been frequently in question, and there had been no mistaking the systematic threatening of judicial independence posed by ultraroyalism. Executive domination had been apparent in administrative despotism from 1820 onwards, and it had reached an apogee with the proposed press laws of January 1827. Given royal anger at the judiciary, it seems apparent that judicial independence would have come under intense scrutiny had the attempt at a coup d'état succeeded in 1830.

Under the July Monarchy, the role of the judiciary was no longer under fundamental question from the executive. Conversely, fixity of judicial tenure had many critics among radical Liberals, and it was only with reluctance that radicals accepted the effective 'shelving' of this issue in August 1830. Thereafter, the role of the judiciary would remain a point of contestation, but threat to judicial independence came principally from the Left, rather than the executive.

Change in the nature of the Chamber of Peers went along two main lines. During the Restoration, the upper house had played an important role, but it was secondary to the lower house. The primacy of the Deputies in budgetary matters had confirmed their superior status, and this had been re-enforced by the fact that Deputies represented the public, who, in turn, could attend debates in the lower house. Nevertheless, the Peers had at times emerged as the main bastion against Villèle's despotism, and they could prove useful in their function as a high court for crimes of treason. For example, in refusing the execution of former members of the Polignac cabinet in late 1830 the Peers took an unpopular decision with which most Deputies probably agreed, but for which they would not be held responsible.

Past experience therefore provided reasons in late 1831 for not abolishing the upper house entirely. Instead, the new regime settled for the continued appointment of Peers by the throne, although the king must choose from a list of notables. Because the number of Peers was not fixed, opposition in the upper house could always be overcome by the executive, giving the Peers something of a subordinate status, but enabling them to continue their role of temporarily blocking measures. The utility of the upper house's ability to slow legislation derived from the point that the composition of the lower house and, by extension, the cabinet, was by nature volatile. Thus the Peers could serve as a safety valve against haste, but they could not prevent the Deputies from having their way if sufficiently determined.

Hereditary peerage was abolished in favour of life appointment. This measure advanced the principle of meritocracy, although the latter was restricted by conditions placed on the lists of notables that reflected priorities also apparent in the *cens* – tax payments in the range of 3,000 francs, or demonstration of capacity through possession of high office. Reconstitution of the personnel of the upper house was not necessarily anti-noble; while the removal of hereditary rights did embody hostility to caste formation, peerage could be accommodated to a Napoleonic formulation of reward for service to the state. Suspicion of politics conducted in private also led to the opening of the upper house to public attendance, a change that brought the two houses more closely in line.

The period of 1827 to 1831 marked a dramatic decline in the percentage of *ancien régime* nobles in the lower house. Most noble Deputies had aligned with ultraroyalism and many would become Legitimist, and hence they were struck by public backlash. As the July Monarchy stabilized, however, the threat of Legitimism and fears over privilege receded, and the electorate became more receptive to noble candidates. Towards the end of the regime, the percentage of nobles in the Chamber of Deputies would again be relatively high, although the figures of the Restoration were a thing of the past.[17]

All of these changes – establishment of constitutional monarchy based on national sovereignty, genuine division of powers, balance between royal and parliamentary government and removal of heredity from peerage – were in accord with Liberal objectives prior to July 1830. They amounted to an extensive systemic change and made France substantially different from the other continental powers. They were also a product of compromise, but the Liberal programme of developing the representative principle would prove far more difficult to achieve through consensus.

Proponents of full manhood suffrage were few because ideas regarding political participation were tied to notions of independence, of which property possession was deemed the essential manifestation. While some allowance was made for capacity, with education or occupation as criteria, direct contribution to the state in the form of tax payment was the favoured means for determining franchise. Within these bounds, however, there was extensive room for debate.

The new *cens* of 200 francs for the national electorate was disappointing to many Liberals. By 1831 the electorate stood at roughly 166,600 voters; about 90 per cent qualified on the basis of the *cens* rather than capacity. In a department such as the Côte-d'Or, the electorate rose from 3,000 to

[17] P. Higonnet, 'La composition de la Chambre des Députés de 1827 à 1831', *Revue Historique*, 239 (1968), pp. 351–78.

5,300 immediately, and to 7,000 towards the end of the regime. In social terms, change increased the proportion of landed middle-class elements – prosperous small-scale merchants and artisans (after they had purchased land) and well-to-do peasants. Notables paying over 1,000 francs in taxes diminished as a part of the electorate to 9 per cent by the late 1840s. Economic growth had increased the national franchise to roughly 241,000 by 1846, but this appeared very restrictive when compared to the extension of the franchise in Britain after the Reform Acts of 1832.

Certain contextual factors made limited expansion more acceptable in the early 1830s. A precedent for further lowering the *cens* had been set, and meanwhile reduction of age qualification to twenty-five for voting and to thirty for candidature, and reduction of the *cens* of eligibility to 500 francs, could be taken as mitigating considerations. Furthermore, the *cens* was but part of a package. From a Liberal standpoint, there was much to be pleased by: abolition of the Double Vote, reduction of the Deputy's mandate from seven to five years, the necessity of seeking re-election in case of appointment or promotion in government service, and election of college presidents.

Optimism over future reform could also be derived from a franchise that included over two million for elections to municipal councils, although mayors remained appointive. In the 1840s there would be 38,000 municipal voters in the Côte-d'Or and close to 50,000 in the Saône-et-Loire, representing 32.7 per cent and 32.5 per cent, respectively, of full manhood suffrage (using the franchise of 1848 as a benchmark). The franchise for electing members of the departmental and *arrondissement* councils was more restrictive; a voter must pay either 200 francs in taxes in total, or 150 francs in direct taxes. Here one can note that the franchise for municipal elections was fixed in March 1831, whereas that for departmental and *arrondissement* councils was determined in June 1833 – evidence of the impact of sustained civil disorder.

Despite such progressive steps, government remained highly centralized and councils continued to be largely consultative, as the desire to weaken the grip of the Napoleonic administrative model weakened in reaction to civil disturbance. All the same the councils did provide a means by which local communities gained more say in taxation and expenditure. For this reason, elections could be fiercely contested and this, in turn, gave a far greater part of the population experience of electoral politics. Election of National Guard officers also marked a step forward for the representative principle. The extent to which local politics reflected national party politics varied, with urban communes more likely than their rural counterparts to take on a clearly partisan cast, but one way or another, the July settlement did lay seeds for future democratization.[18]

The capstone to the July Settlement was the Guizot Education Law of June 1833. Given the anticlerical riots of the early 1830s, the care that Guizot took to include the Catholic Church in primary education may seem surprising. The Society for Elementary Education had been quick to declare support for the July Revolution, and the Chambers thereafter showed themselves disposed to favour mutual schools over their Catholic rivals. Some Liberals did indeed see in the Revolution a victory for mutual schools over those of the Christian brothers, leading Guizot to intervene on behalf of the *frères*, but few Liberals were advocates of laissez-faire when it came to education, and once a state system had been established to end Catholic monopoly, their main objective had been secured. Mutual schools soon went into decline, absorbed by the state.[19]

Guizot sought to avoid the extremes of previous educational systems, and did not want a complete divorce of secular and spiritual considerations. Thus, at the communal level, the priest or pastor would join the mayor and three municipal councillors in a committee which would monitor schools in terms of discipline and salubrity, arrange for the free instruction of children whose parents could not afford to pay, and suspend unsatisfactory teachers. When the bill was presented, much of its substance passed with little debate, but criticism arose as to the role of clergymen on the local committees. Guizot compromised and hence the role of priests or pastors was restricted to general monitoring; they would take no part in decisions concerning the appointment or suspension of teachers.[20]

Once theocracy was truly defeated, much of what had motivated Restoration Liberal hostility to the Church was removed. Revision of the Charter had clarified that Catholicism did not enjoy privileged status, and had underlined the principle of religious toleration. In practical terms, loss of privilege was apparent in the dramatic reduction of the toll the Catholic Church took on national and local budgets. Thereafter, the secular nature of the Orleanist regime led at times to difficult relations with the Church, but it also ensured that France would no longer be troubled by religious missions constantly alluding to the illegitimacy of nationalized lands or secular marriages.

[18] Rosanvallon, *La monarchie*, pp. 105–21 and 279–357; Collingham, *July Monarchy*, pp. 70–115; Lévêque, *Une société*, p. 485, and P. Vigier, 'Elections municipales et prise de conscience politique sous la monarchie de Juillet', in *La France au XIXe siècle: mélanges offerts à Charles Hippolyte Pouthas* (Paris, 1973), pp. 278–86.

[19] Tronchet, *L'enseignement*, III, pp. 177–579.

[20] Johnson, *Guizot*, pp. 122–33.

Although Bourbon governments under Decazes, Martignac and, to a much lesser extent, Villèle had at times sought to temper the demands of theocrats, the power and material resources of the Catholic Church had been steadily enhanced by the Restoration state. All of the gains had gone in one direction, and if one leaves aside the brief interval wherein Charles X tolerated Martignac's relative moderation, ultraroyalism's increasing association of Church and state had characterized all of the 1820s. Ultimately, royalism was itself divided over whether legitimacy was secular or religious in nature, but Bourbon governments did a very poor job of defending the Revolutionary and Napoleonic heritage of the secular state.

Antagonism between the Left and the Church, especially over education, would continue well into the twentieth century. In its early years, the July Monarchy experienced difficulty with the Catholic Church over the clergy's reluctance to take an oath of allegiance to Louis-Philippe, and during the Revolutionary aftermath, when the nature of the regime was being fought over, mission crosses were often the sites of contestation. There were probably several hundred such incidents between 1830 and late 1832. The majority involved moving crosses from public spaces to the interior of churches, but there were many instances in which crosses were damaged or destroyed. Striking as such symbolism was, there does not appear to have been much bloodshed, and the incidents were provoked by a combination of popular elements and middle-class figures often enrolled in the National Guard. To move the crosses from public ground to the interior of churches was typically *juste milieu.* Some Restoration officials had thought along similar lines, but while there might have been a symbolic similarity, what was essential lay in the reality that gave representation its meaning, or lack thereof. The July Monarchy had decisively shed the theocratic underpinnings that too often accompanied Bourbon rule.[21]

The role of the press in Restoration Opposition ensured that freedom of expression would be emphasized in the revised Charter. There would be no return to censorship, and juries would determine the verdict of press trials. Nevertheless, in the Law of 8 October 1830 the Deputies by a wide margin voted to retain Restoration libel laws with a couple of minor revisions, and kept caution money and the stamp duty. By September 1835, after the Corsican radical Guiseppe Fieschi's attempt to assassinate the king had missed its target but left eighteen dead and twenty-two injured, the Deputies had thought again, and laws were made tougher. After the

[21] Kroen, *Politics and Theater*, pp. 285–305, Phayer, 'Politics and popular religion', 351–61, and Pilbeam, *1830*, pp. 99–105, 117–20.

September Laws, provocation of attack on the king or attempts to overthrow the regime would be treated as treason; for lesser offences conviction could be obtained by gaining a simple majority in the jury. Fines were increased, as was the amount of caution money, and public subscriptions to pay fines were prohibited.

One should not, however, emphasize such practices to the point of losing sight of fundamental differences between the Orleanist and Bourbon regimes. At least part of the reaction of the July Monarchy was a product of confronting hate literature; tacit calls for the murder of the king pushed the bounds of what most states can tolerate. More to the point, there was a world of difference in the level of freedom of expression between the 1820s and any period of the Orleanist regime. Under the July Monarchy, the abolition of censorship and trial by jury secured a marked advance in freedom of expression.[22]

Thus the July Revolution and settlement fulfilled, or partly fulfilled, most Restoration Opposition objectives, and to that extent 1830 constituted a victory for Liberals. If one turns from ends to means, however, the July Revolution and its aftermath mostly entailed failure.

## SOURCES OF DIVISION

The Restoration Opposition possessed characteristics that P. Rosanvallon has identified as part of a liberal current in modern French politics. In essence, liberals sought to put Revolutionary ideals into practice by balancing the desire for increased liberty with society's need for stability. Thus they pursued a middle way free of the extremism of the Far Left and the Far Right. Unfortunately, Rosanvallon has interpreted Guizot as the leading exemplar of the liberal current and this seems a poor choice, given that from the Education Act onwards Guizot's primary role was to block reform until it gave way to revolution. All the same, Rosanvallon's project of drawing attention to the liberal current does mark a useful departure, especially if we give as much attention to political practice as to theory.[23]

Restoration Liberals had achieved significant progress by making means suit ends. Their means were pragmatic and reformist, entailing compromise based on a realistic assessment of how much could be achieved given current circumstance. From July 1830 onwards, however, Liberals repeated the errors of the early 1820s as initial enthusiasm for the Revolution gave

[22] Collins, *Government*, pp. 60–99.
[23] Rosanvallon, *Le moment*, pp. 11–31, 265–330, and Johnson, *Guizot*, pp. 26–87.

way to alarm. Sources of tension were principally three: fear of foreign intervention, civil disorders resulting from economic distress, and political agitation resulting from deceived expectations. Under the cumulative pressure of these three sources of tension, Liberals found that maintaining an alliance based on dual respect for liberty and order became increasingly difficult.

Liberals were but one part of the coalition that had blocked Restoration despotism and counter-revolution, and they, in turn, were a combination of moderates and radicals. During the July Settlement differences among former partners sharpened, and they were also reformulated in new political combinations. In the early 1830s there were four main groupings: Legitimists or Carlists (who continued to view the Bourbon monarchy as sovereign), the Party of Resistance (which sought to limit change between regimes), the Party of Movement (which sought more extensive change) and republicans (who sought a regime free of monarchy).

Tracing the political reconfigurations of 1830 is by no means easy, but they can be broadly summarized as follows. Ultraroyalists usually travelled into Legitimism. Moderate royalists splintered, with some following Chateaubriand into Legitimism, while others rallied to the new regime and became part of the Resistance. The latter formed the initial base for the *juste milieu*, a middle ground between democracy and absolutism that, in effect, signified stasis. Moderate Liberals also divided. Initially the majority shifted between Resistance and Movement, but as time passed an increasing number aligned with the Resistance. Radical Liberals entered into the Movement but they were slow to clarify that their opposition was loyal, and hence damaged the Movement's prospects. From the radical Liberal block also sprang the leaders of republicanism.

Nascent divisions first appeared in the Chambers and observers could detect new battle lines being drawn even during the debates that accompanied the drafting of the revised Charter in early August. Nevertheless, one should not overstate such differences; the cabinet of 11 August and the Laffitte cabinet, established on 2 November, contained elements of both the Resistance and Movement. Moreover, the laws of the settlement, up to the Education Law of June 1833, did constitute compromise between the two main blocks.[24]

Dissensions in Paris were often viewed with alarm in the provinces, but similar divisions slowly emerged. Partly because activists competed for a limited number of rewards, but also because appointments were judged as

[24] Collingham, *July Monarchy*, pp. 23–44.

indicative of the nature of the new regime, the scramble for office triggered by the administrative purge marked a beginning.[25]

In the Haute-Garonne, desire for a thorough purge was doubtless partly self-serving, but frustration at the retention of office by former ultraroyalists was justified. Certainly, Opposition figures did well by a purge directed by Guizot. Alphonse Génie became secretary general at the prefecture and Zépherin Picot de Lapeyrousse and Bart became sub-prefects at, respectively, Villefranche and Saint-Gaudens. Joseph Viguerie became mayor of Toulouse, and Gasc, Authier and Théodore Rolland joined him in various capacities at the *mairie.* In September the municipal council became a haven for Liberals, who also 'arrived' in large numbers in the revamped departmental council in January 1831.[26]

While the purge at Toulouse was simplified by the clarity of the battle lines, matters elsewhere were less certain. At Villefranche, the mayor had not joined the provisional commission of August and was subsequently replaced by the notary Théodore Fourtanier, who had been a member. At Saint-Gaudens the barrister Jean-Baptiste Lapenne had been considered a Liberal in 1820 but had become mayor prior to the July Revolution. He had not entered the provisional commission, and on 30 August Théodore Tatareau, who had also been a mayor prior to the July Revolution, replaced Lapenne. Tatareau had also temporarily replaced the sub-prefect of the *arrondissement.* This situation elicited complaints from the *France Méridionale* and was soon rectified, but Tatareau retained his post as mayor until replaced by the venerable Jean-Marie-Gabriel Durand in August 1831.[27]

Some quixotic appointments resulted from poorly informed decisions made in Paris, but it was also true that the early purge was considered too radical, and hence was subsequently altered. In the opinion of the *France Méridionale*, however, change did not go far enough. Tatareau, as interim sub-prefect at Saint-Gaudens, drew criticism because he failed to take action against mayors who initially refused to fly the tricolour. Meanwhile, letters from Villemur denounced a 'lax administration' for compromising 'patriotic spirit', and similar complaints were registered in a petition from Verfeil demanding the removal of Villèle's 'agents'.[28]

[25] See C. Pouthas, 'La réorganisation du ministère de l'Intérieur et la réconstitution de l'administration préfectorale par Guizot en 1830', *Revue d'Histoire Moderne*, 9 n. 4 (1962), pp. 241–63.

[26] ADHG, 1M97, 27 August and 18 September 1830, and *France Méridionale*, 9–11 September 1830, 23 January and 13 February 1831.

[27] ADHG, 1M98, 10 September 1830, 16 August, 4 November 1831 and 9 March 1832, and *France Méridionale*, 14–30 August 1830.

[28] ADHG, 4M97, 19 August 1830, and *France Méridionale*, 12–26 August and 4 September 1830.

The *France Méridionale* was especially keen on a purge of the judiciary. In early August 1830 a government order annulled all previous press convictions, but the journal did not forget that no other court had shown itself to be as hostile to 'our new institutions'. When Hocquart took his oath of allegiance before Louis-Philippe, the journal expressed incredulity. Moreover, it was mystifying that the entire court, including d'Aldéguier, a man entirely dedicated to the old regime, was planning to take the oath. All the same, d'Aldéguier duly led the vast majority of judges in swearing allegiance, leaving the journal to wonder what this might mean for the future.[29]

Liberals also profited by the scramble for office in the Isère. Penet became the first Orleanist mayor of Grenoble in August 1830 and Rivier became the second after Penet had been elected to the Chamber. Renauldon *fils* accepted nomination to the prefecture of the Haut-Rhin in January 1831; Félix Réal became *premier avocat général* at Grenoble, and Joseph Rey became a councillor at the court at Angers, prior to being transferred back to Grenoble in 1831.[30]

Not everyone could be satisfied. By 12 August 1830 Froussard was already writing to Blanc of his anger at 'harpies' who battened on to offices gained by the blood of the people. Blanc later wrote to Victor Cousin criticizing the *conseil universitaire* for forcing the retirement of two presumably republican professors at the *collège* of Grenoble. Why not appoint Froussard? Such complaints were not merely sour grapes; they also expressed ideological disillusionment that was to become widespread. A striking manifestation of similar frustration with the limited scope of change came in January 1831 when forty-two members of the Grenoble National Guard wrote an address to Lafayette expressing indignation that 'counter-revolutionary forces' had forced him to resign as leader of the National Guard for all of France.[31]

Patronage squabbles were intense in the Bas-Rhin, where few Restoration administrators refused to take vows of loyalty to the new regime. Senior officials were rapidly removed: at the end of August Esmangart gave way to Claude Nau de Champlouis, who had recently been elected a Deputy in the Vosges after being purged from the prefectoral corps by the Polignac cabinet. Thereafter Marchand became a judge; Liechtenberger became a *substitut*; Steiner became postmaster of Strasbourg; and Constant ensured that Coulmann was given a place in the Council of State. With the plum of Strasbourg postmaster having gone to Steiner, Stoeber thought he might

[29] *France Méridionale*, 7–28 August, 9–14 September, 2 October and 14 November 1830.

[30] BMUG, N2442, 3 September 1830; R90622, 25 September 1830, and T3938, pp. 106–16.

[31] BMUG, N2136, 12 August 1830; N1723, 22 October 1830, and the address of the National Guardsmen in ADI, J514.

like to try his hand at Dunkirk. When the latter post failed to materialize, he let his anger be known, but fell back into line after a word from Constant.[32]

Jostling for positions thus fostered division in domestic politics, and the ill will that inevitably resulted was heightened by a desire to influence foreign policy during a period of sustained crisis. The Left was inclined to view French revolution as the dawn of universal 'liberation', and, in the euphoria following the July Days, Audry de Puyraveau called in the Chamber for a *levée en masse* as a step towards the revision of the Vienna Settlement. Bellicosity increased in response to the Belgian revolt against union with Holland in October, and Polish rebellion against Russian rule in late November 1830.

For the new regime, survival pivoted on a struggle for patriotic credibility. Key figures in diplomacy had to reconcile unrealistic expectations to the necessity of ensuring that alarm over the return of French revolution did not become a pretext for Allied intervention. Towards finding a middle path, Molé and Talleyrand developed a policy wherein no state (including France) would intervene in France's spheres of influence – Belgium, the German Rhineland states, the northern Italian states and Iberia. To the Left, non-intervention was insufficient in that it did not allow for crusading, but it did in fact foster significant geo-strategic change by limiting the influence of the autocratic states.

Putting policy into practice was difficult. It meant no 'reunification' with Belgium, and while securing Belgian independence did ensure that Britain would have no part in alliance against France, compromise with 'perfidious Albion' was unappealing to elements eager for revenge. Equally problematic was that recognition of geo-strategic reality meant that the French government took no concrete measures on behalf of the Poles even as crowds attacked the Russian embassy in Paris in March 1831.

Matters only worsened when Austrian troops moved into the Italian states to crush revolt. Given that the French government had sought to appease the autocracies by dispersing Italian refugee groups arming forces for war in the homeland, it was not hard to depict Orleanist foreign policy as spineless. For its part, the Left was closely involved with refugee groups, and had helped prepare forces that had fought in Belgium. Moreover, the Laffitte government was as reluctant to confront its critics over foreign issues as domestic, adding to its image of weakness at a time when desire for force was growing. Thus, although the diplomatic course embarked

[32] BN, NAF 24914, 8 October 1830; BCUL Co 1157; Co 1063; Co 3886; Co 3715; Co 1593; Co 1671; Co 2705; Co 2245; Co 2725; Co 1235; *Courrier du Bas-Rhin*, 8–26 August, 5–7 September 1830; Coulmann, *Réminiscences*, II, pp. 123, 205–6, and Ponteil, *L'opposition*, pp. 58–90.

upon held promise, it was doubtful whether the regime would survive long enough to gain the benefits.[33]

Fear of foreign intervention produced high tension in frontier departments. While proclaiming that France was not troubled by the possibility of 'the enterprises of foreigners', the *France Méridionale* nevertheless warned that to maintain peace the nation must prepare for war. By November fear of war was abating, and according to the *France Méridionale*, peace was 'in the nature of things due to the interests of all peoples'. While troop movements in Russia were a cause for alarm, Europe so desired peace that it was difficult to believe that the northern powers would meddle in Belgium.[34]

Belgium became a preoccupation partly because intervention restoring the house of Nassau was seen as a likely precedent for returning the Bourbons to France. By December prospects for peace appeared diminished and an increasingly bellicose posture was apparent. The *France Méridionale* now expected war, but was not fearful because it would be a 'truly national war against old monarchies which France would accept on behalf of [foreign] peoples'. By February 1831 defensive motivation was giving way to aggressive nationalism: 'nature' dictated that Belgium should be part of France, and in mid-March a series of articles dismissed the 'old diplomacy' being exercised in London while calling for France 'to carry liberty' into Poland and Italy in a general assault on 'the old social order'.[35]

Differing visions as to the conduct of foreign policy had a common denominator in the element of fear, and the corrosive impact of fear could also be seen in domestic civil conflicts. Most disorder sprang from economic hardship and was initially unrelated to partisan political alignment. Sources of discontent were many, but it is difficult to gain even a relative grasp of the dimensions of contestation. Listing incidents of conflict does indicate willingness to test a weakened state, and charting participation rates in violent contestation gives a sense of process unfolding, but judging by statistics presented, non-participation was as striking as its opposite, and one historian has suggested that intensity of discontent was far less than in 1847–8.[36]

[33] Collingham, *July Monarchy*, pp. 186–90, and P. Schroeder, *The Transformation of European Politics 1763–1848* (Oxford, 1994), pp. 666–711.

[34] *France Méridionale*, 5 August, 21–6 November 1830, and P. Pilbeam, 'The emergence of opposition to the Orleanist monarchy, August 1830–1 April 1831', *English Historical Review*, 85, n. 334 (1970), pp. 12–28.

[35] *France Méridionale*, 30 November, 7–12 December 1830, 6–8 February, 4–15 March and 19 April 1831.

[36] See the articles by E. Newman, J. Rule and C. Tilly, and J. Merriman, in J. Merriman, ed., *1830 in France* (New York, 1975), pp. 17–118, and R. Price, 'Popular disturbances in the French provinces after the July Revolution of 1830', *European Studies Review*, 1, n. 4 (1971), pp. 323–50.

While the Revolution exacerbated economic depression, it also gave rise to expectations that distress would soon be alleviated. When relief did not come, strikes, market riots and defiance of tax collectors increased. Racked by desertion in the ranks and uncertainty among officers, the army became an unreliable instrument of law enforcement, and the National Guard was as likely to join in disorder as end it. When, however, the Perier ministry began to take a firm line in 1831, partly through the reorganization of the army and the Guard, protest fell off rapidly.

Desire for change was a product of particular grievances, expressed in demands for the expulsion of foreign workers, pay rises or fixed wages in a particular sector, cheaper grain prices, the destruction of machines, or the abolition of the *droits réunis.* Such demands were only occasionally linked to support for a political doctrine. At times they were politically contradictory, in that expulsion of foreign workers could hardly be reconciled with avowals of sympathy for foreign refugees. At times they were economically contradictory: fixing grain prices was unlikely to rest well with peasants.

Some peasants in the Ariège, Alsace and the Doubs did contest the forest codes, and as resistance in the Ariège turned violent, sympathy among at least part of the elite turned into reaction. Did this make the Demoiselles of the Ariège (so-called because they dressed as women) representative of more than willingness to defend their material interests according to a particular context? To attribute governmental refusal to respond to particular demands to 'bourgeois' attitudes simply masks what was a very complicated scenario in a nation of many divergent interests. Certainly there existed nothing like a consensus, inside or outside middle-class circles.[37]

Notions of the state as an agent for social justice through the redistribution of wealth were still in their infancy, and the Left responded to economic grievances with limited political and fiscal solutions. Beyond franchise extension, radical Liberals saw in fiscal reform a means to fulfil both middle-class and popular expectations. According to the *France Méridionale*, an immediate step should be a sharp reduction in the *droits réunis.* Thereafter control over taxation should be decentralized and budgets should be balanced so that the nation was not impoverished by interest payment on loans to rich financiers.

Alongside fiscal frugality, Liberals continued to champion mass education. According to the *France Méridionale*, the condition of the 'poorest classes' should be ameliorated through the extension of primary education in combination with the granting of political rights at the municipal and national levels. In early 1831 came a call for a 'truly national educational

[37] Sahlins, *Forest Rites.*

system' based on the mutual school method. When the municipal council allotted 4,000 francs for the mutual school at Toulouse, the journal expressed a desire to see such institutions spread so that the 'people' could be informed 'of their rights and duties'. When in May 1831 the departmental general council ended the allocation of funds to the archbishopric, and directed 10,000 francs for the development of primary education, the *France Méridionale* was delighted.[38]

The Restoration Liberal Opposition had always been a coalition of diverse groups united primarily by the battle against ultraroyalism and Bourbon despotism. With the threat posed by the latter two forces greatly diminished, if not entirely defeated, in the aftermath of the July Revolution Liberals then found themselves confronted by a host of new problems – disillusionment with the new regime, the possibility of war with the other powers, and civil unrest born of dire economic circumstances. Under the pressure of these challenges, compromise and consensus-building became increasingly difficult.

## CRACKS IN THE OLD COALITION

There was no general election prior to the passage of the new electoral law, but some 113 by-elections between August 1830 and April 1831 did reshape the lower house broadly in favour of the Left. In departments where Legitimism was strong, a desire to maintain coalition lasted longer and signs of division in the Haute-Garonne were scarce in by-elections in October and November 1830. In discussing candidates, the *France Méridionale* spoke favourably of old royalist allies such as Auguste de Cambon and the moderate Liberal Malaret. Election of Alexandre de Cambon at Albi had released voters of Muret and Saint-Gaudens of their debt to him, and thus they could turn to Durand, who had in the past stepped aside for Cambon. Such arguments held sway; at Muret–Saint-Gaudens Lambert Bastide stood aside for Durand, and Théodore Rolland did the same for Malaret at Toulouse. Both Bastide and Rolland were radical Liberals.[39]

Not all endorsement went to old warhorses, and Charles de Rémusat attracted particular enthusiasm. Rémusat's positioning in the aftermath of the Revolution had been broadly in line with that of departmental Liberals: no compromise with the Bourbon monarchy was possible, but France was

[38] *France Méridionale*, 26–31 August, 2–7 September, 9 November, 28 December 1830, 2–7 January, 19 April, 7–19 May 1831 and 12 January 1832.

[39] *France Méridionale*, 23 September, 19–30 October and 2–9 November 1830. See also Beck, *Legislators*, p. 109–10.

not ready for republicanism. Liberal veterans Jean-Pierre Amilhau, a notary and old friend of François-Bernard Boyer-Fonfrède, Durand and Malaret took seats at, respectively, Villefranche, Muret and Toulouse and, in the departmental college, Auguste de Cambon and Rémusat swept through on the first ballot.[40]

Unlike in the Haute-Garonne, the parting of the ways in the Isère was facilitated by a rapid decline of ultraroyalism; retirement from the Chamber by Planelli was political suicide. Meanwhile the moderate leadership of Augustin Perier and Faure ran into trouble as they incurred radical ire by opposing the abolition of hereditary peerage, and taking a conservative position during discussions of the franchise. Thus their ally Teissère was badly beaten by Réal in an election at Grenoble in November 1830.[41]

Favourable prospects for radicals could also be seen in the Bas-Rhin. While his interventions in the Chamber on behalf of freedom of the press were to be expected, Constant's defence of the right of association was strikingly democratic. Political associations at Paris were composed of men who, 'without bad intentions whatsoever', assembled to discuss current and proposed institutions: 'They have the right, otherwise why have you consecrated liberty of the press?' As a Deputy who had accepted a civil service post, Constant stood again for election, and on 21 October he received 208 of 237 votes cast at Strasbourg.[42]

In a letter of congratulation, the members of Constant's 'constitutional committee' revealed frustration with former allies. Constant would lend his experience to the 'popular government', but he would flay the government the moment it forgot the principles that created it. He would always demand 'the rights of the people' and claim all the results of the Revolution of July. Similar sentiments were apparent in letters from Schützenberger, Schweighauser and Walter. According to Schützenberger, people wanted the frank execution of the Charter, less taxation, and local government laws based on 'confidence in, not mistrust of, the people'. Lowering the national *cens* to 200 francs would not be nearly enough. Schweighauser believed the nation wanted a franchise that would 'allow all to be part of elections'. France would then no longer have a Chamber 'which was considered good when confronted by a despotic-Jesuitical government', but was

40 ADHG, 2M24bis, 22–8 October and 6 November 1830, and *France Méridionale*, 23 September, 30 October and 2 November 1830.

41 BMUG, R90720, 21 December 1830, Barral, *Perier*, pp. 118–31, and B. Jacquier, *Le légitimisme dauphinois, 1830–70* (Grenoble, 1976), pp. 135–74.

42 J.-P. Aguet, 'Benjamin Constant, député de Strasbourg, parlementaire sous la monarchie de Juillet (juillet–décembre 1830)', in *Autour*, pp. 79–119.

no longer up to the mark. Walter was convinced that Constant's position in the Chamber was exactly that of the majority of French people, who had passed beyond the Centre-Left (moderate Liberals).[43]

Municipal elections held at Strasbourg in October revealed the new political formations. While Turckheim was now mayor, much of the municipal council was well to the left of him. It would be labelled 'republican' by the administration, though this indicated more clarity than there was. At any event, the council had become a bastion of the Movement, as had the National Guard.

Ceremonies on 9 and 11 September had already indicated fissure. In the first the Guard placed a tricolour on the tomb of the Carbonaro Colonel Caron, after speeches by Liechtenberger and Stoeber. While this could be interpreted as a symbol of despotic injustice righted, there was more than a hint of rebellion sanctified in it. Two days later, Turckheim spoke at ceremonies paying tribute to Revolutionary generals Kléber and Louis-Charles Desaix; this too represented rejection of the Restoration, but there was little of revolutionary conspiracy about it. A third ceremony, however, united the old Opposition at Strasbourg for the last time. On 12 December the *Courrier du Bas-Rhin* announced the death of Constant and four days later Liberals held a funeral ceremony at the Temple Neuf, followed by a march to the Hôtel de l'Esprit. This time there was no floating orchestra, but the crowd numbered 4,000.[44]

In January 1831 Coulmann tried to fill the vacuum created by the death of Constant. Respect for the new monarch was, however, still high and an aide-de-camp of Louis-Philippe gave Coulmann a thrashing at the polls. The official candidate had enjoyed the support not just of the prefect, but also of Humann, Saglio and Turckheim, and radicals would not forgive such 'disloyalty' on the part of their former allies.[45]

By the end of 1830, radicals had begun to register similar impatience at Toulouse. In its first edition of 1831, the *France Méridionale* opined that the Bourbons had fallen because they had failed to keep faith with France. The current regime, which had become too preoccupied with order, should think more carefully about the fate of its predecessor. Similarly, in mid-January 1831 an address of the Toulousain municipal council called on

[43] BCUL, Co 1619; Co 2709; Co 1520; Co 1472; Co 1518, and Co 3753, and *Courrier du Bas-Rhin*, 17 October 1830.

[44] *Courrier du Bas-Rhin*, 12 September and 14–19 December 1830, Leuilliot, '1830', p. 88, and Ben-Amos, *Funerals*, pp. 92–3.

[45] Coulmann, *Réminiscences*, II, pp. 232–4.

Louis-Philippe to press forward completion of the Revolution of 1830. The Charter must be based on popular institutions, with local and national electoral laws truly representative of the nation's desires.

The *France Méridionale* consistently advocated a broader franchise than the regime established, but it did try to find a middle way. In January 1831 the journal opined that proposed legislation was an embarrassment when compared to the laws of the Legislative Assembly of 1791. One had to keep in mind, however, that the Assembly was truly 'great and national', whereas the present Chamber was a product of fraud. Taking this into account, doubling the number of voters and lowering age qualifications did represent significant gains. Matters would be better still if the *cens* for candidates was simply dropped in favour of paying Deputies a salary.

Passage of the electoral law in April gained qualified approval as a step towards future improvement, but in September the *France Méridionale* printed a petition asking why all individuals included in municipal elections should not also be included in the national franchise. After passage in March of the laws for municipal government, the *cens* had been set at 86.5 francs. This level of qualification did not immediately translate into an electorate much greater than the national franchise at Toulouse (2,081 and 1,771 respectively in 1831), but it certainly brought the possibility of voting in the future much closer for many.[46]

One of the more debilitating developments of the Revolutionary aftermath was that compromise and the toleration of opposing views came to be associated with weakness, and even progressive journals such as the *France Méridionale* would soon be trapped by political polarization. Central to this downward spiral in political culture was the issue of freedom of association. Guizot had led resistance by attacking the political clubs that mushroomed in August 1830, calling for the rigorous enforcement of penal laws against permanent associations of more than twenty members. In practice, the new regime had initially been tolerant, ignoring public meetings of the Friends of the People that could draw numbers in the hundreds.

Among the Friends of the People there were portentous fissures. Girondins advocated legal means for pursuing change – propaganda, education of the masses and electoral organization – and hence the difference between them and the Movement was not easily distinguished. Montagnards shared the Girondin mandate and repeatedly denied conspiratorial

[46] *France Méridionale*, 9–12 November 1830, 2–18 January, 18–20 February, 2 June, 23 September and 6 October 1831.

intentions, but they also stockpiled guns. *Enragés* were less concerned by denials and more eager to lead revolt.[47]

Because a small wing of the Left promoted violence, it became increasingly easy for conservatives to associate the entire Left with civil disorder, and some crowd manifestations did indeed have political resonance. Demonstrations in Paris in December 1830 during the trial of the Polignac cabinet ministers had little to do with economic grievance. Anticlerical riots that led to the sacking of the palace of the archbishop of Paris in February 1831 were a riposte to Legitimist ceremonies, although they also placed pressure on the government. Members of the Friends were involved in the riots, although it would be pushing matters to characterize them as specifically republican.[48]

Ministers such as Laffitte found themselves confronted by the same tactics that Liberals had applied to the second Richelieu ministry in the summer of 1820, and historical parallel advanced when the riots of February triggered the advent of the Perier ministry in mid-March 1831. Where the Laffitte government had been irresolute, Perier personified force. Perier was not literally reactionary; he did not intend to reverse the Revolution or revise the Charter in a regressive direction. It was, after all, under his government that the laws on municipal councils, the National Guard, national elections, and the abolition of hereditary peerage were passed, and all of these constituted compromise between the Movement and Resistance. Moreover, matters were finely balanced as the parliamentary session opened; the Resistance candidate defeated the Movement candidate by only five votes in the election of the president of the lower house.

Perier's programme was, nevertheless, pursued by aggressively attacking critics, and whether his strategies prevented or encouraged revolt is an open question. In the short term, Perier's policies did work towards stabilization by associating all opponents with insurrection and blurring the lines between reform and revolt. In the long term, the consequence was to found a regime that could not cope with change, because change had been inextricably linked to fear. Perier's rule was typified by an early piece of legislation. Nineteen members of the Friends had been arrested for their part in the riots of December 1831, but they were acquitted. Perier then responded by pushing through restrictive laws on public demonstrations.[49]

[47] G. Perreux, *Au temps des sociétés secrètes* (Paris, 1931), pp. 1–37, and G. Weil, *Histoire du parti républicain en France de 1814 à 1870* (Paris, 1900), pp. 29–74.

[48] Pilbeam, *1830*, pp. 94–6 and 167–86.

[49] Bury and Tombs, *Thiers*, pp. 42–5; Bourset, *Casimir*, pp. 199–280; Collingham, *July Monarchy*, pp. 55–69, and Higonnet, 'La composition', pp. 364–72.

Perier's appointment was interpreted by the Parisian press to mean that coalition was over, and journalists began to attack the regime itself. Carrel took the *National* to the furthest extreme of the Movement, with a democratic programme and hints that a republic was the ultimate objective. The *Tribune*, the *Révolution* and the *Mouvement* became unabashedly republican. For his part, Perier pursued the Opposition press ferociously, launching repeated charges to break newspapers through attrition. Results were mixed, as juries inclined to leniency, and the main consequence was to push journalists to more extreme positions.

A prime example of how Perier worked could be seen in his destruction of the National Associations. These organizations were stimulated especially by fear of invasion. To some extent they were sparked by Carlist demonstrations in mid-February 1831, but they were also a riposte to the Perier government's refusal to intervene on behalf of revolution abroad. Radicals dominated the movement, but the Associations initially also included moderates, and over the months of March and April they grew rapidly. Ultimately, Associations were formed in over sixty departments and numbers perhaps reached 100,000. Publicity contributed, and here too the old Liberal coalition was apparent as the radical *National, Tribune* and *Révolution* joined the moderate *Constitutionnel, Courrier Français* and *Journal de Commerce* in endorsing the movement.[50]

Perier made clear his opposition in the Chamber. While he did not question the patriotism of those who joined, he underlined that there was no need for the Associations when France possessed an army and a National Guard. He also implied that their real purpose might be to challenge the state, and insisted that government officials either resign or end membership in the Associations. Either way the objective was achieved. Those who resigned thereby lost influence; those who remained recognized they must follow government orders.

Political polarization was the upshot, and in the Bas-Rhin Coulmann received a letter from his young radical supporter Valentin Schneegans expressing exasperation at a government that was driving people towards either Carlism or republicanism. In April Marchand too lamented the purge, and began talks with Coulmann and Voyer d'Argenson over founding a new journal. Silbermann had done his share at the *Courrier du Bas-Rhin* prior to July 1830, but his initial response to the new regime had not been all that might be desired: 'it is not a republic that we demand, nor a democracy with all its possibilities of popular excess'. Subsequently the *Courrier* had

[50] Collins, *Government*, pp. 69–76, and Pilbeam, 'The Emergence', pp. 12–28.

taken a sharp swing leftwards and begun to advocate universal manhood suffrage while interpreting constitutional monarchy as a transitional phase that would eventually give way to a republic.

Radicals were, however, always a step ahead of Silbermann. In January 1831 Schertz had sought to create a 'Patriotic and Political Society of the Bas-Rhin' and announced in the *Courrier* that it would press for universal manhood suffrage and amelioration of the living conditions of workers. Mayor Turckheim had immediately condemned this initiative, linking it to the popular societies of 1793, and plans were aborted. In March the *Courrier* itself had announced the formation of a Patriotic Association, but again Turckheim had responded negatively, blocking attempts to recruit in the National Guard. According to Schertz, the Left needed a journal that would be less concerned by governmental response to such initiatives, and thus when in May he began his own newspaper, *L'Alsacien*, its republicanism was almost as pronounced as its distaste for the 'moderation' of the *Courrier*.[51]

Tempers were flaring throughout France when the Chamber was dissolved in April 1831. Given that by-elections since July had favoured the Movement slightly, there was perhaps reason for optimism when the *France Méridionale* called on electors to choose Deputies who would press for reform. The value of 'loyal' civil servants to the cabinet could, however, be seen in July, when the administration again took up its old role of orchestrating elections for official candidates. The return of the administration as campaign agent more or less put paid to hopes for significant decentralization.[52]

Although Legitimists abstained from voting in the Haute-Garonne, disintegration of the old Restoration Opposition meant that previous large majorities disappeared. The one exception occurred at Muret, where Rémusat emerged as a consummate politician. He was already shifting rightwards in the direction of Perier, but kept this reversal hidden from local supporters. Not all Liberals were as cynical. General Pelet had strong support in both the two old colleges at Toulouse, and he gained election in the first college, comfortably defeating Malaret on the second ballot. It took a run-off in the second college before the *ministériel* Jean-François Chalret defeated Pelet. Toulouse *extra-muros* also required a run-off, at which point Sans defeated Théodore Rolland. Amilhau not only defeated Martin Bernard at Saint-Gaudens, he also won at Villefranche.

[51] BN, NAF 20035, 31 August and 16 September 1831; BCUL, Co. 2712; *Courrier du Bas-Rhin*, 31 August, 16–28 September, 7–16 November, and 2 December 1830, and Coulmann, *Réminiscences*, II, pp. 232–44.

[52] *France Méridionale*, 18 March and 3–21 April 1831.

Results left the *France Méridionale* with mixed emotions. That campaigns by Auguste de Cambon and Malarat had foundered was no cause for grief; previous debt to them had been paid. The journal had supported Rémusat and Pelet, and although it had endorsed Rolland rather than Sans, the latter had the backing of the Movement and would soon gain approval from the *France Méridionale*. Amilhau, however, was a source of vexation because as a Deputy he had voted with the Centre-Right.[53]

Elections in the Bas-Rhin revealed radical ascendancy, but the tenor of campaigning also demonstrated how old allies were fast becoming enemies. Coulmann complained that the Catholic clergy had led entire villages to vote against him; while this was an overstatement, it was true that Restoration royalists were aligning with moderate Restoration Liberals. *Ministériels* also found reason to lament the tactics of their adversaries, as law students staged a *charivari* outside the home of Humann in Strasbourg on 3 May. On the following day satire turned into riot, with students mixing with popular elements, and troops with bayonets fixed had to disperse a mob of some 400. Strasbourgeois attempts at intimidation did no harm, however, to Humann's prospects at Sélestat, where 151 voters signed an address vowing they would re-elect their Deputy.

Although no proponent of violence, one of those who verbally attacked Humann was Silbermann. The *Courrier du Bas-Rhin* now supported candidates Coulmann, Lafayette, Odilon Barrot and local radicals at Sélestat and Wissembourg, but the journal also backed the centrist Saglio, as did Strasbourg radicals in a preliminary poll. Voters at the college then rejected *ministériels* Turckheim and Mathieu-Faviers, and of the radical slate only one failed (against Humann at Sélestat). When Lafayette subsequently opted for Meaux, radical ascendancy was again hammered home as Voyer d'Argenson swept to victory.[54]

Former moderate Liberal leaders did not fare well in the Isère either. Augustin Perier fell to Réal's rising star at Grenoble, and Augustin was also angered by the desertion of his former aide Penet, who had gained election at Saint-Marcellin. Next on the chopping block was Faure, who had refused voter demands that he vote for the abolition of hereditary peerage. Not only was Faure defeated in the July general elections, the republican Etienne Garnier-Pagès also beat him at Vienne in December. In an article in the new opposition journal the *Dauphinois*, the editor Alexandre Crépu gave a revealing explanation of what was transpiring. While respectful of Faure's

[53] ADHG, 2M24bis, 18 May, 9–29 June and 9 July 1831 and election minutes in the same file; *France Méridionale*, 9–30 June, 2–9 July 1831, and Rémusat, *Mémoires*, II, pp. 464–78 and 490–503.

[54] Ponteil, *L'opposition*, pp. 91–201.

past contributions, Crépu argued that he was representative of a moderate leadership vital under the Restoration, but no longer needed.[55]

The parting of the ways between moderate Restoration and radical Liberals thus marked the period immediately following the July Revolution. While the former Centre-Left shifted rightwards to align with *doctrinaires* and former moderate royalists, the former Left provided the basis of the Movement and initially carried a substantial portion of the electorate with it. Division among former Liberal allies resulted from the clarification of previously obscured differences as to what constituted appropriate 'development of the representative principle' in the Charter, but this development was not necessarily problematic and it had the virtue of presenting clear alternatives to voters and the public more generally. More troublesome was the animosity that soon entered the debate, making compromise and mediation among divergent groups more difficult. Worse still, the possibility of future reform was further damaged by former moderate Liberals who fostered polarization, and by fragmentation among former radical Liberals over how to pursue progressive change.

## LOST OPPORTUNITIES

Radicals were strongly positioned immediately after the general elections of 1831, but thereafter their fortunes steadily declined. There were two principal causes for the failure of the radicals to seize opportunities provided by the electorate: successful foreign policy on the part of the government, and association of all the Left with republicanism. Ties to republicanism damaged the Party of Movement because a minority of republicans resorted to insurrection against the regime, and aligned themselves with Legitimists in doing so.

Orleanist governments made progress in weakening the Left's patriotic appeal when France intervened in Belgium in August 1831. Although collaboration with the British had previously secured Belgian independence in the London Conference, diplomatic gains held less appeal for the French public than military intervention. By seeking to reconquer Belgium in August 1831, the Dutch king provided a pretext for a demonstration of French power. Nothing was better to restore morale in the army than an opportunity to point bayonets at foreigners rather than unruly citizens. Furthermore, in addition to the salutary impact of a display of armed force, the government benefited by the Soult Law, introduced in the Chamber in August 1831 and

[55] Barral, *Perier*, pp. 118–31, and Félix-Faure, *Félix Faure*, pp. 137–9 and 143–5.

passed in March 1832. The Soult Law renewed conscription, but there never was any likelihood of creating the large, national army demanded by the Left. Emphasis was instead placed on securing a 'professional' force that would be less vulnerable to the siren songs of republican agitators, and towards this end members of the military were prohibited from participation in political associations.

The appeal of forceful foreign policy could be seen in the *France Méridionale* as the journal reported with obvious pleasure in August that French troops had crossed into Belgium. Readers might have been surprised to learn that the *France Méridionale* viewed war as an unfortunate necessity, especially when it again called for war against the kings of Europe. After the intervention in Belgium had proved less dramatic in its effects, however, a more rational assessment returned to the journal and by January 1832 one could read that the government's policy of maintaining peace abroad was praiseworthy. In pondering the *France Méridionale*'s apparent volte-face over European conflagration, it helps to keep in mind that the journal's bellicosity always had a defensive hue to it. As it became apparent that the British had no intention of abetting plans to use Belgium as a launching pad for an Allied invasion of France, inflated bellicosity deflated rapidly.[56]

As the government slowly improved its public image in foreign affairs, the impact of civil disorder on the electorate gradually undermined radical ability to work for reform. By the time of the trial of the ministers of Charles X in late 1830, divisions had become well established in the press, with the *National* demanding dramatic change, while the *Journal des débats* and the *Constitutionnel* brayed for a crackdown on agitators. Formed in the midst of Parisian uproar, the Laffitte cabinet had managed to prevent mobs from slaughtering the accused in December, though this accomplishment had been achieved more by subterfuge than force. Thereafter the sacking of the archbishop's palace in mid-February 1831 had again revealed official reluctance to intervene against the crowd. In the provinces, officials at Nancy and Chaumont had probably instigated outbreaks of anticlericalism, and while National Guardsmen might have prevented sacking by crowds, they had then conducted their own depredations. The first consequence of disorder had been a shifting towards the right in the government, abetted by resignations from Lafayette and Barrot. All this shuffle had achieved under Laffitte, however, was paralysis and hence Louis-Philippe had reluctantly handed power over to Perier.[57]

[56] *France Méridionale*, 5 August, 17 December 1830, 13 March, 16–19 July, 9 August 1831 and 6 January 1832.

[57] See Pilbeam, *1830*, pp. 105–14.

An advocate of polarization thus confronted the Left, but the Left also played a part in the politics of fear that would destroy their prospects. Members of the Movement did not advocate insurrection, but like moderate Liberals in the 1820s, they were not averse to exploiting alarm. Moreover, radical Liberals were closely tied to republicans in associations based on the legal methods of opposition pioneered during the Restoration. Republicans, in turn, mixed the two Revolutionary traditions and began to spread this to workers. Ultimately, the combination of legal radicals and semi-legal republicans proved disastrous, because it gave Perier and his successors the ground Liberals had taken from Charles X – desire for the rule of law.

Radical sympathy for republicanism was based on a certain amount of shared ideological ground. Republicans wanted a political system in which more of the male population directly participated, and radicals shared this objective, though, as a whole, they were less generous. That there was a common base could be seen in several associations. The Aide-toi, free of the influence of Guizot, supported radicals and republicans alike, as organization was extended to local and National Guard elections. Membership in cantonal committees perhaps reached a high of 20,000 men who engaged in registration campaigns, put forward slates of candidates, and circulated petitions for franchise reform. Similarly, members of the Movement such as Barrot and Maughin combined with republicans such as Voyer d'Argenson and Garnier-Pagès in associations in Paris to provide free education.[58]

Although they shared a good deal of common ground, differences arose between radicals and republicans over the means by which progress should be pursued. Most republicans eschewed violence, and Deputies Garnier-Pagès and Louis-Marie de Cormenin preached against it. Yet republicanism did have an insurrectionary wing, and the cult of Robespierre, as interpreted by Buonarroti, Cavaignac and Blanqui, inevitably brought forward the most divisive historical associations of republicanism. Meanwhile Voyer d'Argenson asked the poor why they did not rise up against the rich in his *Boutade d'un riche à sentiments populaires*, published in 1833. Such advocates of insurrection provided conservatives with precisely the sort of spectre required to turn desire for civil order into blanket rejection of change.[59]

The central question regarding the Movement was whether it would remain loyal in its opposition. Not many Deputies wanted a republic, and in this they reflected those whom they represented, but the Movement

[58] See P. Rosanvallon, 'La république du suffrage universel', in Furet and Ozouf, eds., *Le siècle*, pp. 371–89, Weill, *Histoire*, pp. 56–9, and Huard, *La naissance*, p. 53.

[59] Pilbeam, *Republicanism*, pp. 98–9, and P. Pilbeam, 'The insurrectionary tradition in France, 1, n. 3 1835–48', *Modern and Contemporary France*, 1, n. 3 (1993), pp. 253–64.

did align with republicanism in pressuring the government via extra-parliamentary means. One of the easiest ways to stir the emotions of the crowd was to appeal to its bellicose sentiments, and all of the Left was disposed to do so. Austrian participation in the crushing of revolt in the Italian states in 1831 was thus fraught with potential domestic consequences for the government, and Perier responded by sending a naval squadron to the Italian coast, while French and British diplomats pressured for withdrawal of Austrian forces.

Equally threatening for the government was agitation over Poland. Sympathy for the Poles ran deep in the Left, but there was in fact little that France could do against Russian repression. Nor was the position of the Poles advanced by riots in Paris in September 1831, and at Metz and Strasbourg shortly thereafter, upon news of the Polish capitulation. Franco-British lobbying did 'encourage' Metternich to withdraw troops from Italy by the end of the year, but he immediately reversed this in early 1832 as soon as revolt broke out anew. Perier then sent French troops to Ancona in a manoeuvre that yielded little of substance, but did provide an occasion for flag-waving.

Forceful government action was more evident within France in the form of troop deployments to crush, rather than negotiate with, 'revolt' at Grenoble and Lyons. At Lyons, Perier reversed previous administrative attempts at compromise between *canuts* (silk weavers) and merchants and the result was 169 deaths in street fighting; at Grenoble he backed a prefect whose idea of order was that troops should bayonet fleeing students who had pushed matters too far at carnival. Perier's provocative tactics were designed with the Deputies and the electorate in mind, and he was correct in the main: violent confrontation furthered desire for a government capable of enforcing order.[60]

The less intransigent republicans knew well what Perier was working towards. As president of the Friends of the People, Doctor François-Vincent Raspail fought to direct the club towards peaceful propaganda. Republicans were not, however, so enamoured of legal means that they did not seriously ponder the merits of revolt after the funeral of General Lamarque in early June 1832. While the majority followed Armand Carrel in concluding against, a minority decided to push forward. In a cycle that was to become familiar, Paris was placed in a state of siege while the army did

[60] R. Bezucha, 'The revolution of 1830 and the city of Lyon', in Merriman, ed., *1830*, pp. 119–38, and C. Breunig, 'Casimir Perier and the troubles of Grenoble, March 11–13 1832', *French Historical Studies*, 2, n. 4 (1962), pp. 469–89.

battle with a Carlist–republican alliance, and perhaps some 800 were killed or seriously injured.

If we look at developments surrounding the Lamarque riots, we find why the Movement and republicanism were so closely associated. Previously a left-wing parliamentary committee had drawn up a document known as the *compte rendu* in order to push the government away from the policies of Perier, who had fallen victim to cholera in May. The *compte rendu* criticized the king for failure to promote the Movement, castigated weak foreign policy and criticized purges conducted in the National Guards of Lyons, Grenoble and Perpignan. About 140 Movement and republican Deputies had signed the 'account', although roughly 20 per cent of left-wing Deputies had refused. The doubts of the latter group about the wisdom of this attempt to pressure the king could only have been confirmed thereafter when Laffitte, Barrot and François Arago chose to present Louis-Philippe with the *compte rendu* during the second day of the Lamarque riots. At the very least the timing suggested willingness to exploit mass violence, and to some it suggested connivance in insurgency.

Developments subsequent to the Lamarque riots demonstrated how much good will still remained for the Left to lose at Paris. In the aftermath of the insurrection, military tribunals were established, but appeal to the *cour de cassation* quashed this violation of the Charter. When the government brought leaders of the Friends of the People to trial for holding meetings of more than twenty members, Cavaignac appealed to the jury to decide on the issue of freedom of association. Having recognized that the Friends had broken the law, the jury then declared the accused innocent. The presiding judge insisted on following the law, but the jury had effectively made a case for revising it.

Although the Friends of the People expired shortly thereafter, their demise resulted mostly from drunkenness overcoming patriotism in the absence of leaders. Moreover, government determination to enforce the law of association simply fostered the emergence of the Society of the Rights of Man, which followed the Carbonari example in forming a federation of cells of fewer than twenty members.[61]

In the provinces, members of the Movement found themselves caught in a trap. While paying tribute in his *Réminiscences* to the support of Schertz, Liechtenberger, Marchand and Schützenberger, Coulmann subsequently regretted that their adoption of immediate republicanism had not been based on a realistic appraisal of contemporary politics. All the

[61] Weill, *Histoire*, pp. 67–74, and Ben-Amos, *Funerals*, pp. 93–5.

same, Coulmann himself had signed the *compte rendu.* In August 1832 he, Liechtenberger, Marchand, Schneegans and Schertz brought Barrot for a tour of Alsace, and the cries at a banquet at Strasbourg were combative: 'Down with the *juste milieu*!'[62]

Failure for the Movement, however, lay less in the message than the tactics adopted. A week-long rebellion against tariffs on imports in September 1831 gained sympathy from the *Courrier du Bas-Rhin*, but Silbermann was right to fret over the impact of law-breaking. Schertz, who showed fewer qualms, was soon brought to trial for inciting hatred against the government, and by January 1832 he and *L'Alsacien* were bankrupt. The passing of Polish émigrés through Strasbourg gave rise to repeated threatening demonstrations thereafter, and Saglio was twice the victim of *charivari.* Voters at Sélestat remained unimpressed, and when Humann became Minister of Finance, they re-elected him by 189 votes to 4 for a radical candidate!

In the Haute-Garonne, insurrection slowly drove a wedge between radicals and republicans. Early demonstrations at Toulouse were aimed at Legitimist targets, and during the summer of 1831 crowds protesting against government failure to close a Legitimist café had to be dispersed repeatedly. Events then took a more sinister turn on 30 September when a crowd of roughly 200 paraded in protest at governmental inaction over Poland. The arrival of news of the fall of Warsaw next day led crowds to smash the printing presses of the Legitimist *Mémorial* and *Gazette* while sympathetic National Guardsmen looked on.

By October crowd action had a clearly anti-Orleanist character. 'Minstrels' took to performing at the Capitole, encouraging crowds to join in republican songs, and mayor Viguerie sent in the police and troops to disperse the crowd. On the following night crowds chanting 'Down with Louis-Philippe!' and 'Long live the republic!' attacked the *octroi* offices in the *faubourg* Saint-Etienne, and again troops went into action. The initial response of the *France Méridionale* was to blame Legitimism, but it also warned that the government must move quickly to assure the 'people' of 'the fruits of the revolution'.[63]

The merging of economic protest and political dissent cut ground from under those who advocated franchise reform but eschewed violence, and months of local disorder and the 'catastrophe' of the revolt of the *canuts* at Lyons placed the *France Méridionale* in a difficult position. While expressing hope that a good harvest would ease the plight of workers, the journal also

[62] Coulmann, *Réminiscences*, II, pp. 241–4, and Ponteil, *L'opposition*, pp. 91–201.

[63] *France Méridionale*, 12–28 July and 16 October 1831, and Aminzade, *Toulouse*, pp. 104–6.

urged that watch be kept over those who attempted to stir revolt, and agitation was partly ascribed to left-wing 'anarchists'.

Until the autumn of 1831, the *France Méridionale* was the sole journal occupying the left of the political spectrum, but thereafter it found itself outflanked by the *Patriote de Juillet*, which had pronounced republican tendencies. Initially the *France Méridionale* welcomed the *Patriote*, but shortly thereafter the elder journal lectured the younger: sovereignty resided only partly in the people; it also lay in the laws that were the expression of it. Sometimes the use of force was indeed a 'sacred duty', but when arbitrary rule had ceased, 'citizens must lay down their arms'. The *Patriote* then drew heavy fire for claiming that the 'justice of the people had been blocked' on 22 December when authorities broke up a *charivari* aimed at Amilhau. Amilhau was a bête noire of the *France Méridionale*, but the journal would not endorse intimidation.[64]

The longing for old alliances remained, and subsequently the *France Méridionale* declared there were only two real sides in the current war – the friends of July and Legitimists. In January 1832 the return of the old enemy to the ballot box in by-elections fostered such illusions. There was a reassuring familiarity in seeing Limairac elected as college president, and great satisfaction in watching the old Liberal coalition rally behind Lambert Bastide to defeat the Legitimist Duke of Fitz-James. Yet this was a last hurrah.[65]

Ultraroyalist organization had not simply withered away after July 1830. Immediately following the Revolution, many Legitimists had withdrawn from politics through resignation of government office and abstention from elections. As the prospects for foreign intervention declined, however, this strategy had come to look like defeatism and Legitimists had returned to the political forum.

The key Legitimist organization was the Affiliation Catholique, founded in October 1830. The name echoed the Institut Philanthropique of the 1790s and structure was similar, with Toulouse as a centre for a network that extended to five departments in the south-west, which in turn was connected to a national organization. Directed by a council named the Grand-Prieuré, leadership was noble, with Villèle and the Marquis Pierre d'Hautpoul (another veteran of the White Terror) at the top, but lower-class

[64] *France Méridionale*, 4–20 October and 11–29 December 1831; for an interesting parallel, see the attempt of the Lyonnais *Précurseur* to find a middle position between the Orleanist *juste milieu* and republican insurrection in Popkin, *Press*, pp. 88–103 and 193–228.

[65] AN, F1C III Garonne (Haute-) 7, 8 January 1832; ADHG, 2M24bis, minutes of 8 January 1832, and *France Méridionale*, 13–29 December 1831 and 2–12 January 1832.

elements provided the bulk of the membership. Legitimism also possessed an army along the lines of the *verdets*, and official reports estimated the size of this force at Toulouse at approximately 1,000. Wealthy members of the Affiliation paid a subscription, the funds from which were directed to charity, propaganda and supporting Legitimist newspapers brought to trial.[66]

Legitimist strategy consisted essentially of destabilizing the new regime and election campaigns and public commemoration served to remind the public that a Bourbon king still waited in the wings. Legitimists also supported Spanish Carlists in their civil wars, providing funds, weapons and uniforms. Their opponents were well aware of the general aspects of Legitimist organization. They could hardly fail to be, given Carlist commemorations at Toulouse in January 1831 of the execution of Louis XVI. Some 200 Legitimists had gathered at the *église* Saint-Etienne and had sought to march in a procession, but crowds led by *jeunes gens* singing 'The Marseillaise' had confronted them in a counter-demonstration. Shortly thereafter, 600 National Guardsmen had arrived. Carlist leaders had then marched to the prefecture, where insults were duly exchanged, prior to Legitimists beating a hasty retreat.[67]

Until the summer of 1831, the *France Méridionale* had warned that Legitimist manifestations ran a risk of inciting popular revenge. After disturbances in September and October, however, the journal recognized that crowds were being agitated by a coalition of republicans and Carlists. This was a troubling realization as it shattered belief that the Liberal radical wing and the 'people' were inevitable allies. To combat such splintering, the *France Méridionale* attacked Carlists who sought to exploit misery by adopting the 'language of democracy'.[68]

By combining with Carlists in the Lamarque riots, republican insurgents in Paris had also begun to provoke questions about their patriotism. What was the public to think of such willingness to combine with the old 'anti-national' forces of the Right? Moreover, while republicans dominated the fighting in Paris, Legitimists attempted insurgency in the Midi and, when this fizzled out, in the Vendée. Were republicans merely dupes of Legitimists who, after all, had been more than eager for a third Allied

[66] Aminzade, *Toulouse*, pp. 48–54; J. Lesparre, 'Les partis politiques dans la Haute-Garonne à la fin de la monarchie de juillet', in J. Godeschot, ed., *La Révolution de 1848 à Toulouse et dans la Haute-Garonne* (Toulouse, 1948), pp. 31–5; V. Clarenc, 'Toulouse, capitale du Carlisme Catalan (1830–1840)', *Annales du Midi* (1993), pp. 225–46, and Fourcassié, *Villèle*, pp. 395–440.

[67] ADHG, 4M48, 16 February 1831, and *France Méridionale*, 23 January, 6–23 August 1831.

[68] *France Méridionale*, 20 October, 7–9 December 1831 and 8–12 January 1832.

invasion of France? That the threat of Carlism was largely hollow was illustrated by the futile episode of the Duchess of Berry in the summer and autumn of 1832, but the entire escapade did provide Orleanists such as Thiers with ample opportunity to convince the public that the regime needed support.[69]

Thereafter Legitimists shifted emphasis to electoral organization, and similar republican failures at insurrection from 1832 to 1834 contributed to the formation of a Legitimist–republican electoral alliance in 1834. This change of strategy bore fruit in June 1834 in the election of Pierre-Antoine Berryer at Toulouse, followed by the election of Fitz-James, again at Toulouse, in 1835. When it held, the alliance could gain reward for republicans too, as when the lawyer/journalist Jacques Joly was elected in 1839.

Whether combining forces with Legitimism served the long-term prospects of republicanism was, nevertheless, questionable. Carlists could at times play the role of wrecking agent, especially in departments such as the Gard where religious antagonism and patronage enabled Legitimist nobles to retain influence over Catholic workers. Yet the Gard was exceptional and Legitimists generally constituted a small, unpopular elite in France. For most of the public, Bourbon royalism was indelibly tied to foreign intervention in 1814–15. By way of contrast, Orleanist rapprochement with Britain yielded returns in the Quadruple Alliance of April 1834, joining the French, British, Spanish and Portuguese governments against Carlist forces in Iberia. For most patriots, the Alliance marked a satisfying reversal of French intervention on behalf of reaction in 1823.[70]

Neither Perier's intentionally indiscriminate attack upon the Left nor the Movement's failure to divorce itself clearly from the insurrectionary wing of republicanism was apt to foster reform based on meaningful dialogue and consensus-building. Moreover, republicanism's growing association with Legitimism raised serious questions about the patriotism of the Left generally, and where exactly it was that revolutionaries intended to take France.

## THE LONG MARCH LENGTHENS

Republicanism gradually declined after 1832, and severely damaged the prospects of the entire Left in the process. After the Lamarque riots,

[69] Collingham, *July Monarchy*, pp. 116–31, and Bury and Tombs, *Thiers*, pp. 47–9.

[70] Aminzade, *Toulouse*, pp. 109–11, 133–5, 144–8; S. Henry, 'La campagne des banquets à Toulouse', in Godeschot, ed., *1848*, pp. 55–6; Fitzpatrick, *Catholic Royalism*, pp. 97–181; Jacquier, *Légitimisme*, pp. 135–74, and Schroeder, *Tranformation*, pp. 720–6.

most republicans concluded that propaganda and organization offered better potential than mass violence, and an Association for the Defence of the Patriotic Press concentrated on establishing republican newspapers throughout the provinces. Loosely coordinated by the Parisian chapter, perhaps sixty-seven local affiliates had been established by September 1833. At Strasbourg, the initial call for such an association came from the *Courrier du Bas-Rhin* and Liechtenberger became president of an organization whose members donated funds. Similarity to press expansion in 1828 was striking: by 1834 some 60 of 240 provincial journals were republican, although many were on a shaky financial footing. The progressive nature of republicanism could be seen in Cabet's *Le Populaire*; aimed specifically at workers and sold at two sous per copy, it enjoyed a circulation of 27,000. Although the government maintained the repressive strategies initiated by Perier, juries continued to acquit more frequently than condemn, and most journals managed to carry on.[71]

The Society of the Rights of Man also reached out to the provinces, linking previously established associations and encouraging the formation of new ones. Like Liberals before them, provincial republicans were fond of banquets in honour of Deputies or figures acquitted of state charges. Republicans also maintained enthusiasm by petitioning the Chamber, or collecting subscriptions, especially for causes such as Polish resistance. Organizations on behalf of the Poles, combining republicans and radicals, bore more than a passing resemblance to efforts made on behalf of Greek independence in the 1820s.[72]

Most progress was made in the east and parts of the Midi, whereas response was limited to a couple of cities in the west and little was accomplished in the north. Hard numbers are difficult to come by. Guizot estimated that the Society possessed 3,000 members in 1833, whereas the *Tribune* put the figure at 4,000 for Paris alone. What does appear clear is that, outside of Lyons and Paris, only a limited mass base was gained and very little attention was given to the peasantry. Persistent state harassment meant that the Society could hardly be expected, however, to reach impressive mass dimensions.[73]

One can view the Society of the Rights of Man as part of the long republican march forward. One can also note that republicans

[71] Perreux, *Au temps*, pp. 38–332, Collingham, *July Monarchy*, pp. 132–85, and Huard, *La naissance*, p. 56–9.

[72] M. Brown, 'The Comité Franco-Polonais and the French reaction to the Polish uprising of November 1830', *English Historical Review*, 93 (1978), pp. 774–93.

[73] Weill, *Histoire*, pp. 75–86.

went further than Liberals had done in recruiting non-middle-class elements into political association. In this sense, republicanism was progressive. Nevertheless, republican organizations remained decidedly middle-class, and one can ask whether middle-class agents of politicization were not leading the workers who joined down a path characterized by failure. The achievements of the Society were remarkably similar to those of the Carbonari in the 1820s. Much effort went towards recruitment in the army, especially in the east, with success among non-commissioned officers neutralized by loyalty among senior officers and indifference among the rank and file. More importantly, because its activities were partly public and partly secret, the Society provided a perfect target for conservatives bent on associating legal and illegal modes of opposition.

What progress there was came by moderate means. Development in the Côte-d'Or and Saône-et-Loire could be seen in the evolution of several local newspapers towards republicanism, and at Dijon Cabet and Garnier-Pagès organized a local Society that called for the widening of the franchise but avoided association with insurrection. It was largely middle-class, but, like its counterparts at Metz, Strasbourg and Rouen, recruited among artisans. Conversely, recruitment did not extend to manual workers at Rouen, where there was a sizeable working-class population employed in textile factories. August 1830 had seen extensive industrial unrest in the Seine-Inférieure, a consequence of which was that social conservatism had become pronounced, even among the Left. As part of this trend, in January 1834 members of the Movement backed Laffitte and broke with the Society of the Rights of Man in preparing for elections. In contrast, relations among Burgundian members of the Movement, such as Maughin and Hernoux, and republicans, such as Cabet, remained close. The fortunes of the Movement in the Seine-Inférieure, at least in the short term, would therefore differ from those in Burgundy when the Society launched insurrection at Lyons and Paris in April 1834.

At Lyons, republicanism had made headway partly due to Perier's politicization of an industrial dispute in 1832. Dijonnais National Guardsmen had initially responded to the first Lyonnais revolt with an offer to travel to Lyons to aid the authorities. Thereafter, however, republican leaders convinced 231 Guardsmen to sign a proclamation stating they would have refused to oppose the Lyonnais *canuts* had they known the true nature of the insurrection. When Lyonnais revolt broke out again in April 1834, republicanism was involved from the start. Moreover the uprising was timed to coincide with revolt in Paris. Both insurrections were savagely repressed, with another 421 souls lost at Lyons, but what was crucial about them was their impact on France generally.

Previous prosecution of leaders of the Society of the Rights of Man at Paris had yielded little more than acquittals. By the autumn of 1833, the government had decided to push repression further, proposing a bill enabling it to dissolve associations regardless of whether they held under twenty members. Radicals in the Chamber could protest all they liked, and republicans Voyer d'Argenson and Garnier-Pagès could join Raspail in denial of conspiracy, but lauding the Convention while labelling the current Chamber as 'prostituted' did little to stop the passage of the bill. More prescient were warnings from Pagès de l'Ariège that measures ostensibly designed to combat illegal association would be used to harass legal organization. The government did specify that legislation would not affect electoral committees or preliminary polls among voters, but it was no coincidence that the Aide-toi and the Association for the Defence of the Patriotic Press collapsed shortly thereafter. Most of the Left followed the republican Lafayette in opposition to the legislation, but at this point old allies such as Laffitte and Barrot began to break ranks. Although it was not the sole cause of insurrection in Lyons and Paris, the bill played a part, furthering polarization that now decimated the Left.[74]

After the insurrections of April 1834, republicanism plunged into a rapid downward spiral. Newspapers such as the *Tribune* that had called for revolt suffered the inevitable consequence, and whatever sympathy might have existed for the victims of repression evaporated with Fieschi's brutal attempt to assassinate Louis-Philippe in late July 1835. Behind this atrocity were the *enragés* of the Society of the Rights of Man. It was in this context that the September Laws were proposed, and while they were not passed without strong opposition in the press and Chamber, the trial of the republican conspirators of Lyons and Paris further diminished respect for republicanism and its associates.[75]

Cavaignac and Armand Marrast hurled defiance, underlining that many Orleanists themselves had conspired against the Bourbon monarchy in the Carbonari. The escape from imprisonment of twenty-eight accused, however, argued against their self-righteousness; they were not about to repeat

74 Lévêque, *Une société*, pp. 489–90; Porch, *Army*, pp. 47–117; B. Moss, 'Parisian workers and the origins of republican socialism, 1830–1833', in Merriman, ed., *1830*, pp. 203–17, and Huard, *La naissance*, pp. 53–9, 67–73, 75–81.

75 See J. Lucas-Dubreton, *Louis-Philippe et la machine infernale (1830–1835)* (Paris, 1951).

the martyrdom of the four sergeants of La Rochelle. Meanwhile, revelations of extensive organization, including arms stockpiling, did not please the public any more than it had done in 1822, and by 1835 all hope of further reform was effectively gone, as public backlash against all organization, legal or illegal, set in.

The elections of June 1834 were an unmitigated disaster for the Left, yielding roughly 320 *ministériels*, forty floating Deputies and ninety members of an Opposition in which republicans were but a small minority. Many Deputies who had formerly sat with the Left now sat in the Centre, after listening to their supporters. Reaction to sustained disorder did not consist simply of repressive legislation; insurrection had fostered a political climate in which the electorate was ill disposed to look upon any form of political association favourably. The Chamber would thereafter become increasingly fragmented with the emergence of Thiers' Third Party, and this would pose one more hurdle for establishing reform coalitions.

Reaction has often been described as 'bourgeois', but this all too convenient pejorative term accounts poorly for the results of municipal elections. In his evaluation of municipal elections for France generally in 1834, Thiers noted that conservative notables had been much more successful than in 1831. Although his calculations were impressionistic, scholarly estimation that in 1837 68.7 per cent of municipal councillors were *constitutionnels* (supporters of the regime), whereas 13.1 per cent were Legitimist and 18.2 per cent were from the democratic Opposition, suggests no great divorce between national and municipal electorates.[76]

Burgundian voters made their sentiments clear in the national elections of 1834. Cabet had taken flight to London, but his replacement at Dijon II gained less than one-third of the votes cast. Maughin saw his previous majority at Beaune reduced from 73.6 per cent to 52 per cent. Hernoux carried Dijon I over a conservative by seven votes on the third ballot, whereas in 1831 he had attracted 68.7 per cent of the vote on the first ballot. Overall in the Côte-d'Or and Saône-et-Loire, the Left, republican or radical, gained three of twelve seats when previously it had held six, and results were similar in municipal elections. Conversely, disassociation with the Society of the Rights of Man enabled the Left to fight more effectively at Rouen, securing a seat for Laffitte. All the same, conservative reaction was apparent in the rest of the department and by 1837 Laffitte had lost his seat.[77]

[76] Vigier, 'Elections', pp. 282–4.

[77] Lévêque, *Une société*, pp. 491–504; Gonnet, 'La société', pp. 833–72, and R. Aminzade, *Ballots and Barricades* (Princeton, 1993), pp. 174–77, 254.

Results in the Bas-Rhin were similar. From 1832 to 1834 the Left created a succession of organizations, ranging from a chapter of the Society of the Rights of Man, to a Patriotic *casino*, to an overtly republican association. Repeated riots at Strasbourg led again to the dissolution of the National Guard in July 1834. The formation of an association against taxes on drinks and salt was designed to woo the popular classes, but did not aid electoral prospects. Although radicals retained their strength in the Strasbourg municipal government, by 1833 *constitutionnels* had recovered control of the councils of the department and *arrondissements.* National elections in 1834 then capped the process. With one exception, *ministériels* swept the department, and even the one remaining seat at Wissembourg was lost in January 1835 when an official candidate mauled Coulmann by a vote of eighty-nine to sixteen. The credit held by radicals in the early 1830s had by then been lost, as voters followed moderates such as Saglio back into the orbit of Humann.[78]

In the Isère, results were complicated by the advantages Casimir Perier had given the Left by the endorsement of an unjustifiable use of force. Even here, however, the potential of 1830 was largely wasted. The election of Garnier-Pagès in 1832 and the ability of figures such as Crépu to make the municipal council of Grenoble a republican stronghold until the mid-1830s did appear to herald the Isère's return to the forefront of left-wing politics. Nevertheless, solid *ministériel* advances accompanied spectacular republican victories, and by 1842 *ministériels* had captured the municipal council of Grenoble. The champion of those who wanted reform but remained loyal to the regime was Félix Réal. Having defeated Augustin Perier in 1831, he then crushed Voyer d'Argenson in Grenoble *extra muros* in August 1836.

Other Liberals successfully took an Orleanist track. While Gabriel Prunelle's relations with the central government as mayor of Lyons in the early 1830s were stormy, he took the government line as Deputy for the *arrondissement* of Vienne until 1842. Support of the government posed little problem for Alphonse Perier, who gained election at Grenoble in 1834, defeating a republican and the Legitimist Planelli. A vital cog in the Restoration Liberal organization, Alphonse was then considered more radical than his brothers, but he gradually shifted rightwards, supporting Guizot until this finally cost him his position in the Chamber in 1846.[79]

[78] Ponteil, *L'opposition*, pp. 202–472; Livet and Rapp, *Strasbourg*, pp. 296–30, 311–12, and Coulmann, *Réminiscences*, III, pp. 139–40, 183–7.

[79] Breunig, 'Casimir', pp. 469–89; Barral, *Perier*, pp. 119–24; Bourset, *Casimir*, pp. 265–6, and Jacquier, *Légitimisme*, pp. 16–20, 140.

## DEJA VU

Much as they had done in the mid-1820s, radicals turned away from conspiracy and insurrection in the mid-1830s. From 1835 onwards, politically motivated violence was left to 'professionals' such as Blanqui, whose notions of the revolutionary vanguard ensured that few would be compromised. Press restrictions forced journalists to drop calls for murder, but thereby made criticism of the regime more responsible and ultimately more effective. As civil disorder diminished, the leading proponents of change, including utopian socialists such as Cabet, found that their ideas made headway. By 1837 the Left was back to forming electoral committees and, although such efforts would be set back by the attempt of a self-proclaimed 'conspirator' and 'exterminator of tyrants' to assassinate Louis-Philippe in 1840, recovery of this form of organization would continue thereafter. Similarly, press associations specifically linked to the issue of franchise reform would revive in 1844.[80]

For their part, moderates traumatized by the disorders of the early 1830s settled into support of an Orleanist *juste milieu* that amounted to political stultification. Government in the late 1830s was typified by cabinet instability and policies designed to achieve little in the domestic sphere. Two attempts by Thiers to popularize the regime through foolishly aggressive foreign policy achieved the very reverse, and Guizot thereafter successfully worked electoral patronage to block reform in the 1840s. Public preoccupation with order, however, diminished. The association of monarchy with privilege gained ground with each rejection of reform, at a time when perhaps one-quarter of the adult male population had grown accustomed to holding the vote at the local level.

At Toulouse, republicanism splintered in 1835. The futility of an insurrectionary wing thereafter allowed a reformist group to establish ascendancy and they found that middle-class elements were receptive to their message. As 1848 approached, an alliance developed between republican elements and members of the dynastic opposition over the issue of electoral reform. Such consolidation, with middle-class leaders enjoying extensive lower-class support, was an ominous portent for the regime.

It would take until 1842, the year of Humann's death, for Liechtenberger and Schneegans to begin a revival of republicanism based on calls for electoral reform in the Bas-Rhin. By this stage radical control of the Strasbourg municipal council had been lost; Schützenberger had become a man of

[80] See Huard, *La naissance*, pp. 53–5 and 59–62.

order and hence mayor, and the *Courrier du Bas-Rhin* had returned to moderation. This time the movement refrained from violence in wooing public opinion.

The national banquet campaigns of the 1840s pointed to an emerging elite and a popular coalition as dangerous to the Orleanist regime as it had been to the Bourbon. When the National Guard joined in revolt in 1848, Louis-Philippe recognized that the consensus upon which the July Monarchy had been founded was lost, and wisely departed. At Toulouse, little time was wasted in declaring a republic; resistance was even less apparent than in 1830. In the Bas-Rhin, Liechtenberger was undoubtedly the most popular individual in the department.

As *commissaires géneraux* of the new republic, Jean-Baptiste Froussard of Grenoble and Martin Bernard of Toulouse could seek to give the new regime a solid foundation, but the same basic problems would remain. Blues fell out with Reds as democratic socialism surpassed political republicanism, and violence again played its destructive role. The former Carbonaro turned Orleanist Adolphe Martin could watch ruefully from his window as a Toulousain popular club staged a *charivari* designed to 'convince' him to resign his post as president of the *cour d'appel*, and Pagès de l'Ariège received the same treatment for his 'lukewarm' republicanism, although this did not stop him from gaining re-election in April. If this was progress, it was Louis-Napoleon who would profit by it.[81]

When to call a halt to armed resistance is surely the most difficult question confronted by advocates of change in the midst of revolution. When insurrection succeeds, the temptation is to attribute victory to force, but such a conclusion differs little from the thinking of proponents of a reactionary coup d'état. Judging by the July Revolution, many of the public viewed mass violence as a last resort. When circumstance no longer seemed to warrant such means, longing for order superseded desire for enhanced liberty. Not knowing when to desist in the politics of violence, in turn, played into the hands of reaction, by blurring the lines between those who sought change through convincing the public, and those who wished to force change before the public was ready.

In not searching relentlessly for consensus, Liberals had failed to build upon the legacy they had created during the Restoration. They had thereby lost the opportunity in the early 1830s to found a regime that could recognize

[81] Collingham, *The July Monarchy*, pp. 200–417; Perreux, *Au temps*, pp. 333–85; Pilbeam, *Republicanism*, pp. 129–242; Aminzade, *Toulouse*, pp. 108–15, 135–48; Henry, 'La campagne'; Ponteil, *L'opposition*, pp. 202–472; Livet and Rapp, *Strasbourg*, pp. 296–30, 311–12, and Coulmann, *Réminiscences*, III, pp. 139–40, 183–7.

that change is a permanent necessity, not something to be feared and repressed. Because change in France was synonymous with the Revolution, the very notion of 'terminating' the Revolution was faulty; the essence of politics lay in accommodating perpetual change to the need for stability. No ideology provided a path to perfection, but reform through compromise did enhance the possibility of improvement. At the end of the day, radical Liberals who failed to divorce themselves from the insurrectionary wing of republicanism had complemented the polarization fostered by a moderate Liberal, Casimir Perier. France had benefited by Liberal coalition in July 1830, but would have been better served had Liberals thereafter recognized the means by which progress had been gained.

CONCLUSION

# *Revolutionary tradition*

Two waves of crisis lashed the Second Restoration. The first began with Decazes's decision to alter the Lainé Law in late 1819, and culminated in the arrival of ultraroyalist rule under Villèle in December 1821. The second began with Villèle's decision in October 1827 to call a general election, and culminated in the Revolution of 1830. The first crisis thus fostered executive despotism; the second led to the triumph of parliamentary government.

Crucial to such differing results was the role of the Centre-Right. Under Richelieu in 1820, the Centre-Right allied with the Right and the consequence was a shrewd combination of gradualist counter-revolution and administrative despotism. Confronted by Polignac in 1829, the Centre-Right aligned with the Liberal Opposition, and the consequence was success for the Liberal argument that the Charter was a contract between king and nation. If one asks why the Centre-Right acted so differently, the answer lies less in the Liberal message than in Liberal means. The content of Liberal appeal remained largely consistent during the Restoration, but after 1823 association with insurrection was abandoned. Proposals for change could be well received by both the electorate and the general public, but they had to be put forward by legal reform, not threats of violent upheaval.

The cause of both crises was the influence Liberals gained through electoral success. In 1820 and 1830 Liberals were progressing rapidly towards a majority in the Chamber of Deputies, which meant the question of sovereignty could no longer be fudged. Because the regime collapsed amidst insurrection, it has been tempting to conclude that the Opposition must have been revolutionary. Revolution, in the sense of overthrow of the dynasty, was not, however, what Liberals intended. Conversely, one should not go to the opposite extreme in portraying a reactionary regime as the sole agent of change. Liberals did intend to establish their interpretation of the Charter, including 'development of the representative principle'.

Revolutionary tradition thus took two paths – one reformist and one conspiratorial. The two were not entirely separate, either in objectives or personnel. Between 1820 and 1824, moderate Liberals did not engage in insurrection, but neither did they disassociate themselves from radicals who did. In the early 1830s, members of the Movement did not join in conspiratorial republican societies, but they devoted all their energies to attacking the agents of order/repression, and it was not difficult to draw conclusions concerning where sentiments lay.

The public, except in one instance, consistently reacted unfavourably to insurrection, and revelations of conspiracy led to a backlash against all forms of organization, legal or otherwise, except for the greatest of all organizations – the administration. Even in the latter regard, the public showed a marked aversion for the governmental equivalent of conspiracy – use of agents provocateurs, deployment of the *fonds secrets* for the covert purchase of newspapers, or, worst of all, the idea that the government itself might be the product of Jesuit intrigue. If the greater public differed from the narrow circle of the electorate in these regards, it did not demonstrate such a division when called on to do so by revolutionaries. Hence the 'professional' revolutionaries Blanqui and Barbès changed to strategies that did not depend on anything remotely approximating majority support.

The July Revolution constituted an important exception to negative response to revolt, but in this case the objectives of armed resistance were aligned with public opinion as represented by voters in the elections of June–July. Insurrection was interpreted as a defensive response to aggression; the public was well educated as to the meaning of the July Ordinances. For this reason the Revolution was accepted with alacrity by most of the elite and by most of the general population. Better still, Liberal organization and mass support in the provinces enabled a transition of power that was striking for its orderliness; revolution often entails reprisal and bloodshed, but in this case there was little of either.

The Revolution of 1830 points to the conclusion that belief in oppression must be widespread, and means must be adjudged appropriate to ends, for insurrection to lead to a change in regime. Such conditions, however, were seldom met, and the belief of small groups that their objectives justified violent means in fact repeatedly favoured political reaction. Thus insurrection's primary role was to weaken movements for reform pursued through legal means. Nothing fostered growth in the state's repressive capacity more than fear of armed revolt, as preoccupation with civil order re-enforced expectations of strong government. Fear, in turn, could be used for the purpose of blocking change by presenting it as a threat rather than a source of improvement or inevitable readjustment.

Studies of how change came to France have long been absorbed by the dynamic between the repressive state and revolutionary movements. The inclination to view matters from this perspective has been strengthened by the belief that the state has inevitably been an agent of social oppression, and that this has only been overcome through organized rebellion. Neither of these two perspectives is instructive, however, for understanding the Restoration or the early July Monarchy. Change came to France in 1830 because the public had become convinced of its necessity. One can attribute the Revolution to Bourbon errors, but one should not lose sight of a public unwilling to accept such errors. Unwillingness was a direct result of the Liberal Opposition's powers of persuasion, not coercion.

## LIBERAL OPPOSITION AND PARTY FORMATION

Due to the narrow confines of the electorate, and assumptions that political orientation derives from social status, there has been a pronounced tendency to ignore the *monarchie constitutionelle* in investigation of the process of democratization in France. After all, if only the elite could participate directly in politics, why should the rest of the population take any notice? Hence literature on the Revolutions of 1789 and 1848 dwarfs that of the period 1814–48.[1]

Yet politics consists of more than simply voting, and differences between the elite and the rest of the population have been greatly overstated. Social tensions should not be simply swept aside in analysis, but political divisions were not solely determined along class lines. Restoration royalism did to a certain extent have a mass base, and for most of France the Opposition had a much greater following, a point that was demonstrated in 1815 and again in 1830. The basic fault line was a product of both material interest and ideology or belief systems. This is not to say that every soul intently followed day-to-day battles in the legislature any more than citizens currently do. Nevertheless, the issues debated, and legislation passed or rejected, in the Chambers did affect the interests of all, and government was viewed through the prism of values held by the general populace, not just the electorate.

The troubled issue of the security of nationalized lands, apparent from 1814 to 1830, illustrated how material interests, ideology and political culture combined. Any hint of the question being reopened produced a strong

[1] See P. McPhee, 'Electoral democracy and direct democracy in France, 1789–1851', *European History Quarterly*, 16, n. 1 (1986), pp. 77–96, and M. Edelstein, 'Integrating the French peasants into the nation-state: the transformation of electoral participation (1789–1870)', *History of European Ideas*, 15 n. 1–3 (1992), pp. 319–26.

reaction in urban centres and, especially, in the countryside, where the lands were constantly being sub-divided through family inheritance, multiplying the numbers affected. Villèle's émigré indemnity fell well short of putting an end to the matter, because the principal beneficiary of the revocation of the Charter's guarantee of sanctity would have been the Catholic Church. Anticlericalism was by no means simply a product of material grievance, but the issue of nationalized lands was a major part of it.

When Villèle proposed his bill, Constant attacked it as an affront to the principles of the Revolution. Morever, Liberals inevitably linked generosity to émigrés or the Church in state budgets to alleged poor treatment of that bastion of patriotism – the army. Throughout the Restoration, anticlericalism and patriotism walked hand in hand on the Left, and these were not issues that left the greater public indifferent. Liberal participation in anticlerical demonstrations, in the streets or at the theatre, demonstrated the ties that bound them to groups outside the electorate.

Use of *charivari* perhaps revealed elite culture employing an expression of dissent drawn from popular culture, but this did not begin during the July Monarchy. *Charivari* was used by middle-class elements, particularly students, from at least 1819 onwards as a weapon against religious missions, and it seems probable that such tactics can be traced back at least to the Revolution, as can theatre battles. After 1830 *charivari* was increasingly applied to unpopular politicians, but this was less a cross-cultural fertilization resulting from the July Revolution than a temporary product of weakened state authority. More significantly, at this stage use of *charivari* was no longer simply a defensive response to clerical aggression; it was an act of intimidation that, if the examples of Humann, Saglio, Chalret and Pagès are anything to judge by, was counter-productive when it came to voting. Again, the Liberal use of serenades in the 1830s was nothing new, and it certainly did not constitute a borrowing from popular culture.[2]

Liberals were not a party in the full, modern sense of the term, but this perhaps enhanced their appeal outside the electorate. The issues upon which they focused were basic ones, and their ideological heterogeneity meant that diverse groups could rally to them. They were not tied to obvious sectional interests and they had to base their appeal broadly, given the diversity of French regional economic interests. Uniformly, Liberals claimed to represent the nation, and they were far more apt, and better placed, to do so than royalists, both because they were consciously part

[2] See Sahlins, *Forest Rites*, pp. 83–134 and Kroen, *Politics and Theater*, pp. 291–3.

of the Revolutionary tradition, and because royalism had been restored by foreign intervention.

Liberals did not have what we now consider party discipline and they fell loosely into two camps of moderates and radicals. This generalization, however, tends to mask a complicated relationship. The difference between radicals and moderates often had as much to do with temperament as ideology. Liberals such as Goyet, who were progressive in terms of expanding the franchise, were not necessarily first in line for the barricades. This was not for want of courage; patience and fortitude require their own kind of gumption, and rushing into conflict often results from loss of nerve. It said a great deal that moderate Liberals took the lead in formulating the address of the 221 in early 1830. All the same, radical Liberals did distinguish themselves by demanding more by way of change, and were more inclined to push for rapid results. Liberals with Revolutionary Bonapartist or republican tendencies were more likely to step to the forefront of aggressively contesting ultraroyalism or state authority. Social origins were also a factor. There were obvious exceptions in that Lafayette, Voyer d'Argenson and Corcelles were not exactly born into humble circumstances, and they were highly militant, but the Periers and Turckheims of the Opposition were more typical of Liberal notables, and it was at the lower end of the *cens* that radicalism found its strongest constituency.

The most significant breach between radicals and moderates was the willingness of the former to resort to violence or intimidation. Ultraroyalists were predisposed to link insurrection to ideology, but they were only partly correct and there was no exact correspondence. Nevertheless, certain points do emerge clearly. Legal and conspiratorial Liberal Opposition coexisted, embodied in Constant defending Lafayette in the Chamber, and although insurrectionary opposition took centre stage for a time, legal opposition continued. Nor were the two ever entirely separate; while certain Liberals entered into conspiracy, many of them also continued to fight by legal means. Furthermore, while Liberals who stuck to the straight and narrow could see the damage done to their cause by insurrection, relations seldom were entirely severed. When the republican conspirator Froussard lost his teaching position at Mont-Fleury in the Isère, he found a defender in Augustin Perier, and an employer in Casimir. After the period of insurrection had ended, its instigators returned to the legal fold with little difficulty.

Thus there was a certain amount of flexibility in the Opposition that could make the two blocks complementary, but could also make Liberalism vulnerable to the centrist wooing of Decazes and Martignac. Both the latter cabinet leaders sought to detach moderates through progressive legislation, but ultimately their efforts failed due to Liberal determination to make the representative principle in the Charter a genuine reflection of national sovereignty. Bound up as it has been in emphasis on the social aspects of counter-revolution, much Restoration history has overlooked this fundamental political dividing point.

If the Liberal Opposition was not a modern political party, it did make major advances in party formation. In his discussion of the Aide-toi, Pouthas made the mistake of attributing Liberal organization in 1827 to young former members of the Carbonari, and this error has become typical of general accounts. Pouthas, however, overlooked the advances made by Liberals prior to 1820. The key to Opposition success lay in grassroots organization. Because Liberal strategies – patriotic oaths, formation of registration committees, transactions and preliminary ballots – were partly a product of the *régime censitaire*, historians have overlooked them, while focusing on Parisian-based 'high politics', or insurrection. Yet they all did serve towards organizing the vote, and committing Deputies to certain broad policy lines.

Liberal banquets, serenades, petitions and subscriptions were means of encouraging political commitment and activism that could be transferred to more democratic electoral systems. Particularly important was the way in which the press, especially the local press, could facilitate the organization of politics along partisan lines. In its appeal to *constitutionnels* or 'patriots' the press seldom distinguished between electors and non-electors, but it did frequently remind voters that in performing their duty they were acting on national interests. Beyond raising political consciousness through coherent integration of a host of issues, the press could also foster an early form of party discipline. Moreover, with each step that Decazes or Martignac took in reducing repression, Liberal organization became progressively more public.

One should avoid excessive claims. Many of the strategies deployed by Restoration Liberals harked back to the Revolution, and doubtless could be traced further to any occasion when people voted in sizeable numbers – be it for the Estates (General or provincial) or in village councils. Precedents for Liberal practices such as electoral committees, registration drives, banquets, transactions, preliminary polls, slates of candidates and battles over electoral bureaux can all be found in the early 1790s.[3]

[3] See, for example, Crook, *Elections*, pp. 8–130, P. Gueniffey, 'Revolutionary democracy and the elections', in R. Waldinger, P. Dawson and I. Woloch, eds., *The French Revolution and the Meaning of Citizenship* (Westport, Conn., and London, 1993), pp. 89–103, and Woloch, *New Regime*, pp. 60–94.

The broad political scenario of the Directory, especially after 1797, was remarkably similar to that of the Restoration as the dynamic of organizational battle between royalists and neo-Jacobins gave an increasingly partisan cast to elections. Brief acceptance of official candidature and increasing press participation in campaigns pushed party politics further. Neo-Jacobin *cercles constitutionnels* in provincial centres such as Le Mans established subcommittees throughout the department in order to organize campaigns and it was such experience that Charles Goyet, via his mentor Rigomer Bazin, drew upon in the early Restoration. More striking still was the way in which the Directory set the stage for subsequent state attempts to control the electorate by using *commissaires* (forerunners of the prefects) to act as campaign managers for official candidates (often themselves). Français de Nantes denounced these developments in 1799 and, despite his happy conversion to Imperial notability, would fight them again in the Restoration. Thus the Directory had entered into a phase of tripartite politics that presaged those of the Restoration.[4]

There were, of course, differences. Violation of the secrecy of the ballot – such a vital issue to Liberals – tended to work against democratization during the Restoration, whereas neo-Jacobins, as a rule, had preferred oral voting in the 1790s. More significantly, the restored Bourbons inherited a much more formidable state apparatus from Napoleon and, from Decazes onwards, the administration became a tool for electoral organization far more sophisticated than anything developed during the Revolution. In a sense, the state itself fostered politicization, but its objective was to turn the electorate into a herd of sheep; it was initially ultraroyalism and then the Liberal Opposition that encouraged genuine politicization through the promotion of voter independence.[5]

The essential difference between the Directory and the Restoration lay in the relative stability of the latter's electoral regime. Unlike in the Directorial secondary assemblies, the Restoration electorate remained largely the same group of individuals and simple passage of time gave the Opposition opportunity to develop, coordinate and refine the political practices that worked. Many initiatives came first from the local level, but they could then be spread via the press and Parisian committees, often including departmental Deputies, to the rest of France. Ultraroyalists were the first group, early in the Second Restoration, to combine electoral politics with demonstrations of broad public support, but this was a device that Liberals were far better

[4] See Crook, *Elections*, pp. 165–89, and Woloch, *New Regime*, pp. 95–112.

[5] See Edelstein, 'Integrating', pp. 323–5.

placed to exploit in most of France and they repeatedly did so thereafter. From 1817 onwards Liberal grassroots organization rapidly surpassed ultraroyalist mass organization and, indeed, ultraroyalism became increasingly reliant upon state despotism.

Historians of Revolutionary elections, naturally enough, tend to focus on issues of mass democratization through the exercise of voting rights. Yet one should be careful over linking electoral participation with politicization too exclusively. That the Left could muster substantial mass support was demonstrated most clearly in 1815 and 1830, but examples of Liberals reaching beyond the electorate litter the Restoration. The latter tendency was manifest in sustained attachment to Revolutionary and Napoleonic symbols, but it was given substance by shared material interests. When push came to shove, those who would have benefited by reversion to *ancien régime* privilege were a distinct minority.

That voting remained meaningful was a crucial victory of the Restoration Opposition; Restoration parliaments did possess power and this would be increased in the July Monarchy. By preserving the measure of genuine parliamentary government afforded by the Charter, Liberals reversed a process of parliamentary emasculation begun under the Directory and continued under Napoleon until the First Restoration. During the Hundred Days, Louis XVIII had promised parliament to abide by the Charter and Napoleon had then upped the liberal ante with the *Acte additionnel*. Thereafter, however, Restoration governments began a drive to short-circuit the division of powers through use of the administration to control the electorate so that official candidates, promoted by the executive, would inevitably form the majority in the lower house. Had this succeeded, the vote would have been no more meaningful than under the First Empire.

The essential Liberal contribution, in the long term, was that Liberals revivified the means of organization and persuasion that countered the executive drive towards the destruction of voter independence. They did not originate such means, but they made them more sophisticated and carried them onwards into the July Monarchy. In the early 1830s radical Liberals repeated their errors of the early 1820s and, for a time, this lapse contributed to a conservative programme that amounted to stultification. Nevertheless, the methods of 'legal liberty' remained, and were effectively redeployed from the late 1830s onwards.

Among the many themes of political history has been the question of when political parties were born. The answer of course pivots on definitions which can be endlessly debated, but one can at least submit observations drawn from evidence too long ignored or simply unknown, and criteria developed by S. Berstein in a recent essay provide a useful means for pondering to what extent the Liberal Opposition constituted a party. Berstein identifies four main criteria. Firstly, a party must exist beyond the lifetime of its founders, indicating that it responds to a 'profound tendency within public opinion'. As a rule of thumb, it should last for more than a generation. Secondly, a party should possess a hierarchical organization in which permanent relations are maintained between a national leadership and local structures that give direction to a part of the population. Thirdly, a party must aspire to the exercise of power and, towards that end, must put forward a plan capable of gaining the approval of the nation as a whole. As part of this process, a party must be able to mediate among the divergent interests of its supporters. Finally, a party must search for popular support, either by giving direction to activists, or by attracting voters.[6]

In terms of duration, the Liberal Opposition splintered in the aftermath of the July Revolution; it was a forerunner of most the main political groupings that followed, save Legitimism, but effectively it ended with the separation of its constituent parts. The Liberal Opposition did not survive the existence of its founders, and it did not endure for more than a generation. All the same, it did respond to a profound tendency within public opinion, and indeed its success in this regard (the establishment of national sovereignty) was a major reason for its end.

If we turn to spatial extension, evaluation yields similarly mixed conclusions, but here we begin to fill in major historical lacunae. The Liberal Opposition did have a structure linking national leadership and local committees of activists capable of triggering political manifestations by significant numbers, both inside and outside the electorate. The Opposition was not a parliamentary group lacking connections in the country, and local committees were not simply representatives of parochial, local interests. Conversely, the element of hierarchy was distinctly lacking. The *comité directeur* was more a coordinating body than a party executive capable of issuing commands with the expectation that they would be heeded. Nor did the *comité* have the means to discipline those who ignored directives, advice or pleadings. The term 'independent' had great resonance at the grassroots level; discipline and hierarchy were more characteristic of administrative despotism.

Rather ironically, given general historical interpretation, discipline tended to flow more towards Deputies from their grassroots supporters.

[6] S. Berstein 'Les partis', in R. Rémond, ed., *Pour une histoire politique* (Paris, 1988), pp. 49–95.

The Liberal Opposition was founded on Independent promises to reflect the will of voters – apparent in the adoption of patriotic oaths that outlined broad policy commitments, and promises to submit to re-election should government office or promotion provide temptation as to allegiance. Very early on, Liberals took to the 'preliminary polls' by which they determined their votes, often by way of 'transactions'. Although this was partly a work of coordination, it was also true that the merits of individual candidates were discussed, whether they attended or not. Thus certain broad understandings could be reached, and Liberal newspapers were not shy about reminding Deputies when they appeared to fail in such undertakings. The performance of Deputies in the battle over whether to admit Grégoire was scrutinized in the Isère to the point of bringing printed denials from the supporters of Français de Nantes when he was accused of not fighting hard enough.

Such commitments were at the heart of Liberal Opposition, and they would become more sophisticated from 1827 onwards. Much has been made of the point that certain candidates (Grégoire in 1820 and Guizot in 1830) did not need to campaign locally to secure election. Yet behind each election was a local committee more or less certain that it already possessed the commitment it desired. In neither case was support a matter of patronage from above; rather, it indicated the opposite. There was little of largesse to be expected from Grégoire or Guizot, and local Liberals were actually inclined to keep these two candidates away from the scene. Of all the Liberal Deputies, perhaps the most assiduous in constituency work was Constant; he knew to what extent he had to reflect the wishes of his local *équipe*, and in the example made of Humann in the Bas-Rhin he could see the limits of local patronage. There were countless variations, as many as Liberal Deputies and local committees, but Constant was much closer to the norm than has generally been recognized.

Exactly what was meant by representation was often at issue, and one can note a certain penchant in the Opposition for direct democracy that moderate Liberals disliked, but to which they increasingly had to submit. While this does bring to mind the *sans-culottes* of the Revolution, we should bear in mind that the Liberal Opposition was a different group with a good deal more historical experience to draw upon. Liberal insistence on secrecy of the ballot constituted rejection of the sort of intimidation for which *sans-culottes*, and the Restoration administration, were renowned.

In an analysis of the development of representative government, it is not unnatural to focus on the 'modern' features of western democracies. Historically, however, the chief opponent of representative government has usually been located in the state itself. The scenario of two or more parties, distinct from the state, waging electoral battle for control of government, is a relatively recent one. During the Restoration, the state apparatus was effectively deployed towards achieving the rough contemporary equivalent of a one-party state. Given this, the Liberal Opposition was drawn towards mechanisms of direct democracy to secure independence of the state. One does not need to think long and hard to see that the battle Liberals waged was similar to that which currently goes on in much of the 'developing' world; in this sense the experience of the Liberal Opposition, confronted by the Napoleonic administrative model, was more relevant to contemporary politics than one might originally have thought. Moreover, the Opposition's battle against use of the state for the promotion of privilege was a universal one.

The third and fourth of Berstein's criteria fit remarkably comfortably with the Liberal Opposition. Liberals certainly aspired to the exercise of power, and they were willing to search for support amidst the general population in this pursuit. More tellingly, given its loose ideological character, the Liberal Opposition was a 'mediator' in the sense of representing a wide variety of interests. The latter point takes on more significance if we consider the fissures within post-Revolutionary France. Although it did have fundamental, unifying values, the Liberal Opposition was exceptionally heterogeneous in social and doctrinal terms. As a political phenomenon, this makes it all the more worthy of attention in a country known for fragmentation. Ultimately, there was something very 'modern' about the way in which Liberals eschewed doctrinal clarity and division in favour of pragmatism, compromise and opportunism.

At the very least, it is apparent that many of the features identified by Berstein in other countries as crucial to the transition to modern politics, such as the local registration associations that sprang up in Britain in 1832, were already apparent in Restoration France. When such practices returned to France in the early Third Republic, they may have been applied to a greater degree, but they were not different in kind from Restoration practices – a particular manifestation of the general observation that French political *moeurs* had their origins in the *monarchie censitaire*. Too narrow a definition of Revolutionary tradition has meant that the reform tradition that was part of it has yet to be systematically studied.

Was the Liberal Opposition a political party? It was a major step in the direction of a modern party, partly fulfilling the criteria, but not completely. It certainly represented a much greater advance than historians have recognized.

That the Liberal Opposition developed a tradition of seeking to detach change from fear was, however, more significant. The strategy of 'legal liberty' sought to promote reform by accommodating liberty to order through respect for the rule of law while advocating change. It was based on gradualism, but not stasis, and belief that progress could be made by convincing, rather than threatening, the public. The roots of such a tradition can be traced back at least as far as the Enlightenment. The Revolution had seen a first great flowering of what proved to be a very fragile plant, but to Restoration Liberals went credit for developing a hardier strain based on grafting appropriate practices onto high ideals.

Liberal Opposition also had an intransigent, insurrectionary side. In its dual nature, it reflected the Revolutionary tradition, just as ultraroyalism inherited the dual character of counter-revolutionary tradition. Resort to force, either through insurrection or state repression, could be found on either side. Ultimately, the Liberal Opposition triumphed in 1830 because its willingness to compromise made it the better 'mediator' of the many interests that comprised France. Thereafter, the destruction of coalition through return to insurrection would undermine ability to mediate. All the same, the reform path of Restoration Liberal Opposition, based on organization and appeal to public opinion, had been shown to work, and would serve as a model for other groups and generations to follow.

It is unlikely that all interests in any state will ever be one and indivisible, or that there ever will be complete agreement as to ultimate ends. The objective of politics is not to achieve utopia; it is to find the means to accommodate the permanent need for change with pursuit of a workable consensus. In its emphasis on 'legal liberty' the Liberal Opposition found the way to put ideals into practice. This was no small step, but it would not be an easy one to follow, as the struggle to understand the essence of the Revolutionary tradition continued.

# *Bibliography*

## PRIMARY SOURCES

### NATIONAL ARCHIVES (AN)

AFIV 1937 Secrétairerie D'Etat Impériale, an VIII – an 1815

BB2 8–15 Evénements politiques, 1815–16
BB3 118–39 Affaires prévôtales
BB3 140–66 Délits politiques, an VIII–1816
BB3 167–77 Rapports politiques des procureurs généraux, 1819–35
BB30 179–272 Mélange conçernant l'Empire et la Restauration

F1A 581–9 Evénements de 1814–15 dans les départements

F1B I 145 Fonctionnaires de l'administration préfectorale
F1B 231 Conseils généraux et conseils d'arrondissement: organisation et personnel
F1B II Garonne (Haute-) 7 Personnel administratif
F1B II Garonne (Haute-) 8 Personnel administratif

F1C I 11 Comtes rendus administratifs, 1814–30
F1C I 24–6 Rapports et correspondances relatifs à divers manifestations de l'esprit public, 1790–1821
F1C I 27–31 Adresses au Roi, 1817–30
F1C I 32 Adresses au Général Lafayette, 1830
F1C II 47–53 Elections. Formation du jury criminel, 1814–31

F1C III Garonne (Haute-) 6–7 Elections, 1813–77
F1C III Garonne (Haute-) 9 Comtes rendus administratifs, 1812–70
F1C III Garonne (Haute-) 14 Correspondance et divers
F1C III Isère 3 Correspondance politique
F1C III Isère 4 Correspondance politique
F1C III Isère 5 Correspondance politique
F1C III Isère 9 Correspondance et divers
F1C III Rhin (Bas-) 3 Elections, 1808–15
F1C III Rhin (Bas-) 4 Elections, 1816–30
F1C III Rhin (Bas-) 8 comtes rendus administratifs, 1809–70

F1C III Rhin (Bas-) 14 Correspondance et divers, an VI – 1815
F1C III Rhin (Bas-) 15 Correspondance et divers, 1816–70
F1C III Seine-Inférieure 4 Elections, 1815–24
F1C III Seine-Inférieure 5 Elections, 1827–30
F1C III Seine-Inférieure 16 Correspondance et divers, an X – 1854

F1C V Garonne (Haute-) 2 Conseils généraux, 1807–23

F7 3616–18 Garde Nationale, an IV – 1815
F7 3677–86 Police générale, an VII – 1820
F7 3679–98 Police générale
F7 3734–7 Minutes de bulletins
F7 3784–98 Police générale: bulletins de police, 1814–1830
F7 3821–7 Rapports hebdomadaires des départements (October–December 1815)
F7 3932 Gendarmerie. Bulletins
F7 4006 Rapports de gendarmerie
F7 4029–32 Rapports de gendarmerie
F7 4133–4 Rapports de gendarmerie
F7 6684–89 Sociétés secrètes
F7 6692–93 Troubles dans les théâtres et étudiants des facultés
F7 6694–6701 Associations, loges maçonniques, 1816–34
F7 6702–3 Surveillance des militaires, 1816–30
F7 6704–6 Ecrits et objets séditieux
F7 6707–15 Conventionnels régicides, 1815–30
F7 6718–20 Députés
F7 6722 Sociétés philhelléniques
F7 6726 Affaire de Belfort
F7 6740–1 Elections et esprit public
F7 6742 Journaux
F7 6745–6 Affaire Louvel
F7 6750 Lettres anonymes
F7 6753–5 Fonds de la police secrète
F7 6767–72 Situation politique: rapports des préfets
F7 6776 Associations contre le paiement de l'impôt
F7 6777–8 Rapports des légions de gendarmerie
F7 7069–89 Rapports sur les journaux, 1821–30
F7 9636 Situation des départements
F7 9649 Situation des départements
F7 9659 Situation des départements
F7 9667 Situation des départements
F7 9693 Situation des départements

F9 515–16 Garde Nationale
F9 538–9 Garde Nationale

F15 3618–9 Enquête sur les caisses de secours

DEPARTMENTAL ARCHIVES OF THE HAUTE-GARONNE (ADHG)

1M60 Maires et adjoints
1M65 Ordres du Commissaire Extraordinaire, Cent-Jours
1M67 Arrondissement de Muret, avril 1815
1M69 Arrondissement de Saint-Gaudens
1M72–5 Maires et adjoints
1M96–99 Maires et adjoints
2M19–24bis Elections
2Mbis2 Conseils d'arrondissement et conseil générale, 1815–16
4M34–49 Police générale, 1814–32
13M57bis Etat de police, 1815–30
6T1–4 Imprimeurs et libraires

DEPARTMENTAL ARCHIVES OF THE ISÈRE (ADI)

Fonds Chaper: J514–15; J528–9; J551; IIJ
Fonds Chaper Supplément: 4J19–4J21
Fonds Edmond Maignien: 5J32

4M11–13 Listes électorales
7M1–2 Circulaires, instructions, an X – 1830
8M3–6 Renseignements généraux, décrets, etc., 1815–31
10M1 Circulaires, correspondance des sous-préfets, an VIII – 1834
11M1 Notes bibliographiques, an VIII – 1871
12M1 Conseils d'arrondissements, an VIII – 1834
13M1 Notes bibliographiques, an VIII – 1871
14M5 Renseignements personnels
51M–55M Police générale
97M Associations: sociétés secrètes
97M1 Loges maçonniques, an X – 1877

DEPARTMENTAL ARCHIVES OF THE SEINE-MARITIME (ADSM)

1M153–78 Situation morale et politique du département, 1814–30
1M642 Pratique religieuse
3M44–63 Listes électorales
3M149–71 Plébiscites et élections, 1815–30
4M116–17 Rapports de police, 1814–27
4M207 Colportage, 1816–87
4M632 Saisis d'interdictions, an VIII – 1831
4M636 Situation de l'imprimerie et de la librairie, 1815–19
4M638 Statistiques et enquêtes conçernant les imprimeurs, 1815–54
4M643 Enquêtes conçernant la presse
4M655 Contrôle de l'information, an VIII – 1862
4M2684 Surveillance des personalités politiques, 1814–25
4M2703 Associations politiques, 1824–88

### DEPARTMENTAL ARCHIVES OF THE BAS-RHIN (ADBR)

1M2 Préfets
1M6 Sécrétaires généraux
1M8–13 Sous-préfets
1M17–18 Conseils de préfecture
1M26–31 Conseils généraux
1M36–45 Conseils d'arrondissement
1M88–103 Maires et conseils municipaux (Restauration)
1M147–8 Maires et conseils municipaux (Monarchie de Juillet)
2M11–20 Elections
3M10–22 Police générale
10M1 Maçons
15MII 9 Administration générale: supplément

### NATIONAL LIBRARY IN PARIS (BN): MANUSCRIPTS

Lb46 396 Fédération Alsacienne: relation des journées
Lc9.10 (15) Prospectus for *Le Patriote Alsacien*
Nouvelles Acquisitions françaises (NAF), 20033–20037. Recueil de lettres autographes de personnes nées ou ayant vécu en Alsace du XVIIe siècle au XIXe siècle
Nouvelles Acquisitions françaises (NAF), 24914: correspondance de Coulmann et papiers de B. Constant

### CANTONAL AND UNIVERSITY LIBRARY OF LAUSANNE – DORIGNY; INSTITUT BENJAMIN CONSTANT: FONDS CONSTANT (BCUL)

#### Letters to Benjamin Constant

Co 159–64; 993; 1024–7; 1028–30; 1035–6; 1037–8; 1054–5; 1063; 1076; 1082–7; 1097–8; 1112; 1123–4; 1155; 1157–8; 1162; 1207–8; 1231; 326; 1327–47; 1352; 1365; 1370; 1378; 1401; 1415; 1450–1; 1472; 1478; 1489; 1515; 1518; 1520; 1532; 1536–8; 1593; 1610; 1619; 1634; 1639; 1643; 1673; 1698; 1903; 1923; 1929–62; 1964; 1966–8; 1972; 1975–7; 1982; 1983; 2002–3; 2005; 2006; 2008; 2010; 2013; 2026–7; 2050; 2051; 2110; 2205; 2245; 2314; 2321; 2450; 2502; 2550; 2566; 2604; 2625–6; 2703; 2705–6; 2708–9; 2712; 2719–22; 2723–5; 3379; 3572; 3577; 3640; 3688; 3690–2; 3704; 3712; 3715; 3748; 3753; 3756; 3807; 3813; 3885; 3886; 3915; 4024; 4600\6–10; 4639; 4640; 4643; 4654; 4742\7–11

#### Letters to others in possession of Benjamin Constant

Co 1421; 1065; 1235; 1422

#### Letters from Benjamin Constant

Co 166; 3935; 4021; Is 4216; 4282; 4517; 4743; 4882; Ms 286\1–3

Documents, petitions, etc.

Co 2015; 3271; 3756; 4506; 4508; 4545\1; 4546; 4551; 4553; 4554; 4557; 4581; 4600\1–11; 4679; 4746

#### MUNICIPAL AND UNIVERSITY LIBRARY OF GRENOBLE (BMUG): MANUSCRIPTS

R4735; R4737; R7380; R7453; R7906 – R8198; R8226; R8324; R8439; R8473; R8772; R9035; R9109; R9466; R9513; R9676; R9874; R10418; R10475; R10582; R95026; R90546; R90576; R90616; R90617; R90618; R90619; R90620; R90622; R90623; R90626; R90630–31; R90671; R90697; R90720

T3938–49; T3957; T3972–3

N1549; N1596; N1600–2; N1684; N1690; N1692; N1723; N1730; N1782–3; N1788; N1895; N1924–5; N1942; N1993; N2005; N2043; N2086; N2135–6; N2198; N2359; N2361; N2372; N2402; N2442; N2451; N2467; N2495; N2506; N2599; N2861; N2901; N2938; N3065; N3119; N3120; N3153

#### NATIONAL AND UNIVERSITY LIBRARY OF STRASBOURG (BNUS): MANUSCRIPTS

Mss. 1169–82; 1504; 1508; 1534; 1535; 3586; D. 121 616; M. 112 933; M. 113 383; M. 113 441; M. 121 121; G. 114 .869

#### MUNICIPAL LIBRARY OF TOULOUSE (BMT): MANUSCRIPTS

LmC 4756; LmC 4764; LmC 8799; LmC 13232; LmC 13232 (3); LmD 3129

## CONTEMPORARY PUBLISHED SOURCES: THE PRESS

*Courrier du Bas-Rhin*, 1816–30
*L'Echo des Alpes*, 1819–20
*Journal de Rouen*, 1814–30
*Journal de Grenoble*, 1815–30
*Journal libre de l'Isère*, 1820–2
*Journal politique et littéraire de Toulouse et de la Haute-Garonne*, 1815–30
*La France Méridionale*, 1828–32
*La Nacelle*, 1822–3
*Le Neustrien*, 1826–30
*Le Patriote Alsacien*, 1820

## MEMOIRS, CORRESPONDENCE AND PRINTED SOURCES

Barante, Amable-Guillaume-Prosper, baron de, *Souvenirs du Baron de Barante, 1782–1866*, 8 vols. (Paris, 1890–1901).

Barrot, Odilon, *Mémoires posthumes*, 4 vols. (Paris, 1875–6).

Bérenger de la Drôme, Alphonse-Marie, *De la justice criminelle en France* (Paris, 1818).

Berriat-Saint-Prix, Jacques, *Napoléon I à Grenoble* (Paris, 1861).

Boyer-Fonfrède, François-Bernard, 'Des avantages d'une constitution libérale' (Paris, 1814).

Cabet, Etienne, *Révolution de 1830 et situation présente* (Paris, 1833).

Champollion-Figéac, Jacques-Joseph, *Fourier et Napoléon* (Paris, 1844).

Constant, Benjamin, *De l'état actuel de la France et des bruits qui circulent* (Paris, 1819).

*Cours de politique constitutionnelle*, edited by Edouard Laboulaye (Paris, 1872).

Coulmann, Jean-Jacques, *Réminiscences*, 3 vols. (Paris, 1862–9).

Duchesne, Antoine-Louis-Hippolyte, 'Réflexions d'un royaliste constitutionnel' (Paris, 1814).

'Nouvelles réflexions d'un royaliste constitutionnel' (Paris, 1814).

'Vote d'un Dauphinois sur l'Acte Additionnel aux constitutions de l'Empire' (Grenoble, 1815).

Dupin, Charles, *Forces productives et commerciales de la France* (Paris, 1827).

Frénilly, Auguste-François-Faveau, marquis de, *Recollections of Baron de Frénilly* (New York, 1909).

Harpaz, Ephraïm, ed., *Benjamin Constant et Goyet de la Sarthe: Correspondance 1818–1822* (Geneva, 1973).

Haussez, Charles Lemercher de Longpré, baron, d', *Mémoires de Baron d'Haussez* (Paris, 1896–7).

Montbel, Guillaume-Isadore, comte de, *Souvenirs du Comte de Montbel* (Paris, 1913).

Noailles, Hélie-Guillaume-Hubert, marquis de, ed., *Le Comte Molé: sa vie, ses mémoires*, 6 vols. (Paris, 1922–30).

Pagès, Jean-Pierre, *Principes généraux du droit politique* (Paris, 1817).

Palmer, R. R., ed., *From Jacobin to Liberal: Marc-Antoine Jullien, 1775–1848* (Princeton, 1993).

Pasquier, Etienne-Denis, baron de, *Histoire de mon temps: mémoires du Chancelier Pasquier*, 6 vols. (Paris, 1893–6).

Rémusat, Charles de, *Mémoires de ma vie*, 5 vols. (Paris, 1958).

Rémusat, Paul de, ed., *Correspondance de M. de Rémusat pendant les premières années de la Restauration*, 5 vols. (Paris, 1883–4).

Stoeber, Ehrenfried, 'La correspondance d'Ehrenfried Stoeber', in *La vie en Alsace*, 7 (July 1934), pp. 163–8, and 8 (August 1934), p. 192.

Thiers, Adolphe, *Les Pyrénées et le Midi de la France, pendant les mois de novembre et décembre 1822* (Paris, 1823).

Villèle, Joseph, comte de, *Mémoires et correspondance du Comte de Villèle*, 5 vols. (Paris, 1887–90).

Weiss, Charles, *Journal, 1815–1822* (Besançon, 1972).

*Journal, 1823–1833* (Besançon, 1981).

Zickel-Koechlin, F., 'Souvenirs d'un contemporain sur les événements de 1816 à 1823 en Alsace', *Revue d'Alsace*, 1 (1850), pp. 508–9, 543–56, and 2 (1851), pp. 76–96, 115–32, 253–64, 357–69.

## SECONDARY SOURCES

Aguet, Jean-Pierre, 'Benjamin Constant, député de Strasbourg, parlementaire sous la monarchie de Juillet (juillet–décembre 1830)', in Société Savante d'Alsace et des Régions de l'Est, *Autour des 'Trois Glorieuses' en 1830: Strasbourg, l'Alsace et la liberté* (Strasbourg, 1981), pp. 79–125.

Albert, Madeleine, *La Première Restauration dans la Haute-Garonne* (Paris, 1932).

Alexander, R. S., *Bonapartism and Revolutionary Tradition in France: The fédérés of 1815* (Cambridge, 1991).

*Napoleon* (London, 2001).

'The Federations of 1815 and the continuity of anti-Bourbon personnel, 1789–1830', *Proceedings of the Annual Meeting of the Western Society for French History*, 17 (1990), pp. 286–94.

'Restoration republicanism reconsidered', *French History*, 8, n. 4 (1994), pp. 442–69.

'"No Minister": French Restoration rejection of authoritarianism', in David Laven and Lucy Riall, eds., *Napoleon's Legacy* (Oxford, 2000), pp. 29–47.

Aminzade, Ronald, *Class, Politics and Early Industrial Capitalism: A Study of Mid-Nineteenth-Century Toulouse, France* (Albany, N.Y., 1981).

*Ballots and Barricades* (Princeton, 1993).

Artz, Frederick B., *France under the Bourbon Restoration, 1814–1830*, (Cambridge, Mass., 1931).

Avezou, Robert, 'Un grand parlementaire dauphinois Charles Sapey', *Evocations*, 33–8 (1948), pp. 370–5, 396–401, 434–42.

Bagge, Dominique, *Les idées politiques en France sous la Restauration* (Paris, 1952).

Barral, Pierre, *Les Perier dans l'Isère au XIXe siècle d'après leur correspondance familiale* (Paris, 1964).

Barthélemy, Joseph, *L'introduction du régime parlementaire en France sous Louis XVIII et Charles X* (Paris, 1904).

Bastid, Paul, *Les institutions politiques de la monarchie parlementaire française (1814–1848)* (Paris, 1954).

Beach, Vincent, *Charles X of France* (Boulder, Colo., 1971).

Beck, Thomas, *French Legislators 1800–1834* (Berkeley, 1974).

Bellanger, Claude *et al.*, *Histoire générale de la presse française*, 4 vols. (Paris, 1969).

Ben-Amos, Avner, *Funerals, Politics, and Memory in Modern France, 1789–1996* (Oxford, 2000).

Berstein, Serge, 'Les partis', in René Rémond, ed., *Pour une histoire politique* (Paris, 1988), pp. 49–95.

Bertier de Sauvigny, Guillaume de, *Le Comte Ferdinand de Bertier (1782–1864) et l'énigme de la congrégation* (Paris, 1948).

*The Bourbon Restoration* (Philadelphia, 1966).

'L'image de la Révolution Française dans "Le Conservateur"', in Roger Dufraisse and Elisabeth Müller-Luckner, eds., *Révolution und Gegenrévolution 1789–1830* (Munich, 1991), pp. 143–53.

Bezucha, Robert J., 'The revolution of 1830 and the city of Lyon', in John Merriman, ed., *1830 in France* (New York, 1975), pp. 119–38.

Bluche, Frédéric, *Le Bonapartisme* (Paris, 1980).

*Le plébiscite des Cent-Jours* (Paris, 1980).

Bourset, Madelaine, *Casimir Perier* (Paris, 1994).

Bouton, André, 'Luttes dans l'ouest entre les chevaliers de la Foi et les chevaliers de la Liberté', *Revue des Travaux de l'Académie des Sciences Morales et Politiques*, 115, n. 2 (1962), pp. 1–13.

Breunig, Charles, 'Casimir Perier and the troubles of Grenoble, March 11–13 1832', *French Historical Studies*, 2, n. 4 (1962), pp. 469–89.

Brown, Mark, 'The Comité Franco-Polonais and the French reaction to the Polish uprising of November 1830', *English Historical Review*, 93 (1978), pp. 774–93.

Bury, J. P. T. and R. P. Tombs, *Thiers 1797–1877: A Political Life* (London, 1986).

Calmette, A., 'Les Carbonari en France sous la Restauration, 1821–1830', *La Révolution de 1848*, 9 (1912–13), pp. 401–17; 10 (1913–14), pp. 52–73, 117–38, 214–30.

Cappadocia, Ezio, 'The Liberals and Madame de Staël in 1818', in R. Herr and H. Parker, eds., *Essays Presented to Louis Gottschalk* (Durham, N.C., 1965), pp. 182–98.

Charbonneau, Roger, 'Les élections de 1827 dans les Deux-Sèvres', *Bulletin de la Société Historique et Scientifique des Deux-Sèvres*, 51, n. 10 (1956), pp. 234–9.

Chaumié, Jacqueline, 'Les Girondins et les Cent Jours', *Annales Historiques de la Révolution Française*, 43, n. 205 (1971), pp. 329–65.

Clarenc, Véronique, 'Toulouse, capitale du Carlisme Catalan (1830–1840)', *Annales du Midi* (1993), pp. 225–46.

Collingham, H. A. C., *The July Monarchy* (London, 1988).

Collins, Irene, *The Government and the Newspaper Press in France 1814–1881* (Oxford, 1959).

Crauffon, Jehan, *La Chambre des Députés sous la Restauration, son recrutement et son organisation* (Paris, 1908).

Crémieux, Adolphe, *La censure en 1820 et en 1821* (Paris, 1912).

Crook, Malcolm, *Elections in the French Revolution: An Apprenticeship in Democracy, 1789–1799* (Cambridge, 1996).

Cubitt, Geoffrey, *The Jesuit Myth* (Oxford, 1993).

Darmon, Pierre, *La rumeur de Rodez* (Paris, 1991).

Daudet, Ernest, *Louis XVIII et le duc Decazes* (Paris, 1899).

Day, C. R., 'The development of Protestant primary education in France under the constitutional monarchy, 1815–1848', *Canadian Journal of History*, 16, n. 2 (1981), pp. 215–36.

Day-Hickman, Barbara-Ann, *Napoleonic Art: Nationalism and the Spirit of Rebellion in France (1815–1848)* (Newark, N.J., 1999).

Doyle, William, *The Oxford History of the French Revolution* (Oxford, 1989).

Dumolard, Henry, *La Terreur Blanche dans l'Isère: Jean-Paul Didier et la conspiration de Grenoble* (Grenoble, 1928).
Duprat, Annie, 'Une guerre des images: Louis XVIII, Napoléon et la France en 1815,' *Revue d'Histoire Moderne et Contemporaine*, 47, n. 3 (2000), pp. 487–504.
Duvergier de Hauranne, Prosper, *Histoire du governement parlementaire en France*, 10 vols. (Paris, 1857–72).
Edelstein, Melvin, 'Integrating the French peasants into the nation-state: the transformation of electoral participation (1789–1870)', *History of European Ideas*, 15, n. 1–3 (1992), pp. 319–26.
Espié, Roseline, 'La conspiration du 19 août d'après les mémoires inédits de Joseph Rey de Grenoble' (DES, University of Grenoble, 1965).
Eude, Robert, 'Un archevêque de Rouen au XIXe siècle: le Cardinal-Prince de Croy (1824–1844)', *Précis Analytique des Travaux de l'Académie de Rouen, 1951–3*, (1955), pp. 229–47.
Eydoux, Louis, *L'assassinat du général Ramel* (Toulouse, 1905).
Fauchille, Paul, 'Comment se préparaient des élections en 1818', *Revue de Paris* (July, 1902), pp. 154–74.
Félix-Faure, Jacques, *Un compagnon de Stendhal: Félix Faure, pair de France* (Aran, 1978).
Fitzpatrick, Brian, *Catholic Royalism in the Department of the Gard* (Cambridge, 1983).
Fizaine, Simone, *La vie politique dans la Côte-d'Or sous Louis XVIII, les élections et la presse* (Dijon and Paris, 1931).
Fontana, Biancamaria, *Benjamin Constant and the Post-Revolutionary Mind* (New Haven and London, 1991).
Ford, Caroline, 'Private lives and public order in Restoration France: the seduction of Emily Loveday', *American Historical Review*, 99, n. 1 (1994), pp. 21–43.
Fourcassié, Jean, *Une ville à l'époque romantique, Toulouse* (Paris, 1953).
*Villèle* (Paris, 1954).
Gildea, Robert, *Education in Provincial France 1800–1914* (Oxford, 1983).
Girard, Louis, *La garde nationale 1814–1871* (Paris, 1964).
*Les libéraux français, 1814–75* (Paris, 1984).
'La réélection des députés promus à des fonctions publiques (1828–1831)', in *Mélanges offerts à Charles H. Pouthas* (Paris, 1973), pp. 227–44.
Glachant, Victor, *Benjamin Constant sous l'oeil du guet* (Paris, 1906).
Goblot, Jean-Jacques, *La jeune France libérale. Le Globe et son groupe littéraire 1824–1830* (Paris, 1995).
Godeschot, Jacques, ed., *La Révolution de 1848 à Toulouse et dans la Haute-Garonne* (Toulouse, 1948).
*The Counter-Revolution: Doctrine and Action* (Princeton, 1971).
Gonnard, P., 'La légende napoléonienne et la presse libérale: La Minerve', *Revue des Etudes Napoléoniennes*, 3, n. 1 (1914), pp. 28–49.
Gonnet, Paul, 'Esquisse de la crise économique en France de 1827 à 1832', *Revue d'Histoire Economique et Sociale*, 33 (1955), pp. 249–92.
'La société dijonnaise au XIXe siècle' (Thèse, University of Paris, 1974).

Gras, Albin, *Grenoble en 1814 et 1815* (Grenoble, 1854).

Gueniffey, Patrice, 'Revolutionary democracy and the elections', in Renée Waldinger, Philip Dawson and Isser Woloch, eds., *The French Revolution and the Meaning of Citizenship* (Westport, Conn. and London, 1993), pp. 89–103.

Guillon, Edouard, *Les complots militaires sous la Restauration* (Paris, 1895).

Harpaz, Ephraïm, *L'école libérale sous la Restauration, le Mercure et la Minerve, 1817–1820* (Geneva, 1968).

Hemardinquer, J.-J., 'Affaires et politique sous la Monarchie censitaire. Un Libéral: F.-B. Boyer-Fonfrède (1767–1845)', *Annales du Midi*, 73, n. 54 (1961), pp. 165–218.

Henry, Simone, 'La campagne des banquets à Toulouse', in Jacques Godeschot, ed., *La Révolution de 1848 à Toulouse et dans la Haute-Garonne* (Toulouse, 1948), pp. 53–62.

Higgs, David, *Ultraroyalism in Toulouse* (Baltimore, 1973).

'Politics and charity at Toulouse, 1750–1850', in John Bosher, ed., *French Government and Society, 1500–1850* (London, 1973), pp. 191–207.

'Bonapartism lower-class in the Haute-Garonne', unpublished paper presented at the annual meeting of the Society for French Historical Studies, Vancouver, March 1990.

Higonnet, Patrice, 'La composition de la Chambre des Députés de 1827 à 1831', *Revue Historique*, 239 (1968), pp. 351–78.

Holroyd, Richard, 'The Bourbon army, 1815–1830', *Historical Journal*, 14, n. 3 (1971), pp. 529–52.

Houssaye, Henry, *1815* (Paris, 1902).

Huard, Raymond, *La naissance du parti politique en France* (Paris, 1996).

Hudson, Nora, *Ultra-Royalism and the French Restoration* (Cambridge, 1936).

Jacquier, Bernard, *Le légitimisme dauphinois, 1830–70* (Grenoble, 1976).

Jardin, André, *Histoire du libéralisme politique* (Paris, 1985).

Jardin, André and André-Jean Tudesq, *Restoration and Reaction* (Cambridge and New York, 1984).

Johnson, Douglas, *Guizot: Aspects of French History, 1787–1874* (London, 1963).

Kayser, Jacques, *Les grands batailles du radicalisme (1820–1901)* (Paris, 1962).

Kent, Sherman, *The Election of 1827 in France* (Cambridge, Mass., 1975).

Kroen, Sheryl, *Politics and Theater: The Crisis of Legitimacy in Restoration France, 1815–1830* (Berkeley, 2000).

Langeron, Roger, *Decazes, ministre du roi* (Paris, 1960).

Laven, David and Lucy Riall, eds., *Napoleon's Legacy* (Oxford, 2000).

*La vie en Alsace*, July 1929 and July–August 1934.

Le Gallo, Emile, *Les Cent-Jours* (Paris, 1923).

Le Gallo, Yves, 'Anticléricalisme et structures urbaines et militaires à Brest sous la Monarchie constitutionnelle', *Actes du 91e Congrès de la Société des Savantes, Rennes 1966*, 3 (1969), pp. 75–139.

Legoy, Jean, 'Un espace révolutionnaire: le théâtre du Havre, 1789–1850', in *Révolutions et mouvements révolutionnaires en Normandie. Actes du XXIe*

*Congrès des sociétés historiques et archéologiques de Normandie tenus au Havre du 24 au 29 octobre 1989* (Le Havre, 1990), pp. 275–84.

Lesparre, Jeanne, 'Les partis politiques dans la Haute-Garonne à la fin de la monarchie de juillet', in Jacques Godeschot, ed., *La Révolution de 1848 à Toulouse et dans la Haute-Garonne* (Toulouse, 1948), pp. 29–40.

Leuilliot, Paul, *La Première Restauration et les Cent Jours en Alsace* (Paris, 1958).

*L'Alsace au début du XIXe siècle*, 3 vols. (Paris, 1959).

'L'Alsace et la révolution de 1830', *La Vie en Alsace* (1929), pp. 73–94.

'La dissolution de la garde nationale de Strasbourg en 1817', *Revue d'Alsace*, 81 (1934), pp. 383–99.

'L'opposition libérale en Alsace à la fin de la Restauration', in *Deux siècles d'Alsace française, 1648–1848* (Strasbourg, 1948), pp. 291–314.

'L'Alsace sous la Restauration', *Revue d'Alsace*, 96 (1957), pp. 106–30.

Lévêque, Pierre, *Une société provinciale: la Bourgogne sous la Monarchie de Juillet* (Paris, 1983).

Lewis, Gwynne, *The Second Vendée* (Oxford, 1978).

Liggio, Leonard P., 'Charles Dunoyer and French classical liberalism', *Journal of Libertarian Studies*, 1, n. 3 (1977), pp. 153–78.

Livet, Georges and Francis Rapp, eds., *Histoire de Strasbourg* (Toulouse, 1987).

Loubet, Jean, 'Le gouvernement toulousain du duc d'Angoulême après les Cent-Jours', *La Révolution Française*, 64 (1913), pp. 149–65 and 337–66.

Lucas-Dubreton, J., *Louis-Philippe et la machine infernale (1830–1835)* (Paris, 1951).

*Le culte de Napoléon, 1815–1848* (Paris, 1960).

'Le complot de Canuel à Lyon (1817)', *Revue des Deux Mondes*, n. 19 (1959), pp. 443–9.

Lyons, Martyn, *Revolution in Toulouse* (Berne, 1978).

'Fires of expiation: book-burnings and Catholic missions in Restoration France', *French History*, 10, n. 1 (1996), pp. 240–66.

Macia-Widemann, Marie-Pascale, 'Le Comité philhellénique et la politique intérieure française (1824–1829)', *Revue de la Société d'Histoire de la Restauration et de la Monarchie Constitutionnelle*, 5 (1991), pp. 27–41.

McCord, Norman, *British History 1815–1906* (Oxford, 1991).

McPhee, Peter, 'Electoral democracy and direct democracy in France, 1789–1851', *European History Quarterly*, 16, n. 1 (1986), pp. 77–96.

Maget-Dedominici, Maryse, 'La "loi de justice et d'amour" ou la liberté de la presse? Etude d'un mouvement oppositionnel en France (1826–27)', *Schweizerische Zeitschrift für Geschichte*, 40, n. 1 (1990), pp. 1–28.

Mansel, Philip, *Louis XVIII* (London, 1981).

*Paris Between Empires 1814–1852* (London, 2001).

Mellon, Stanley, *The Political Uses of History* (Stanford, 1958).

Ménager, Bernard, *Les Napoléon du peuple* (Paris, 1988).

Merriman, John M., *1830 in France* (New York, 1975).

'The Norman fires of 1830: incendiaries and fear in rural France', *French Historical Studies*, 9, n. 3 (1976), pp. 451–66.

Moss, Bernard H., 'Parisian workers and the origins of republican socialism', in John Merriman, ed., *1830 in France* (New York, 1975), pp. 203–17.
Mouchet, Jean, 'L'esprit public dans le Morbihan sous la Restauration', *Annales de Bretagne*, 45 (1938), pp. 89–182.
Moulard, Jacques, *Le Comte Camille de Tournon* (Paris, 1914).
Neely, Sylvia, *Lafayette and the Liberal Ideal 1814–1824* (Carbondale and Edwardsville, Ill., 1991).
'Rural politics in the early Restoration: Charles Goyet and the Liberals of the Sarthe', *European Historical Quarterly*, 16, n. 3 (1986), pp. 313–42.
'The politics of liberty in the old world and the new: Lafayette's return to America in 1824', *Journal of the Early Republic*, 6 (Summer 1986), pp. 151–71.
'Lafayette: the soldier of two worlds', in L. Kramer, ed., *The French-American Connection: 200 Years of Cultural and Intellectual Interaction* (Chapel Hill, N.C., 1994), pp. 6–19.
Newman, Edgar, 'Republicanism during the Bourbon Restoration in France, 1814–1830' (Ph.D. dissertation, University of Chicago, 1969).
'The blouse and the frock coat: the alliance of the common people of Paris with the liberal leadership and the middle class during the last years of the Bourbon Restoration', *Journal of Modern History*, 46, n. 1 (1974), pp. 26–69.
Nordmann, Jean-Thomas, *Histoire des Radicaux (1820–1973)* (Paris, 1974).
Oechslin, Jean-Jacques, *Le mouvement ultra-royaliste sous la Restauration, son idéologie et son action politique* (Paris, 1960).
Perreux, Gabriel, *Au temps des sociétés secrètes* (Paris, 1931).
Perrin, René, *L'esprit public dans le département de la Meurthe de 1814 à 1816* (Paris, 1913).
Phayer, J. Michael, 'Politics and popular religion: the cult of the cross in France, 1815–1840', *Journal of Social History*, 11, n. 1 (1978), pp. 346–65.
Pilbeam, Pamela, *The 1830 Revolution in France* (London, 1991).
*Republicanism in Nineteenth-Century France* (London 1995).
'The emergence of opposition to the Orleanist monarchy, August 1830–1 April 1831', *English Historical Review*, 85, n. 334 (1970), pp. 12–28.
'The insurrectionary tradition in France 1835–48', *Modern and Contemporary France*, 1, n. 3 (1993), pp. 253–64.
'Revolutionary movements in western Europe', in Pamela Pilbeam, ed., *Themes in Modern European History 1780–1830* (London, 1995), pp. 125–50.
Pilenco, A., *Les moeurs électorales en France* (Paris, 1928).
Pinkney, David, *The French Revolution of 1830* (Princeton, 1972).
Ponteil, Félix, *L'opposition politique à Strasbourg sous la monarchie de juillet (1830–48)* (Paris, 1932).
*Georges Humann, 1780–1842* (Paris, 1977).
Popkin, Jeremy D., *Press, Revolution and Social Identities in France, 1830–1835* (University Park, Pa., 2002).
'Un grand journal de province à l'époque de la révolution de 1830: *Le Précurseur de Lyon*, 1826–1834', in Michel Biard *et al.*, eds., *Hommages à Jean-Paul Bertaud* (Paris, 2002), pp. 185–96.

Porch, Douglas, *Army and Revolution, France 1815–1848* (London, 1974).
Pouthas, Charles, *Guizot pendant la Restauration: préparation de l'homme d'état (1814–1830)* (Paris, 1923).
'La réorganisation du ministère de l'Intérieur et la réconstitution de l'administration préfectorale par Guizot en 1830', *Revue d'Histoire Moderne*, 9, n. 4 (1962), pp. 241–63.
Price, Roger, 'Popular disturbances in the French provinces after the July Revolution of 1830', *European Studies Review*, 1, n. 4 (1971), pp. 323–50.
'The French army and the Revolution of 1830', *European Studies Review*, 3, n. 3 (1973), pp. 243–67.
Putz, H., 'Les élections de 1824 en Seine-Inférieure. Action gouvernementale et propagande royaliste', *Annales de Normandie*, 5, n. 1 (1955), pp. 59–72.
Rader, Daniel L., *The Journalists and the July Revolution in France* (The Hague, 1973).
'The Breton association and the press: propaganda for "legal resistance" before the July Revolution', *French Historical Studies* 2, n. 1 (1961), pp. 64–82.
Rémond, René, *L'anticléricalisme en France de 1815 à nos jours* (Paris, 1976).
ed., *Pour une histoire politique* (Paris, 1988).
Resnick, Daniel, *The White Terror and the Political Reaction after Waterloo* (Cambridge, Mass., 1966).
Ribe, Georges, *L'opinion publique et la vie politique à Lyon lors des premières années de la Seconde Restauration* (Paris, 1957).
Ribner, Jonathan P., *Broken Tablets. The Cult of the Law in French Art from David to Delacroix* (Berkeley and Oxford, 1993).
Richard, Gabriel, 'Une conspiration policière à Nancy en 1816', *Annales de l'Est*, 10 (1959), pp. 173–88.
Richard, Michel, 'La bourgeoisie protestante de Strasbourg à l'époque de Benjamin Constant', in Société Savante d'Alsace et des Régions de l'Est, *Autour des 'Trois Glorieuses' en 1830: Strasbourg, l'Alsace et la liberté* (Strasbourg, 1981), pp. 151–67.
Richardson, Nicholas, *The French Prefectoral Corps, 1814–1830* (Cambridge, 1966).
Roberts, J. M., *The Mythology of Secret Societies* (London, 1972).
Roberts, James, *The Counter-Revolution in France 1787–1830* (New York, 1990).
Rolland, M., 'Le département de l'Isère sous la Chambre Introuvable,' (DES, University of Grenoble, 1955).
Rosanvallon, Pierre, *Le moment Guizot* (Paris, 1985).
*Le sacre du citoyen: histoire du suffrage universel en France* (Paris, 1992).
*La monarchie impossible* (Paris, 1994).
'La république du suffrage universel', in François Furet and Mona Ozouf, eds., *Le siècle de l'avènement républicain* (Paris, 1993), pp. 371–89.
Sahlins, Peter, *Forest Rites. The War of the Demoiselles in Nineteenth-Century France* (Cambridge, Mass., and London, 1994).
Savigear, P., 'Carbonarism and the French army, 1815–24', *History*, 54 (June 1969), pp. 198–211.
Schermerhorn, Elizabeth, *Benjamin Constant* (Boston and New York, 1924).

Schroeder, Paul, *The Transformation of European Politics 1763–1848* (Oxford, 1994).

Sevrin, Ernest, *Les missions religieuses en France sous la Restauration, 1815–1830*, 2 vols. (Paris, 1948–59).

Shumway, Anna, *A Study of the Minerve Française* (Philadelphia, 1934).

Simms, Brendan, 'The eastern empires from the challenge of Napoleon to the Restoration, c. 1806–30', in Pamela Pilbeam, ed., *Themes in Modern European History 1780–1830* (London, 1995), pp. 85–106.

Société Savante d'Alsace et des Régions de l'Est, *Autour des 'Trois Glorieuses' en 1830: Strasbourg, l'Alsace et la liberté* (Strasbourg, 1981).

Spitzer, Alan B., *Old Hatreds and Young Hopes: The French Carbonari against the Bourbon Restoration* (Cambridge, Mass., 1971).

*The French Generation of 1820* (Princeton, 1987).

'Restoration political theory and debate over the law of the double vote', *Journal of Modern History*, 55, n. 1 (1983), pp. 54–70.

'The elections of 1824 and 1827 in the Department of the Doubs', *French History*, 1989, 3, n. 2 (1989), pp. 153–76.

'La république souterraine', in François Furet and Mona Ozouf, eds., *Le siècle de l'avènement républicain* (Paris, 1993), pp. 345–69.

'Malicious memories: Restoration politics and a prosopography of turncoats', *French Historical Studies*, 24, n. 1 (2001), pp. 37–61.

Sutherland, D. M. G., *France 1789–1815: Revolution and Counterrevolution* (London, 1985).

Thureau-Dangin, Paul, *Le parti libéral sous la Restauration* (Paris, 1876).

Tronchet, Raymond, *L'enseignement mutuel en France de 1815 à 1833*, 3 vols. (Lille, 1973).

Tudesq, André-Jean, *La démocratie en France depuis 1815* (Paris, 1971).

'Les comportements électoraux sous le régime censitaire', in Daniel Gaxie, ed., *Explication du vote: un bilan des études électorales en France* (Paris, 1985).

Vaulabelle, Achille de, *Histoire des deux restaurations*, 8 vols. (Paris, 1858).

Vergnaud, Maurice, 'Agitation politique et crise de subsistances à Lyon de septembre 1816 à juin 1817', *Cahiers d'Histoire*, 2 (1957), pp. 163–77.

Vidalenc, Jean, *Le département de l'Eure sous la monarchie constitutionnelle* (Paris, 1952).

*Les demi-solde: étude d'une catégorie sociale* (Paris, 1955).

Vigier, Philippe, 'Elections municipales et prise de conscience politique sous la monarchie de Juillet', in *La France au XIXe siècle: mélanges offerts à Charles Hippolyte Pouthas* (Paris, 1973), pp. 278–86.

Wahl, Henri, 'Les manifestations de l'opposition libérale et les complots militaires dans le Haut-Rhin sous la Restauration (1820–1824)', *Revue d'Alsace*, 92 (1953), pp. 102–32.

Waquet, Françoise, *Les fêtes royales sous la Restauration, ou l'ancien régime retrouvée* (Geneva, 1981).

Waresquiel, Emmanuel, 'Un paradoxe politique. La Chambre "introuvable" et la naissance de parlementarisme français (octobre 1815–avril 1816)', *Commentaire*, 15, n. 58 (1992), pp. 409–16.

'Une introduction à l'iconographie politique de la Restauration', *Revue de la Société d'Histoire de la Restauration et de la Monarchie Constitutionnelle*, 8 (1996), pp. 11–20.

Waresquiel, Emmanuel de and Benoît Yvert, *Histoire de la Restauration 1814–1830* (Paris, 1996).

Weil, Georges-Denis, *Les élections législatives depuis 1789* (Paris, 1895).

Weill, Georges, *Histoire du parti républicain en France de 1814 à 1870* (Paris, 1900).

'L'idée républicaine en France pendant la Restauration', *Revue d'Histoire Moderne*, 2 (1927), pp. 321–48.

'Les mémoires de Joseph Rey', *Revue Historique*, 157 (1928), pp. 291–307.

Wisner, David A., 'Law, legislative politics and royal patronage in the Bourbon Restoration: the commission to decorate the *conseil d'état* chambers, 1825–1827', *French History*, 12, n. 2 (1998), pp. 149–71.

Wolff, Philippe, ed., *Histoire de Toulouse* (Toulouse, 1974).

Woloch, Isser, *The New Regime* (New York, 1994).

*Napoleon and his Collaborators* (New York and London, 2001).

Wood, Dennis, *Benjamin Constant* (London, 1993).

Woolf, Otto, *Ouvrard* (New York, 1962).

Woolf, Stuart, *Napoleon's Integration of Europe* (London, 1991).

Yvert, Jean-Benoît, 'Decazes et la politique du juste-milieu: "royaliser la nation, nationaliser la royauté" (1815–1820)', in Roger Dufraisse and Elisabeth Müller-Luckner, eds., *Révolution und Gegenrévolution 1789–1830* (Munich, 1991), pp. 193–210.

# Index

## NEW STUDIES IN EUROPEAN HISTORY

*Books in the series*

Royalty and Diplomacy in Europe, 1890–1914
RODERICK R. MCLEAN

Catholic Revival in the Age of the Baroque
Religious Identity in Southwest Germany, 1550–1750
MARC R. FORSTER

Helmuth von Moltke and the Origins of the First World War
ANNIKA MOMBAUER

Peter the Great
The Struggle for Power, 1671–1725
PAUL BUSHKOVITZ

Fatherlands
State Building and Nationhood in Nineteenth-Century Germany
ABIGAIL GREEN

The French Second Empire
An Anatomy of Political Power
ROGER PRICE

Origins of the French Welfare State
The Struggle for Social Reform in France, 1914–47
PAUL V. DUTTON

Ordinary Prussians
Brandenburg Junkers and Villagers, 1500–1840
WILLIAM W. HAGEN

Liberty and Locality in Revolutionary France
Rural Life and Politics, 1760–1820
PETER JONES

From Reich to State
The Rhineland in the Revolutionary Age, 1780–1830
MICHAEL ROWE

Rewriting the French Revolutionary Tradition
ROBERT ALEXANDER

9 780521 801225